*the sociology
of
the possible*

the sociology
of
the possible

edited by

Richard Ofshe

University of California, Berkeley

Prentice-Hall, Inc.
Englewood Cliffs, New Jersey

Prentice-Hall sociology series
Neil J. Smelser, editor

© *1970 by Prentice-Hall, Inc., Englewood Cliffs, New Jersey*

C–13–821496–4
P–13–821488–3

Library of Congress Catalog Card Number 75–118810

Printed in the United States of America

Current printing (last digit);
15   14   13   12   11   10   9   8   7   6   5   4   3   2   1

Prentice-Hall International, Inc., London
Prentice-Hall of Australia, Pty. Ltd., Sydney
Prentice-Hall of Canada, Ltd., Toronto
Prentice-Hall of India Private Limited, New Delhi
Prentice-Hall of Japan, Inc., Tokyo

Selections from Harry Harrison, *The Streets of Ashkelon,* copyright, 1962, by Nova Publications, Ltd.; reprinted by permission of the author and the author's agent, Robert P. Mills.

Selections from Daniel Keyes, *Flowers for Algernon,* copyright, 1959, by Mercury Press, Inc.; reprinted by permission of the author and the author's agent, Robert P. Mills.

Philip José Farmer, "My Sister's Brother," from *Strange Relations,* copyright © 1960 by Ballantine Books, Inc. Published by Ballantine Books, Inc. Permission granted by Victor Gollancz Ltd.

Selection from *Walden Two* reprinted with permission of The Macmillan Company from *Walden Two* by B. F. Skinner. Copyright 1948 by B. F. Skinner.

One ought to think about building a society in much the same manner as one builds a structure out of Tinker Toys. If a part doesn't quite go, chuck it out and try another.

Jason Peacock

contents

substantive contents

The contents of the book are organized below in terms of a set of standard subdivisions of the discipline and major themes of selections listed in the regular Table of Contents. In some cases a selection appears in more than one subdivision.

preface

Ideally, there are many ways in which to approach the study of sociology, psychology, other social sciences, or, for that matter, any discipline. In practice, however, a painful orthodoxy exists in the manner in which undergraduate courses are taught and the manner in which they are received. I am not suggesting that courses ought necessarily to be designed primarily to be meaningful life experiences with "real here and now" interaction, as some of my teaching assistants have suggested, nor that students ought primarily to be sent out into the "real world" to see what it is all about. The results that I have seen of the application of these approaches are typically as pedestrian as the results of courses built on the notion that students ought to read at least a thousand pages of a double-column textbook and take a two-hour final examination that consists of 150 multiple-choice questions.

The orthodoxy to which I refer is one not of teaching style but rather of the apparently traditional agreement between student and instructor that students should read, or memorize, or interact, or observe, but that they are not required to attempt to think in any serious or creative fashion about the subject designated in the course title.

The purpose of the book is to provoke its readers into thinking about sociology —more precisely, into thinking about sociology in a certain fashion: how things could be rather than only how they are and how they came to be that way. What is interesting, even exciting, about the subject is what it can be used for.

Unlike most scientific disciplines, sociology has developed to its present state without having had to generate solutions to problems that are later implemented and thereby tested—and without having had the advantages that attend such a process. The reasons for this are complicated, but probably the major one is that sociologists have never had the political power necessary to implement the social experiments they would have liked to undertake, and those who have had the power have been more concerned with the realities of political survival or personal fortune than with the good that might be accomplished through fostering social change.

The fact that social scientists are more frequently being asked their opinions on important issues, even if their advice is only rarely acted upon, suggests that one of two things has occurred. Either recognition has developed that social scientists understand the dynamics of society better than those who have no formal training, or things have gotten so bad, and it is so clear that as a society we are *up against the wall,* that the Establishment is willing to listen to almost anyone.

As reliance on sociologists to provide solutions to problems grows, the possibility of a new approach to the development of the discipline is also growing. Until now, sociologists have been forced to try to build their discipline primarily by culling out of available information the data necessary to construct and evaluate explanations of social phenomena or by observing or asking questions about naturally occurring events. Since the causes of social phenomena are often multivariate, available data on crucial points, are frequently inadequate and since in natural settings several variables are usually changing simultaneously, it is difficult to identify causes or to relate variables in a precise manner.

More important, if you want to find new solutions to old problems and more desirable ways of organizing a society, you cannot hope to succeed if you examine only existing solutions and study only existing forms of social organization. It could be argued that the fastest way in which to develop a body of reliable sociological theory is to attempt to create new states of affairs in the real world—that is, attempt to specify some condition that we wish to bring about, design a plan using the best available theory for how to accomplish it, set to work, and see if the plan works. If it does not, the problem is to devise a modified plan that corrects mistaken assumptions about how the world behaves and to attempt to move closer to the desired condition. This condition can be something as trivial as the successful introduction of a new toothpaste into the market or as important as the successful education of children from black ghettos. In my opinion, it is much easier to construct a plan for changing a society from what it is now than to explain how it developed to the point at which you find it.

In putting this book together I have attempted to collect materials that deal with the possible—not the future, just the possible. I did not intend this book to attempt predictions of the future, nor even to provide speculations on the possibilities. I have been concerned mainly with the value of the selections as treatments of social possibilities, independent of the probability of their being achieved. The selections are intended to provide a basis for exercises in sociological analysis and to illustrate the types of social arrangement about which some exceedingly intelligent and creative men have thought.

Some selections seem to demonstrate that their authors were first-rate sociologists. Their analyses of what would happen to a social system if some changes were introduced are perceptive, and the societies that they create would probably function using the principles they set down. In other selections, the sociology seems quite naive. In all cases, however, I have tried to select materials in which it is possible to analyze why the predicted change would or would not come about, why the society would or would not function in the manner the designer expected, what unanticipated problems are inherent in the social structure of the created society, and why an individual would react to a situation as the writer expects.

My goal is to provide a context in which students may explore the conceptual consequences and, I hope, the possible real consequences of changes in the social order—a context in which a student may *think* about the principles and possible applications of sociology in a creative fashion.

This book was put together with the assistance of many people who helped me in many different fashions. I am indebted primarily to John Messer, who worked on this project from start to finish. The major task in creating this book was that of sifting through several thousand volumes of science fiction and actually reading several hundred books. Anyone who has ever attempted to live on a steady diet of science fiction for several months, reading book after book with no intellectual break, will realize that permanent damage may be done to mind and psyche. Shifting from social system to social system, experiencing a series of planet-wide devastations, and surviving all sorts of disorienting situations makes it difficult to distinguish the literary unreality of science fiction from the everyday unreality of what we call the real world. John and my wife Lynne made most of this trip with me. I hope they were wise enough to stop before the damage became irreversible.

In trying to cut short the search for potentially usable materials, I attempted to get help from some of the science fiction "heads" who abound on the Berkeley campus. I found one person in particular, Steven Compton, who was a great help.

Many examples of what I think to be both first-rate social-science fiction and first-rate sociology might have been included in this volume but were impossible to condense or excerpt in a manner that permitted their inclusion. Among the works from which I would most have liked to include excerpts were Isaac Asimov's "Foundation trilogy" *(Foundation, Foundation and Empire,* and *Second Foundation),* Robert Heinlein's *Stranger in a Strange Land,* Jack Vance's *To Live Forever* and *The Languages of Pao,* Kurt Vonnegut's *Player Piano,* and John Christopher's *No Blade of Grass.* If anyone feels outraged that I have omitted from this list, or from this book, a work that is as good as any that are included, please take the trouble to let me know.

Finally, I must acknowledge the help and encouragement I received from my publisher. Both Ed Stanford and Alan B. Lesure of Prentice-Hall were frequently at my side, encouraging me to meet my deadline as well as giving aid.

designs for a society:

introduction

In his ethnography of Erehwonian society, Samuel Butler[1] describes the principles of Erehwon's system of higher education. Although educational systems utilizing the same basic principles were in operation in Butler's own society and are clearly in evidence in most countries of today's world, the Erehwonians are the only people known to have extended these principles to the fullest and to have joined them with a set of concrete educational practices. Butler describes the organization of their system into two major lines of study:

> The main feature in their system is the prominence which they give to a study which I can only translate by the word "hypothetics." They argue thus—that to teach a boy merely the nature of the things which exist in the world around him, and about which he will have to be conversant during his whole life, would be giving him but a narrow and shallow conception of the universe, which it is urged might contain all manner of things which are not now to be found therein. To open his eyes to these possibilities, and so to prepare him for all sorts of emergencies, is the object of this system of hypothetics. To imagine a set of utterly strange and impossible contingencies, and require the youths to give intelligent answers to the questions that arise therefrom, is reckoned the fittest conceivable way of preparing them for the actual conduct of their affairs in after life (pp. 206–7).

The second major focus of Erehwonian educational practice was the study of unreason:

> The arguments in favor of the deliberate development of the unreasoning faculties were much more cogent. But here they depart from the principles on which they justify their study of hypothetics; for they base the importance which they assign to hypothetics upon the fact of their being a preparation for the extraordinary, while

[1]Samuel Butler, *Erehwon,* first published in 1872 (New York: The Modern Library, 1933).

their study of Unreason rests upon its developing those faculties which are required for the daily conduct of affairs. Hence their professorships of Inconsistency and Evasion, in both of which studies the youths are examined before being allowed to proceed to their degree of hypothetics. The more earnest and conscientious students attain to a proficiency in these subjects which is quite surprising; there is hardly any inconsistency so glaring but they soon learn to defend it, or injunction so clear that they cannot find some pretext for disregarding it.

Life, they urge, would be intolerable if men were to be guided in all they did by reason and reason only. Reason betrays men into the drawing of hard and fast lines, and to the defining by language—language being like the sun, which rears and then scorches. Extremes are alone logical, but they are always absurd; the mean is illogical, but an illogical mean is better than the sheer absurdity of an extreme. There are no follies and no unreasonableness so great as those which can apparently be irrefragably defended by reason itself, and there is hardly an error into which men may not easily be led if they base their conduct upon reason only (pp. 208–9).

Unfortunately, Butler's parody of English educational practices in the mid-1800s is a reasonable parody of the principles and practices of higher education today. The cry for relevance in education may do something to produce a change in the direction of introducing some correlation between what students are told to learn by their instructors, what is going on in the world around them, and what issues in that world need to be thought about.

Relevance in sociology takes two forms. On the one hand is the question of the structure of social reality as it now exists; on the other is the question of the nature of this (or any) social reality. On the one hand is a need to create in the minds of a society's members some realistic picture of their social world as it is now constituted, so that they may understand something of the true conditions of their environment. This kind of knowledge is immediately relevant, and like all descriptions of social systems it soon becomes an inadequate representation of current reality. On the other hand is a need to develop an understanding of, and to teach about, the principles by which social systems operate, so that members of a society may better understand how their environment is changing and, perhaps, act to shape it in a particular direction.

If this book is relevant, it is relevant in the second sense of the word. Sociology as a discipline has been concerned mainly with two issues: how a society arrived at a certain state, and how it functions now. Relatively little attention has been paid to the questions how social systems might be constituted, whether certain sets of arrangements could be used, and what advantages and disadvantages inhere in drastically different forms of social organization. These questions are relevant to the future.

It is difficult to imagine a person who has not tried to devise a way of changing social arrangements that he feels need changing. The difficulty in such an endeavor is that selecting the best route to a certain social end requires the most sophisticated type of sociological knowledge. To succeed, a person must be able to predict with considerable accuracy whether the change he proposes will affect aspects of the social system that he does not wish to affect, and if it will do so, whether the main goal will be achieved and whether the net result will be a gain or a loss. To change an inefficient industrial system for an efficient system *and* a fascist government would probably constitute a net loss. To succeed at introducing change, moreover, a person must be able to gauge the extent to which individuals who enjoy advantages in the current state of affairs will object to losing them, and whether those who stand to gain by the change will recognize their interest in it and how much support they will give.

Thinking about sociological issues in this way should be a viable means of developing an understanding of the principles by which a system operates. It requires a person to apply what he believes to be true about the dynamics of society in a creative fashion. A plan for modification of a system or creation of an entirely new system can be examined in the light of what is known about how the social world operates. Thinking about sociological issues in this fashion should also serve at least to make students aware that, theoretically, there is no reason the social world must be organized in the manner in which they find it, that alternative forms of social organization are possible, and that they cannot be attained by fiat. The problem is not so much to design a social system that seems more humane, desirable, and fair; it is to figure out how to build it.

— *BITS* —

social psychology
and interpersonal relations

part I

from deviant
to deviant
to deviant

The status of social deviant is sometimes acquired when a person makes a more or less conscious choice; sometimes it is the result of a long sequence of minor actions that culminates in the person's moving into a subculture that has norms different from those of the larger society. A man who chooses to steal from his company in order to maintain or improve his standard of living is taking the first path to deviant status. In a currently fashionable example of the second pattern, a student is first introduced to and then becomes a member of a group whose practice it is to use pot and later finds that he no longer accepts the larger society's definition of pot as a substance to be suppressed.

Deviant status can be obtained in a third way. Unlike a deviant status that results from conscious choice or gradual movement, it is not an *achieved* status. It is *ascribed,* for it is a characteristic with which the individual is born. In the same sense that one's status as a male or a female is (usually) an ascribed status, some people are assigned at birth to certain categories of social deviance. The physically or mentally abnormal are social deviants in this sense. They are, to use Erving Goffman's term, *stigmatized.* The role of ascribed deviant is unusual, for it does not require that the individual reject society's norms, as do the thief and the pot-head; the society rejects the deviant. Everyone else reacts to the stigmatized in terms of a set of norms different from those that typically govern interaction.

In his story, "Flowers for Algernon," Daniel Keyes views the world from the perspective of an ascribed deviant. The unique aspect of the story is that Keyes presents the deviant's view of the world from the bottom looking up, from the top looking down, and provides something of the experience of moving between the end points. Keyes's central character, Charlie, makes the transition from the status of idiot, with an IQ of 68, to that of genius and back again.

It seems appropriate to describe Charlie's mobility as a movement upward followed by a movement downward, as if one were describing the progress of a mountain climber. The significance of being at the bottom or the top is similar —you can see more and farther from the top than from the bottom. The worlds in which Charlie moves as an idiot and as a genius are no different physically, but they are vastly different psychologically. The difference is a function of Charlie's being able, as an idiot, to understand relatively little about how his physical and social worlds operate, and being able, as a genius, to understand a great deal about the dynamics of both worlds.

Keyes's story makes a particular point extraordinarily well and provides a stimulus that leads to the consideration of two interesting and frightening questions. Assume that it is reasonable to conceive an idiot's world in the manner Keyes has chosen. When reading the story you can easily understand Charlie's misperceptions of his social world, and therefore you can understand his actions. Consider the world from the perspective of a genius. Is it possible that this analogy is appropriate?—the world of a genius is to the world of a normal as the world of a normal is to the world of an idiot. If the analogy is appropriate, then relative to a genius, a man of normal intelligence must seem as pathetic as Charlie does to a normal man.

Consider a second point: to what extent is the account of the transition from genius to idiot a reasonable description of what it would be like to lose a substantial proportion of your mental abilities? What would it be like to have an automobile accident and recover to find yourself able to function only in a manner equivalent to Charlie's ability level as an idiot?

"flowers for algernon"

by Daniel Keyes

progris riport 1—martch 5, 1965

Dr. Strauss says I shud rite down what I think and evrey thing that happins to me from now on. I dont know why but he says its importint so they will see if they will use me. I hope they use me. Miss Kinnian says maybe they can make me smart. I want to be smart. My name is Charlie Gordon. I am 37 years old and 2 weeks ago was my brithday. I have nuthing more to rite now so I will close for today.

progris riport 2—martch 6

I had a test today. I think I faled it. and I think that maybe now they wont use me. What happind is a nice young man was in the room and he had some white cards with ink spillled all over them. He sed Charlie what do you see on this card. I was very skared even tho I had my rabits foot in my pockit because when I was a kid I always faled tests in school and I spillled ink to.

I told him I saw a inkblot. He said yes and it made me feel good. I thot that was all but when I got up to go he stopped me. He said now sit down Charlie we are not thru yet. Then I don't remember so good but he wantid me to say what was in the ink. I dint see nuthing in the ink but he said there was picturs there other pepul saw some picturs. I couldnt see any picturs. I reely tryed to see. I held the card close up and then far away. Then I said if I had my glases I could see better I usully only ware my glases in the movies or TV but I said they are in the closit in the hall. I got them. Then I said let me see that card agen I bet Ill find it now.

I tryed hard but I still coudnt find the pictures I only saw the ink. I told him maybe I need new glases. He rote somthing down on a paper and I got skared of faling the test. I told him it was a very nice inkblot with little points all around the eges. He looked very sad so that wasnt it. I said please let me try agen. Ill get it in a few minits becaus Im not so fast somtimes. Im a slow reeder too in Miss Kinnians class for slow adults but I'm trying very hard.

He gave me a chance with another card that had 2 kinds of ink spilled on it red and blue.

He was very nice and talked slow like Miss Kinnian does and he explaned it to me that it was a *raw shok*. He said pepul see things in the ink. I said show me where. He said think. I told him I think a inkblot but that wasnt rite eather. He said what does it remind you—pretend something. I closd my eyes for a long time to pretend. I told him I pretned a fowntan pen with ink leeking all over a table cloth. Then he got up and went out.

I dont think I passd the *raw shok* test.

progris report 3—martch 7

. . . Some men in white coats took me to a difernt part of the hospitil and gave me a game to play. It was like a race with a white mouse. They called the mouse Algernon. Algernon was in a box with a lot of twists and turns like all kinds of walls and they gave me a pencil and a paper with lines and lots of boxes. On one side it said START and on the other end it said FINISH. They said it was *amazed* and that Algernon and me had the same *amazed* to do. I dont see how we could have the same *amazed* if Algernon had a box and I had a paper but I dint say nothing. Anyway there wasnt time because the race started.

One of the men had a watch he was trying to hide so I wouldnt see it so I tryed not to look and that made me nervous.

Anyway that test made me feel worser than all the others because they did it over 10 times with difernt *amazeds* and Algernon won every time. I dint know that mice were so smart. Maybe thats because Algernon is a white mouse. Maybe white mice are smarter then other mice.

progris riport 4—Mar 8

Their going to use me! Im so exited I can hardly write. Dr Nemur and Dr Strauss had a argament about it first. Dr Nemur was in the office when Dr Strauss brot me in. Dr Nemur was worryed about using me but Dr Strauss told him Miss Kinnian rekemmended me the best from all the people who was teaching. I like Miss Kinnian becaus shes a very smart teacher. And she said Charlie your going to have a second chance. If you volenteer for this experament you mite get smart. They dont know if it will be perminint but theirs a chance. Thats why I said ok even when I was scared because she said it was an operashun. She said dont be scared Charlie you done so much with so little I think you deserv it most of all.

So I got scaird when Dr Nemur and Dr Strauss argud about it. Dr Strauss said I had something that was very good. He said I had a good *motor-vation*. I never even knew I had that. I felt proud when he said that not every body with an eye-q of 68 had that thing. I dont know what it is or where I got it but he said Algernon had it too. Algernons *motor-vation* is the cheese they put in his box. But it cant be that because I didnt eat any cheese this week.

Then he told Dr Nemur something I dint understand so while they were talking I wrote down some of the words.

He said Dr Nemur I know Charlie is not what you had in mind as the first of your new brede of intelek** (coudnt get the word) superman. But most people of his low ment** are host** and uncoop** they are usualy dull apath** and hard to reach. He has a good natcher hes intristed and eager to please.

Dr Nemur said remember he will be the first human beeng ever to have his intelijence trippled by surgicle meens.

Dr Strauss said exakly. Look at how well hes lerned to read and write for his low mentel age its as grate an acheve** as you and I lerning einstines therey of **vity without help. That shows the intenss motor-vation. Its comparat** a tremen* achev** I say we use Charlie.

I dint get all the words and they were talking to fast but it sounded like Dr Strauss was on my side and like the other one wasnt.

Then Dr Nemur nodded he said all right maybe your right. We will use Charlie. When he said that I got so exited I jumped up and shook his hand for being so good to me. I told him thank you doc you wont be sorry for giving me a second chance. And I mean it like I told him. After the operashun Im gonna try to be smart. Im gonna try awful hard.

progris ript 5—Mar 10

. . . I asked Dr Strauss if Ill beat Algernon in the race after the operashun and he said maybe. If the operashun works Ill show that mouse I can be as smart as he is. Maybe smarter. Then Ill be abel to read better and spell the words good and know lots of things and be like other people. I want to be smart like other people. If it works perminint they will make everybody smart all over the wurld.

They dint give me anything to eat this morning. I dont know what that eating has to do with getting smart. Im very hungry and Dr Nemur took away my box of candy. That Dr Nemur is a grouch. Dr Strauss says I can have it back after the operashun. You cant eat befor a operashun . . .

Progress Report 6—Mar 15

The operashun dint hurt. He did it while I was sleeping. They took off the bandijis from my eyes and my head today so I can make a PROGRESS REPORT. Dr Nemur who looked at some of my other ones sayd I spell PROGRESS wrong and he told me how to spell it and REPORT too. I got to try and remember that.

I have a very bad memary for spelling. Dr Strauss says its ok to tell about all the things that happin to me but he says I shoud tell more about what I feel and what I think. When I told him I dont know how to think he said try. All the time when the bandijis were on my eyes I tryed to think. Nothing happened. I dont know what to think about. Maybe if I ask him he will tell me how I can think now that Im suppose to get smart. What do smart people think about. Fancy things I suppose. I wish I knew some fancy things alredy.

Progress Report 7—mar 19

Nothing is happining. I had lots of tests and different kinds of races with Algernon. I hate that mouse. He always beats me. Dr Strauss said I got to play those games. And he said some time I got to take those tests over again. Thse inkblots are stupid. . . .

I got a headache from trying to think so much. I thot Dr Strauss was my frend but he dont help me. He dont tell me what to think or when Ill get smart. Miss Kinnian dint come to see me. I think writing these progress reports are stupid too.

Progress Report 8—Mar 23

Im going back to work at the factery. They said it was better I shud go back to work but I cant tell anyone what the operashun was for and I have to come to the hospitil for an hour evry night after work. They are gonna pay me mony evry month for lerning to be smart.

Im glad Im going back to work because I miss my job and all my frends and all the fun we have there.

Dr Strauss says I shud keep writing things down but I dont have to do it every day just when I think of something or something speshul happins. He says dont get discoridged because it takes time and it happins slow. He says it took a long time with Algernon before he got 3 times smarter then he was before. Thats why Algernon beats me all the time because he had that operashun too. That makes me feel better. I coud probly do that *amazed* faster than a reglar mouse. Maybe some day Ill beat Algernon. Boy that would be something. So far Algernon looks like he mite be smart perminent.

Mar 25   (I dont have to write PROGRESS REPORT on top any more just when I hand it in once a week for Dr Nemur to read. I just have to put the date on. That saves time)

We had a lot of fun at the factery today. Joe Carp said hey look where Charlie had his operashun what did they do Charlie put some brains in. I was going to tell him but I remembered Dr Strauss said no. Then Frank Reilly said what did you do Charlie forget your key and open your door the hard way. That made me laff. Their really my friends and they like me.

Sometimes somebody will say hey look at Joe or Frank or George he really pulled a Charlie Gordon. I dont know why they say that but they always laff. This morning Amos Borg who is the 4 man at Donnegans used my name when he shouted at Ernie the office boy. Ernie lost a packige. He said Ernie for godsake what are you trying to be a Charlie Gordon. I dont understand why he said that. I never lost any packiges.

Mar 28   Dr Strauss came to my room tonight to see why I dint come in like I was suppose to. I told him I dont like to race with Algernon any more. He said I dont have to for a while but I shud come in. He had a present for me only it wasnt a present but just for lend. I thot it was a little television but it wasnt. He said I got to turn it on when I got to sleep. I said your kidding why shud I turn it on when Im going to sleep. Who ever herd of a thing like that. But he said if I want to get smart I got to do what he says. I told him I dont think I was going to get smart and he put his hand on my sholder and said Charlie you dont know it yet but your getting smarter all the time. You wont notice for a while. I think he was just being nice to make me feel good because I dont look any smarter. . . .

Mar 29   That crazy TV kept me up all night. How can I sleep with something yelling crazy things all night in my ears. And the nutty pictures. Wow. I dont know what it says when Im up so how am I going to know when Im sleeping.

Dr Strauss says its ok. He says my brains are lerning when I sleep and that will help me when Miss Kinnian starts my lessons in the hospitl (only I found out it isnt a hospitil its a labatory). I think its all crazy. If you can get smart when your sleeping why do people go to school. That thing I dont think will work. I use to watch the late show and the late late show on TV all the time and it never made me smart. Maybe you have to sleep while you watch it.

Progress Report 9—April 3

Dr Strauss showed me how to keep the TV turned low so now I can sleep. I dont hear a thing. And I still dont understand what it says. A few times I play it over in the morning to find out what I lerned when I was sleeping and I dont think so. Miss Kinnian says Maybe its another langwidge or something. But most times it sounds american. It talks so fast faster then even Miss Gold who was my teacher in 6 grade and I remember she talked so fast I coudnt understand her.

I told Dr Strauss what good is it to get smart in my sleep. I want to be smart when Im awake. He says its the same thing and I have two minds. Theres the *subconscious* and the *conscious* (that's how you spell it). And one dont tell the other one what its doing. They dont even talk to each other. Thats why I dream. And boy have I been having crazy dreams. Wow. Ever since that night TV. The late late late late late show.

I forgot to ask him if it was only me or if everybody had those two minds.

(I just looked up the word in the dictionary Dr Strauss gave me. The word is *subconscious. adj. Of the nature of mental operations yet not present in consciousness; as, subconscious conflict of desires.*) Theres more but I still don't know what it means. This isnt a very good dictionary for dumb people like me. . . .

April 6 I beat Algernon! I dint even know I beat him until Burt the tester told me. Then the second time I lost because I got so exited I fell off the chair before I finished. But after that I beat him 8 more times. I must be getting smart to beat a smart mouse like Algernon. But I dont feel smarter.

I wanted to race Algernon some more but Burt said thats enough for one day. They let me hold him for a minit. Hes not so bad. Hes soft like a ball of cotton. He blinks and when he opens his eyes their black and pink on the eges.

I said can I feed him because I felt bad to beat him and I wanted to be nice and make friends. But said no Algernon is a very specshul mouse with an operashun like mine, and he was the first of all the animals to stay smart so long. He told me Algernon is so smart that every day he has to solve a test to get his food. Its a thing like a lock on a door that changes every time Algernon goes in to eat so he has to lern something new to get his food. That made me sad because if he coudnt lern he would be hungry.

I dont think its right to make you pass a test to eat. How would Dr Nemur like it to have to pass a test every time he wants to eat. I think Ill be frends with Algernon.

April 10 Miss Kinnian teaches me to spell better. She says look at a word and close your eyes and say it over and over until you remember. I have lots of truble with *through* that you say *threw* and *enough* and *tough* that you dont say *new* and *tew*. You got to say *enuff* and *tuff*. Thats how I use to write it before I started to get smart. Im confused but Miss Kinnian says theres no reason in spelling.

April 15 Miss Kinnian says Im lerning fast. She read some of the Progress Reports and she looked at me kind of funny. She says Im a fine person and Ill show them all. I asked her why. She said never mind but I shoudnt feel bad if I find out that everybody isnt nice like I think. She said for a person who god gave so little to you done more then a lot of people with brains they never even used. I said all my frends are smart people but there good. They like me and they never did anything that wasnt nice. . . .

Apr 16 Today, I lerned, the *comma,* this is a comma (,) a period, with a tail, Miss Kinnian, says its important, because, it makes writing, better, she said, somebody, could lose, a lot of money, if a comma, isnt, in the, right place, I dont have, any money, and I dont see, how a comma, keeps you, from losing it,

But she says, everybody, uses commas, so Ill use, them too,

Apr 17 I used the comma wrong. Its punctuation. Miss Kinnian told me to look up long words in the dictionary to lern to spell them. I said whats the difference if you can read it anyway. She said its part of your education so now on Ill look up all the words Im not sure how to spell. It takes a long time to write that way but I think Im remembering. I only have to look up once and after that I get it right. Anyway thats how come I got the word *punctuation* right. (Its that way in the dictionary). Miss Kinnian says a period is punctuation too, and there are lots of other marks to lern. I told her I thot all the periods had to have tails but she said no.

You got to mix them up, she showed?me" how. to mix! them (up,. and now; I can! mix up all kinds" of punctuation, in! my writing? There, are lots! of rules? to lern; but I'm gettin'g them in my head.

One thing I? like about, Dear Miss Kinnian: (thats the way it goes in a business letter if I ever go into business) is she, always gives me' a reason" when — I ask. She's a gen'ius! I wish! I cou'd be smart" like, her;

(Punctuation, is; fun!)

April 18 What a dope I am! I didn't even understand what she was talking about. I read the grammar book last night and it explanes the whole thing. Then I saw it was the same way as Miss Kinnian was trying to tell me, but I didn't get it. I got up in the middle of the night, and the whole thing straightened out in my mind.

Miss Kinnian said that the TV working in my sleep helped out. She said I reached a plateau. Thats like the flat top of a hill.

After I figgered out how punctuation worked, I read over all my old Progress Reports from the beginning. Boy, did I have crazy spelling and punctuation! I told Miss Kinnian I ought to go over the pages and fix all the mistakes but she said, "No, Charlie, Dr. Nemur wants them just as they are. That's why he let you keep them after they were photostated, to see your own progress. You're coming along fast, Charlie."

That made me feel good. After the lesson I went down and played with Algernon. We don't race any more.

April 20 I feel sick inside. Not sick like for a doctor, but inside my chest it feels empty like getting punched and a heartburn at the same time.

I wasn't going to write about it, but I guess I got to, because it's important. Today was the first time I ever stayed home from work.

Last night Joe Carp and Frank Reilly invited me to a party. There were lots of girls and some men from the factory. I remembered how sick I got last time I drank too much, so I told Joe I didn't want anything to drink. He gave me a plain Coke instead. It tasted funny, but I thought it was just a bad taste in my mouth.

We had a lot of fun for a while. Joe said I should dance with Ellen and she would teach me the steps. I fell a few times and I couldn't understand why because no one else was dancing besides Ellen and me. And all the time I was tripping because somebody's foot was always sticking out.

Then when I got up I saw the look on Joe's face and it gave me a funny feeling in my stomack. "He's a scream," one of the girls said. Everybody was laughing.

Frank said, "I ain't laughed so much since we sent him off for the newspaper that night at Muggsy's and ditched him."

"Look at him. His face is red."

"He's blushing. Charlie is blushing."

"Hey, Ellen, what'd you do to Charlie? I never saw him act like that before."

I didn't know what to do or where to turn. Everyone was looking at me and laughing and I felt naked. I wanted to hide myself. I ran out into the street and I threw up. Then I walked home. It's a funny thing I never knew that Joe and Frank and the others liked to have me around all the time to make fun of me.

Now I know what it means when they say "to pull a Charlie Gordon." I'm ashamed.

Progress Report 11

April 21   Still didn't go into the factory. I told Mrs. Flynn my landlady to call and tell Mr. Donnegan I was sick. Mrs. Flynn looks at me very funny lately like she's scared of me.

I think it's a good thing about finding out how everybody laughs at me. I thought about it a lot. It's because I'm so dumb and I don't even know when I'm doing something dumb. People think it's funny when a dumb person can't do things the same way they can.

Anyway, now I know I'm getting smarter every day. I know punctuation and I can spell good. I like to look up all the hard words in the dictionary and I remember them. I'm reading a lot now, and Miss Kinnian says I read very fast. Sometimes I even understand what I'm reading about, and it stays in my mind. There are times when I can close my eyes and think of a page and it all comes back like a picture.

Besides history, geography, and arithmetic, Miss Kinnian said I should start to learn a few foreign languages. Dr. Strauss gave me some more tapes to play while I sleep. I still don't understand how that conscious and unconscious mind works, but Dr. Strauss says not to worry yet. He asked me to promise that when I start learning college subjects next week I wouldn't read any books on psychology—that is, until he gives me permission.

I feel a lot better today, but I guess I'm still a little angry that all the time people were laughing and making fun of me because I wasn't so smart. When I become intelligent like Dr. Strauss says, with three times my I.Q. of 68, then maybe I'll be like everyone else and people will like me and be friendly.

I'm not sure what an I.Q. is. Dr. Nemur said it was something that measured how intelligent you were—like a scale in the drugstore weighs pounds. But Dr. Strauss had a big argument with him and said an I.Q. didn't weigh intelligence at all. He said an I.Q. showed how much intelligence you could get, like the numbers on the outside of a measuring cup. You still had to fill the cup up with stuff.

Then when I asked Burt, who gives me my intelligence tests and works with Algernon, he said that both of them were wrong (only I had to promise not to tell them he said so). Burt says that the I.Q. measures a lot of different things including some of the things you learned already, and it really isn't any good at all.

So I still don't know what I.Q. is except that mine is going to be over 200 soon. I didn't want to say anything, but I don't see how if they don't know *what* it is, or *where* it is—I don't see how they know *how much* of it you've got.

Dr. Nemur says I have to take a *Rorschach Test* tomorrow. I wonder what *that* is.

April 22   I found out what a *Rorschach* is. It's the test I took before the operation—the one with the inkblots on the pieces of cardboard. The man who gave me the test was the same one.

I was scared to death of those inkblots. I knew he was going to ask me to find the pictures and I knew I wouldn't be able to. I was thinking to myself, if only there was some way of knowing what kind of pictures were hidden there. Maybe there weren't any pictures at all. Maybe it was just a trick to see if I was dumb enough to look for something that wasn't there. Just thinking about that made me sore at him.

"All right, Charlie," he said, "you've seen these cards before, remember?"

"Of course I remember."

The way I said it, he knew I was angry, and he looked surprised. "Yes, of course. Now I want you to look at this one. What might this be? What do you see on this card? People see all sorts of things in these inkblots. Tell me what it might be for you—what it makes you think of."

I was shocked. That wasn't what I had expected him to say at all. "You mean there are no pictures hidden in those inkblots?"

He frowned and took off his glasses. "What?"

"Pictures. Hidden in the inkblots. Last time you told me that everyone could see them and you wanted me to find them too."

He explained to me that the last time he had used almost the exact same words he was using now. I didn't believe it, and I still have the suspicion that he misled me at the time just for the fun of it. Unless—I don't know any more—could I have been *that* feeble-minded?

We went through the cards slowly. One of them looked like a pair of bats tugging at something. Another one looked like two men fencing with swords. I imagined all sorts of things. I guess I got carried away. But I didn't trust him any more, and I kept turning them around and even looking on the back to see if there was anything there I was supposed to catch. While he was making his notes, I peeked out of the corner of my eye to read it. But it was all in code that looked like this:

$$WF + A \; DdF - Ad \; orig. \; WF - A \; SF + obj$$

The test still doesn't make sense to me. It seems to me that anyone could make up lies about things that they didn't really see. How could he know

I wasn't making a fool of him by mentioning things that I didn't really imagine? Maybe I'll understand it when Dr. Strauss lets me read up on psychology.

April 27   . . . Dr. Strauss and Dr. Nemur don't seem to be getting along so well. They're arguing all the time. This evening when I came in to ask Dr. Strauss [something] I heard him shouting. Dr. Nemur was saying that it was *his* experiment and *his* research, and Dr. Strauss was shouting back that he contributed just as much, because he found me through Miss Kinnian and he performed the operation. Dr. Strauss said that someday thousands of neurosurgeons might be using his technique all over the world.

Dr. Nemur wanted to publish the results of the experiment at the end of this month. Dr. Strauss wanted to wait a while longer to be sure. Dr. Strauss said that Dr. Nemur was more interested in the Chair of Psychology at Princeton than he was in the experiment. Dr. Nemur said that Dr. Strauss was nothing but an opportunist who was trying to ride to glory on *his* coattails.

When I left afterwards, I found myself trembling. I don't know why for sure, but it was as if I'd seen both men clearly for the first time. I remember hearing Burt say that Dr. Nemur had a shrew of a wife who was pushing him all the time to get things published so that he could become famous. Burt said that the dream of her life was to have a big-shot husband.

Was Dr. Strauss really trying to ride on his coattails?

Progress Report 12

April 30 I've quit my job with Donnegan's Plastic Box Company. Mr. Donnegan insisted that it would be better for all concerned if I left. What did I do to make them hate me so?

The first I knew of it was when Mr. Donnegan showed me the petition. Eight hundred and forty names, every one connected with the factory, except Fanny Girden. Scanning the list quickly, I saw at once that hers was the only missing name. All the rest demanded that I be fired.

Joe Carp and Frank Reilly wouldn't talk to me about it. No one else would either, except Fanny. She was one of the few people I'd known who set her mind to something and believed it no matter what the rest of the world proved, said, or did—and Fanny did not believe that I should have been fired. She had been against the petition on principle and despite the pressure and threats she'd held out.

"Which don't mean to say," she remarked, "that I don't think there's something mighty strange about you, Charlie. Them changes. I don't know. You used to be a good, dependable, ordinary man—not too bright maybe, but honest. Who knows what you done to yourself to get so smart all of a sudden. Like everybody around here's been saying, Charlie, it's not right."

"But how can you say that, Fanny? What's wrong with a man becoming intelligent and wanting to acquire knowledge and understanding of the world around him?"

She stared down at her work and I turned to leave. Without looking at me, she said: "It was evil when Eve listened to the snake and ate from the tree of knowledge. It was evil when she saw that she was naked. If not for that none of us would ever have to grow old and sick, and die."

Once again now I have the feeling of shame burning inside me. This intelligence has driven a wedge between me and all the people I once knew and loved. Before, they laughed at me and despised me for my ignorance and dullness; now, they hate me for my knowledge and understanding. What in God's name do they want of me?

They've driven me out of the factory. Now I'm more alone than ever before. . . .

May 15 Dr. Strauss is very angry at me for not having written any progress reports in two weeks. He's justified because the lab is now paying me a regular salary. I told him I was too busy thinking and reading. When I pointed out that writing was such a slow process that it made me impatient with my poor handwriting, he suggested that I learn to type. It's much easier to write now because I can type nearly seventy-five words a minute. Dr. Strauss continually reminds me of the need to speak and write simply so that people will be able to understand me.

I'll try to review all the things that happened to me during the last two weeks. Algernon and I were presented to the American Psychological Association sitting in convention with the World Psychological Association last Tuesday. We created quite a sensation. Dr. Nemur and Dr. Strauss were proud of us.

I suspect that Dr. Nemur, who is sixty—ten years older than Dr. Strauss —finds it necessary to see tangible results of his work. Undoubtedly the result of pressure by Mrs. Nemur.

Contrary to my earlier impressions of him, I realize that Dr. Nemur is not at all a genius. He has a very good mind, but it struggles under the spectre of self-doubt. He wants people to take him for a genius. Therefore, it is important for him to feel that his work is accepted by the world. I believe that Dr. Nemur was afraid of further delay because he worried that someone else might make a discovery along these lines and take the credit from him.

Dr. Strauss on the other hand might be called a genius, although I feel that his areas of knowledge are too limited. He was educated in the tradition of narrow specialization; the broader aspects of background were neglected far more than necessary—even for a neurosurgeon.

I was shocked to learn that the only ancient languages he could read were Latin, Greek, and Hebrew, and that he knows almost nothing of mathematics beyond the elementary levels of the calculus of variations. When he admitted this to me, I found myself almost annoyed. It was as if he'd hidden this part of himself in order to deceive me, pretending—as do many people I've discovered—to be what he is not. No one I've ever known is what he appears to be on the surface.

Dr. Nemur appears to be uncomfortable around me. Sometimes when I try to talk to him, he just looks at me strangely and turns away. I was angry at first when Dr. Strauss told me I was giving Dr. Nemur an inferiority complex. I thought he was mocking me and I'm oversensitive at being made fun of.

How was I to know that a highly respected psychoexperimentalist like Nemur was unacquainted with Hindustani and Chinese? It's absurd when you consider the work that is being done in India and China today in the very field of his study.

I asked Dr. Strauss how Nemur could refute Rahajamati's attack on his method and results if Nemur couldn't even read them in the first place. That strange look on Dr. Strauss' face can mean only one of two things. Either he doesn't want to tell Nemur what they're saying in India, or else —and this worries me—Dr. Strauss doesn't know either. I must be careful to speak and write clearly and simply so that people won't laugh.

May 20 I would not have noticed the new dishwasher, a boy of about sixteen, at the corner diner where I take my evening meals if not for the incident of the broken dishes.

They crashed to the floor, shattering and sending bits of white china under the tables. The boy stood there, dazed and frightened, holding the empty tray in his hand. The whistles and catcalls from the customers (the cries of "hey, there go the profits!" . . . "*Mazeltov!*" . . . and "well, *he* didn't work here very long . . . " which invariably seem to follow the breaking of glass or dishware in a public restaurant) all seemed to confuse him.

When the owner came to see what the excitement was about, the boy cowered as if he expected to be struck and threw up his arms as if to ward off the blow.

"All right! All right, you dope," shouted the owner, "don't just stand there! Get the broom and sweep that mess up. A broom . . . a broom, you idiot! It's in the kitchen. Sweep up all the pieces."

The boy saw that he was not going to be punished. His frightened expression disappeared and he smiled and hummed as he came back with the broom to sweep the floor. A few of the rowdier customers kept up the remarks, amusing themselves at his expense.

"Here, sonny, over here there's a nice piece behind you . . . "

"C'mon, do it again . . . "

"He's not so dumb. It's easier to break 'em than to wash 'em . . . "

As his vacant eyes moved across the crowd of amused onlookers, he slowly mirrored their smiles and finally broke into an uncertain grin at the joke which he obviously did not understand.

I felt sick inside as I looked at his dull, vacuous smile, the wide, bright eyes of a child, uncertain but eager to please. They were laughing at him because he was mentally retarded.

And I had been laughing at him too.

Suddenly, I was furious at myself and all those who were smirking at him. I jumped up and shouted, "Shut up! Leave him alone! It's not his fault he can't understand! He can't help what he is! But for God's sake . . . he's still a human being!"

The room grew silent. I cursed myself for losing control and creating a scene. I tried not to look at the boy as I paid my check and walked out without touching my food. I felt ashamed for both of us.

How strange it is that people of honest feelings and sensibility, who would not take advantage of a man born without arms or legs or eyes— how such people think nothing of abusing a man born with low intelligence. It infuriated me to think that not too long ago I, like this boy, had foolishly played the clown.

And I had almost forgotten.

I'd hidden the picture of the old Charlie Gordon from myself because now that I was intelligent it was something that had to be pushed out of my mind. But today in looking at that boy, for the first time I saw what I had been. *I was just like him!*

Only a short time ago, I learned that people laughed at me. Now I can see that unknowingly I joined with them in laughing at myself. That hurts most of all.

I have often reread my progress reports and seen the illiteracy, the childish naivete, the mind of low intelligence peering from a dark room, through the keyhole, at the dazzling light outside. I see that even in my dullness I knew that I was inferior, and that other people had something I lacked—something denied me. In my mental blindness, I thought that it was somehow connected with the ability to read and write, and I was sure that if I could get those skills I would automatically have intelligence too.

Even a feeble-minded man wants to be like other men.

A child may not know how to feed itself, or what to eat, yet it knows of hunger.

This then is what I was like, I never knew. Even with my gift of intellectual awareness, I never really knew.

This day was good for me. Seeing the past more clearly, I have decided to use my knowledge and skills to work in the field of increasing human intelligence levels. Who is better equipped for this work? Who else has lived in both worlds? These are my people. Let me use my gift to do something for them.

Tomorrow, I will discuss with Dr. Strauss the manner in which I can work in this area. I may be able to help him work out the problems of widespread use of the technique which was used on me. I have several good ideas of my own.

There is so much that might be done with this technique. If I could be made into a genius, what about thousands of others like myself? What fantastic levels might be achieved by using this technique on normal people? On *geniuses?*

There are so many doors to open. I am impatient to begin.

Progress Report 13

May 23   It happened today. Algernon bit me. I visited the lab to see him as I do occasionally, and when I took him out of his cage, he snapped at my hand. I put him back and watched him for a while. He was unusally disturbed and vicious.

May 24   Burt, who is in charge of the experimental animals, tells me that Algernon is changing. He is less co-operative; he refuses to run the maze any more; general motivation has decreased. And he hasn't been eating. Everyone is upset about what this may mean.

May 25   They've been feeding Algernon, who now refuses to work the shifting-lock problem. Everyone identifies me with Algernon. In a way we're both the first of our kind. They're all pretending that Algernon's behavior is not necessarily significant for me. But it's hard to hide the fact that some of the other animals who were used in this experiment are showing strange behavior.

Dr. Strauss and Dr. Nemur have asked me not to come to the lab any more. I know what they're thinking but I can't accept it. I am going ahead with my plans to carry their research forward. With all due respect to both of these fine scientists, I am well aware of their limitations. If there is an answer, I'll have to find it out for myself. Suddenly, time has become very important to me.

May 29   I have been given a lab of my own and permission to go ahead with the research. I'm on to something. Working day and night. I've had a cot moved into the lab. Most of my writing time is spent on the notes which I keep in a separate folder, but from time to time I feel it necessary to put down my moods and my thoughts out of sheer habit.

I find the *calculus of intelligence* to be a fascinating study. Here is the place for the application of all the knowledge I have acquired. In a sense it's the problem I've been concerned with all my life.

May 31   Dr. Strauss thinks I'm working too hard. Dr. Nemur says I'm trying to cram a lifetime of research and thought into a few weeks. I know I should rest, but I'm driven on by something inside that won't let me stop. I've got to find the reason for the sharp regression in Algernon. I've go to know *if* and *when* it will happen to me.

June 4   Letter to Dr. Strauss *(copy)*
Dear Dr. Strauss:
   Under separate cover I am sending you a copy of my report entitled, "The Algernon-Gordon Effect: A Study of Structure and Function of Increased Intelligence," which I would like to have you read and have published.
   As you see, my experiments are completed. I have included in my report all of my formulae, as well as mathematical analysis in the appendix. Of course, these should be verified.
   Because of its importance to both you and Dr. Nemur (and need I say to myself, too?) I have checked and rechecked my results a dozen times in the hope of finding an error. I am sorry to say the results must stand. Yet for the sake of science, I am grateful for the little bit that I here add to the knowledge of the function of the human mind and of the laws governing the artificial increase of human intelligence.
   I recall your once saying to me that an experimental *failure* or the *disproving* of a theory was as important to the advancement of learning as a success would be. I know now that this is true. I am sorry, however, that my own contribution to the field must rest upon the ashes of the work of two men I regard so highly.

Yours truly,
Charles Gordon
encl.: rept.

June 5   I must not become emotional. The facts and the results of my experiments are clear, and the more sensational aspects of my own rapid climb cannot obscure the fact that the tripling of intelligence by the surgical technique developed by Drs. Strauss and Nemur must be viewed as having little or no practical applicability (at the present time) to the increase of human intelligence.
   As I review the records and data on Algernon, I see that although he is still in his physical infancy, he has regressed mentally. Motor activity is impaired; there is a general reduction of glandular activity; there is an accelerated loss of co-ordination.

There are also strong indications of progressive amnesia.

As will be seen by my report, these and other physical and mental deterioration syndromes can be predicted with statistically significant results by the application of my formula.

The surgical stimulus to which we were both subjected has resulted in an intensification and acceleration of all mental processes. The unforeseen development, which I have taken the liberty of calling the *Algernon-Gordon Effect*, is the logical extention of the entire intelligence speed-up. The hypothesis here proven may be described simply in the following terms: Artificially increased intelligence deteriorates at a rate of time directly proportional to the quantity of the increase.

I feel that this, in itself, is an important discovery.

As long as I am able to write, I will continue to record my thoughts in these progress reports. It is one of my few pleasures. However, by all indications, my own mental deterioration will be very rapid.

I have already begun to notice signs of emotional instability and forgetfulness, the first symptoms of the burnout.

June 10 Deterioration progressing. I have become absent-minded. Algernon died two days ago. Dissection shows my predictions were right. His brain had decreased in weight and there was a general smoothing out of cerebral convolutions as well as a deepening and broadening of brain fissures.

I guess the same thing is or will soon be happening to me. Now that it's definite, I don't want it to happen.

I put Algernon's body in a cheese box and buried him in the back yard. I cried.

June 15 Dr. Strauss came to see me again. I wouldn't open the door and I told him to go away. I want to be left to myself. I have become touchy and irritable. I feel the darkness closing in. It's hard to throw off thoughts of suicide. I keep telling myself how important this introspective journal will be.

It's a strange sensation to pick up a book that you've read and enjoyed just a few months ago and discover that you don't remember it. I remembered how great I thought John Milton was, but when I picked up *Paradise Lost* I couldn't understand it at all. I got so angry I threw the book across the room.

I've got to try to hold on to some of it. Some of the things I've learned. Oh, God, please don't take it all away.

June 21 Why can't I remember? I've got to fight. I lie in bed for days and I don't know who or where I am. Then it all comes back to me in

a flash. Fugues of amnesia. Symptoms of senility—second childhood. I can watch them coming on. It's so cruelly logical. I learned so much and so fast. Now my mind is deteriorating rapidly. I won't let it happen. I'll fight it. I can't help thinking of the boy in the restaurant, the blank expression, the silly smile, the people laughing at him. No—please—not that again.
. . .

June 22   I'm forgetting things that I learned recently. It seems to be follow-ing the classic pattern—the last things learned are the first things forgotten. Or is that the pattern? I'd better look it up again. . . .

I reread my paper on the *Algernon-Gordon Effect* and I get the strange feeling that it was written by someone else. There are parts I don't even understand.

Motor activity impaired. I keep tripping over things and it becomes in-creasingly difficult to type.

June 23   I've given up using the typewriter completely. My co-ordination is bad. I feel that I'm moving slower and slower. Had a terrible shock today. I picked up a copy of an article I used in my research, Krueger's *Uber psychische Ganzheit,* to see if it would help me understand what I had done. First I thought there was something wrong with my eyes. Then I realized I could no longer read German. I tested myself in other languages. All gone.

June 30   A week since I dared to write again. It's slipping away like sand through my fingers. Most of the books I have are too hard for me now. I get angry with them because I know that I read and understood them just a few weeks ago.

I keep telling myself I must keep writing these reports so that somebody will know what is happening to me. But it gets harder to form the words and remember spellings. I have to look up even simple words in the dictionary now and it makes me impatient with myself.

Dr. Strauss comes around almost every day, but I told him I wouldn't see or speak to anybody. He feels guilty. They all do. But I don't blame anyone. I knew what might happen. But how it hurts.

July 10   My landlady Mrs Flynn is very worried about me. She says the way I lay around all day and don't do anything I remind her of her son before she threw him out of the house. She said she doesnt like loafers. If Im sick its one thing, but if Im a loafer thats another thing and she wont have it. I told her I think Im sick.

I try to read a little bit every day, mostly stories, but sometimes I have to read the same thing over and over again because I dont know what it means. And its hard to write. I know I should look up all the words in the dictionary but its so hard and Im so tired all the time.

Then I got the idea that I would only use the easy words instead of the long hard ones. That saves time. I put flowers on Algernons grave about once a week. Mrs Flynn thinks Im crazy to put flowers on a mouses grave but I told her that Algernon was special.

July 14   Its sunday again. I dont have anything to do to keep me busy now because my television set is broke and I dont have any money to get it fixed. (I think I lost this months check from the lab. I dont remember)

I get awful headaches and asperin doesnt help me much. Mrs Flynn knows Im really sick and she feels very sorry for me. Shes a wonderful woman whenever someone is sick.

July 22   Mrs Flynn called a strange doctor to see me. She was afraid I was going to die. I told the doctor I wasnt too sick and that I only forget some-times. He asked me did I have any friends or relatives and I said no I dont have any. I told him I had a friend called Algernon once but he was a mouse and we used to run races together. He looked at me kind of funny like he thought I was crazy.

He smiled when I told him I used to be a genius. He talked to me like I was a baby and he winked at Mrs Flynn. I got mad and chased him out because he was making fun of me the way they all used to.

July 24   I have no more money and Mrs. Flynn says I got to go to work somewhere and pay the rent because I havent paid for over two months. I dont know any work but the job I used to have at Donnegans Plastic Box Company. I dont want to go back there because they all knew me when I was smart and maybe theyll laugh at me. But I dont know what else to do to get money.

July 27   Mr Donnegan was very nice when I came back and asked him for my old job of janitor. First he was very suspicious but I told him what happened to me then he looked very sad and put his hand on my shoulder and said Charlie Gordon you got guts.

Everybody looked at me when I came downstairs and started working in the toilet sweeping it out like I used to. I told myself Charlie if they make fun of you dont get sore because you remember their not so smart as you once thot they were. And besides they were once your friends and if they laughed at you that doesnt mean anything because they liked you too.

One of the new men who came to work there after I went away made a nasty crack he said hey Charlie I hear your a very smart fella a real quiz kid. Say something intelligent. I felt bad but Joe Carp came over and grabbed him by the shirt and said leave him alone you lousy cracker or Ill break your neck. I didnt expect Joe to take my part so I guess hes really my friend.

ideology,
cognitive consistency,
and crucial experiment

Social psychologists have long been interested in the dynamics of cognitive organization, particularly in the manner in which individuals integrate new ideas or facts with existing belief systems. Knowledge of this process could provide a basis for understanding the manner in which attitudes and beliefs initially develop; it is certainly the key to understanding how cognitive structures are modified by new information. The problem of accounting for the way in which individuals assimilate new information is particularly intriguing, for some evidence suggests that individuals strive for a certain consistency among their cognitions, and other evidence indicates that they frequently maintain sets of beliefs that are psycho-logically inconsistent.

Considerable research has been done on the manner in which beliefs about a certain topic—say, beliefs about the qualities possessed by a friend or an acquaintance—are interrelated and on the extent to which the evaluation of one facet of an issue, or one aspect of a man's character, determines expectations about other facets of the issue or aspects of his character. If, for example, a person's experience with another leads him to believe that the other is honest in his business dealings, he will be more likely to expect the other to possess additional positive attributes, rather than negative ones. If additional information indicates that the person is miserly and treats his family badly, it will cause considerable discomfort for the person who at first possessed only positive information about his acquaintance. An attempt to attain cognitive consistency will typically follow receipt of the new information. Under these circumstances, it is likely that some thought will be given to the question whether the initial impression of honesty was erroneous. Usually, the individual will seek some way of reconciling the psycho-logical inconsistency of a man's being both honest and miserly.

The various strategies that individuals use in attempting to reconcile distressing cognitive inconsistencies have been only minimally charted, and even less is known about the conditions under which two or more inconsistent beliefs, belief systems, or sets of beliefs and actions can be maintained. It is, for example, not clearly understood how a man is able to feel no great psychological stress when he claims to be committed to the revolution of a society and the abolition of economic capitalism and yet permits himself to be supported by the income from stock investments made for him by his parents. In the same vein, little is understood of the psychological mechanisms that permit a man to claim to adhere to a value system in which material possessions are considered irrelevant and yet define his life in terms of his possessions.

Harry Harrison's story, "The Streets of Ashkelon," deals with the effects on a nonhuman species of the introduction of two sets of beliefs that are commonly held by humans and that contradict one another.

"the streets of ashkelon"

by Harry Harrison

Somewhere above, hidden by the eternal clouds of Wesker's World, a thunder rumbled and grew. Trader John Garth stopped when he heard it. . . .

"That noise is the same as the noise of your sky-ship," Itin said, with stolid Wesker logicality, slowly pulverizing the idea in his mind and turning over the bits one by one for closer examination. "But your ship is still sitting where you landed it. It must be, even though we cannot see it, because you are the only one who can operate it. And even if anyone else could operate it we would have heard it rising into the sky. Since we did not, and if this sound is a sky-ship sound, then it must mean . . . "

"Yes, another ship," Garth said, too absorbed in his own thoughts to wait for the laborious Weskerian chains of logic to clank their way through to the end. . . .

"You better go ahead, Itin," he said. "Use the water so you can get to the village quickly. Tell everyone to get back into the swamps, well clear of the hard ground. That ship is landing on instruments and anyone underneath at touchdown is going to be cooked."

This immediate threat was clear enough to the little Wesker amphibian. Before Garth finished speaking Itin's ribbed ears had folded like a bat's wing and he slipped silently into the nearby canal. Garth squelched on through the mud, making as good time as he could over the clinging surface. He had just reached the fringes of the village clearing when the rumbling grew to a head-splitting roar and the spacer broke through the low-hanging layer of clouds above. Garth shielded his eyes from the down-reaching tongue of flame and examined the growing form of the grey-black ship with mixed feelings.

After almost a standard year on Wesker's World he had to fight down a longing for human companionship of any kind. While this buried fragment of herd-spirit chattered for the rest of the monkey tribe, his trader's mind was busily drawing a line under a column of figures and adding up the total. This could very well be another trader's ship, and if it were his monopoly of the Wesker trade was at an end. Then again, this might not be a trader at all, which was the reason he stayed in the shelter of the giant fern and loosened his gun in its holster.

The ship baked dry a hundred square metres of mud, the roaring blast died, and the landing feet crunched down through the crackling crust. Metal creaked and settled into place while the cloud of smoke and steam slowly drifted lower in the humid air.

"Garth, where are you?" the ship's speaker boomed. The lines of the spacer had looked only slightly familiar, but there was no mistaking the rasping tones of that voice. Garth wore a smile when he stepped out into the open and whistled shrilly through two fingers. A directional microphone ground out of its casing on the ship's fin and turned in his direction.

"What are you doing here, Singh?" he shouted towards the mike.

. . .

"I am on course to a more fairly atmosphered world where a fortune is waiting to be made. I only stopped here since an opportunity presented to turn an honest credit by running a taxi service. I bring you friendship, the perfect companionship, a man in a different line of business who might help you in yours. I'd come out and say hello myself, except I would have to decon for biologicals. I'm cycling the passenger through the lock so I hope you won't mind helping with his luggage."

At least there would be no other trader on the planet now, that worry was gone. But Garth still wondered what sort of passenger would be taking one-way passage to an uninhabited world. And what was behind that concealed hint of merriment in Singh's voice? He walked around to the far side of the spacer where the ramp had dropped, and looked up at the man in the cargo lock who was wrestling ineffectually with a large crate. The man turned towards him and Garth saw the clerical dog-collar and knew just what it was Singh had been chuckling about.

"What are you doing here?" Garth asked; in spite of his attempt at self control he snapped the words. If the man noticed this he ignored it, because he was still smiling and putting out his hand as he came down the ramp.

"Father Mark," he said. "Of the Missionary Society of Brothers. I'm very pleased to . . . "

"I said what are you doing here." Garth's voice was under control now, quiet and cold. He knew what had to be done, and it must be done quickly or not at all.

"That should be obvious," Father Mark said, his good nature still unruffled. "Our missionary society has raised funds to send spiritual emissaries to alien worlds for the first time. I was lucky enough . . . "

"Take your luggage and get back into the ship. You're not wanted here and have no permission to land. You'll be a liability and there is no one on Wesker to take care of you. Get back into the ship."

"I don't know who you are sir, or why you are lying to me," the priest said. He was still calm but the smile was gone. "But I have studied galactic law and the history of this planet very well. There are no diseases or beasts here that I should have any particular fear of. It is also an open planet, and until the Space Survey changes that status I have as much right to be here as you do."

The man was of course right, but Garth couldn't let him know that. He had been bluffing, hoping the priest didn't know his rights. But he did. There was only one distasteful course left for him, and he had better do it while there was still time.

"Get back in that ship," he shouted, not hiding his anger now. With a smooth motion his gun was out of the holster and the pitted black muzzle only inches from the priest's stomach. The man's face turned white, but he did not move.

"What the hell are you doing, Garth!" Singh's shocked voice grated from the speaker. "The guy paid his fare and you have no rights at all to throw him off the planet."

"I have this right," Garth said, raising his gun and sighting between the priest's eyes. "I give him thirty seconds to get back aboard the ship or I pull the trigger."

"Well I think you are either off your head or playing a joke," Singh's exasperated voice rasped down at them. "If a joke, it is in bad taste, and either way you're not getting away with it. Two can play at that game, only I can play it better."

There was the rumble of heavy bearings and the remote-controlled four-gun turret on the ship's side rotated and pointed at Garth. "Now—down gun and give Father Mark a hand with the luggage," the speaker commanded, a trace of humour back in the voice now. "As much as I would like to help, Old Friend, I cannot. I feel it is time you had a chance to talk to the father; after all, I have had the opportunity of speaking with him all the way from Earth."

Garth jammed the gun back into the holster with an acute feeling of loss. Father Mark stepped forward, the winning smile back now and a bible taken from a pocket of his robe, in his raised hand. "My son," he said.

"I'm not your son," was all Garth could choke out as defeat welled up in him. His fist drew back as the anger rose, and the best he could do was open the fist so he struck only with the flat of his hand. Still the blow sent the priest crashing to the ground and fluttered the pages of the book splattering into the thick mud.

Itin and the other Weskers had watched everything with seemingly emotionless interest, and Garth made no attempt to answer their unspoken questions. He started towards his house, but turned back when he saw they were still unmoving.

"A new man has come," he told them. "He will need help with the things he has brought. If he doesn't have any place for them, you can put them in the big warehouse until he has a place of his own."

He watched them waddle across the clearing towards the ship, then went inside and gained a certain satisfaction from slamming the door hard enough to crack one of the panes. There was an equal amount of painful pleasure in breaking out one of the remaining bottles of Irish whiskey that he had been saving for a special occasion. Well this was special enough, though not really what he had had in mind. The whiskey was good and burned away some of the bad taste in his mouth, but not all of it. If his tactics had worked, success would have justified everything. But he had failed and in addition to the pain of failure there was the acute feeling that he had made a horse's ass out of himself. Singh had blasted off without any good-byes. There was no telling what sense he had made of the whole matter, though he would surely carry some strange stories back to the trader's lodge. Well, that could be worried about the next time Garth signed in. Right now he had to go about setting things right with the missionary. Squinting out through the rain he saw the man struggling to erect a collapsible tent while the entire population of the village stood in ordered ranks and watched. Naturally none of them offered to help.

By the time the tent was up and the crates and boxes stowed inside it the rain had stopped. The level of fluid in the bottle was a good bit lower and Garth felt more like facing up to the unavoidable meeting. In truth, he was looking forward to talking to the man. This whole nasty business aside, after an entire solitary year any human companionship looked good. *Will you join me now for dinner. John Garth,* he wrote on the back of an old invoice. But maybe the guy was too frightened to come? Which was no way to start any kind of relationship. Rummaging under the bunk, he found a box that was big enough and put his pistol inside. Itin was of course waiting outside the door when he opened it, since this was his tour as Knowledge Collector. He handed him the note and the box.

"Would you take these to the new man," he said.

"Is the new man's name New Man?" Itin asked.

"No, it's not!" Garth snapped. "His name is Mark. But I'm only asking you to deliver this, not get involved in conversation."

As always when he lost his temper, the literal minded Weskers won the round. "You are not asking for conversation," Itin said slowly, "but Mark may ask for conversation. And others will ask me his name, if I do not know his na . . . " The voice cut off as Garth slammed the door. This didn't work in the long run either because next time he saw Itin—a day, a week, or even a month later—the monologue would be picked up on the very word it had ended and the thought rambled out to its last frayed end. Garth cursed under his breath and poured water over a pair of the tastier concentrates that he had left.

"Come in," he said when there was a quiet knock on the door. The priest entered and held out the box with the gun.

"Thank you for the loan, Mr. Garth, I appreciate the spirit that made you send it. I have no idea of what caused the unhappy affair when I landed, but I think it would be best forgotten if we are going to be on this planet together for any length of time."

"Drink?" Garth asked, taking the box and pointing to the bottle on the table. He poured two glasses full and handed one to the priest. "That's about what I had in mind, but I still owe you an explanation of what happened out there." He scowled into his glass for a second, then raised it to the other man. "It's a big universe and I guess we have to make out as best we can. Here's to Sanity."

"God be with you," Father Mark said, and raised his glass as well.

"Not with me or with this planet," Garth said firmly. "And that's the crux of the matter." He half-drained the glass and sighed.

"Do you say that to shock me?" the priest asked with a smile. "I assure you it doesn't."

"Not intended to shock. I meant it quite literally. I suppose I'm what you would call an atheist, so revealed religion is no concern of mine. While these natives, simple and unlettered stone-age types that they are, have managed to come this far with no superstitions or traces of deism whatsoever. I had hoped that they might continue that way."

"What are you saying?" the priest frowned. "Do you mean they have no gods, no belief in the hereafter? They must die . . . ?"

"Die they do, and to dust returneth like the rest of the animals. They have thunder, trees and water without having thunder-gods, tree sprites, or water nymphs. They have no ugly little gods, taboos, or spells to hag-ride and limit their lives. They are the only primitive people I have ever encountered that are completely free of superstition and appear to be much happier and sane because of it. I just wanted to keep them that way."

"You wanted to keep them from God—from salvation?" The priest's eyes widened and he recoiled slightly.

"No," Garth said. "I wanted to keep them from superstition until they knew more and could think about it realistically without being absorbed and perhaps destroyed by it."

"You're being insulting to the Church, sir, to equate it with superstition
. . ."

"Please," Garth said, raising his hand. "No theological arguments. I
don't think your society footed the bill for this trip just to attempt a
conversion on me. Just accept the fact that my beliefs have been arrived
at through careful thought over a period of years, and no amount of
undergraduate metaphysics will change them. I'll promise not to try and
convert you—if you will do the same for me."

"Agreed, Mr. Garth. As you have reminded me, my mission here is to
save these souls, and that is what I must do. But why should my work
disturb you so much that you try and keep me from landing? Even
threaten me with your gun and . . ." the priest broke off and looked into
his glass.

"And even slug you?" Garth asked, suddenly frowning. "There was no
excuse for that, and I would like to say that I'm sorry. Plain bad manners
and an even worse temper. Live alone long enough and you find yourself
doing that kind of thing." He brooded down at his big hands where they
lay on the table, reading memories into the scars and calluses patterned
there. "Let's just call it frustration, for lack of a better word. In your
business you must have had a lot of chance to peep into the darker places
in men's minds and you should know a bit about motives and happiness.
I have had too busy a life to ever consider settling down and raising a
family, and right up until recently I never missed it. Maybe leakage radiation is softening up my brain, but I had begun to think of these furry and
fishy Weskers as being a little like my own children, that I was somehow
responsible to them."

"We are all His children," Father Mark said quietly.

"Well, here are some of His children that can't even imagine His existence," Garth said, suddenly angry at himself for allowing gentler emotions to show through. Yet he forgot himself at once, leaning forward with
the intensity of his feelings. "Can't you realize the importance of this?
Live with these Weskers awhile and you will discover a simple and happy
life that matches the state of grace you people are always talking about.
They get *pleasure* from their lives—and cause no one pain. By circumstances they have evolved on an almost barren world, so have never had
a chance to grow out of a physical stone age culture. But mentally they
are our match—or perhaps better. They have all learned my language so
I can easily explain the many things they want to know. Knowledge and
the gaining of knowledge gives them real satisfaction. They tend to be
exasperating at times because every new fact must be related to the structure of all other things, but the more they learn the faster this process
becomes. Someday they are going to be man's equal in every way, perhaps
surpass us. If—would you do me a favour?"

"Whatever I can."

"Leave them alone. Or teach them if you must—history and science, philosophy, law, anything that will help them face the realities of the greater universe they never even knew existed before. But don't confuse them with your hatreds and pain, guilt, sin, and punishment. Who knows the harm . . . "

"You are being insulting, sir!" the priest said, jumping to his feet. The top of his grey head barely came to the massive spaceman's chin, yet he showed no fear in defending what he believed. Garth, standing now himself, was no longer the penitent. They faced each other in anger, as men have always stood, unbending in the defence of that which they think right.

"Yours is the insult," Garth shouted. "The incredible egotism to feel that your derivative little mythology, differing only slightly from the thousands of others that still burden men, can do anything but confuse their still fresh minds! Don't you realize that they believe in truth—and have never heard of such a thing as a lie. They have not been trained yet to understand that other kinds of minds can think differently from theirs. Will you spare them this . . . ?"

"I will do my duty which is His will, Mr. Garth. These are God's creatures here, and they have souls. I cannot shirk my duty, which is to bring them His word, so that they may be saved and enter into the kingdom of heaven."

When the priest opened the door the wind caught it and blew it wide. He vanished into the stormswept darkness and the door swung back and forth and a splatter of raindrops blew in. Garth's boots left muddy footprints when he closed the door, shutting out the sight of Itin sitting patiently and uncomplaining in the storm, hoping only that Garth might stop for a moment and leave with him some of the wonderful knowledge of which he had so much.

By unspoken consent that first night was never mentioned again. After a few days of loneliness, made worse because each knew of the other's proximity, they found themselves talking on carefully neutral grounds. Garth slowly packed and stowed away his stock and never admitted that his work was finished and he could leave at any time. He had a fair amount of interesting drugs and botanicals that would fetch a good price. And the Wesker Artifacts were sure to create a sensation in the sophisticated galactic market. Crafts on the planet here had been limited before his arrival, mostly pieces of carving painfully chipped into the hard wood with fragments of stone. He had supplied tools and a stock of raw metal from his own supplies, nothing more than that. In a few months the Weskers had not only learned to work with the new materials, but had translated their own designs and forms into the most alien—but most beautiful—artifacts that he had ever seen. All he had to do was release these on the market to create a primary demand, then return for a new supply. The Weskers wanted only books and tools and knowledge in return, and through their own efforts he knew they would pull themselves into the galactic union.

This is what Garth had hoped. But a wind of change was blowing through the settlement that had grown up around his ship. No longer was he the centre of attention and focal point of the village life. He had to grin when he thought of his fall from power; yet there was very little humour in the smile. Serious and attentive Weskers still took turns of duty as Knowledge Collectors, but their recording of dry facts was in sharp contrast to the intellectual hurricane that surrounded the priest.

Where Garth had made them work for each book and machine, the priest gave freely. Garth had tried to be progressive in his supply of knowledge, treating them as bright but unlettered children. He had wanted them to walk before they could run, to master one step before going on the next.

Father Mark simply brought them the benefits of Christianity. The only physical work he required was the construction of a church, a place of worship and learning. More Weskers had appeared out of the limitless planetary swamps and within days the roof was up, supported on a framework of poles. Each morning the congregation worked a little while on the walls, then hurried inside to learn the all-promising, all-encompassing, all-important facts about the universe.

Garth never told the Weskers what he thought about their new interest, and this was mainly because they never asked him. Pride or honour stood in the way of his grabbing a willing listener and pouring out his grievances. Perhaps it would have been different if Itin was on Collecting duty; he was the brightest of the lot; but Itin had been rotated the day after the priest had arrived and Garth had not talked to him since.

It was a surprise then when after seventeen of the trebly-long Wesker days, he found a delegation at his doorstep when he emerged after breakfast. Itin was their spokesman, and his mouth was open slightly. Many of the other Weskers had their mouths open as well, one even appearing to be yawning, clearly revealing the double row of sharp teeth and the purple-black throat. The mouths impressed Garth as to the seriousness of the meeting: this was the one Wesker expression he had learned to recognize. An open mouth indicated some strong emotion; happiness, sadness, anger, he could never be really sure which. The Weskers were normally placid and he had never seen enough open mouths to tell what was causing them. But he was surrounded by them now.

"Will you help us, John Garth," Itin said. "We have a question."

"I'll answer any question you ask," Garth said, with more than a hint of misgiving. "What is it?"

"Is there a God?"

"What do you mean by 'God'?" Garth asked in turn. What should he tell them?

"God is our Father in Heaven, who made us all and protects us. Whom we pray to for aid, and if we are saved will find a place . . . "

"That's enough," Garth said. "There is no God."

All of them had their mouths open now, even Itin, as they looked at Garth and thought about his answer. The rows of pink teeth would have been frightening if he hadn't known these creatures so well. For one instant he wondered if perhaps they had been already indoctrinated and looked upon him as a heretic, but he brushed the thought away.

"Thank you," Itin said, and they turned and left.

Though the morning was still cool, Garth noticed that he was sweating and wondered why.

The reaction was not long in coming. Itin returned that same afternoon. "Will you come to the church?" he asked. "Many of the things that we study are difficult to learn, but none as difficult as this. We need your help because we must hear you and Father talk together. This is because he says one thing is true and you say another is true and both cannot be true at the same time. We must find out what is true."

"I'll come, of course," Garth said, trying to hide the sudden feeling of elation. He had done nothing, but the Weskers had come to him anyway. There could still be grounds for hope that they might yet be free.

It was hot inside the church, and Garth was surprised at the number of Weskers who were there, more than he had seen gathered at any one time before. There were many open mouths. Father Mark sat at a table covered with books. He looked unhappy but didn't say anything when Garth came in. Garth spoke first.

"I hope you realize this is their idea—that they came to me of their own free will and asked me to come here?"

"I know that," the priest said resignedly. "At times they can be very difficult. But they are learning and want to believe, and that is what is important."

"Father Mark, Trader Garth, we need your help," Itin said. "You both know many things that we do not know. You must help us come to religion which is not an easy thing to do." Garth started to say something, then changed his mind. Itin went on. "We have read the bibles and all the books that Father Mark gave us, and one thing is clear. We have discussed this and we are all agreed. These books are very different from the ones that Trader Garth gave us. In Trader Garth's books there is the universe which we have not seen, and it goes on without God, for he is mentioned nowhere; we have searched very carefully. In Father Mark's books He is everywhere and nothing can go without Him. One of these must be right and the other must be wrong. We do not know how this can be, but after we find out which is right then perhaps we will know. If God does not exist . . . "

"Of course He exists, my children," Father Mark said in a voice of

heartfelt intensity. "He is our Father in Heaven who has created us all
. . ."

"Who created God?" Itin asked and the murmur ceased and everyone
of the Weskers watched Father Mark intensely. He recoiled a bit under
the impact of their eyes, then smiled.

"Nothing created God, since He is the Creator. He always was . . ."

"If He always was in existence—why cannot the universe have always
been in existence? Without having had a creator?" Itin broke in with a
rush of words. The importance of the question was obvious. The priest
answered slowly, with infinite patience.

"Would that the answers were that simple, my children. But even the
scientists do not agree about the creation of the universe. While they
doubt—we who have seen the light *know*. We can see the miracle of
creation all about us. And how can there be a creation without a Creator?
That is He, our Father, our God in Heaven. I know you have doubts; that
is because you have souls and free will. Still, the answer is so simple. Have
faith, that is all you need. Just believe."

"How can we believe without proof?"

"If you cannot see that this world itself is proof of His existence, then
I say to you that belief needs no proof—if you have faith!"

A babble of voices arose in the room and more of the Wesker mouths
were open now as they tried to force their thoughts through the tangled
skein of words and separate the thread of truth.

"Can you tell us, Garth?" Itin asked, and the sound of his voice quieted
the hubbub.

"I can tell you to use the scientific method which can examine all things
—including itself—and give you answers that can prove the truth or fal-
sity of any statement."

"That is what we must do," Itin said, "we had reached the same conclusion." He held a thick book before him and a ripple of nods ran across
the watchers. "We have been studying the bible as Father Mark told us
to do, and we have found the answer. God will make a miracle for us,
thereby proving that He is watching us. And by this sign we will know
Him and go to Him."

"That is the sin of false pride," Father Mark said. "God needs no
miracles to prove His existence."

"But *we* need a miracle!" Itin shouted, and though he wasn't human
there was need in his voice. "We have read here of many smaller miracles,
loaves, fishes, wine, snakes—many of them, for much smaller reasons.
Now all He need do is make a miracle and He will bring us all to Him
—the wonder of an entire new world worshipping at His throne as you
have told us, Father Mark. And you have told us how important this is.
We have discussed this and find that there is only one miracle that is best
for this kind of thing."

His boredom at the theological wrangling drained from Garth in an instant. He had not been really thinking or he would have realized where all this was leading. He could see the illustration in the bible where Itin held it open, and knew in advance what picture it was. He rose slowly from his chair, as if stretching, and turned to the priest behind him.

"Get ready!" he whispered. "Get out the back and get to the ship; I'll keep them busy here. I don't think they'll harm me."

"What do you mean . . . ?" Father Mark asked, blinking in surprise.

"Get out, you fool!" Garth hissed. "What miracle do you think they mean? What miracle is supposed to have converted the world to Christianity?"

"No!" Father Mark said. "It cannot be. It just cannot be . . . !"

"GET MOVING!" Garth shouted, dragging the priest from the chair and hurling him towards the rear wall. Father Mark stumbled to a halt, turned back. Garth leaped for him, but it was already too late. The amphibians were small, but there were so many of them. Garth lashed out and his fist struck Itin, hurling him back into the crowd. The others came on as he fought his way towards the priest. He beat at them but it was like struggling against waves. The furry, musky bodies washed over and engulfed him. He fought until they tied him, and he still struggled until they beat on his head until he stopped. Then they pulled him outside where he could only lie in the rain and curse and watch.

Of course the Weskers were marvellous craftsmen, and everything had been constructed down to the last detail, following the illustration in the bible. There was the cross, planted firmly on the top of a small hill, the gleaming metal spikes, the hammer. Father Mark was stripped and draped in a carefully pleated loincloth. They led him out of the church.

At the sight of the cross he almost fainted. After that he held his head high and determined to die as he had lived, with faith.

Yet this was hard. It was unbearable even for Garth, who only watched. It is one thing to talk of crucifixion and look at the gentle carved bodies in the dim light of prayer. It is another to see a man naked, ropes cutting into his skin where he hangs from a bar of wood. And to see the needle-tipped spike raised and placed against the soft flesh of his palm, to see the hammer come back with the calm deliberation of an artisan's measured stroke. To hear the thick sound of metal penetrating flesh.

Then to hear the screams.

Few are born to be martyrs; Father Mark was not one of them. With the first blows, the blood ran from his lips where his clenched teeth met. Then his mouth was wide and his head strained back and the guttural horror of his screams sliced through the susurration of the falling rain. It resounded as a silent echo from the masses of watching Weskers, for whatever emotion opened their mouths was now tearing at their bodies with all its force, and row after row of gaping jaws reflected the crucified priest's agony.

Mercifully he fainted as the last nail was driven home. Blood ran from the raw wounds, mixing with the rain to drip faintly pink from his feet as the life ran out of him. At this time, somewhere at this time, sobbing and tearing at his own bonds, numbed from the blows on the head, Garth lost consciousness.

He awoke in his own warehouse and it was dark. Someone was cutting away the woven ropes they had bound him with. The rain still dripped and splashed outside.

"Itin," he said. It could be no one else.

"Yes," the alien voice whispered back. "The others are all talking in the church. Lin died after you struck his head, and Inon is very sick. There are some that say you should be crucified too, and I think that is what will happen. Or perhaps killed by stoning on the head. They have found in the bible where it says . . . "

"I know." With infinite weariness. "An eye for an eye. You'll find lots of things like that once you start looking. It's a wonderful book." His head ached terribly.

"You must go, you can get to your ship without anyone seeing you. There has been enough killing." Itin as well, spoke with a new-found weariness.

Garth experimented, pulling himself to his feet. He pressed his head to the rough wood of the wall until the nausea stopped. "He's dead." He said it as a statement, not a question.

"Yes, some time ago. Or I could not have come away to see you."

"And buried of course, or they wouldn't be thinking about starting on me next."

"And buried!" There was almost a ring of emotion in the alien's voice, an echo of the dead priest's. "He is buried and he will rise on High. It is written and that is the way it will happen. Father Mark will be so happy that it has happened like this." The voice ended in a sound like a human sob.

Garth painfully worked his way towards the door, leaning against the wall so he wouldn't fall.

"We did the right thing, didn't we?" Itin asked. There was no answer. "He will rise up, Garth, won't he rise?"

Garth was at the door and enough light came from the brightly lit church to show his torn and bloody hands clutching at the frame. Itin's face swam into sight close to his, and Garth felt the delicate, many fingered hands with the sharp nails catch at his clothes.

"He will rise, won't he, Garth?"

"No," Garth said, "he is going to stay buried right where you put him. Nothing is going to happen because he is dead and he is going to stay dead."

The rain runnelled through Itin's fur and his mouth was opened so wide that he seemed to be screaming into the night. Only with effort could he talk, squeezing out the alien thoughts in an alien language.

"Then we will not be saved? We will not become pure?"

"You were pure," Garth said, in a voice somewhere between a sob and a laugh. "That's the horrible ugly dirty part of it. You were pure. Now you are . . ."

"Murderers," Itin said, and the water ran down from his lowered head and streamed away into the darkness.

— 3 —

a difference
that makes
a difference

The ways in which men of different races, cultures, ethnic groups, and statuses relate to one another and the varieties of belief systems and interaction patterns that develop in connection with relations between groups are subjects of considerable interest to social scientists and of considerable importance to the rest of the world's population. Clearly, conflicts drawn along lines of group identification have occurred frequently throughout recorded history. The fact that conflicts of this sort occur, generate effects that tend to endure, and frequently increase antipathy between groups is one of the more pathetic aspects of the human condition.

Accounting for the existence of hostilities between individuals who identify themselves as members of different groups, in any particular case, requires identifying the specific sociological variables and historical conditions that generated the antagonisms and tracing the changes in variables and historical events that determined whether the antagonisms grew or diminished. To explain why hostilities between groups come about in general—that is, to understand the phenomenon independent of any particular case—requires much more. The distinction between accounting for a particular instance of conflict and understanding the phenomenon in general is equivalent to the distinction between knowing history, being able to trace a sequence of events through time, and knowing sociology, understanding why a particular combination of social and historical conditions produced a certain outcome and being able to predict how changing any of the social or historical conditions would change the outcome.

To understand conflict between groups generally requires us not only to understand how social variables (such as economic competition) and historical events (such as the assassination of a certain individual) affect conflict, but also to construct a theory how stereotypes develop and how they are modified. A peculiar relationship seems to exist between the conditions necessary to generate hostilities between groups and the conditions necessary to maintain them. Unfortunately, the objective causes of antagonisms (such as competition for scarce goods between members of two groups) result in hostilities that typically give rise to stereotypes of the members of the opposing group. These stereotypes are consistent with the hostile feelings that exist between members of the two groups. Unfortunately, negative stereotypes tend to persist even after objective causes for antagonisms between groups cease to exist.

The sequence is something like this: Some realistic competition generates hostilities. In order to justify the hatred they feel for members of the opposing group, men convince themselves that their opponents are evil, dirty, uncivilized, cruel— that is, that they possess all the characteristics required of first-class villains. It is, after all, much easier to hate someone who is entirely despicable than someone who is only about as despicable as you are. The problem is that once this image of the members of another race, ethnic group, or social class has been created, it becomes a justification for treating these people differently from members of one's own group. The undesirable characteristics they are *known* to possess seem to justify treating members of the other group as essentially different from members of one's own group. The stereotype becomes the basis for maintaining hostility.

Hostilities between groups can come about for reasons far less understandable than competition for scarce resources or political domination. Hostilities can be the end-product of interactions between men of different groups who simply operate with reference to different norms and values.

Whether because of learned reaction or, as some zoologists claim, because of universal wariness of organisms that are substantially different in appearance or manner from oneself, interacting with a creature that is unfamiliar is anxiety-provoking. Its reactions, motivations, and desires cannot be assumed to be the same as one's own, and therefore its behavior cannot be predicted. A movement that would not provoke anxiety when made by a friend or even a casual acquaintance can provoke an extreme response when made by a stranger. Given that situations involving unknown quantities are inherently anxiety-provoking, it is relatively easy to understand how actions can be interpreted to mean something quite different from what the person who performed the act intended.

Accept for the moment the proposition that the greater the apparent physical or social distance between two individuals, the greater the inherent anxiety in their initial interactions. It therefore follows that the more the cultures of two men differ, the greater will be the stress generated by their interaction. In the same manner, the more physically different two men are, the greater the potential fear of each other and the easier it is to generate misunderstandings. The range of variation across human cultures and the range of variation in physical characteristics of varieties of the human species are relatively so small that it may be difficult to detect easily in oneself the uneasiness that accompanies these differences. The possible variations between different species of intelligent life are, however, infinite. In "My Sister's Brother," Philip José Farmer proposes a situation in which the great cultural and physical differences between characters make it easier to detect the egocentrism of the human actor, his physical and cultural biases, and to follow the reasoning, motivations, and fears that lead him to act as he does.

"my sister's brother"

by Philip José Farmer

When he opened his eyes, he knew he was not alone. He saw a Martian.

A hole had appeared in the wall of the tube to his left. It was a round section about four feet across, and it had sunk in as if it were a plug being pulled inwards, as indeed it was.

A moment later a head popped out of the hole. The size of a Georgia watermelon, it was shaped like a football and was as pink as a baby's bottom. Its two eyes were as large as coffee cups and each was equipped with two vertical lids. It opened its two parrot-like beaks, ran out a very long tubular tongue, withdrew the tongue, and snapped the beak shut. Then it scuttled out from the hole to reveal a body also shaped like a football and only three times as large as its head. The pinkish body was supported three feet from the ground on ten spindly spidery legs, five on each side. Its legs ended in broad round pads on which it ran across the jellymire surface, sinking only slightly. Behind it streamed at least fifty others.

These picked up the little plants that Lane had upset in his struggles and licked them clean with narrow round tongues that shot out at least two feet. They also seemed to communicate by touching their tongues, as insects do with antennae.

As he was in the space between two rows, he was not involved in the setting up of the dislodged plants. Several of them ran their tongues over his helmet, but these were the only ones that paid him any attention. It was then that he began to stop dreading that they might attack him with their powerful looking beaks. Now he broke into a sweat at the idea that they might ignore him completely.

That was just what they did. After gently embedding the thin roots of the plantlets in the sticky stuff, they raced off towards the hole in the tube.

Lane, overwhelmed with despair, shouted after them, though he knew they couldn't hear him through his helmet and the thin air even if they had hearing organs.

"Don't leave me here to die!"

Nevertheless, that was what they were doing. The last one leaped through the hole, and the entrance stared at him like the round black eye of Death itself.

He struggled furiously to lift himself from the mire, not caring that he was only exhausting himself.

Abruptly, he stopped fighting and stared at the hole.

A figure had crawled out of it, a figure in a pressure-suit.

Now he shouted with joy. Whether the figure was Martian or not, it was built like a member of homo sapiens. It could be presumed to be intelligent and therefore curious.

He was not disappointed. The suited being stood up on two hemispheres of shiny red metal and began walking towards him in a sliding fashion. Reaching him, it handed him the end of a plastic rope it was carrying under its arm.

He almost dropped it. His rescuer's suit was transparent. It was enough of a shock to see clearly the details of the creature's body, but the sight of the two heads within the helmet caused him to turn pale.

The Martian slidewalked to the tube from which Lane had leaped. It jumped lightly from the two bowls on which it had stood, landed on the three-foot high top of the tube, and began hauling Lane out from the mess. He came out slowly but steadily and soon was scooting forward, gripping the rope. When he reached the foot of the tube, he was hauled on up until he could get his feet in the two bowls. It was easy to jump from them to a place beside the biped.

It unstrapped two more bowls from its back, gave them to Lane, then lowered itself on the two in the garden. Lane followed it across the mire.

Entering the hole, he found himself in a chamber so low he had to crouch. Evidently, it had been constructed by the dekapeds and not by his companion for it, too, had to bend its back and knees.

Lane was pushed to one side by some dekapeds. They picked up the thick plug, made of the same grey stuff as the tube walls, and sealed the entrance with it. Then they shot out of their mouths strand after strand of grey spiderwebby stuff to seal the plug.

The biped motioned Lane to follow, and it slid down a tunnel which plunged into the earth at a forty-five degree angle. It illuminated the passage with a flashlight which it took from its belt. They came into a large chamber which contained all of the fifty dekapeds. These were waiting motionless. The biped, as if sensing Lane's curiosity, pulled off its glove and held it before several small vents in the wall. Lane removed his glove and felt warm air flowing from the holes.

Evidently this was a pressure chamber, built by the ten-legged things. But such evidence of intelligent engineering did not mean that these things had the individual intelligence of a man. It could mean group intelligence such as Terrestrial insects possess.

After a while, the chamber was filled with air. Another plug was pulled;

Lane followed the dekapeds and his rescuer up another forty-five degree tunnel. He estimated that he would find himself inside the tube from which the biped had first come. He was right. He crawled through another hole into it.

And a pair of beaks clicked as they bit down on his helmet!

Automatically, he shoved at the thing, and under the force of his blow the dekaped lost its bite and went rolling on the floor, a bundle of thrashing legs.

Lane did not worry about having hurt it. It did not weigh much, but its body must be tough to be able to plunge without damage from the heavy air inside the tube into the almost-stratospheric conditions outside.

However, he did reach for the knife at his belt. But the biped put its hand on his arm and shook one of its heads.

Later, he was to find out that the seeming bite must have been an accident. Always—with one exception—the leggers were to ignore him.

He was also to find that he was lucky. The leggers had come out to inspect their garden because, through some unknown method of detection, they knew that the plantlets had been disturbed. The biped normally would not have accompanied them. However, today, its curiosity aroused because the leggers had gone out three times in three days, it had decided to investigate.

The biped turned out its flashlight and motioned to Lane to follow. Awkwardly, he obeyed. There was light, but it was dim, a twilight. Its source was the many creatures that hung from the ceiling of the tube. These were three feet long and six inches thick, cylindrical, pinkish-skinned, and eyeless. A dozen frondlike limbs waved continuously, and their motion kept air circulating in the tunnel.

Their cold firefly glow came from two globular pulsing organs which hung from both sides of the round loose-lipped mouth at the free end of the creature. Slime drooled from the mouth and dripped on to the floor or into a narrow channel which ran along the lowest part of the sloping floor. Water ran in the six-inch deep channel, the first native water he had seen. The water picked up the slime and carried it a little way before it was gulped up by an animal that lay on the bottom of the channel.

Lane's eyes adjusted to the dimness until he could make out the water-dweller. It was torpedo-shaped and without eyes or fins. It had two openings in its body; one obviously sucked in water, the other expelled it.

He saw at once what this meant. The water at the North Pole melted in the summertime and flowed into the far end of the tube system. Helped by gravity and by the pumping action of the line of animals in the channel, the water was passed from the edge of the Pole to the equator.

Leggers ran by him on mysterious errands. Several, however, halted beneath some of the downhanging organisms. They reared up on their hind five legs and their tongues shot out and into the open mouths by the glowing balls. At once the fireworm—as Lane termed it—its cilia waving wildly, stretched itself to twice its former length. Its mouth met the beak of the legger, and there was an exchange of stuff between their mouths.

Impatiently, the biped tugged at Lane's arm. He followed it down the tube. Soon they entered a section where pale roots came down out of holes in the ceiling and spread along the curving walls, gripping them, then becoming a network of many thread-thin rootlets that crept across the floor and into the water of the channel.

Here and there a dekaped chewed at a root and then hurried off to offer a piece to the mouths of the fire-worms.

After walking for several minutes, the biped stepped across the stream. It then began walking as closely as possible to the wall, meanwhile looking apprehensively at the other side of the tunnel, where they had been walking.

Lane also looked but could see nothing at which to be alarmed. There was a large opening at the base of the wall which evidently led into a tunnel. This tunnel, he presumed, ran underground into a room, or rooms, for many leggers dashed in and out of it. And about a dozen, larger than average, paced back and forth like sentries before the hole.

When they had gone about fifty yards past the opening, the biped relaxed. After it had led Lane along for ten minutes, it stopped. Its naked hand touched the wall. He became aware that the hand was small and delicately shaped, like a woman's.

A section of the wall swung out. The biped turned and bent down to crawl into the hole, presenting buttocks and legs femininely rounded, well shaped. It was then that he began thinking of it as a female. Yet the hips, though padded with fatty tissue, were not broad. The bones were not widely separated to make room to carry a child. Despite their curving, the hips were relatively as narrow as a man's.

Behind them, the plug swung shut. The biped did not turn on her flashlight, for there was illumination at the end of the tunnel. The floor and walls were not of the hard grey stuff nor of packed earth. They seemed vitrified, as if glassed by heat.

She was waiting for him when he slid off a three-foot high ledge into a large room. For a minute he was blinded by the strong light. After his eyes adjusted, he searched for the source of light but could not find it. He did observe that there were no shadows in the room.

The biped took off her helmet and suit and hung them in a closet. The door slid open as she approached and closed when she walked away.

She signalled that he could remove his suit. He did not hesitate. Though the air might be poisonous, he had no choice. His tank would soon be empty. Moreover, it seemed likely that the atmosphere contained enough oxygen. Even then he had grasped the idea that the leaves of the umbrella plants, which grew out of the top of the tubes, absorbed sunlight and traces of carbon dioxide. Inside the tunnels, the roots drew up water from the channel and absorbed the great quantity of carbon dioxide released by the dekapeds. Energy of sunlight converted gas and liquid into glucose and oxygen, which were given off in the tunnels.

Even here, in this deep chamber which lay beneath and to one side of the tube, a thick root penetrated the ceiling and spread its thin white web over the walls. He stood directly beneath the fleshy growth as he removed his helmet and took his first breath of Martian air. Immediately afterwards, he jumped. Something wet had dropped on his forehead. Looking up, he saw that the root was excreting liquid from a large pore. He wiped the drop off with his finger and tasted it. It was sticky and sweet. Well, he thought, the tree must normally drop sugar in water. But it seemed to be doing so abnormally fast, because another drop was forming.

Then it came to him that perhaps this was so because it was getting dark outside and therefore cold. The umbrella trees might be pumping the water in their trunks into the warm tunnels. Thus, during the bitter sub-zero night, they'd avoid freezing and swelling up and cracking wide open.

It seemed a reasonable theory.

He looked around. The place was half living quarters, half biological laboratory. There were beds and tables and chairs and several unidentifiable articles. . . .

The biped took a large green ceramic bowl from a cupboard and set it on a table. Lane eyed her curiously, wondering what she was going to do. By now he had seen that the second head belonged to an entirely separate creature. Its slim four foot length of pinkish skin was coiled about her neck and torso; its tiny flat-faced head turned towards Lane; its snaky light blue eyes glittered. Suddenly its mouth opened and revealed toothless gums, and its bright red tongue, mammalian, not at all reptilian, thrust out at him.

The biped, paying no attention to the worm's actions, lifted it from her. Gently, cooing a few words in a soft many-vowelled language, she placed it in the bowl. It settled inside and looped around the curve, like a snake in a pit.

The biped took a pitcher from the top of a box of red plastic. Though the box was not connected to any visible power source, it seemed to be a stove. The pitcher contained warm water which she poured into the bowl, half filling it. Under the shower, the worm closed its eyes as if it were purring soundless ecstasy.

Then the biped did something that alarmed Lane.

She leaned over the bowl and vomited into it.

He stepped towards her. Forgetting the fact that she couldn't understand him, he said, 'Are you sick?'

She revealed human-looking teeth in a smile meant to reassure him, and she walked away from the bowl. He looked at the worm, which had its head dipped into the mess. Suddenly, he felt sick, for he was sure that it was feeding off the mixture. And he was equally certain that she fed the worm regularly with regurgitated food.

It didn't cancel his disgust to reflect that he shouldn't react to her as he would to a Terrestrial. He knew that she was totally alien and that it was inevitable that some of her ways would repel, perhaps even shock him. Rationally, he knew this. But if his brain told him to understand and forgive, his belly said to loathe and reject.

His aversion was not much lessened by a close scrutiny of her as she took a shower in a cubicle set in the wall. She was about five feet tall and slim as a woman should be slim, with delicate bones beneath rounded flesh. Her legs were human; in nylons and high heels they would have been exciting—other things being equal. However, if the shoes had been toeless, her feet would have caused much comment. They had four toes.

Her long beautiful hands had five fingers. These seemed nailless, like the toes, though a closer examination later showed him they did bear rudimentary nails.

She stepped from the cubicle and began towelling herself, though not before she motioned to him to remove his suit and also to shower. He stared intently back at her until she laughed a short embarrassed laugh. It was feminine, not at all deep. Then she spoke.

He closed his eyes and was hearing what he had thought he would not hear for years: a woman's voice. Hers was extraordinary: husky and honeyed at the same time.

But when he opened his eyes, he saw her for what she was. No woman. No man. What? It? No. The impulse to think *her, she,* was too strong.

This, despite her lack of mammaries. She had a chest, but no nipples, rudimentary or otherwise. Her chest was a man's, muscled under the layer of fat which subtly curved to give the impression that beneath it . . . budding breasts?

No, not this creature. She would never suckle her young. She did not even bear them alive, if she *did* bear. Her belly was smooth, undimpled with a navel.

Smooth also was the region between her legs, hairless, unbroken, as innocent of organ as if she were a nymph painted for some Victorian children's book.

It was that sexless joining of the legs that was so horrible. Like the white belly of a frog, thought Lane, shuddering.

At the same time, his curiosity became even stronger. How did this thing mate and reproduce?

Again she laughed and smiled with fleshy pale-red humanly everted lips and wrinkled a short, slightly uptilted nose and ran her hand through thick straight red-gold fur. It was fur, not hair, and it had a slightly oily sheen, like a water-dwelling animal's.

The face itself, though strange, could have passed for human, but only passed. Her cheekbones were very high and protruded upwards in an unhuman fashion. Her eyes were dark blue and quite human. This meant nothing. So were an octupus's eyes.

She walked to another closet, and as she went away from him he saw again that though the hips were curved like a woman's they did not sway with the pelvic displacement of the human female.

The door swung momentarily open, revealed the carcasses of several dekapeds, minus their legs, hanging on hooks. She removed one, placed it on a metal table, and out of the cupboard took a saw and several knives and began cutting.

Because he was eager to see the anatomy of the dekaped, he approached the table. She waved him to the shower. Lane removed his suit. When he came to the knife and axe he hesitated, but, afraid she might think him distrustful, he hung up the belt containing his weapons beside the suit. However, he did not take off his clothes because he was determined to view the inner organs of the animal. Later, he would shower.

The legger was not an insect, despite its spidery appearance. Not in the terrestrial sense, certainly. Neither was it a vertebrate. Its smooth hairless skin was an animal's, as lightly pigmented as a blond Swede's. But, though it had an endo-skeleton, it had no backbone. Instead, the body bones formed a round cage. Its thin ribs radiated from a cartilaginous collar which adjoined the back of the head. The ribs curved outwards, then in, almost meeting at the posterior. Inside the cage were ventral lung sacs, a relatively large heart, and liver-like and kidney-like organs. Three arteries, instead of the mammalian two, left the heart. He couldn't be sure with such a hurried examination, but it looked as if the dorsal aorta, like some terrestrial reptiles, carried both pure and impure blood.

There were other things to note. The most extraordinary was that, as far as he could discern, the legger had no digestive system. It seemed to lack both intestines and anus unless you would define as a intestine a sac which ran straight through from the throat half-way into the body. Further, there was nothing he could identify as reproductive organs, though this did not mean that it did not possess them. The creature's long tubular tongue, cut open by the biped, exposed a canal running down the length of tongue from its open tip to a bladder at its base. Apparently these formed part of the excretory system.

Lane wondered what enabled the legger to stand the great pressure differences between the interior of the tube and the Martian surface. At the same time he realized that this ability was no more wonderful than the biological mechanism which gave whales and seals the power to endure without harm the enormous pressures a half mile below the sea's surface.

The biped looked at him with round and very pretty blue eyes, laughed, and then reached into the chopped open skull and brought out the tiny brain.

"*Hauaimi*," she said slowly. She pointed to her head, repeated. "*Hauaimi*," and then indicated his head. "*Hauaimi.*"

Echoing her, he pointed at his own head. "*Hauaimi.* Brain."

"Brain," she said, and she laughed again.

She proceeded to call out the organs of the legger which corresponded to hers. Thus, the preparations for the meal passed swiftly as he proceeded from the carcass to other objects in the room. By the time she had fried the meat and boiled strips of the membranous leaf of the umbrella plant, and also added from cans various exotic foods, she had exchanged at least forty words with him. An hour later, he could remember twenty.

There was one thing yet to learn. He pointed to himself and said, "Lane."

Then he pointed to her and gave her a questioning look.

"Mahrseeya," she said.

"Martia?" he repeated. She corrected him, but he was so struck by the resemblance that always afterwards he called her that. After a while, she would give up trying to teach him the exact pronunciation.

Martia washed her hands and poured him a bowlful of water. He used the soap and towel she handed him, then walked to the table where she stood waiting. On it was a bowl of thick soup, a plate of fried brains, a salad of boiled leaves and some unidentifiable vegetables, a plate of ribs with thick dark legger meat, hard-boiled eggs and little loaves of bread.

Martia gestured for him to sit down. Evidently her code did not allow her to sit down before her guest did. He ignored his chair, went behind her, put his hand on her shoulder, pressed down, and with the other hand slid her chair under her. She turned her head to smile up at him. Her fur slid away to reveal one lobeless pointed ear. He scarcely noticed it, for he was too intent on the half-repulsive, half-heartquickening sensation he got when he touched her skin. It had not been the skin itself that caused that, for she was soft and warm as a young girl. It had been the *idea* of touching her.

Part of that, he thought as he seated himself, came from her nakedness. Not because it revealed her sex but because it revealed her lack of it. No breasts, no nipples, no navel, no pubic fold or projection. The absence of these seemed wrong, very wrong, unsettling. It was a shameful thing that she had nothing of which to be ashamed.

That's a queer thought, he said to himself. And for no reason, he became warm in the face.

Martia, unnoticing, poured from a tall bottle a glassful of dark wine. He tasted it. It was exquisite, no better than the best Earth had to offer but as good.

Martia took one of the loaves, broke it into two pieces, and handed him one. Holding the glass of wine in one hand and the bread in the other, she bowed her head, closed her eyes, and began chanting.

He stared at her. This was a prayer, a grace-saying. Was it the prelude to a sort of communion, one so like Earth's it was startling?

Yet, if it were, he needn't be surprised. Flesh and blood, bread and wine: the symbolism was simple, logical, and might even be universal.

However it was possible that he was creating parallels that did not exist. She might be enacting a ritual whose origin and meaning were like nothing of which he had ever dreamed.

If so, what she did next was equally capable of misinterpretation. She nibbled at the bread, sipped the wine and then plainly invited him to do the same. He did so. Martia took a third and empty cup, spat a piece of wine-moistened bread into the cup, and indicated that he was to imitate her.

After he did, he felt his stomach draw in on itself. For she mixed the stuff from their mouths with her finger and then offered it to him. Evidently, he was to put the finger in his mouth and eat from it.

So the action was both physical and metaphysical. The bread and the wine were the flesh and blood of whatever divinity she worshipped. More, she, being imbued with the body and the spirit of the god, now wanted to mingle hers and that of the god's with his. . . .

He took her proffered finger in his mouth and sucked the paste off it.

Then obeying her gestures, he dipped his own finger into the bowl and put it between her lips.

She closed her eyes and gently mouthed the finger. When he began to withdraw it, he was stopped by her hand on his wrist. He did not insist on taking the finger out, for he wanted to avoid offending her. Perhaps a long time interval was part of the rite.

But her expression seemed so eager and at the same time so ecstatic, like a hungry baby just given the nipple, that he felt uneasy. After a minute, seeing no indication on her part that she meant to quit, he slowly but firmly pulled the finger loose. She opened her eyes and sighed, but she made no comment. Instead, she began serving his supper.

The hot thick soup was delicious and invigorating. Its texture was somewhat like the plankton soup that was becoming popular on hungry Earth, but it had no fishy flavour. The brown bread reminded him of rye. The legger meat was like wild rabbit, though it was sweeter and had an unidentifiable tang. He took only one bite of the leaf salad and then frantically poured wine down his throat to wash away the burn. Tears came to his eyes, and he coughed until she spoke to him in an alarmed tone. He smiled back at her but refused to touch the salad again. The wine not only cooled his mouth, it filled his veins with singing. He told himself he should take no more. Nevertheless, he finished his second cup before he remembered his resolve to be temperate.

By then it was too late. The strong liquor went straight to his head; he felt dizzy and wanted to laugh. The events of the day, his near-escape from death, the reaction to knowing his comrades were dead, his realization of his present situation, the tension caused by his encounters with the dekapeds, and his unsatisfied curiosity about Martia's origin and the location of others of her kind, all these combined to produce in him a half-stupor, half-exuberance.

He rose from the table and offered to help Martia with the dishes. She shook her head and put the dishes in a washer. In the meantime, he decided that he needed to wash off the sweat, stickiness, and body odour left by two days of travel. On opening the door to the shower cubicle, he found that there wasn't room enough to hang his clothes in it. So, uninhibited by fatigue and wine also mindful that Martia, after all, was *not* a female, he removed his clothes.

Martia watched him, and her eyes became wider with each garment shed. Finally, she gasped and stepped back and turned pale.

"It's not that bad," he growled, wondering what had caused her reaction. "After all, some of the things I've seen around here aren't too easy to swallow."

She pointed with a trembling finger and asked him something in a shaky voice.

Perhaps it was his imagination, but he could swear she used the same inflection as would an English speaker.

"Are you sick? Are the growths malignant?"

He had no words with which to explain, nor did he intend to illustrate function through action. Instead, he closed the door of the cubicle after him and pressed the plate that turned on the water. The heat of the shower, and the feel of the soap, of grime and sweat being washed away, soothed him somewhat, so that he could think about matters he had been too rushed to consider.

First, he would have to learn Martia's language or teach her his. Probably both would happen at the same time. Of one thing he was sure. That was that her intentions towards him were, at least at present, peaceful. When she had shared communion with him, she had been sincere. He did not get the impression that it was part of her cultural training to share bread and wine with a person she intended to kill.

Feeling better, though still tired and a little drunk, he left the cubicle. Reluctantly, he reached for his dirty shorts. Then he smiled. They had been cleaned while he was in the shower. Martia, however, paid no attention to his smile of pleased surprise but, grim-faced, she motioned to him to lie down on the bed and sleep. Instead of lying down herself, however, she picked up a bucket and began crawling up the tunnel. He decided to follow her, and, when she saw him, she only shrugged her shoulders.

On emerging into the tube, Martia turned on her flashlight. The tunnel was in absolute darkness. Her beam, playing on the ceiling, showed that the glowworms had turned out their lights. There were no leggers in sight.

She pointed the light at the channel so he could see that the jetfish were still taking in and expelling water. Before she could turn the beam aside, he put his hand on her wrist and with his other hand lifted a fish from the channel. He had to pull it loose with an effort, which was explained when he turned the torpedo-shaped creature over and saw the colum of flesh hanging from its belly. Now he knew why the reaction of the propelled water did not shoot them backwards. The ventral-foot acted as a suction pad to hold them to the floor of the channel.

Somewhat impatiently, Martia pulled away from him and began walking swiftly back up the tunnel. He followed her until she came to the opening in the wall which had earlier made her so apprehensive. Crouching, she entered the opening, but before she had gone far she had to move a tangled heap of leggers to one side. There were the large great-beaked ones he had seen guarding the entrance. Now they were asleep at the post.

If so, he reasoned, then the thing they guarded against must also be asleep.

What about Martia? How did she fit into their picture? Perhaps she didn't fit into their picture at all. She was absolutely alien, something for which their instinctual intelligence was not prepared and which, therefore, they ignored. That would explain why they had paid no attention to him when he was mired in the garden.

Yet there must be an exception to that rule. Certainly Martia had not wanted to attract the sentinels' notice the first time she had passed the entrance.

A moment later he found out why. They stepped into a huge chamber which was at least two hundred feet square. It was as dark as the tube, but during the waking period it must have been very bright because the ceiling was jammed with glowworms.

Martia's flash raced around the chamber, showing him the piles of sleeping leggers. Then, suddenly it stopped. He took one look, and his heart raced, and the hairs on the back of his neck rose.

Before him was a worm three feet high and twenty feet long.

Without thinking, he grabbed hold of Martia to keep her from coming closer to it. But even as he touched her, he dropped his hand. She must know what she was doing.

Martia pointed the flash at her own face and smiled as if to tell him not to be alarmed. And she touched his arm with a shyly affectionate gesture.

For a moment he didn't know why. Then it came to him that she was glad because he had been thinking of her welfare. Moreover, her reaction showed she had recovered from her shock at seeing him unclothed.

He turned from her to examine the monster. It lay on the floor, asleep, its great eyes closed behind vertical slits. It had a huge head, football-shaped like those of the little leggers around it. Its mouth was big, but the beaks were very small, horny warts on its lips. The body, however, was that of a caterpillar worm's, minus the hair. Ten little useless legs stuck out of its side, too short even to reach the floor. Its sides bulged as if pumped full of gas.

Martia walked past the monster and paused by its posterior. Here she lifted up a fold of skin. Beneath it was a pile of a dozen leathery-skinned eggs, held together by a sticky secretion.

"Now I've got it," muttered Lane. "Of course. The egg-laying queen. She specializes in reproduction. That is why the others have no reproductive organs, or else they're so rudimentary I couldn't detect them. The leggers are animals, all right, but in some things they resemble terrestrial insects.

"Still, that doesn't explain the absence also of a digestive system."

Martia put the eggs in her bucket and started to leave the room. He stopped her and indicated he wanted to look around some more. She shrugged and began to lead him around. Both had to be careful not to step on the dekapeds, which lay everywhere.

They came to an open bin made of the same grey stuff as the walls. Its interior held many shelves, on which lay hundreds of eggs. Strands of the spiderwebby stuff kept the eggs from rolling off.

Nearby was another bin that held water. At its bottom lay more eggs. Above them minnow-sized torpedo shapes flitted about in the water.

Lane's eyes widened at this. The fish were not members of another genus but were the larvae of the leggers. And they could be set in the channel not only to earn their keep by pumping water which came down from the North Pole but to grow until they were ready to metamorphose into the adult stage.

However, Martia showed him another bin which made him partially revise his first theory. This bin was dry, and the eggs were laid on the floor. Martia picked one up, cut its tough skin open with her knife, and emptied its contents into one hand.

Now his eyes did get wide. This creature had a tiny cylindrical body, a suction pad at one end, a round mouth at the other, and two globular organs hanging by the mouth. A young glowworm.

Martia looked at him to see if he comprehended. Lane held out his hands and hunched his shoulders with an I-don't-get-it air. Beckoning, she walked to another bin to show him more eggs. Some had been ripped from within, and the little fellows whose hard beaks had done it were staggering around weakly on ten legs.

Energetically, Martia went through a series of charades. Watching her, he began to understand.

The embryos that remained in the eggs until they fully developed went through three main metamorphoses: the jetfish stage, the glowworm stage, and finally the baby dekaped stage. If the eggs were torn open by the adult nurses in one of the first two stages, the embryo remained fixed in that form, though it did grow larger.

What about the queen? he asked her by pointing to the monstrously egg-swollen body.

For answer, Martia picked up one of the newly-hatched. It kicked its many legs but did not otherwise protest, being, like all its kind, mute. Martia turned it upside down and indicated a slight crease in its posterior. Then she showed him the same spot on one of the sleeping adults. The adult's rear was smooth, innocent of the crease.

Martia made eating gestures. He nodded. The creatures were born with rudimentary sexual organs, but these never developed. In fact, they atrophied completely unless the young were given a special diet, in which case they matured into egg-layers.

But the picture wasn't complete. If you had females, you had to have males. It was doubtful if such highly developed animals were self-fertilizing or reproduced parthenogenetically.

Then he remembered Martia and began doubting. She gave no evidence of reproductive organs. Could her kind be self-producing? Or was she a Martian, her natural fulfillment diverted by diet?

It didn't seem likely, but he couldn't be sure that such things were not possible in her scheme of Nature.

Lane wanted to satisfy his curiosity. Ignoring her desire to get out of the chamber, he examined each of the five baby dekapeds. All were potential females.

Suddenly Martia, who had been gravely watching him, smiled and took his hand, and led him to the rear of the room. Here, as they approached another structure, he smelled a strong odour which reminded him of clorox.

Closer to the structure, he saw that it was not a bin but a hemispherical cage. Its bars were of the hard grey stuff, and they curved up from the floor to meet at a central point. There was no door. Evidently the cage had been built around the thing in it, and its occupant must remain until he died.

Martia soon showed him why this thing was not allowed freedom. It—he—was sleeping, but Martia reached through the bars and struck it on the head with her fist. The thing did not respond until it had been hit five more times. Then, slowly, it opened its sidewise lids to reveal great staring eyes, bright as fresh arterial blood.

Martia threw one of the eggs at the thing's head. Its beak opened swiftly, the egg disappeared, the beak closed, and there was a noisy gulp.

Food brought it to life. It sprang up on its ten long legs, clacked its beak, and lunged against the bars again and again.

Though in no danger, Martia shrank back before the killer's lust in the scarlet eyes. Lane could understand her reaction. It was a giant, at least two feet higher than the sentinels. Its back was on a level with Martia's; its beaks could have taken her head in between them.

Lane walked around the cage to get a good look at its posterior. Puzzled, he made another circuit without seeing anything of maleness about it except its wild fury like that of a stallion locked in a barn during the mating season. Except for its size, red eyes, and a cloaca, it looked like one of the guards.

He tried to communicate to Martia his puzzlement. By now, she seemed to anticipate his desires. She went through another series of pantomimes, some of which were so energetic and comical that he had to smile.

First, she showed him two eggs on a nearby ledge. These were larger than the others and were speckled with red spots. Supposedly, they held male embryos.

Then she showed him what would happen if the adult male got loose. Making a face which was designed to be ferocious but only amused him, clicking her teeth and clawing with her hands, she imitated the male running amok. He would kill everybody in sight. Everybody, the whole colony, queen, workers, guards, larvae, eggs, bite off their heads, mangle them, eat them all up, all, all. And out of the slaughterhouse he would charge into the tube and kill every legger he met, devour the jetfish, drag down the glowworms from the ceiling, rip them apart, eat them, eat the roots of the trees. Kill, kill, kill, eat, eat, eat!

That was all very well, sighed Lane. But how did. . . . ?

Martia indicated that, once a day, the workers rolled, literally rolled the queen across the room to the cage. There they arranged her so that she presented her posterior some few inches from the bars and the enraged male. And the male, though he wanted to do nothing but get his beak into her flesh and tear her apart, was not master of himself. Nature took over; his will was betrayed by his nervous system.

Lane nodded to show he understood. In his mind was a picture of the legger that had been butchered. It had had one sac at the internal end of the tongue. Probably the male had two, one to hold excretory matter, the other to hold seminal fluid.

Suddenly Martia froze, her hands held out before her. She had laid the flashlight on the floor so she could act freely; the beam splashed on her paling skin.

"What is it?" said Lane, stepping towards her.

Martia retreated, holding out her hands before her. She looked horrified.

"I'm not going to harm you," he said. However, he stopped so she could see he didn't mean to get any closer to her.

What was bothering her? Nothing was stirring in the chamber itself besides the male, and he was behind her.

Then she was pointing, first at him and then at the raging dekaped. Seeing this unmistakable signal of identification, he comprehended. She had perceived that he, like the thing in the cage, was male, and now she perceived structure and function in him.

What he didn't understand was why that should make her so frightened of him. Repelled, yes. Her body, its seeming lack of sex, had given him a feeling of distaste bordering on nausea. It was only natural that she should react similarly to his body. However, she had seemed to have got over her first shock.

Why this unexpected change, this horror of him?

Behind him, the beak of the male clicked as it lunged against the bars. The click echoed in his mind.

Of course, the monster's lust to kill!

Until she had met him, she had known only one male creature. That was the caged thing. Now, suddenly, she had equated him with the monster. A male was a killer.

Desperately, because he was afraid that she was about to run in a panic out of the room, he made signs that he was not like this monster; he shook his head no, no, no. He wasn't, he wasn't, he wasn't!

Martia, watching him intently, began to relax. Her skin regained its pinkish hue. Her eyes became their normal size. She even managed a strained smile.

To get her mind off the subject, he indicated that he would like to know why the queen and her consort had digestive systems, though the workers did not. For answer, she reached up into the downhanging mouth of the worm suspended from the ceiling. Her hand, withdrawn, was covered with secretion. After smelling her fist, she gave it to him to sniff also. He took it, ignoring her slight and probably involuntary flinching when she felt his touch.

The stuff had an odour such as you would expect from predigested food.

Martia then went to another worm. The two light organs of this one were not coloured red, like the other, but had a greenish tint. Martia tickled its tongue with her finger and held out her cupped hands. Liquid trickled into the cup.

Lane smelled the stuff. No odour. When he drank the liquid, he discovered it to .be a thick sugar water.

Martia pantomimed that the glowworms acted as the digestive systems for the workers. They also stored food away for them. The workers derived part of their energy from the glucose excreted by the roots of the trees. The proteins and vegetable matter in their diet originated from the eggs and from the leaves of the umbrella plant. Strips of the tough membranous leaf were brought into the tubes by harvesting parties which ventured forth in the daytime. The worms partially digested the eggs, dead leggers, and leaves and gave it back in the form of a soup. The soup, like the glucose, was swallowed by the workers and passed through the walls of their throats or into the long straight sac which connected the throat to the larger blood vessels. The waste products were excreted through the skin or emptied through the canal in the tongue.

Lane nodded and then walked out of the room. Seemingly relieved, Martia followed him. When they had crawled back into her quarters, she put the eggs in a refrigerator and poured two glasses of wine. She dipped her finger in both, then touched the finger to her lips and to his. Lightly, he touched the tip with his tongue. This, he gathered, was one more ritual, perhaps a bedtime one, which affirmed that they were at one and at peace. It might be that it had an even deeper meaning, but if so, it escaped him.

Martia checked on the safety and comfort of the worm in the bowl. By now it had eaten all its food. She removed the worm, washed it, washed the bowl, half-filled it with warm sugar water, placed it on a table by the bed, and put the creature back in. Then she lay down on the bed and closed her eyes. She did not cover herself and apparently did not expect him to expect a cover. . . .

During their next period of wakefulness Lane and Mahrseeya establish a rudimentary form of communication. Lane discovers that Mahrseeya's species, the Eeltau, are not native Martians, that they have been observing Earth from Mars for a period of time, and that they have withdrawn their outpost from Mars in order not to be discovered by the explorers; he also learns the circumstances under which Mahrseeya was left behind. Lane convinces himself that Mahrseeya does not intend to permit his return to Earth.

As he fell asleep, he was thinking that perhaps Martia and he would be the two ambassadors to bring their people together in peace. After all, both of them were highly civilized, essentially pacifistic, and devoutly religious. There was such a thing as the brotherhood, not only of man, but of all sentient beings throughout the cosmos, and . . .

Pressure on his bladder woke him up. He opened his eyes. The ceiling and walls expanded and contracted. His wristwatch was distorted. Only by extreme effort could he focus his eyes enough to straighten the arms on his watch. The piece, designed to measure the slightly longer Martian day, indicated midnight.

Groggily, he rose. He felt sure that he must have been drugged and that he would still be sleeping if the bladder pain hadn't been so sharp. If only he could take something to counteract the drug, he could carry out his plans now. But first he had to get to the toilet.

To do so, he had to pass close to Martia's bed. She did not move but lay on her back, her arms flung out and hanging over the sides of the bed, her mouth open wide.

He looked away, for it seemed indecent to watch when she was in such a position.

But something caught his eye—a movement, a flash of light like a gleaming jewel in her mouth.

He bent over her, looked, and recoiled in horror.

A head rose from between her teeth.

He raised his hand to snatch at the thing but froze in the posture as he recognized the tiny pouting round mouth and little blue eyes. It was the worm.

At first, he thought Martia was dead. The thing was not coiled in her mouth. Its body disappeared into her throat.

Then he saw her chest was rising easily and that she seemed to be in no difficulty.

Forcing himself to come close to the worm, though his stomach muscles writhed and his neck muscles quivered, he put his hand close to its lips.

Warm air touched his fingers, and he heard a faint whistling.

Martia was breathing through it!

Hoarsely, he said, "God!" and he shook her shoulder. He did not want to touch the worm because he was afraid that it might do something to injure her. In that moment of shock he had forgotten that he had an advantage over her, which he should use.

Martia's lids opened; her large grey-blue eyes stared blankly.

"Take it easy," he said soothingly.

She shuddered. Her lids closed, her neck arched back, and her face contorted.

He could not tell if the grimace was caused by pain or something else.

"What is this—this monster?" he said. "Symbiote? Parasite?"

He thought of vampires, of worms creeping into one's sleeping body and there sucking blood.

Suddenly she sat up and held out her arms to him. He seized her hands, saying, "What is it?"

Martia pulled him towards her at the same time lifting her face to his.

Out of her open mouth shot the worm, its head pointed towards his face, its little lips formed into an O.

It was reflex, the reflex of fear that made Lane drop her hands and spring back. He had not wanted to do that, but he could not help himself.

Abruptly, Martia came wide awake. The worm flopped its full length from her mouth and fell into a heap between her legs. There it thrashed for a moment before coiling itself like a snake, its head resting on Martia's thigh, its eyes turned upwards to Lane.

There was no doubt about it. Martia looked disappointed, frustrated.

Lane's knees, already weak, gave way. However, he managed to continue to his destination. When he came out, he walked as far as Martia's bed, where he had to sit down. His heart was thudding against his ribs and he was panting hard.

He sat behind her, for he did not want to be where the worm could touch him.

Martia made motions for him to go back to his bed and they would all sleep. Evidently, he thought, she found nothing alarming in the incident.

But he knew he could not rest until he had some kind of explanation. He handed her paper and pen from the bedside table and then gestured fiercely. Martia shrugged and began sketching while Lane watched over her shoulder. By the time she had used up five sheets of paper, she had communicated her message.

His eyes were wide, and he was even paler.

So—Martia *was* a female. Female at least in the sense that she carried eggs—and, at times, young—within her.

And there was the so-called worm. So called? What could he call it? It could not be designated under one category. It was many things in one. It was a larva. It was a phallus. It was also her offspring, of her flesh and blood.

But not of her genes. It was not descended from her.

She had given birth to it, yet she was not its mother. She was neither one of its mothers.

The dizziness and confusion he felt was not caused altogether by his sickness. Things were coming too fast. He was thinking furiously, trying to get this new information clear, but his thoughts kept going back and forth, getting nowhere.

"There's no reason to get upset," he told himself. "After all, the splitting of animals into two sexes is only one of the ways of reproduction tried on Earth. On Martia's planet Nature—God—has fashioned another method for the higher animals. And only He knows how many other designs for reproduction He has fashioned on how many other worlds."

Nevertheless, he was upset.

This worm, no, this larva, this embryo outside its egg and its secondary mother . . . well, call it, once and for all, larva, because it did metamorphose later.

This particular larva was doomed to stay in its present form until it died of old age.

Unless Martia found another adult of the Eeltau.

And unless she and this other adult felt affection for each other.

Then, according to the sketch she'd drawn, Martia and her friend, or lover, would lie down or sit together. They would caress and kiss as much as Terrestrial man and woman do. . . .

Then, unlike the Terran custom, a third would enter the union to form a highly desired and indeed indispensable and eternal triangle.

The larva, blindly, brainlessly obeying its instincts, aroused by mutual fondling by the two, would descend tail first into the throat of one of the two Eeltau. Inside the body of the lover a fleshy valve would open to admit the slim body of the larva. Its open tip would touch the ovary of the host. The larva, like an electric eel, would release a tiny current. The hostess would go into an ecstasy, its nerves stimulated electro-chemically. The ovary would release an egg no larger than a pencil dot. It would disappear into the open tip of the larva's tail, there to begin a journey up a canal towards the centre of its body, urged on by the contraction of muscle and whipping of cilia.

Then the larva slid out of the first hostess' mouth and went tail first into the other, there to repeat the process. Sometimes the larva garnered eggs, sometimes not, depending upon whether the ovary had a fully developed one to release.

When the process was successful, the two eggs moved towards each other but did not quite meet.

Not yet.

There must be other eggs collected in the dark incubator of the larva, collected by pairs, though not necessarily from the same couple of donors.

These would number anywhere from twenty to forty pairs.

Then, one day, the mysterious chemistry of the cells would tell the larva's body that it had gathered enough eggs.

A hormone was released, the metamorphosis begun. The larva swelled enormously, and the mother, seeing this, placed it tenderly in a warm place and fed it plenty of predigested food and sugar water.

Before the eyes of its mother, the larva then grew shorter and wider. Its tail contracted; its cartilaginous vertebrae, widely separated in its larval stage, shifted closer to each other and hardened. A skeleton formed, ribs, shoulders. Legs and arms budded and grew and took humanoid shape. Six months passed, and there lay in its crib something resembling a baby of homo sapiens.

From then until its fourteenth year, the Eeltau grew and developed much as its Terran counterpart.

Adulthood, however, initiated more strange changes. Hormone released hormone until the first pair of gametes, dormant these fourteen years, moved together.

The two fused, the chromatin of one uniting with the chromatin of the other. Out of the two—a single creature, wormlike, four inches long, released into the stomach of its hostess.

Then, nausea. Vomiting. And so, comparatively painlessly, the bringing forth of a genetically new being.

It was this worm that would be both foetus and phallus and would give ecstasy and draw into its own body the eggs of loving adults and would metamorphose and become infant, child, and adult.

And so on and so on.

He rose and shakily walked to his own bed. There he sat down, his head bowed, while he muttered to himself.

"Let's see now. Martia gave birth to, brought forth, or up, this larva. But the larva actually doesn't have any of Martia's genes. Martia was just the hostess for it.

"However, if Martia has a lover, she will, by means of this worm, pass on her heritable qualities. This worm will become an adult and bring forth, or up, Martia's child."

He raised his hands in despair.

"How do the Eeltau reckon ancestry? How keep track of their relatives? Or do they care? Wouldn't it be easier to consider your foster mother, your hostess, your real mother? As, in the sense of having borne you, she is?

"And what kind of sexual code do these people have? It can't, I would think, be much like ours. Nor is there any reason why it should be.

"But who is responsible for raising the larva and child? Its pseudo-mother? Or does the lover share in the duties? And what about property and inheritance laws? And, and . . . "

Helplessly, he looked at Martia.

Fondly stroking the head of the larva, she returned his stare.

Lane shook his head.

"I was wrong. Eeltau and Terran couldn't meet on a friendly basis. My people would react to yours as to disgusting vermin. Their deepest prejudices would be aroused, their strongest taboos would be violated. They could not learn to live with you or consider you even faintly human.

"And as far as that goes, could you live with us? Wasn't the sight of me naked a shock? Is that reaction a part of why you don't make contact with us?"

Martia put the larva down and stood up and walked over to him and kissed the tips of his fingers. Lane, though he had to fight against visibly flinching, took her fingers and kissed them. Softly, he said to her, "Yet . . . individuals could learn to respect each other, to have affection for each other. And masses are made of individuals."

He lay back on the bed. The grogginess, pushed aside for a while by excitement, was coming back. He couldn't fight off sleep much longer.

"Fine noble talk," he murmured. "But it means nothing. The Eeltau don't think they should deal with us. And we are, unknowingly, pushing out towards them. What will happen when we are ready to make the interstellar jump? War? Or will they be afraid to let us advance even to that point and destroy us before then. After all, one cobalt bomb."

He looked again at Martia, at the not-quite-human yet beautiful face, the smooth skin of the chest, abdomen, and loins, innocent of nipple, navel, or labia. From far off she had come, from a possibly terrifying place

across terrifying distances. About her, however, there was little that was terrifying and much that was warm, generous, companionable, attractive.
. . .

He turned over so his back was to her, and he pounded his fist against the bed.

"Oh dear God why couldn't it be so?"

A long time he lay there, his face pressed into the mattress. Something had happened; the overpowering fatigue was gone; his body had drawn strength from some reservoir. Realizing this, he sat up and beckoned to Martia, smiling at the same time.

She rose slowly and started to walk to him, but he signalled that she should bring the larva with her. At first, she looked puzzled. Then her expression cleared, to be replaced by understanding. Smiling delightedly, she walked to him, and though he knew it must be a trick of his imagination, it seemed to him that she swayed her hips as a woman would.

She halted in front of him and then stooped to kiss him full on the lips. Her eyes were closed.

He hesitated for a fraction of a second. She—no, it, he told himself —looked so trusting, so loving, so womanly, that he could not do it.

He brought the edge of his palm hard against the side of her neck.

She crumpled forward against him, her face sliding into his chest. Lane caught her under the armpits and laid her face down on the bed. The larva, which had fallen from her hand to the the floor, was writhing about as if hurt. Lane picked it up by its tail and, in a frenzy that owed its violence to the fear he might not be able to do it, snapped it like a whip. There was a crack as the head smashed into the floor, and blood spurted from its eyes and mouth. Lane placed his heel on the head and stepped down until there was a flat mess beneath his foot.

Then, quickly . . . , he ran to the cabinet. Snatching a narrow towel out of it, he ran back and gagged her. After that he tied her hands behind her back with the rope.

"Now, you bitch!" he panted. "We'll see who comes out ahead! You would do that with me, would you! You deserve this; your monster deserves to die!"

Furiously he began packing. In fifteen minutes he had the suits, helmets, tanks, and food rolled into two bundles. He searched for the weapon she had talked about and found something that might conceivably be it. It had a butt that fitted to his hand, a dial that might be a rheostat for controlling degrees of intensity of whatever it shot, and a bulb at the end. The bulb, he hoped, expelled the stunning and killing energy. Of course, he might be wrong. It could be fashioned for an entirely different purpose.

Martia had regained consciousness. She sat on the edge of the bed, her shoulders hunched, her head drooping, tears running down her cheeks and into the towel around her mouth. Her wide eyes were focused on the smashed worm by her feet.

Roughly, Lane seized her shoulder and pulled her upright. She gazed wildly at him, and he gave her a little shove. He felt sick within him, knowing that he had killed the larva when he did not have to do so and that he was handling her so violently because he was afraid, not of her, but of himself. If he had been disgusted because she had fallen into the trap he set for her, he was so because he, too, beneath his disgust, had wanted to commit that act of love. Commit, he thought, was the right word. It contained criminal implications.

Martia whirled around, almost losing her balance because of her tied hands. Her face worked, and sounds burst from the gag.

"Shut up!" he howled, pushing her again. She went sprawling and only saved herself from falling on her face by dropping on her knees. Once more, he pulled her to her feet, noting as he did so that her knees were skinned. The sight of the blood instead of softening him, enraged him even more.

"Behave yourself, or you'll get worse!" he snarled.

She gave him one more questioning look, threw back her head, and made a strange strangling sound. Immediately, her face took on a bluish tinge. A second later, she fell heavily on the floor.

Alarmed, he turned her over. She was choking to death.

He tore off the gag and reached into her mouth and grabbed the root of her tongue. It slipped away and he seized it again, only to have it slide away as if it were a live animal that defied him.

Then he had pulled her tongue out of her throat; she had swallowed it in an effort to kill herself. . . .

At that moment, hearing an unfamiliar noise, he looked up. There were two Eeltau in pressure suits standing there, and another crawling out of the tunnel. Each had a bulb-tipped handgun in her hand.

Desperately, Lane snatched at the weapon he carried in his belt. With his left hand he twisted the rheostat on the side of the barrel, hoping this would turn it on full force. Then he raised the bulb towards the group.
. . .

He woke flat on his back, clad in his suit, except for the helmet, and strapped to a stretcher. His body was helpless, but he could turn his head. He did so, and saw many Eeltau dismantling the room. The one who had stunned him with her gun before he could fire was standing by him.

She spoke in English that held only a trace of foreign accent. "Settle down, Mr. Lane. You're in for a long ride. You'll be more comfortably situated once we're in our ship."

He opened his mouth to ask her how she knew his name but closed it when he realized she must have read the entries in the log at the base. And it was to be expected that some Eeltau would be trained in Earth languages. For over a century their sentinel spaceships had been tuning in to radio and TV.

It was then that Martia spoke to the captain. Her face was wild and reddened with weeping and marks where she had fallen. The interpreter said to Lane, "Mahrseeya asks you to tell her why you killed her . . . baby. She cannot understand why you thought you had to do so."

"I cannot answer," said Lane. His head felt very light, almost as if it were a balloon expanding. And the room began slowly to turn around.

"I will tell her why," answered the interpreter. "I will tell her that it is the nature of the beast."

"That is not so!" cried Lane. "I am no vicious beast. I did what I did because I had to! I could not accept her love and still remain a man! Not the kind of man. . . . "

"Mahrseeya," said the interpreter, "will pray that you be forgiven the murder of her child and that you will someday, under our teaching, be unable to do such a thing. She herself, though she is stricken with grief for her dead baby, forgives you. She hopes the time will come when you will regard her as a—sister. She thinks there is some good in you."

Lane clenched his teeth together and bit the end of his tongue until it bled while they put his helmet on. He did not dare to try to talk, for that would have meant he would scream and scream. He felt as if something had been planted in him and had broken its shell and was growing into something like a worm. It was eating him, and what would happen before it devoured all of him he did not know.

— 4 —

on the effects
of improved communication

A common theme in the writings of those who design possible societies is the social effect of the ability to communicate with complete accuracy. It is often proposed that if such communication could be established, it would change every aspect of society as we know it and possibly bring the solution to most inter-personal problems. The necessity of relying on a relatively crude medium of communication, language, it is argued, makes it impossible for anyone ever to convey his cognitions precisely to another.

Consider the following idealized view of human communication: the thoughts of a person, P, can be conceived of as a pattern of electrical impulses in his brain. In order to communicate these thoughts to O, P must try to use symbols (words) that will stimulate the same pattern of electrical activity in O's brain. To the extent that the pattern stimulated in O is different from P's original pattern, communica-tion between P and O will be imperfect. If O must choose some action on the basis of his understanding of P's message, and communication is imperfect, O may choose what he thinks to be a reasonable action, but P may find it unsatisfac-tory. Hence, hostility is often not desired, but results from the inability of two people to communicate adequately.

When writers of social-science fiction treat the possibility of perfect communica-tion, it is frequently as a concomitant of the ability to read the thoughts of another. In the usual situation, not only is it possible for one individual to transfer his thoughts to another without loss of information, but it is impossible for anyone to prevent his thoughts from being read. Some writers have treated the type of normative system that might develop in order to reestablish privacy under these conditions.[1] Others have described how a society might be affected initially if this

---

[1] One of the most interesting science-fiction novels in which this theme appears is *The Demolished*

ability were to become available to everyone overnight, or what set of stable norms for interpersonal behavior a society might develop if this ability were acquired gradually and new rules had time to evolve.

It is interesting to consider the effects of sudden acquisition of this ability on a society geared to verbal communication. The most obvious effect would be complete loss of the only sort of privacy that really matters—a person's ability to monitor his communications to others. Consider the extent to which every sort of human interaction would be affected if it were not possible to privately consider alternative statements or courses of action before choosing how to behave in public. The distinction between private thought and public action would cease to exist. The immediate results are obvious. The strategies we know for governing human interaction would become useless: lying, deceit, being kind by politely avoiding mention of a sensitive issue, suppressing hostile reactions to someone's behavior, masking emotions. The results of a transformation of this type could be both comical and shattering for those involved. If such a change occurred suddenly, for some period afterward the frequency with which humans interacted would probably fall to its lowest level in the history of man.

One of the earliest treatments of the effects on social organization of perfect communication and complete loss of cognitive privacy is "To Whom This May Come," by Edward Bellamy. Bellamy considers how a society might operate if the ability to perfectly understand another individual was one of the conditions under which the norms of the society developed.

"to whom this may come"

by Edward Bellamy

It is now about a year since I took passage at Calcultta in the ship Adelaide for New York. We had baffling weather till New Amsterdam Island was sighted, where we took a new point of departure. Three days later, a terrible gale struck us. Four days we flew before it, whither, no one knew, for neither sun, moon, nor stars were at any time visible, and we could take no observation. Toward midnight of the fourth day, the glare of lightning revealed the Adelaide in a hopeless position, close in upon a low-lying shore, and driving straight toward it. All around and astern far out to sea was such a maze of rocks and shoals that it was a miracle we

---

Man, by Alfred Bester (London: Penguin Books, 1953). A novel in which the theme of the effects of improved communication is developed is *The Primal Urge,* by Brian Aldiss (New York: Ballantine Books, 1961). Aldiss considers the effects on British society of equipping all inhabitants of the country with emotional registers surgically inset into each person's forehead and designed to glow with different intensities depending on the person's degree of sexual stimulation.

had come so far. Presently the ship struck, and almost instantly went to pieces, so great was the violence of the sea. I gave myself up for lost, and was indeed already past the worst of drowning, when I was recalled to consciousness by being thrown with a tremendous shock upon the beach. I had just strength enough to drag myself above the reach of the waves, and then I fell down and knew no more.

When I awoke, the storm was over. The sun, already halfway up the sky, had dried my clothing, and renewed the vigor of my bruised and aching limbs. On sea or shore I saw no vestige of my ship or my companions, of whom I appeared the sole survivor. I was not, however, alone. A group of persons, apparently the inhabitants of the country, stood near, observing me with looks of friendliness which at once freed me from apprehension as to my treatment at their hands. They were a white and handsome people, evidently of a high order of civilization, though I recognized in them the traits of no race with which I was familiar.

Seeing that it was evidently their idea of etiquette to leave it to strangers to open conversation, I addressed them in English, but failed to elicit any response beyond deprecating smiles. I then accosted them successively in the French, German, Italian, Spanish, Dutch, and Portuguese tongues, but with no better results. I began to be very much puzzled as to what could possibly be the nationality of a white and evidently civilized race to which no one of the tongues of the great seafaring nations was intelligible. The oddest thing of all was the unbroken silence with which they contemplated my efforts to open communication with them. It was as if they were agreed not to give me a clue to their language by even a whisper; for while they regarded one another with looks of smiling intelligence, they did not once open their lips. But if this behavior suggested that they were amusing themselves at my expense, that presumption was negatived by the unmistakable friendliness and sympathy which their whole bearing expressed.

A most extraordinary conjecture occurred to me. Could it be that these strange people were dumb? Such a freak of nature as an entire race thus afflicted had never indeed been heard of, but who could say what wonders the unexplored vasts of the great Southern Ocean might thus far have hid from human ken? Now, among the scraps of useless information which lumbered my mind was an acquaintance with the deaf-and-dumb alphabet, and forthwith I began to spell out with my fingers some of the phrases I had already uttered to so little effect. My resort to the sign language overcame the last remnant of gravity in the already profusely smiling group. The small boys now rolled on the ground in convulsions of mirth, while the grave and reverend seniors, who had hitherto kept them in check, were fain momentarily to avert their faces, and I could see their bodies shaking with laughter. The greatest clown in the world never received a more flattering tribute to his powers to amuse than had been called forth by mine to make myself understood. Naturally, however, I was not flattered, but on the contrary entirely discomfited. Angry I could not well be, for the deprecating manner in which all, excepting of course the boys, yielded to their perception of the ridiculous, and the distress they showed at their failure in self-control, made me seem the aggressor. It was as if they were very sorry for me, and ready to put themselves wholly at my service, if I would only refrain from reducing them to a state of disability by being so exquisitely absurd. Certainly this evidently amiable race had a very embarrassing way of receiving strangers.

Just at this moment, when my bewilderment was fast verging on exasperation, relief came. The circle opened, and a little elderly man, who had evidently come in haste, confronted me, and, bowing very politely, addressed me in English. His voice was the most pitiable abortion of a voice I had ever heard. While having all the defects in articulation of a child's who is just beginning to talk, it was not even a child's in strength of tone, being in fact a mere alternation of squeaks and whispers inaudible a rod away. With some difficulty I was, however, able to follow him pretty nearly.

"As the official interpreter," he said, "I extend you a cordial welcome to these islands. I was sent for as soon as you were discovered, but being at some distance, I was unable to arrive until this moment. I regret this, as my presence would have saved you embarrassment. My countrymen desire me to intercede with you to pardon the wholly involuntary and uncontrollable mirth provoked by your attempts to communicate with them. You see, they understood you perfectly well, but could not answer you."

"Merciful heavens!" I exclaimed, horrified to find my surmise correct; "can it be that they are all thus afflicted? Is it possible that you are the only man among them who has the power of speech?"

Again it appeared that, quite unintentionally, I had said something excruciatingly funny; for at my speech there arose a sound of gentle laughter from the group, now augmented to quite an assemblage, which drowned the plashing of the waves on the beach at our feet. Even the interpreter smiled.

"Do they think it so amusing to be dumb?" I asked.

"They find it very amusing," replied the interpreter, "that their inability to speak should be regarded by any one as an affliction; for it is by the voluntary disuse of the organs of articulation that they have lost the power of speech, and, as a consequence, the ability even to understand speech."

"But," said I, somewhat puzzled by this statement, "didn't you just tell me that they understood me, though they could not reply, and are they not laughing now at what I just said?"

"It is you they understood, not your words," answered the interpreter.

"Our speech now is gibberish to them, as unintelligible in itself as the growling of animals; but they know what we are saying, because they know our thoughts. You must know that these are the islands of the mind-readers."

Such were the circumstances of my introduction to this extraordinary people. The official interpreter being charged by virtue of his office with the first entertainment of shipwrecked members of the talking nations, I became his guest, and passed a number of days under his roof before going out to any considerable extent among the people. My first impression had been the somewhat oppressive one that the power to read the thoughts of others could be possessed only by beings of a superior order to man. It was the first effort of the interpreter to disabuse me of this notion. It appeared from his account that the experience of the mind-readers was a case simply of a slight acceleration, from special causes, of the course of universal human evolution, which in time was destined to lead to the disuse of speech and the substitution of direct mental vision on the part of all races. This rapid evolution of these islanders was accounted for by their peculiar origin and circumstances.

Some three centuries before Christ, one of the Parthian kings of Persia, of the dynasty of the Arsacidae, undertook a persecution of the soothsayers and magicians in his realms. These people were credited with supernatural powers by popular prejudice, but in fact were merely persons of special gifts in the way of hypnotizing, mind-reading, thought transference, and such arts, which they exercised for their own gain.

Too much in awe of the soothsayers to do them outright violence, the king resolved to banish them, and to this end put them, with their families, on ships and sent them to Ceylon. When, however, the fleet was in the neighborhood of that island, a great storm scattered it, and one of the ships, after being driven for many days before the tempest, was wrecked upon one of an archipelago of uninhabited islands far to the south, where the survivors settled. Naturally, the posterity of the parents possessed of such peculiar gifts had developed extraordinary psychical powers.

Having set before them the end of evolving a new and advanced order of humanity, they had aided the development of these powers by a rigid system of stirpiculture. The result was that, after a few centuries, mind-reading became so general that language fell into disuse as a means of communicating ideas. For many generations the power of speech still remained voluntary, but gradually the vocal organs had become atrophied, and for several hundred years the power of articulation had been wholly lost. Infants for a few months after birth did, indeed, still emit inarticulate cries, but at an age when in less advanced races these cries began to be articulate, the children of the mind-readers developed the power of direct vision, and ceased to attempt to use the voice.

The fact that the existence of the mind-readers had never been found out by the rest of the world was explained by two considerations. In the first place, the group of islands was small, and occupied a corner of the Indian Ocean quite out of the ordinary track of ships. In the second place, the approach to the islands was rendered so desperately perilous by terrible currents, and the maze of outlying rocks and shoals, that it was next to impossible for any ship to touch their shores save as a wreck. No ship at least had ever done so in the two thousand years since the mind-readers' own arrival, and the Adelaide had made the one hundred and twenty-third such wreck.

Apart from motives of humanity, the mind-readers made strenuous efforts to rescue shipwrecked persons, for from them alone, through the interpreters, could they obtain information of the outside world. Little enough this proved when, as often happened, the sole survivor of the shipwreck was some ignorant sailor, who had no news to communicate beyond the latest varieties of forecastle blasphemy. My hosts gratefully assured me that, as a person of some little education, they considered me a veritable godsend. No less a task was mine than to relate to them the history of the world for the past two centuries, and often did I wish, for their sakes, that I had made a more exact study of it.

It is solely for the purpose of communicating with shipwrecked strangers of the talking nations that the office of the interpreters exists. When, as from time to time happens, a child is born with some powers of articulation, he is set apart, and trained to talk in the interpreters' college. Of course the partial atrophy of the vocal organs, from which even the best interpreters suffer, renders many of the sounds of language impossible for them. None, for instance, can pronounce *v, f,* or *s;* and as to the sound represented by *th,* it is five generations since the last interpreter lived who could utter it. But for the occasional intermarriage of shipwrecked strangers with the islanders, it is probable that the supply of interpreters would have long ere this quite failed.

I imagine that the very unpleasant sensations which followed the realization that I was among people who, while inscrutable to me, knew my every thought, were very much what any one would have experienced in the same case. They were very comparable to the panic which accidental nudity causes a person among races whose custom it is to conceal the figure with drapery. I wanted to run away and hide myself. If I analyzed my feeling, it did not seem to arise so much from the consciousness of any particularly heinous secrets, as from the knowledge of a swarm of fatuous, ill-natured, and unseemly thoughts and half thoughts concerning those around me, and concerning myself, which it was insufferable that any person should peruse in however benevolent a spirit. But while my chagrin and distress on this account were at first intense, they were also very short-lived, for almost immediately I discovered that the very knowledge that my mind was overlooked by others operated to check thoughts that might be painful to them, and that, too, without more effort of the will than a kindly person exerts to check the utterance of disagreeable remarks. As a very few lessons in the elements of courtesy cures a decent person of inconsiderate speaking, so a brief experience among the mind-readers went far in my case to check inconsiderate thinking. It must not be supposed, however, that courtesy among the mind-readers prevents them from thinking pointedly and freely concerning one another upon serious occasions, any more than the finest courtesy among the talking races restrains them from speaking to one another with entire plainness when it is desirable to do so. Indeed, among the mind-readers, politeness never can extend to the point of insincerity, as among talking nations, seeing that it is always one another's real and inmost thought that they read. I may fitly mention here, though it was not till later that I fully understood why it must necessarily be so, that one need feel far less chagrin at the complete revelation of his weaknesses to a mind-reader than at the slightest betrayal of them to one of another race. For the very reason that the mind-reader reads all your thoughts, particular thoughts are judged with reference to the general tenor of thought. Your characteristic and habitual frame of mind is what he takes account of. No one need fear being misjudged by a mind-reader on account of sentiments or emotions which are not representative of the real character or general attitude. Justice may, indeed, be said to be a necessary consequence of mind-reading.

As regards the interpreter himself, the instinct of courtesy was not long needed to check wanton or offensive thoughts. In all my life before, I had been very slow to form friendships, but before I had been three days in the company of this stranger of a strange race, I had become enthusiastically devoted to him. It was impossible not to be. The peculiar joy of friendship is the sense of being understood by our friend as we are not by others, and yet of being loved in spite of the understanding. Now here was one whose every word testified to a knowledge of my secret thoughts and motives which the oldest and nearest of my former friends had never, and could never, have approximated. Had such a knowledge bred in him contempt of me, I should neither have blamed him nor been at all surprised. Judge, then, whether the cordial friendliness which he showed was likely to leave me indifferent.

Imagine my incredulity when he informed me that our friendship was not based upon more than ordinary mutual suitability of temperaments. The faculty of mind-reading, he explained, brought minds so close together, and so heightened sympathy, that the lowest order of friendship between mind-readers implied a mutual delight such as only rare friends enjoyed among other races. He assured me that later on, when I came to know others of his race, I should find, by the far greater intensity of sympathy and affection I should conceive for some of them, how true this saying was.

It may be inquired how, on beginning to mingle with the mind-readers in general, I managed to communicate with them, seeing that, while they could read my thoughts, they could not, like the interpreter, respond to them by speech. I must here explain that, while these people have no use for a spoken language, a written language is needful for purposes of record. They consequently all know how to write. Do they, then, write Persian? Luckily for me, no. It appears that, for a long period after mind-reading was fully developed, not only was spoken language disused, but also written, no records whatever having been kept during this period. The delight of the people in the newly found power of direct mind-to-mind vision, whereby pictures of the total mental state were communicated, instead of the imperfect descriptions of single thoughts which words at best could give, induced an invincible distaste for the laborious impotence of language.

When, however, the first intellectual intoxication had, after several generations, somewhat sobered down, it was recognized that records of the past were desirable, and that the despised medium of words was needful to preserve it. Persian had meanwhile been wholly forgotten. In order to avoid the prodigious task of inventing a complete new language, the institution of the interpreters was now set up, with the idea of acquiring through them a knowledge of some of the languages of the outside world from the mariners wrecked on the islands.

Owing to the fact that most of the castaway ships were English, a better knowledge of that tongue was acquired than of any other, and it was adopted as the written language of the people. As a rule, my acquaintances wrote slowly and laboriously, and yet the fact that they knew exactly what was in my mind rendered their responses so apt that, in my conversations with the slowest speller of them all, the interchange of thought was as rapid and incomparably more accurate and satisfactory than the fastest talkers attain to.

It was but a very short time after I had begun to extend my acquaintance among the mind-readers before I discovered how truly the interpreter had told me that I should find others to whom, on account of greater natural congeniality, I should become more strongly attached than I had been to him. This was in no wise, however, because I loved him less, but them more. I would fain write particularly of some of these beloved friends, comrades of my heart, from whom I first learned the undreamed-of possibilities of human friendship, and how ravishing the satisfactions of sympathy may be. Who, among those who may read this, has not known that sense of a gulf fixed between soul and soul which mocks love! Who has not felt that loneliness which oppresses the heart that loves it best! Think no longer that this gulf is eternally fixed, or is any necessity of human nature. It has no existence for the race of our fellowmen which I describe, and by that fact we may be assured that eventually it will be bridged also for us. Like the touch of shoulder to shoulder, like the clasping of hands, is the contact of their minds and their sensation of sympathy.

I say that I would fain speak more particularly of some of my friends, but waning strength forbids, and moreover, now that I think of it, another consideration would render any comparison of their characters rather confusing than instructive to a reader. This is the fact that, in common with the rest of the mind-readers, they had no names. Every one had, indeed, an arbitrary sign for his designation in records, but it has no sound value. A register of these names is kept, so they can at any time be ascertained, but it is very common to meet persons who have forgotten titles which are used solely for biographical and official purposes. For social intercourse names are of course superfluous, for these people accost one another merely by a mental act of attention, and refer to third persons by transferring their mental pictures,—something as dumb persons might by means of photographs. Something so, I say, for in the pictures of one another's personalities which the mind-readers conceive, the physical aspect, as might be expected with people who directly contemplate each other's minds and hearts, is a subordinate element.

I have already told how my first qualms of morbid self-consciousness at knowing that my mind was an open book to all around me disappeared as I learned that the very completeness of the disclosure of my thoughts and motives was a guarantee that I would be judged with a fairness and a sympathy such as even self-judgment cannot pretend to, affected as that is by so many subtle reactions. The assurance of being so judged by every one might well seem an inestimable privilege to one accustomed to a world in which not even the tenderest love is any pledge of comprehension, and yet I soon discovered that open-mindedness had a still greater profit than this. How shall I describe the delightful exhilaration of moral health and cleanness, the breezy oxygenated mental condition, which resulted from the consciousness that I had absolutely nothing concealed! Truly I may say that I enjoyed myself. I think surely that no one needs to have had my marvelous experience to sympathize with this portion of it. Are we not all ready to agree that this having a curtained chamber where we may go to grovel, out of the sight of our fellows, troubled only by a vague apprehension that God may look over the top, is the most demoralizing incident in the human condition? It is the existence within the soul of this secure refuge of lies which has always been the despair of the saint and the exultation of the knave. It is the foul cellar which taints the whole house above, be it never so fine.

What stronger testimony could there be to the instinctive consciousness that concealment is debauching, and openness our only cure, than the world-old conviction of the virtue of confession for the soul, and that the uttermost exposing of one's worst and foulest is the first step toward moral health? The wickedest man, if he could but somehow attain to writhe himself inside out as to his soul, so that its full sickness could be seen, would feel ready for a new life. Nevertheless, owing to the utter impotence of the words to convey mental conditions in their totality, or to give other than mere distortions of them, confession is, we must needs admit, but a mockery of that longing for self-revelation to which it testifies. But think what health and soundness there must be for souls among a people who see in every face a conscience which, unlike their own, they cannot sophisticate, who confess one another with a glance, and shrive with a smile! Ah, friends, let me now predict, though ages may elapse before the slow event shall justify me, that in no way will the mutual vision of minds, when at last it shall be perfected, so enhance the blessedness of mankind as by rending the veil of self, and leaving no spot of darkness in the mind for lies to hide in. Then shall the soul no longer be a coal smoking among ashes, but a star in a crystal sphere.

From what I have said of the delights which friendship among the mind-readers derives from the perfection of the mental rapport, it may be imagined how intoxicating must be the experience when one of the friends is a woman, and the subtle attractions and correspondences of sex touch with passion the intellectual sympathy. With my first venturing into society I had begun, to their extreme amusement, to fall in love with the women right and left. In the perfect frankness which is the condition of all intercourse among this people, these adorable women told me that what I felt was only friendship, which was a very good thing, but wholly different from love, as I should well know if I were beloved. It was difficult to believe that the melting emotions which I had experienced in their company were the result merely of the friendly and kindly attitude of their minds toward mine; but when I found that I was affected in the same way by every gracious woman I met, I had to make up my mind that they must be right about it, and that I should have to adapt myself to a world in which, friendship being a passion, love must needs be nothing less than rapture.

The homely proverb, "Every Jack has his Gill," may, I suppose, be taken to mean that for all men there are certain women expressly suited by mental and moral as well as by physical constitution. It is a thought painful, rather than cheering, that this may be the truth, so altogether do the chances preponderate against the ability of these elect ones to recognize each other even if they meet, seeing that speech is so inadequate and so misleading a medium of self-revelation. But among the mind-readers, the search for one's ideal mate is a quest reasonably sure of being crowned with success, and no one dreams of wedding unless it be; for so to do, they consider, would be to throw away the choicest blessing of life, and not alone to wrong themselves and their unfound mates, but likewise those whom they themselves and those undiscovered mates might wed. Therefore, passionate pilgrims, they go from isle to isle till they find each other, and, as the population of the islands is but small, the pilgrimage is not often long.

When I met her first we were in company, and I was struck by the sudden stir and the looks of touched and smiling interest with which all around turned and regarded us, the women with moistened eyes. They had read her thought when she saw me, but this I did not know, neither what was the custom in these matters, till afterward. But I knew, from the moment she first fixed her eyes on me, and I felt her mind brooding upon mine, how truly I had been told by those other women that the feeling with which they had inspired me was not love.

With people who become acquainted at a glance, and old friends in an hour, wooing is naturally not a long process. Indeed, it may be said that between lovers among mind-readers there is no wooing, but merely recognition. The day after we met, she became mine.

Perhaps I cannot better illustrate how subordinate the merely physical element is in the impression which mind-readers form of their friends than by mentioning an incident that occurred some months after our union. This was my discovery, wholly by accident, that my love, in whose society I had almost constantly been, had not the least idea what was the color of my eyes, or whether my hair and complexion were light or dark. Of course, as soon as I asked her the question, she read the answer in my mind, but she admitted that she had previously had no distinct impression on those points. On the other hand, if in the blackest midnight I should come to her, she would not need to ask who the comer was. It is by the mind, not the eye, that these people know one another. It is really only in their relations to soulless and inanimate things that they need eyes at all.

It must not be supposed that their disregard of one another's bodily aspect grows out of any ascetic sentiment. It is merely a necessary consequence of their power of directly apprehending mind, that whenever mind is closely associated with matter the latter is comparatively neglected on account of the greater interest of the former, suffering as lesser things always do when placed in immediate contrast with greater. Art is with them confined to the inanimate, the human form having, for the reason mentioned, ceased to inspire the artist. It will be naturally and quite correctly inferred that among such a race physical beauty is not the important factor in human fortune and felicity that it elsewhere is. The absolute openness of their minds and hearts to one another makes their happiness far more dependent on the moral and mental qualities of their companions than upon their physical. A genial temperament, a wide-grasping, godlike intellect, a poet soul, are incomparably more fascinating to them than the most dazzling combination conceivable of mere bodily graces.

A woman of mind and heart has no more need of beauty to win love in these islands than a beauty elsewhere of mind or heart. I should mention here, perhaps, that this race, which makes so litttle account of physical beauty, is itself a singularly handsome one. This is owing doubtless in part to the absolute compatibility of temperaments in all the marriages, and partly also to the reaction upon the body of a state of ideal mental and moral health and placidity.

Not being myself a mind-reader, the fact that my love was rarely beautiful in form and face had doubtless no little part in attracting my devotion. This, of course, she knew, as she knew all my thoughts, and, knowing my limitations, tolerated and forgave the element of sensuousness in my passion. But if it must have seemed to her so little worthy in comparison with the high spiritual communion which her race know as love, to me it became, by virtue of her almost superhuman relation to me, an ecstasy more ravishing surely than any lover of my race tasted before. The ache at the heart of the intensest love is the impotence of words to make it perfectly understood to its object. But my passion was without this pang, for my heart was absolutely open to her I loved. Lovers may imagine, but I cannot describe, the ecstatic thrill of communion into which this consciousness transformed every tender emotion. As I considered what mutual love must be where both parties are mind-readers, I realized the high communion which my sweet companion had sacrificed for me. She might indeed comprehend her lover and his love for her, but the higher satisfaction of knowing that she was comprehended by him and her love understood, she had foregone. For that I should ever attain the power of mind-reading was out of the question, the faculty never having been developed in a single lifetime.

Why my inability should move my dear companion to such depths of pity I was not able fully to understand until I learned that mind-reading is chiefly held desirable, not for the knowledge of others which it gives its possessors, but for the self-knowledge which is its reflex effect. Of all they see in the minds of others, that which concerns them most is the reflection of themselves, the photographs of their own characters. The most obvious consequence of the self-knowledge thus forced upon them is to render them alike incapable of self-conceit or self-depreciation. Every one must needs always think of himself as he is, being no more able to do otherwise than is a man in a hall of mirrors to cherish delusions as to his personal appearance.

But self-knowledge means to the mind-readers much more than this,— nothing less, indeed, than a shifting of the sense of identity. When a man sees himself in a mirror, he is compelled to distinguish between the bodily self he sees and his real self, which is within and unseen. When in turn the mind-reader comes to see the mental and moral self reflected in other minds as in mirrors, the same thing happens. He is compelled to distinguish between this mental and moral self which has been made objective to him, and can be contemplated by him as impartially as if it were another's, from the inner ego which still remains subjective, unseen, and indefinable. In this inner ego the mind-readers recognize the essential identity and being, the noumenal self, the core of the soul, and the true hiding of its eternal life, to which the mind as well as the body is but the garment of a day.

The effect of such a philosophy as this—which, indeed, with the mind-readers is rather an instinctive consciousness than a philosophy—must obviously be to impart a sense of wonderful superiority to the vicissitudes of this earthly state, and a singular serenity in the midst of the haps and mishaps which threaten or befall the personality. They did indeed appear to me, as I never dreamed men could attain to be, lords of themselves.

It was because I might not hope to attain this enfranchisement from the false ego of the apparent self, without which life seemed to her race scarcely worth living, that my love so pitied me.

But I must hasten on, leaving a thousand things unsaid, to relate the lamentable catastrophe to which it is owing that, instead of being still a resident of those blessed islands, in the full enjoyment of that intimate and ravishing companionship which by contrast would forever dim the pleasures of all other human society, I recall the bright picture as a memory under other skies.

Among a people who are compelled by the very constitution of their minds to put themselves in the places of others, the sympathy which is the inevitable consequence of perfect comprehension renders envy, hatred, and uncharitableness impossible. But of course there are people less genially constituted than others, and these are necessarily the objects of a certain distaste on the part of associates. Now, owing to the unhindered impact of minds upon one another, the anguish of persons so regarded, despite the tenderest consideration of those about them, is so great that they beg the grace of exile, that, being out of the way, people may think less frequently upon them. There are numerous small islets, scarcely more than rocks, lying to the north of the archipelago, and on these the unfortunates are permitted to live. Only one lives on each islet, as they cannot endure each other even as well as the more happily constituted can endure them. From time to time supplies of food are taken to them, and of course, any time they wish to take the risk, they are permitted to return to society.

Now, as I have said, the fact which, even more than their out-of-the-way location, makes the islands of the mind-readers unapproachable, is the violence with which the great antarctic current, owing probably to some configuration of the ocean bed, together with the innumerable rocks and shoals, flows through and about the archipelago.

Ships making the islands from the southward are caught by this current and drawn among the rocks, to their almost certain destruction; while, owing to the violence with which the current sets to the north, it is not possible to approach at all from that direction, or at least it has never been accomplished. Indeed, so powerful are the currents that even the boats which cross the narrow straits between the main islands and the islets of the unfortunate, to carry the latter their supplies, are ferried over by cables, not trusting to oar or sail.

The brother of my love had charge of one of the boats engaged in this transportation, and, being desirous of visiting the islets, I accepted an invitation to accompany him on one of his trips. I know nothing of how the accident happened, but in the fiercest part of the current of one of the straits we parted from the cable and were swept out to sea. There was no question of stemming the boiling current, our utmost endeavors barely sufficing to avoid being dashed to pieces on the rocks. From the first, there was no hope of our winning back to the land, and so swiftly did we drift that by noon—the accident having befallen in the morning—the islands, which are low-lying, had sunk beneath the southwestern horizon.

Among these mind-readers, distance is not an insuperable obstacle to the transfer of thought. My companion was in communication with our friends, and from time to time conveyed to me messages of anguish from my dear love; for, being well aware of the nature of the currents and the unapproachableness of the islands, those we had left behind, as well as we ourselves, knew well we should see each other's faces no more. For five days we continued to drift to the northwest, in no danger of starvation, owing to our lading of provisions, but constrained to unintermitting watch and ward by the roughness of the weather. On the fifth day my companion died from exposure and exhaustion. He died very quietly,—indeed, with great appearance of relief. The life of the mind-readers while yet they are in the body is so largely spiritual that the idea of an existence wholly so, which seems vague and chill to us, suggests to them a state only slightly more refined than they already know on earth.

After that I suppose I must have fallen into an unconscious state, from which I roused to find myself on an American ship bound for New York, surrounded by people whose only means of communicating with one another is to keep up while together a constant clatter of hissing, guttural, and explosive noises, eked out by all manner of facial contortions and bodily gestures. I frequently find myself staring open-mouthed at those who address me, too much struck by their grotesque appearance to bethink myself of replying.

I find that I shall not live out the voyage, and I do not care to. From my experience of the people on the ship, I can judge how I should fare on land amid the stunning Babel of a nation of talkers. And my friends, —God bless them! how lonely I should feel in their very presence! Nay, what satisfaction or consolation, what but bitter mockery, could I ever more find in such human sympathy and companionship as suffice others and once sufficed me,—I who have seen and known what I have seen and. known! Ah, yes, doubtless it is far better I should die; but the knowledge of the things that I have seen I feel should not perish with me. For hope's sake, men should not miss the glimpse of the higher, sun-bathed reaches of the upward path they plod. So thinking, I have written out some account of my wonderful experience, though briefer far, by reason of my weakness, than fits the greatness of the matter. The captain seems an honest, well-meaning man, and to him I shall confide the narrative, charging him, on touching shore, to see it safely in the hands of some one who will bring it to the world's ear.

Note.—The extent of my own connection with the foregoing document is sufficiently indicated by the author himself in the final paragraph.

—E. B.

— PIECES —
social institutions

part II

—5—

the psycho-engineering of personalities

The psychologist B.F. Skinner created a utopian community called Walden Two. An excerpt from his book, *Walden Two,* describes the community's educational institutions and the procedures used to socialize children into the community. Because Skinner is an eminent psychologist and because some principles of his reinforcement-based psychology have been obviously applied in the design of the community's procedures for socializing and educating its members, the plan for Walden Two may be regarded as the most serious attempt by any designer of possible societies whose work is represented in this book to specify how social-science knowledge might be applied. Even Skinner's outline for Walden Two should, however, be viewed as an oversimplified sketch of a small segment of a social system that utilized the procedures he proposed. Walden Two does not provide a detailed plan that could be put directly into operation.

One fear that is often voiced about the effects of the development of a powerful social science (it is frequently echoed in the work of writers of science fiction) is that once the processes of socialization and education are understood and can be controlled, human automatons will be produced whose "free wills" have been destroyed, or at least men will be shaped to fit into their societies. The fear is that knowledge will permit control, and that control will destroy the "natural" process whereby children become adults. In order to see the issue in perspective we have to recognize that two separate components must be considered. The first is the extent to which an individual's *self* is the result of a sequence of socializing experiences. The second is the consequences of controlling this set of experiences.

Proposals for revision of educational systems or for introduction of conscious methods of socialization frequently generate great controversy. One reason for controversy is that such proposals occasion some thought about the tremendous effects of socialization and education. Giving serious thought to how much one's personality, personal preferences, beliefs, and opinions are determined by his socialization and his educational experiences makes it difficult to maintain certain cherished myths about freedom of the individual will.

For most people in our society the socialization process is a set of experiences that are unique to each person. Even educational experiences introduce only a minimum core of common experiences; because educational environments are enormously diverse, only relatively small numbers of people have even this much of a common set of experiences. A young man attending an Eastern prep school for the offspring of the power elite, one attending a military school which advertises that it will produce *men of character,* another attending a suburban, middle-class high school, and a fourth attending an urban ghetto school can hardly be considered to be experiencing equivalent socializations even with regard to their educational experiences. It could be argued that even when class differences are held constant, regional variations are sufficiently great to destroy comparability across school settings. It is unlikely that the social environment of a middle-class school in Georgia is indistinguishable from the social environment of a middle-class school in Los Angeles, or even that a Los Angeles school is interchangeable with one in San Francisco in terms of social environment. The products of each of these socializing environments are usually more like each other than they are like the products of different environments, and this demonstrates that the particular environment has a substantial effect on the end-product.

The great diversity of socialization patterns (experiences within families, experiences within schools, and so on) in our society makes it difficult to identify the causes of variations in adult personality and belief systems. Therefore, the myth remains that our *social selves* are something other than simply the products of our society, our social-class positions within that society, and the specific set of experiences that mark our personal histories. Attempts to identify the causal forces involved in personality development, and proposals to adopt specified sets of socializing experiences designed to create adults with certain personal characteristics, make clear the cause-and-effect nature of social development. This threatens the myth of essential individuality.

Productive objections to the proposals could be made in terms of whether the innovations would produce the intended effects, or whether some other end-product was more desirable. But objections are rarely productive in this sense; rather, they simply suggest that the designer is touching on a taboo subject.

In addition to a certain unwillingness to admit that those aspects of a person's *self* that seem most personal and unique are merely the result of largely accidental experiences, objections are frequently raised on the grounds that up to the limits of assault and battery and other treatment generally recognized as inhumane, parents have the right to do with their children as they please. If a man is a racist, he will object quite strenuously to his society's taking action to prevent him from passing on this delightful social perspective to his children. A second objection is that parents do not like anyone to say, or even to imply, that they are unfit and are producing disturbed children. In every generation a large number of people get *hung up, messed up, screwed up,* or more or less destroyed in the process of being socialized. One result ensured by our not trying to control the socialization process more than we do is that the casualties of one generation will produce casualties in the next generation.

The psychologist Harry Harlow carried out a series of interesting experiments on this point.[1] His research dealt with the effects of rearing infant monkeys in socially abnormal environments. Some monkeys were reared with hostile surrogate mothers, some with no maternal contact, and some under other unusual conditions. The monkeys reacted to these experiences by behaving as adults in ways that could be described as severely disturbed. Some of these monkeys displayed behavior patterns that ranged from periods of complete inactivity to periods of violent self-mutilation. The female monkeys that matured and mated treated their own offspring in a manner more brutal than the manner in which they had been reared. There was little doubt that the second generation would be at least as disturbed as the first.

A great inequity results from society's leaving the socialization process relatively uncontrolled. Parents have certain rights to control their children's minds. Except in the most extreme cases, however, children have virtually no protection from the damage that can be done to them in the process of socialization. Even granting that this damage usually is inflicted accidentally, it would seem that children ought to be protected if possible. Beyond the question of mere protection, it also seems reasonable that if it were possible to help individuals to be put together better, it would be proper to do so. The argument could be made that just as minimum standards of physical health and health practices are required for the protection of the population, minimum standards of socialization standards should be required for the protection of a person's mental health.

One sense in which fear of a powerful social science is justified is that a greater understanding of the roots of personality and cognitive development could lead to more efficient methods of programing individuals to have specific personality traits and beliefs. Therefore, whoever determines what type of personality traits and beliefs are to be produced has tremendous power. There is some protection in having a hodgepodge of vaguely planned but mainly accidental experiences leading to the production of adult personalities. Such a mixture is very difficult to manipulate, control, and thereby determine what is produced.

When we have enough knowledge about the dynamics of personality formation and the development of belief systems to affect the socialization process in order to generate predictable products, a choice will have to be made. The choice will be: continue to manufacture individuals so that it is not obvious that the manufacturing is being carried out, with each person being handled individually, and with very little idea how the product will turn out; or attempt to introduce some quality control, and at least eliminate the lemons.

---

[1]Harry Harlow and Margaret Harlow, "A Study of Animal Affection," *Natural History,* 70, 10 (December 1961), 48–55.

The excerpt from *Walden Two* describes how some aspects of a controlled socialization process might be carried out. The group taking part in the discussion includes eight people. Only four of them are frequent speakers—Frazier (the designer of Walden Two and formerly a graduate student with Professor Burris), Professor Burris (a psychologist and a visitor at Walden Two), Professor Castle (a philosopher, also a visitor), and Mrs. Nash (a worker in the nursery).

walden two

by B.F. Skinner

A young woman in a white uniform met us in a small waiting room near the entrance. Frazier addressed her as Mrs. Nash.

"I hope Mr. Frazier has warned you," she said with a smile, "that we're going to be rather impolite and give you only a glimpse of our babies. We try to protect them from infection during the first year. It's especially important when they are cared for as a group."

"What about the parents?" said Castle at once. "Don't parents see their babies?"

"Oh, yes, so long as they are in good health. Some parents work in the nursery. Others come around every day or so, for at least a few minutes. They take the baby out for some sunshine, or play with it in a play room." Mrs. Nash smiled at Frazier. "That's the way we build up the baby's resistance," she added.

She opened a door and allowed us to look into a small room, three walls of which were lined with cubicles, each with a large glass window. Behind the windows we could see babies of various ages. None of them wore more than a diaper, and there were no bedclothes. In one cubicle a small red newborn was asleep on its stomach. Some of the older babies were awake and playing with toys. Near the door a baby on all fours pressed its nose against the glass and smiled at us.

"Looks like an aquarium," said Castle.

"And very precious fish they are," said Mrs. Nash, as if the comparison were not unfamiliar.

"Which is yours?" asked Frazier.

"Over there asleep," said Mrs. Nash, pointing to a far corner. "Almost ready to graduate, too. He'll be a year old next month." She drew the door gently shut before we had satisfied our curiosity.

"I can show you one of the units in the isolation room, which isn't being used," she said, leading the way along the corridor. She opened another door and we entered. Two of the cubicles stood against the wall.

"This is a much more efficient way of keeping a baby warm than the usual practice of wrapping it in several layers of cloth," said Mrs. Nash, opening a safety-glass window to permit Barbara and Mary to look inside. "The new-born baby needs moist air at about 88 or 90 degrees. At six months, 80 is about right."

"How do you know that?" said Castle, rather belligerently.

"The baby tells us," said Mrs. Nash pleasantly, as if the question were also familiar.

"You know the story about the bath water, don't you, Mr. Castle?" Frazier interrupted. "The temperature's all right if the baby doesn't turn red or blue."

"But I hope—" Castle began.

"It's only a matter of a degree or two," said Mrs. Nash quickly. "If the baby's too warm, it does turn rather pinkish, and it usually cries. It always stops crying when we lower the temperature." She twisted the dial of a thermostat on the front of a cubicle.

"And I suppose if frost forms around the nose it's too cold," said Castle, getting himself under control.

"The baby turns rather pale," said Mrs Nash laughing, "and takes a curious posture with its arms along its sides or slightly curled up. With a little practice we can tell at a glance whether the temperature is right or not."

"But why don't you put clothes on them?" said Barbara.

"What for? It would mean laundry for us and discomfort for the child. It's the same with sheets and blankets. Our babies lie on a stretched plastic cloth which doesn't soak up moisture and can be wiped clean in a moment."

"It looks terribly comfortable," I said. "Why don't you all sleep that way?"

"We're working on that," said Frazier, apparently quite seriously. "It would save no end of laundry, and, as you say, it would be comfortable."

"Clothing and blankets are really a great nuisance," said Mrs. Nash. "They keep the baby from exercising, they force it into uncomfortable postures —"

"When a baby graduates from our Lower Nursery," Frazier broke in, "it knows nothing of frustration, anxiety, or fear. It never cries except when sick, which is very seldom, and it has a lively interest in everything."

"But is it prepared for life?" said Castle. "Surely you can't continue to protect it from frustration or frightening situations forever."

"Of course not. But it can be prepared for them. We can build a tolerance for frustration by introducing obstacles gradually as the baby grows strong enough to handle them. But I'm getting ahead of our story. Have you any other point to make, Mrs. Nash?"

"I suppose you'd like to have them know how much work is saved. Since the air is filtered, we only bathe the babies once a week, and we never need to clean their nostrils or eyes. There are no beds to make, of course. And it's easy to prevent infection. The compartments are sound-proofed, and the babies sleep well and don't disturb each other. We can keep them on different schedules, so the nursery runs smoothly. Let me see, is there anything else?"

"I think that's quite enough," said Frazier. "We have a lot of ground to cover this morning."

"Not so fast, if you please," said Castle. "I'm not satisfied yet. Aren't you raising a lot of very inadequate organisms? Controlled temperature, noiseless sleep—aren't these babies going to be completely at the mercy of a normal environment? Can you go on coddling them forever?"

"I can answer that, Mrs. Nash," said Frazier. "The answer is *no*. Our babies are especially resistant. It's true that a constant annoyance may develop a tolerance, but the commoner result is that the baby is worn down or enervated. We introduce annoyances slowly, according to the ability of the baby to take them. It's very much like inoculation."

"Another thing," said Castle. "What about mother love?"

Frazier and Mrs. Nash looked at each other and laughed.

"Are you speaking of mother love as an essence, Mr Castle?" said Frazier.

"I am not!" said Castle, bristling. "I'm speaking of a concrete thing. I mean the love which the mother gives her baby—the affection—well, to be really concrete, the kisses, the fondling, and so on, I suppose you'd say. You can't expect me to give you the physical dimensions of mother love!" He was confused and flushed. "It's real enough to the baby, I'll bet!" he added blackly.

"Very real," said Frazier quietly. "And we supply it in liberal doses. But we don't limit it to mothers. We go in for father love, too—for every-body's love—community love, if you wish. Our children are treated with affection by everyone—and thoughtful affection too, which isn't marred by fits of temper due to overwork or careless handling due to ignorance."

"But the personal relation between the mother and the child—Isn't there some sort of patterning? I thought the whole personality could be shaped in that way?" Castle appealed to me for professional support, but I failed him.

"You mean what the Freudian calls 'identification,' I think," said Frazier. "I agree that it's important, and we use it very effectively in our educational system. But unless you're a strict Freudian, we're talking in the wrong room. Let's wait till we see another age group. Can you come to the Upper Nursery, Mrs. Nash?"

"Let me check my staff," said Mrs. Nash. She disappeared into the "aquarium," returned almost immediately, and led us to another wing.

The quarters for children from one to three consisted of several small playrooms with Lilliputian furniture, a child's lavatory, and a dressing and locker room. Several small sleeping rooms were operated on the same principle as the baby-cubicles. The temperature and the humidity were controlled so that clothes or bedclothing were not needed. The cots were double-decker arrangements of the plastic mattresses we had seen in the cubicles. The children slept unclothed, except for diapers. There were more beds than necessary, so that the children could be grouped according to developmental age or exposure to contagious diseases or need for supervision, or for educational purposes.

We followed Mrs. Nash to a large screened porch on the south side of the building, where several children were playing in sandboxes and on swings and climbing apparatuses. A few wore "training pants"; the rest were naked. Beyond the porch was a grassy play yard enclosed by closely trimmed hedges, where other children, similarly undressed, were at play. Some kind of marching game was in progress.

As we returned, we met two women carrying food hampers. They spoke to Mrs. Nash and followed her to the porch. In a moment five or six children came running into the playrooms and were soon using the lavatory and dressing themselves. Mrs. Nash explained that they were being taken on a picnic.

"What about the children who don't go?" said Castle. "What do you do about the green-eyed monster?"

Mrs. Nash was puzzled.

"Jealousy. Envy." Castle elaborated. "Don't the children who stay home ever feel unhappy about it?"

"I don't understand," said Mrs. Nash.

"And I hope you won't try," said Frazier, with a smile. "I'm afraid we must be moving along."

We said good-bye, and I made an effort to thank Mrs. Nash, but she seemed to be puzzled by that too, and Frazier frowned as if I had committed some breach of good taste.

"I think Mrs. Nash's puzzlement," said Frazier, as we left the building, "is proof enough that our children are seldom envious or jealous. Mrs. Nash was twelve years old when Walden Two was founded. It was a little late to undo her early training, but I think we were successful. She's a good example of the Walden Two product. She could probably recall the experience of jealousy, but it's not part of her present life."

"Surely that's going too far!" said Castle. "You can't be so godlike as all that! You must be assailed by emotions just as much as the rest of us!"

"We can discuss the question of godlikeness later, if you wish," replied Frazier. "As to emotions—we aren't free of them all, nor should we like to be. But the meaner and more annoying—the emotions which breed unhappiness—are almost unknown here, like unhappiness itself. We don't need them any longer in our struggle for existence, and it's easier on our circulatory system, and certainly pleasanter, to dispense with them."

"If you've discovered how to do that, you are indeed a genius," said Castle. He seemed almost stunned as Frazier nodded assent. "We all know that emotions are useless and bad for our peace of mind and our blood pressure," he went on. "But how arrange things otherwise?"

"We arrange them otherwise here," said Frazier. He was showing a mildness of manner which I was coming to recognize as a sign of confidence.

"But emotions are—fun!" said Barbara. "Life wouldn't be worth living without them."

"Some of them, yes," said Frazier. "The productive and strengthening emotions—joy and love. But sorrow and hate—and the high-voltage excitements of anger, fear and rage—are out of proportion with the needs of modern life, and they're wasteful and dangerous. Mr. Castle has mentioned jealousy—a minor form of anger, I think we may call it. Naturally we avoid it. It has served its purpose in the evolution of man; we've no further use for it. If we allowed it to persist, it would only sap the life out of us. In a cooperative society there's no jealousy because there's no need for jealousy."

"That implies that you all get everything you want," said Castle. "But what about social possessions? Last night you mentioned the young man who chose a particular girl or profession. There's still a chance for jealousy there, isn't there?"

"It doesn't imply that we get everything we want," said Frazier. "Of course we don't. But jealousy wouldn't help. In a competitive world there's some point to it. It energizes one to attack a frustrating condition. The impulse and the added energy are an advantage. Indeed, in a competitive world emotions work all too well. Look at the singular lack of success of the complacent man. He enjoys a more serene life, but it's less likely to be a fruitful one. The world isn't ready for simple pacifism or Christian humility, to cite two cases in point. Before you can safely train out the destructive and wasteful emotions, you must make sure they're no longer needed."

"How do you make sure that jealousy isn't needed in Walden Two?" I said.

"In Walden Two problems can't be solved by attacking others," said Frazier with marked finality.

"That's not the same as eliminating jealousy, though," I said.

"Of course it's not. But when a particular emotion is no longer a useful part of a behavioral repertoire, we proceed to eliminate it."

"Yes, but how?"

"It's simply a matter of behavioral engineering," said Frazier.

"Behavioral engineering?"

"You're baiting me, Burris. You know perfectly well what I mean. The techniques have been available for centuries. We use them in education and in the psychological management of the community. But you're forcing my hand," he added. "I was saving that for this evening. But let's strike while the iron is hot."

We had stopped at the door of the large children's building. Frazier shrugged his shoulders, walked to the shade of a large tree, and threw himself on the ground. We arranged ourselves about him and waited.

"Each of us," Frazier began, "is engaged in a pitch battle with the rest of mankind."

"A curious premise for a Utopia," said Castle. "Even a pessimist like myself takes a more hopeful view than that."

"You do, you do," said Frazier. "But let's be realistic. Each of us has interests which conflict with the interests of everybody else. That's our original sin, and it can't be helped. Now, 'everybody else' we call 'society.' It's a powerful opponent, and it always wins. Oh, here and there an individual prevails for a while and gets what he wants. Sometimes he storms the culture of a society and changes it slightly to his own advantage. But society wins in the long run, for it has the advantage of numbers and of age. Many prevail against one, and men against a baby. Society attacks early, when the individual is helpless. It enslaves him almost before he has tasted freedom. The 'ologies' will tell you how it's done. Theology calls it building a conscience or developing a spirit of selflessness. Psychology calls it the growth of the superego.

"Considering how long society has been at it, you'd expect a better job. But the campaigns have been badly planned and the victory has never been secure. The behavior of the individual has been shaped according to revelations of 'good conduct,' never as the result of experimental study. But why not experiment? The questions are simple enough. What's the best behavior for the individual so far as the group is concerned? And how can the individual be induced to behave in that way? Why not explore these questions in a scientific spirit?

"We could do just that in Walden Two. We had already worked out a code of conduct—subject, of course, to experimental modification. The code would keep things running smoothly if everybody lived up to it. Our job was to see that everybody did. Now, you can't get people to follow a useful code by making them into so many jacks-in-the-box. You can't foresee all future circumstances, and you can't specify adequate future conduct. You don't know what will be required. Instead you have to set up certain behavioral processes which will lead the individual to design his own 'good' conduct when the time comes. We call that sort of thing 'self-control.' But don't be misled, the control always rests in the last analysis in the hands of society.

"One of our Planners, a young man named Simmons, worked with me.

It was the first time in history that the matter was approached in an experimental way. Do you question that statement, Mr. Castle?"

"I'm not sure I know what you are talking about," said Castle.

"Then let me go on. Simmons and I began by studying the great works on morals and ethics—Plato, Aristotle, Confucius, the New Testament, the Puritan divines, Machiavelli, Chesterfield, Freud—there were scores of them. We were looking for any and every method of shaping human behavior by imparting techniques of self-control. Some techniques were obvious enough, for they had marked turning points in human history. 'Love your enemies' is an example—a psychological invention for easing the lot of an oppressed people. The severest trial of oppression is the constant rage which one suffers at the thought of the oppressor. What Jesus discovered was how to avoid these inner devastations. His technique was to *practice the opposite emotion.* If a man can succeed in 'loving his enemies' and 'taking no thought for the morrow,' he will no longer be assailed by hatred of the oppressor or rage at the loss of his freedom or possessions. He may not get his freedom or possessions back, but he's less miserable. It's a difficult lesson. It comes late in our program."

"I thought you were opposed to modifying emotions and instincts until the world was ready for it," said Castle. "According to you, the principle of 'love your enemies' should have been suicidal."

"It would have been suicidal, except for an entirely unforeseen consequence. Jesus must have been quite astonished at the effect of his discovery. We are only just beginning to understand the power of love because we are just beginning to understand the weakness of force and aggression. But the science of behavior is clear about all that now. Recent discoveries in the analysis of punishment—but I am falling into one digression after another. Let me save my explanation of why the Christian virtues—and I mean merely the Christian techniques of self-control—have not disappeared from the face of the earth, with due recognition of the fact that they suffered a narrow squeak within recent memory.

"When Simmons and I had collected our techniques of control, we had to discover how to teach them. That was more difficult. Current educational practices were of little value, and religious practices scarcely any better. Promising paradise or threatening hell-fire is, we assumed, generally admitted to be unproductive. It is based upon a fundamental fraud which, when discovered, turns the individual against society and nourishes the very thing it tries to stamp out. What Jesus offered in return for loving one's enemies was heaven *on earth,* better known as peace of mind.

"We found a few suggestions worth following in the practices of the clinical psychologist. We undertook to build a tolerance for annoying experiences. The sunshine of midday is extremely painful if you come from a dark room, but take it in easy stages and you can avoid pain altogether. The analogy can be misleading, but in much the same way it's possible to build a tolerance to painful or distasteful stimuli, or to frustration, or to situations which arouse fear, anger or rage. Society and nature throw these annoyances at the individual with no regard for the development of tolerances. Some achieve tolerances, most fail. Where would the science of immunization be if it followed a schedule of accidental dosages?

"Take the principle of 'Get thee behind me, Satan,' for example," Frazier continued. "It's a special case of self-control by altering the environment. Subclass A 3, I believe. We give each child a lollipop which has been dipped in powdered sugar so that a single touch of the tongue can be detected. We tell him he may eat the lollipop later in the day, provided it hasn't already been licked. Since the child is only three or four, it is a fairly diff —"

"Three or four!" Castle exclaimed.

"All our ethical training is completed by the age of six," said Frazier quietly. "A simple principle like putting temptation out of sight would be acquired before four. But at such an early age the problem of not licking the lollipop isn't easy. Now, what would you do, Mr. Castle, in a similar situation?"

"Put the lollipop out of sight as quickly as possible."

"Exactly. I can see you've been well trained. Or perhaps you discovered the principle for yourself. We're in favor of original inquiry wherever possible, but in this case we have a more important goal and we don't hesitate to give verbal help. First of all, the children are urged to examine their own behavior while looking at the lollipops. This helps them to recognize the need for self-control. Then the lollipops are concealed, and the children are asked to notice any gain in happiness or any reduction in tension. Then a strong distraction is arranged—say, an interesting game. Later the children are reminded of the candy and encouraged to examine their reaction. The value of the distraction is generally obvious. Well, need I go on? When the experiment is repeated a day or so later, the children all run with the lollipops to their lockers and do exactly what Mr. Castle would do—a sufficient indication of the success of our training."

"I wish to report an objective observation of my reaction to your story," said Castle, controlling his voice with great precision. "I find myself revolted by this display of sadistic tyranny."

"I don't wish to deny you the exercise of an emotion which you seem to find enjoyable," said Frazier. "So let me go on. Concealing a tempting, but forbidden object is a crude solution. For one thing, it's not always feasible. We want a sort of psychological concealment—covering up the candy by paying no attention. In a later experiment the children wear their lollipops like crucifixes for a few hours."

. . . "Some of us learn control, more or less by accident. The rest of us go all our lives not even understanding how it is possible, and blaming our failure on being born the wrong way."

"How do you build up a tolerance to an annoying situation?" I said.

"Oh, for example, by having the children 'take' a more and more painful shock, or drink cocoa with less and less sugar in it until a bitter concoction can be savored without a bitter face."

"But jealousy or envy—you can't administer them in graded doses," I said.

"And why not? Remember, we control the social environment, too, at this age. That's why we get our ethical training in early. Take this case. A group of children arrive home after a long walk tired and hungry. They're expecting supper; they find, instead, that it's time for a lesson in self-control: they must stand for five minutes in front of steaming bowls of soup.

"The assignment is accepted like a problem in arithmetic. Any groaning or complaining is a wrong answer. Instead, the children begin at once to work upon themselves to avoid any unhappiness during the delay. One of them may make a joke of it. We encourage a sense of humor as a good way of not taking an annoyance seriously. The joke won't be much, according to adult standards—perhaps the child will simply pretend to empty the bowl of soup into his upturned mouth. Another may start a song with many verses. The rest join in at once, for they've learned that it's a good way to make time pass."

Frazier glanced uneasily at Castle, who was not to be appeased.

"That also strikes you as a form of torture, Mr. Castle?" he asked.

"I'd rather be put on the rack," said Castle.

"Then you have by no means had the thorough training I supposed. You can't imagine how lightly the children take such an experience. It's a rather severe biological frustration, for the children are tired and hungry and they must stand and look at food; but it's passed off as lightly as a five-minute delay at curtain time. We regard it as a fairly elementary test. Much more difficult problems follow."

"I suspected as much," muttered Castle.

"In a later stage we forbid all social devices. No songs, no jokes—merely silence. Each child is forced back upon his own resources—a very important step."

"I should think so," I said. "And how do you know it's successful? You might produce a lot of silently resentful children. It's certainly a dangerous stage."

"It is, and we follow each child carefully. If he hasn't picked up the necessary techniques, we start back a little. A still more advanced stage"—Frazier glanced again at Castle, who stirred uneasily—"brings me to my point. When it's time to sit down to the soup, the children count off—heads and tails. Then a coin is tossed and if it comes up heads, the 'heads' sit down and eat. The 'tails' remain standing for another five minutes."

Castle groaned.

"And you call that envy?" I asked.

"Perhaps not exactly," said Frazier. "At least there's seldom any aggression against the lucky ones. The emotion, if any, is directed against Lady Luck herself, against the toss of the coin. That, in itself, is a lesson worth learning, for it's the only direction in which emotion has a surviving chance to be useful. And resentment toward things in general, while perhaps just as silly as personal aggression, is more easily controlled. Its expression is not socially objectionable."

Frazier looked nervously from one of us to the other. He seemed to be trying to discover whether we shared Castle's prejudice. I began to realize, also, that he had not really wanted to tell this story. He was vulnerable. He was treading on sanctified ground, and I was pretty sure he had not established the value of most of these practices in an experimental fashion. He could scarcely have done so in the short space of ten years. He was working on faith, and it bothered him.

I tried to bolster his confidence by reminding him that he had a professional colleague among his listeners. "May you not inadvertently teach your children some of the very emotions you're trying to eliminate?" I said. "What's the effect, for example, of finding the anticipation of a warm supper suddenly thwarted? Doesn't that eventually lead to feelings of uncertainty, or even anxiety?"

"It might. We had to discover how often our lessons could be safely administered. But all our schedules are worked out experimentally. We watch for undesired consequences just as any scientist watches for disrupting factors in his experiments.

"After all, it's a simple and sensible program," he went on in a tone of appeasement. "We set up a system of gradually increasing annoyances and frustrations against a background of complete serenity. An easy environment is made more and more difficult as the children acquire the capacity to adjust."

"But *why?*" said Castle. "Why these deliberate unpleasantnesses—to put it mildly? I must say I think you and your friend Simmons are really very subtle sadists."

"You've reversed your position, Mr. Castle," said Frazier in a sudden flash of anger with which I rather sympathized. Castle was calling names, and he was also being unaccountably and perhaps intentionally obtuse. "A while ago you accused me of breeding a race of softies," Frazier continued. "Now you object to toughening them up. But what you don't understand is that these potentially unhappy situations are never very annoying. Our schedules make sure of that. You wouldn't understand, however, because you're not so far advanced as our children."

Castle grew black.

"But what do your children get out of it?" he insisted, apparently trying to press some vague advantage in Frazier's anger.

"What do they get out of it!" exclaimed Frazier, his eyes flashing with a sort of helpless contempt. His lips curled and he dropped his head to look at his fingers, which were crushing a few blades of grass.

"They must get happiness and freedom and strength," I said, putting myself in a ridiculous position in attempting to make peace.

"They don't sound happy or free to me, standing in front of bowls of Forbidden Soup," said Castle, answering me parenthetically while continuing to stare at Frazier.

"If I must spell it out," Frazier began with a deep sigh, "what they get is escape from the petty emotions which eat the heart out of the unprepared. They get the satisfaction of pleasant and profitable social relations on a scale almost undreamed of in the world at large. They get immeasurably increased efficiency, because they can stick to a job without suffering the aches and pains which soon beset most of us. They get new horizons, for they are spared the emotions characteristic of frustration and failure. They get —" His eyes searched the branches of the trees. "Is that enough?" he said at last.

"And the community must gain their loyalty," I said, "when they discover the fears and jealousies and diffidences in the world at large."

"I'm glad you put it that way," said Frazier. "You might have said that they must feel superior to the miserable products of our public schools. But we're at pains to keep any feeling of superiority or contempt under control, too. Having suffered most acutely from it myself, I put the subject first on our agenda. We carefully avoid any joy in a personal triumph which means the personal failure of somebody else. We take no pleasure in the sophistical, the disputative, the dialectical." He threw a vicious glance at Castle. "We don't use the motive of domination, because we are always thinking of the whole group. We could motivate a few geniuses that way—it was certainly my own motivation—but we'd sacrifice some of the happiness of everyone else. Triumph over nature and over oneself, yes. But over others, never."

"You've taken the mainspring out of the watch," said Castle flatly.

"That's an experimental question, Mr. Castle, and you have the wrong answer."

Frazier was making no effort to conceal his feeling. If he had been riding Castle, he was now using his spurs. Perhaps he sensed that the rest of us had come round and that he could change his tactics with a single holdout. But it was more than strategy, it was genuine feeling. Castle's undeviating skepticism was a growing frustration.

"Are your techniques really so very new?" I said hurriedly. "What about the primitive practice of submitting a boy to various tortures before granting him a place among adults? What about the disciplinary techniques of Puritanism? Or of the modern school, for that matter?"

"In one sense you're right," said Frazier. "And I think you've nicely answered Mr. Castle's tender concern for our little ones. The unhappinesses we deliberately impose are far milder than the normal unhappinesses from which we offer protection. Even at the height of our ethical training, the unhappiness is ridiculously trivial—to the well-trained child.

"But there's a world of difference in the way we use these annoyances," he continued. "For one thing, we don't punish. We never administer an unpleasantness in the hope of repressing or eliminating undesirable behavior. But there's another difference. In most cultures the child meets up with annoyances and reverses of uncontrolled magnitude. Some are imposed in the name of discipline by persons in authority. Some, like hazings, are condoned though not authorized. Others are merely accidental. No one cares to, or is able to, prevent them.

"We all know what happens. A few hardy children emerge, particularly those who have got their unhappiness in doses that could be swallowed. They become brave men. Others become sadists or masochists of varying degrees of pathology. Not having conquered a painful environment, they become preoccupied with pain and make a devious art of it. Others submit —and hope to inherit the earth. The rest—the cravens, the cowards—live in fear for the rest of their lives. And that's only a single field—the reaction to pain. I could cite a dozen parallel cases. The optimist and the pessimist, the contented and the disgruntled, the loved and the unloved, the ambitious and the discouraged—these are only the extreme products of a miserable system.

"Traditional practices are admittedly better than nothing," Frazier went on. "Spartan or Puritan—no one can question the occasional happy result. But the whole system rests upon the wasteful principle of selection. The English public school of the nineteenth century produced brave men—by setting up almost insurmountable barriers and making the most of the few who came over. But selection isn't education. Its crops of brave men will always be small, and the waste enormous. Like all primitive principles, selection serves in place of education only through a profligate use of material. Multiply extravagantly and select with rigor. It's the philosophy of the 'big litter' as an alternative to good child hygiene.

"In Walden Two we have a different objective. We make every man a brave man. They all come over the barriers. Some require more preparation than others, but they all come over. The traditional use of adversity is to select the strong. We control adversity to build strength. And we do it deliberately, no matter how sadistic Mr. Castle may think us, in order to prepare for adversities which are beyond control. Our children eventually experience the 'heartache and the thousand natural shocks that flesh is heir to.' It would be the cruelest possible practice to protect them as long as possible, especially when we *could* protect them so well."

Frazier held out his hands in an exaggerated gesture of appeal.

"What alternative *had* we?" he said, as if he were in pain. "What else could we do? For four or five years we could provide a life in which no important need would go unsatisfied, a life practically free of anxiety or frustration or annoyance. What would *you* do? Would you let the child enjoy this paradise with no thought for the future—like an idolatrous and pampering mother? Or would you relax control of the environment and let the child meet accidental frustrations? *But what is the virtue of accident?* No, there was only one course open to us. We had to *design* a series of adversities, so that the child would develop the greatest possible self-control. Call it deliberate, if you like, and accuse us of sadism; there was no other course." Frazier turned to Castle, but he was scarcely challenging him. He seemed to be waiting, anxiously, for his capitulation. But Castle merely shifted his ground.

"I find it difficult to classify these practices," he said. Frazier emitted a disgruntled "Ha!" and sat back. "Your system seems to have usurped the place as well as the techniques of religion."

"Of religion and family culture," said Frazier wearily. "But I don't call it usurpation. Ethical training belongs to the community. As for techniques, we took every suggestion we could find without prejudice as to the source. But not on faith. We disregarded all claims of revealed truth and put every principle to an experimental test. And by the way, I've very much misrepresented the whole system if you suppose that any of the practices I've described are fixed. We try out many different techniques. Gradually we work toward the best possible set. And we don't pay much attention to the apparent success of a principle in the course of history. History is honored in Walden Two only as entertainment. It isn't taken seriously as food for thought. Which reminds me, very rudely, of our original plan for the morning. Have you had enough of emotion? Shall we turn to intellect?"

. . . The living quarters and daily schedules of the older children furnished a particularly good example of behavioral engineering. At first sight they seemed wholly casual, almost haphazard, but as Frazier pointed out their significant features and the consequences of each, I began to make out a comprehensive, almost Machiavellian design.

The children passed smoothly from one age group to another, following a natural process of growth and avoiding the abrupt changes of the home-and-school system. The arrangements were such that each child emulated children slightly older than himself and hence derived motives and patterns for much of his early education without adult aid.

The control of the physical and social environment, of which Frazier had made so much, was progressively relaxed—or, to be more exact, the control was transferred from the authorities to the child himself and to the other members of his group. After spending most of the first year in an air-conditioned cubicle, and the second and third mainly in an air-conditioned room with a minimum of clothing and bedding, the three- or four-year-old was introduced to regular clothes and given the care of a small standard cot in a dormitory. The beds of the five- and six-year-olds were grouped by threes and fours in a series of alcoves furnished like rooms and treated as such by the children. Groups of three or four seven-year-olds occupied small rooms together, and this practice was continued, with frequent change of roommates, until the children were about thirteen, at which time they took temporary rooms in the adult building, usually in pairs. At marriage, or whenever the individual chose, he could participate in building a larger room for himself or refurnishing an old room which might be available.

A similar withdrawal of supervision, proceeding as rapidly as the child acquired control of himself, could be seen in the dining arrangements. From three through six, the children ate in a small dining room of their own. The older children, as we had observed on our first day at Walden Two, took their meals at specified times in the adult quarters. At thirteen all supervision was abandoned, and the young member was free to eat when and where he pleased.

We visited some of the workshops, laboratories, studies, and reading rooms used in lieu of classrooms. They were occupied, but it was not entirely clear that the children were actually in school. I supposed that the few adults to be seen about the building were teachers, but many of them were men, contrary to my conception of schoolteachers at that age level, and more often than not they were busy with some private business. Since Frazier had requested that we avoid questions or discussions in the presence of the children, we proceeded from one room to another in growing puzzlement. I had to admit that an enormous amount of learning was probably going on, but I had never seen a school like it before.

We inspected a well-equipped gymnasium, a small assembly room, and other facilities. The building was . . . very simply decorated, but there was a pleasant "non-institutional" character about it. The doors and many of the windows stood open, and a fair share of the schoolwork, or whatever it was, took place outside. Children were constantly passing in and out. Although there was an obvious excitement about the place, there was little of the boisterous confusion which develops in the ordinary school when discipline is momentarily relaxed. Everyone seemed to be enjoying extraordinary freedom, but the efficiency and comfort of the whole group were preserved.

I was reminded of children on good behavior and was on the point of asking how often the pressure reached the bursting point. But there was a difference, too, and my question slowly evaporated. I could only conclude that this happy and productive atmosphere was probably the usual thing. Here again, so far as I could see, Frazier—or someone—had got things under control.

When we returned to our shade tree, I was primed with questions, and so, I am sure, was Castle. But Frazier had other plans. He had either forgotten how remarkable was the spectacle we had just witnessed, or he was intentionally allowing our wonderment and curiosity to ferment. He began from a very different point of view.

"When we discussed the economics of community life," he said, "I should have mentioned education. Teachers are, of course, workers, and I'm willing to defend all that I said about our economic advantage as specifically applied to education. God knows, the outside world is not exactly profligate in the education of its children. It doesn't spend much on equipment or teachers. Yet in spite of this penny-wise policy, there's still enormous waste. A much better education would cost less if society were better organized.

"We can arrange things more expeditiously here because we don't need to be constantly re-educating. The ordinary teacher spends a good share of her time changing the cultural and intellectual habits which the child acquires from its family and surrounding culture. Or else the teacher duplicates home training, in a complete waste of time. Here we can almost say that the school is the family, and vice versa.

"We can adopt the best educational methods and still avoid the administrative machinery which schools need in order to adjust to an unfavorable social structure. We don't have to worry about standardization in order to permit pupils to transfer from one school to another, or to appraise or control the work of particular schools. We don't need 'grades.' Everyone knows that talents and abilities don't develop at the same rate in different children. A fourth-grade reader may be a sixth-grade mathematician. The grade is an administrative device which does violence to the nature of the developmental process. Here the child advances as rapidly as he likes in any field. No time is wasted in forcing him to participate in, or be bored by, activities he has outgrown. And the backward child can be handled more efficiently too.

"We also don't require all our children to develop the same abilities or skills. We don't insist upon a certain set of courses. I don't suppose we have a single child who has had a 'secondary school education,' whatever that means. But they've all developed as rapidly as advisable, and they're well educated in many useful respects. By the same token we don't waste time in teaching the unteachable. The fixed education represented by a diploma is a bit of conspicuous waste which has no place in Walden Two. We don't attach an economic or honorific value to education. It has its own value or none at all.

"Since our children remain happy, energetic, and curious, we don't need to teach 'subjects' at all. We teach only the techniques of learning and thinking. As for geography, literature, the sciences—we give our children opportunity and guidance, and they learn them for themselves. In that way we dispense with half the teachers required under the old system, and the education is incomparably better. Our children aren't neglected, but they're seldom, if ever, *taught* anything.

"Education in Walden Two is part of the life of the community. We don't need to resort to trumped-up life experiences. Our children begin to work at a very early age. It's no hardship; it's accepted as readily as sport or play. And a good share of our education goes on in workshops, laboratories, and fields. It's part of the Walden Two Code to encourage children in all the arts and crafts. We're glad to spend time in instructing them, for we know it's important for the future of Walden Two and our own security."

"What about higher education?" I said.

"We aren't equipped for professional training, of course," said Frazier. "Those who want to go on to graduate study in a university are given special preparation. Entrance requirements are always tyrannical, though perhaps inevitable in a mass-production system. So far, we've been able to find graduate schools that will take our young people as special students, and as they continue to make excellent records, we expect fewer difficulties. If worse comes to worst, we shall organize as a college and get ourselves accredited. But can you imagine the stupid changes we should have to make?" Frazier snorted with impatience. "Oh, well. Tongue in cheek. Tongue in cheek."

"Don't you mean 'chin up'?" I asked.

"We'd have to set up a 'curriculum,' require a 'C average,' a 'foreign language,' 'so many years of residence,' and so on, and so on. It would be most amusing. No, 'tongue in cheek' was what I meant."

"Your people don't go to college, then?"

"We have no more reason to distinguish between college and high school than between high school and grade school. What are these distinctions, anyway, once you have separated education from the administration of education? Are there any natural breaks in a child's development? Many of our children naturally study more and more advanced material as they grow older. We help them in every way short of teaching them. We give them new techniques of acquiring knowledge and thinking. In spite of the beliefs of most educators, our children are taught to think. We give them an excellent survey of the methods and techniques of thinking, taken from logic, statistics, scientific method, psychology, and mathematics. That's all the 'college education' they need. They get the rest by themselves in our libraries and laboratories."

"But what about libraries and laboratories, though?"

"As to a library, we pride ourselves on having the best books, if not the most. Have you ever spent much time in a large college library? What trash the librarian has saved up in order to report a million volumes in the college catalogue! Bound pamphlets, old journals, ancient junk that even the shoddiest secondhand bookstore would clear from its shelves—all saved on the flimsy pretext that some day someone will want to study the 'history of a field.' Here we have the heart of a great library—not much to please the scholar or specialist, perhaps, but enough to interest the intelligent reader for life. Two or three thousand volumes will do it."

Frazier challenged me with a stare, but I did not wish to fight on such difficult terrain.

"The secret is this," he continued. "We subtract from our shelves as often as we add to them. The result is a collection that never misses fire. We all get something vital every time we take a book from the shelves. If anyone wants to follow a special interest we arrange for loans. If anyone wants to browse, we have half a barnful of discarded volumes.

"Our laboratories are good because they are real. Our workshops are really small engineering laboratories, and anyone with a genuine bent can go farther in them than the college student. We teach anatomy in the slaughterhouse, botany in the field, genetics in the dairy and poultry house, chemistry in the medical building and in the kitchen and dairy laboratory. What more can you ask?"

"And all this is just for the fun of it? You don't feel that some disciplined study is necessary?" said Castle.

"What for?" asked Frazier in unsuccessfully pretended surprise.

"To provide techniques and abilities which will be valuable later," said Castle. "For example, the study of a language."

"Why 'later'? Why not acquire a language when it's valuable? We acquire our own tongue that way! Of course you're thinking of an educational process which comes to a dead stop sometime around the middle of June in one's last year in college. In Walden Two education goes on forever. It's part of our culture. We can acquire a technique whenever we need it.

"As to languages," Frazier continued, "you must know that even in our largest universities a language department considers itself very well off if two or three students at any one time approach fluency. We can do better than that. A member of Walden Two who once lived in France has interested several of our members, from ten to fifty years old, in the language. You may run into them during your stay. I hear them buzzing around the dining room every now and then, and they add a pleasantly cosmopolitan touch. And I'm told they're developing a good feeling for the French language and French literature. They'll never get any grades or credits, but they're getting French. Is there really any choice? Either French is worth learning, *at the time you learn it,* or it's not. And let's be sensible."

"I'm still skeptical," said Castle. "Of course, I'm still at a disadvantage in arguing against an accomplished fact." Frazier nodded his head violently. "But not everything has been accomplished," Castle went on.

"Your pleasant schoolrooms, your industrious and contented children—
these we must accept. But it would take us a long time to find out how
well-educated your children really are according to our standards."
Frazier made a move to speak, but Castle hurried on. "I'll admit these
standards won't tell us everything. We couldn't ask your children to take
our examinations, because they haven't been learning the same things,
even in such a field as French. Your students would probably do no better
on a second-year French examination than the average Parisian. I'll admit
that, and I confess with all the humility I can muster that the kind of
learning you've described is the better—if a comparison is possible. It's
the ideal which every college teacher glimpses now and then when he
looks up from the dance of death in which he has been caught. But I can't
swallow the system you've described because I don't see what keeps the
motors running. Why do your children learn anything at all? What are
your substitutes for our standard motives?"

"Your 'standard motives'—exactly," said Frazier. "And there's the
rub. An educational institution spends most of its time, not in presenting facts or imparting techniques of learning, but in trying to make its
students learn. It has to create spurious needs. Have you ever stopped
to analyze them? What are the 'standard motives,' Mr. Castle?"

"I must admit they're not very attractive," said Castle. "I suppose
they consist of fear of one's family in the event of low grades or expul-
sion, the award of grades and honors, the snob value of a cap and gown,
the cash value of a diploma."

"Very good, Mr. Castle," said Frazier. "You're an honest man. And
now to answer your question—our substitute is simply the absence of
these devices. We have had to *uncover* the worth-while and truly productive motives—the motives which inspire creative work in science and
art outside the academies. No one asks how to motivate a baby. A baby
naturally explores everything it can get at, unless restraining forces have
already been at work. And this tendency doesn't die out, it's *wiped* out.

"We made a survey of the motives of the unhampered child and
found more than we could use. Our engineering job was to *preserve*
them by fortifying the child against discouragement. We introduce discouragement as carefully as we introduce any other emotional situation,
beginning at about six months. Some of the toys in our air-conditioned
cubicles are designed to build perseverance. A bit of a tune from a
music box, or a pattern of flashing lights, is arranged to follow an appropriate response—say, pulling on a ring. Later the ring must be pulled
twice, later still three or five or ten times. It's possible to build up
fantastically perseverative behavior without encountering frustration or
rage. It may not surprise you to learn that some of our experiments
miscarried; the resistance to discouragement became almost stupid or
pathological. One takes some risks in work of this sort, of course. Fortu-

nately, we were able to reverse the process and restore the children to a satisfactory level.

"Building a tolerance for discouraging events proved to be all we needed," Frazier continued. "The motives in education, Mr. Castle, are the motives in all human behavior. Education should be only life itself. We don't need to create motives. We avoid the spurious academic needs you've just listed so frankly, and also the escape from threat so widely used in our civil institutions. We appeal to the curiosity which is characteristic of the unrestrained child, as well as the alert and inquiring adult. We appeal to that drive to control the environment which makes a baby continue to crumple a piece of noisy paper and the scientist continue to press forward with his predictive analyses of nature. We don't need to motivate anyone by creating spurious needs."

"I've known a few men with the kind of motivation you mean," I said.

"The contemporary culture produces a few by accident," said Frazier quickly, "just as it produces a few brave or happy men."

"But I've never understood them." I said rather faintly.

"Why should you, any more than unhappy people can understand the happy ones?"

"But isn't there a real need for the spurious satisfactions?" I said. "Little signs of personal success, money—personal domination, too, if you like. Most of what I do, I do to avoid undesirable consequences, to evade unpleasantnesses, or to reject or attack forces which interfere with my freedom."

"All the unhappy motives," said Frazier.

"Unhappy, perhaps, but powerful. I think the very thing which seems most unpromising in your system is its happiness. Your people are going to be too happy, too successful. But why won't they just go to sleep? Can we expect real achievements from them? Haven't the great men of history been essentially unhappy or maladjusted or neurotic?"

"I have little interest in conclusions drawn from history," said Frazier, "but if you must play that game, I'll play it too. For every genius you cite whose greatness seems to have sprung from a neurosis, I will undertake to cite similar acts of greatness without neurosis. Turn it around and I'll agree. A man with a touch of genius will be so likely to attack existing institutions that he'll be called unbalanced or neurotic. The only geniuses produced by the chaos of society are those who do something about it." Frazier paused, and I wondered if he were thinking of himself. "Chaos breeds geniuses. It offers a man something to be a genius about. But here, we have better things to do."

"But what about the cases where unhappiness has led to artistic or scientific achievement?" I asked.

"Oh, I daresay a few first-rate sonnets would have remained unwritten had the lady yielded," said Frazier. "But not so many, at that. Not many works of art can be traced to the lack of satisfaction of the basic needs. It's not plain sex that gives rise to art, but personal relations which are social or cultural rather than biological. Art deals with something less obvious than the satisfaction to be found in a square meal." Frazier laughed explosively, as if he had perhaps said more than he intended.

"We shall never produce so satisfying a world that there will be no place for art," he continued. "On the contrary, Walden Two has demonstrated very nicely that as soon as the simple necessities of life are obtained with little effort, there's an enormous welling up of artistic interest. And least of all do we need to fear that simple satisfactions will detract from the scientific conquest of the world. What scientist worth the name is engaged, as scientist, in the satisfaction of his own basic needs? He may be thinking of the basic needs of others, but his own motives are clearly cultural. There can be no doubt of the survival value of the inquiring spirit —of curiosity, or exploration, of the need to dominate media, of the urge to control the forces of nature. The world will never be wholly known, and man can't help trying to know more and more of it."

The topic seemed to have grown too vague to stimulate further discussion, but Castle soon offered a substitute.

"I'm torn between two questions which seem incompatible yet equally pressing," he said. "What do you do about differences among your children in intellect and talent? And what do you do to avoid producing a lot of completely standardized young people? Which question should I ask, and what's your answer?"

"They're both good questions," said Frazier, "and quite compatible." I made a move to speak and Frazier said, "I see that Mr. Burris wants to help with the answers."

"My guess is," I said, "that differences are due to environmental and cultural factors and that Mr. Frazier has no great problem to solve. Give all your children the excellent care we have just been witnessing and your differences will be negligible."

"No, you're wrong, Burris," said Frazier. "That's one question we have answered to our satisfaction. Our ten-year-olds have all had the same environment since birth, but the range of their IQ's is almost as great as in the population at large. This seems to be true of other abilities and skills as well."

"And of physical prowess, of course," said Castle.

"Why do you say 'of course'?" said Frazier, with marked interest.

"Why, I suppose because physical differences are generally acknowledged."

"All differences are physical, my dear Mr. Castle. We think with our bodies, too. You might have replied that differences in prowess have always been obvious and impossible to conceal, while other differences have customarily been disguised for the sake of prestige and family pride.

We accept our gross physical limitations without protest and are reasonably happy in spite of them, but we may spend a lifetime trying to live up to a wholly false conception of our powers in another field, and suffer the pain of a lingering failure. Here we accept ourselves as we are."

"Aren't the untalented going to be unhappy?"

"But we don't go in for personal rivalry; individuals are seldom compared. We never develop a taste much beyond a talent. Our parents have little reason to misrepresent their children's abilities to themselves or others. It's easy for our children to accept their limitations—exactly as they have always accepted the gross differences which Mr. Castle called physical prowess. At the same time our gifted children aren't held back by organized mediocrity. We don't throw our geniuses off balance. The brilliant but unstable type is unfamiliar here. Genius can express itself."

— 6 —

biological and social manufacturing for social stability

In *Brave New World,* Aldous Huxley creates an anti-utopian society designed to have stable social institutions, in which individuals are to be free of tension and in which neither warfare nor political change was to occur. One might use several approaches to creating a society with these characteristics. The two extreme strategies would be to design social arrangements to which individuals respond in the desired manner or to design individuals that are ideal for the selected set of social arrangements. Huxley designs a set of procedures intended to carry out the second strategy.

In Huxley's anti-utopia, people are manufactured, biologically and socially, to fit into the society. That society provides a workable—though distasteful—solution to a number of social problems. For example, alternative stratification systems can be thought of as attempts to solve the problem of how to motivate individuals who have relatively scarce talents to fill essential social roles, so that the talent available in the population is utilized efficiently and people are willing to exchange their labor for the rewards they are offered. In Huxley's society, no problem arises in supplying needed people to staff essential positions; they are simply manufactured to specification. Since socialization is completely controlled, no question arises, either, of motivating people to participate in the society; motivation, like ability, can be built in. Individuals can be produced to match the requirements of their occupations; a man who is to run an elevator is built with a limited intelligence so that he will not become bored by the job, and he is made to believe that he is performing an important and interesting task.

Brave New World depicts the other side of the coin from *Walden Two.* It is an extreme case of the danger that arises when control over the manufacturing of men is introduced. However, by introducing biological control Huxley goes one step further in his direction than Skinner went along his path. For Skinner, knowledge of the dynamics of socialization makes it possible to devise procedures that lead to results considered either desirable or undesirable. For Huxley, knowledge of prenatal physical development makes it possible to change a fetus' normal environment in order to protect it from birth defects or to introduce agents that produce desired defects.

The industrialization of reproduction is one of the procedures employed to guarantee a stable society. The excerpt from *Brave New World* describes how the manufacturing process works.

brave new world

by Aldous Huxley

A squat grey building of only thirty-four stories. Over the main entrance the words, *Central London Hatchery and Conditioning Centre,* and, in a shield, the World State's motto, *Community, Identity, Stability.*

The enormous room on the ground floor faced towards the north. . . . The overalls of the workers were white, their hands gloved with a pale corpse-coloured rubber. The light was frozen, dead, a ghost. Only from the yellow barrels of the microscopes did it borrow a certain rich and living substance, lying along the polished tubes like butter, streak after luscious streak in long recession down the work tables.

"And this," said the Director opening the door, "is the Fertilizing Room."

Bent over their instruments, three hundred Fertilizers were plunged, as the Director of Hatcheries and Conditioning entered the room, in the scarcely breathing silence, the absent-minded, soliloquizing hum or whistle, of absorbed concentration. A troop of newly arrived students, very young, pink and callow, followed nervously, rather abjectly, at the Director's heels. Each of them carried a notebook, in which, whenever the great man spoke, he desperately scribbled. Straight from the horse's mouth. It was a rare privilege. The D.H.C. for Central London always made a point of personally conducting his new students round the various departments.

"Just to give you a general idea," he would explain to them. For of course some sort of general idea they must have if they were to do their work intelligently—though as little of one, if they were to be good and happy members of society, as possible. For particulars, as every one knows, make for virtue and happiness; generalities are intellectually necessary evils. Not philosophers but fret-sawyers and stamp collectors compose the backbone of society.

"To-morrow," he would add, smiling at them with a slightly menacing geniality, "you'll be settling down to serious work. You won't have time for generalities. Meanwhile . . ."

Meanwhile, it was a privilege. Straight from the horse's mouth into the notebook. The boys scribbled like mad. . . .

"I shall begin at the beginning," said the D.H.C. and the more zealous students recorded his intention in their notebooks: *Begin at the beginning.* "These," he waved his hand, "are the incubators." And opening an insulated door he showed them racks upon racks of numbered test-tubes. "The week's supply of ova. Kept," he explained, "at blood heat; whereas the male gametes," and here he opened another door, "they have to be kept at thirty-five instead of thirty-seven. Full blood heat sterilizes." Rams wrapped in theremogene beget no lambs.

Still leaning against the incubators he gave them, while the pencils scurried illegibly across the pages, a brief description of the modern fertilizing process; spoke first, of course, of its surgical introduction—"the operation undergone voluntarily for the good of Society, not to mention the fact that it carries a bonus amounting to six months' salary"; continued with some account of the technique for preserving the excised ovary alive and actively developing; passed on to a consideration of optimum temperature, salinity, viscosity; referred to the liquor in which the detached and ripened eggs were kept; and, leading his charges to the work tables, actually showed them how this liquid was drawn off from the test-tubes; how it was let out drop by drop onto the specially warmed slides of the microscopes; how the eggs which it contained were inspected for abnormalities, counted and transferred to a porous receptacle; how (and he now took them to watch the operation) this receptacle was immersed in a warm bouillon containing free-swimming spermatozoa—at a minimum concentration of one hundred thousand per cubic centimetre, he insisted; and how, after ten minutes, the container was lifted out of the liquor and its contents reexamined; how, if any of the eggs remained unfertilized, it was again immersed, and, if necessary, yet again; how the fertilized ova went back to the incubators; where the Alphas and Betas remained until definitely bottled; while the Gammas, Deltas and Epsilons were brought out again, after only thirty-six hours, to undergo Bokanovsky's Process.

"Bokanovsky's Process," repeated the Director, and the students underlined the words in their little notebooks.

One egg, one embryo, one adult—normality. But a bokanovskified egg will bud, will proliferate, will divide. From eight to ninety-six buds, and every bud will grow into a perfectly formed embryo, and every embryo into a full-sized adult. Making ninety-six human beings grow where only one grew before. Progress.

"Essentially," the D.H.C. concluded, "bokanovskification consists of a series of arrests of development. We check the normal growth and, paradoxically enough, the egg responds by budding."

Responds by budding. The pencils were busy.

He pointed. On a very slowly moving band a rack-full of test-tubes was entering a large metal box, another rack-full was emerging. Machinery faintly purred. It took eight minutes for the tubes to go through, he told them. Eight minutes of hard X-rays being about as much as an egg can stand. A few died; of the rest, the least susceptible divided into two; most put out four buds; some eight; all were returned to the incubators, where the buds began to develop; then, after two days, were suddenly chilled, chilled and checked. Two, four, eight, the buds in their turn budded; and having budded were dosed almost to death with alcohol; consequently burgeoned again and having budded—bud out of bud out of bud—were thereafter—further arrest being generally fatal—left to develop in peace. By which time the original egg was in a fair way to becoming anything from eight to ninety-six embryos—a prodigious improvement, you will agree, on nature. Identical twins—but not in piddling twos and threes as in the old viviparous days, when an egg would sometimes accidentally divide; actually by dozens, by scores at a time.

"Scores," the Director repeated and flung out his arms, as though he were distributing largesse. "Scores."

But one of the students was fool enough to ask where the advantage lay.

"My good boy!" The Director wheeled sharply round on him. "Can't you see? Can't you *see?*" He raised a hand; his expression was solemn. "Bokanovsky's Process is one of the major instruments of social stability!"

Major instruments of social stability.

Standard men and women; in uniform batches. The whole of a small factory staffed with the products of a single bokanovskified egg.

"Ninety-six identical twins working ninety-six identical machines!" The voice was almost tremulous with enthusiasm. "You really know where you are. For the first time in history." He quoted the planetary motto. "Community, Identity, Stability." Grand words. "If we could bokanovskify indefinitely the whole problem would be solved."

Solved by standard Gammas, unvarying Deltas, uniform Epsilons. Millions of identical twins. The principle of mass production at last applied to biology.

"But, alas," the Director shook his head, "we *can't* bokanovskify indefinitely."

Ninety-six seemed to be the limit; seventy-two a good average. From the same ovary and with gametes of the same male to manufacture as many batches of identical twins as possible—that was the best (sadly a second best) that they could do. And even that was difficult.

"For in nature it takes thirty years for two hundred eggs to reach maturity. But our business is to stabilize the population at this moment, here and now. Dribbling out twins over a quarter of a century—what would be the use of that?"

Obviously, no use at all. But Podsnap's Technique had immensely accelerated the process of ripening. They could make sure of at least a hundred and fifty mature eggs within two years. Fertilize and bokanovskify—in other words, multiply by seventy-two—and you get an average of nearly eleven thousand brothers and sisters in a hundred and fifty batches of identical twins, all within two years of the same age.

"And in exceptional cases we can make one ovary yield us over fifteen thousand adult individuals."

Beckoning to a fair-haired, ruddy young man who happened to be passing at the moment, "Mr. Foster," he called. The ruddy young man approached. "Can you tell us the record for a single ovary, Mr. Foster?"

"Sixteen thousand and twelve in this Centre," Mr. Foster replied without hesitation. He spoke very quickly, had a vivacious blue eye, and took an evident pleasure in quoting figures. "Sixteen thousand and twelve; in one hundred and eighty-nine batches of identicals. But of course they've done much better," he rattled on, "in some of the tropical Centres. Singapore has often produced over sixteen thousand five hundred; and Mombasa has actually touched the seventeen thousand mark. But then they have unfair advantages. You should see the way a negro ovary responds to pituitary! It's quite astonishing, when you're used to working with European material. Still," he added, with a laugh (but the light of combat was in his eyes and the lift of his chin was challenging), "still, we mean to beat them if we can. I'm working on a wonderful Delta-Minus ovary at this moment. Only just eighteen months old. Over twelve thousand seven hundred children already, either decanted or in embryo. . . . "

In the Bottling Room all was harmonious bustle and ordered activity. Flaps of fresh sow's peritoneum ready cut to the proper size came shooting up in little lifts from the Organ Store in the sub-basement. Whizz and then, click! the lift-hatches flew open; the bottle-liner had only to reach out a hand, take the flap, insert, smooth-down, and before the lined bottle had had time to travel out of reach along the endless band, whizz, click! another flap of peritoneum had shot up from the depths, ready to be slipped into yet another bottle, the next of that slow interminable procession on the band.

Next to the Liners stood the Matriculators. The procession advanced; one by one the eggs were transferred from their test-tubes to the larger containers; deftly the peritoneal lining was slit, the morula dropped into place, the saline solution poured in . . . and already the bottle had passed, and it was the turn of the labellers. Heredity, date of fertilization, membership of Bokanovsky Group—details were transferred from test-tube to bottle. No longer anonymous, but named, identified, the procession marched slowly on; on through an opening in the wall, slowly on into the Social Predestination Room.

"Eighty-eight cubic metres of card-index," said Mr. Foster with relish, as they entered.

"Containing *all* the relevant information," added the Director.
"Brought up to date every morning."
"And coordinated every afternoon."
"On the basis of which they make their calculations."
"So many individuals, of such and such quality," said Mr. Foster.
"Distributed in such and such quantities."
"The optimum Decanting Rate at any given moment."
"Unforeseen wastages promptly made good."
"Promptly," repeated Mr. Foster. "If you knew the amount of overtime
I had to put in after the last Japanese earthquake!" He laughed good-
humouredly and shook his head.
"The Predestinators send in their figures to the Fertilizers."
"Who give them the embryos they ask for."
"And the bottles come in here to be predestinated in deatail."
"After which they are sent down to the Embryo Store."
"Where we now proceed ourselves."
And opening a door Mr. Foster led the way down a staircase into the
basement.
The temperature was still tropical. They descended into a thickening
twilight. Two doors and a passage with a double turn insured the cellar
against any possible infiltration of the day.
"Embryos are like photograph film," said Mr. Foster waggishly, as he
pushed open the second door. "They can only stand red light."
And in effect the sultry darkness into which the students now followed
him was visible and crimson, like the darkness of closed eyes on a summer's afternoon. The bulging flanks of row on receding row and tier above
tier of bottles glinted with innumerable rubies, and among the rubies
moved the dim red spectres of men and women with purple eyes and all
the symptoms of lupus. The hum and rattle of machinery faintly stirred
the air.
"Give them a few figures, Mr. Foster," said the Director, who was tired
of talking.
Mr. Foster was only too happy to give them a few figures.
Two hundred and twenty metres long, two hundred wide, ten high. He
pointed upwards. Like chickens drinking, the students lifted their eyes
towards the distant ceiling.
Three tiers of racks: ground floor level, first gallery, second gallery.
The spidery steel-work of gallery above gallery faded away in all directions into the dark. Near them three red ghosts were busily unloading
demijohns from a moving staircase.
The escalator from the Social Predestination Room.
Each bottle could be placed on one of the fifteen racks, each rack,
though you couldn't see it, was a conveyor travelling at the rate of thirty-
three and a third centimetres an hour. Two hundred and sixty-seven days

at eight metres a day. Two thousand one hundred and thirty-six metres in all. One circuit of the cellar at ground level, one on the first gallery, half on the second, and on the two hundred and sixty-seventh morning, daylight in the Decanting Room. Independent existence—so called.

"But in the interval," Mr. Foster concluded, "we've managed to do a lot to them. Oh, a very great deal." His laugh was knowing and triumphant.

"That's the spirit I like," said the Director once more. "Let's walk round. You tell them everything, Mr. Foster."

Mr. Foster duly told them.

Told them of the growing embryo on its bed of peritoneum. Made them taste the rich blood surrogate on which it fed. Explained why it had to be stimulated with placentin and thyroxin. Told them of the *corpus luteum* extract. Showed them the jets through which at every twelfth metre from zero to 2040 it was automatically injected. Spoke of those gradually increasing doses of pituitary administered during the final ninety-six metres of their course. Described the artificial maternal circulation installed on every bottle at Metre 112; showed them the reservoir of blood-surrogate, the centrifugal pump that kept the liquid moving over the placenta and drove it through the synthetic lung and waste-product filter. Referred to the embryo's troublesome tendency to anemia, to the massive doses of hog's stomach extract and foetal foal's liver with which, in consequence, it had to be supplied.

Showed them the simple mechanism by means of which, during the last two metres out of every eight, all the embryos were simultaneously shaken into familiarity with movement. Hinted at the gravity of the so-called "trauma of decanting," and enumerated the precautions taken to minimize, by a suitable training of the bottled embryo, that dangerous shock. Told them of the tests for sex carried out in the neighbourhood of metre 200. Explained the system of labelling—a T for the males, a circle for the females, and for those who were destined to become freemartins a question mark, black on a white ground.

"For of course," said Mr. Foster, "in the vast majority of cases, fertility is merely a nuisance. One fertile ovary in twelve hundred—that would really be quite sufficient for our purposes. But we want to have a good choice. And of course one must always leave an enormous margin of safety. So we allow as many as thirty per cent of the female embryos to develop normally. The others get a dose of male sex-hormone every twenty-four metres for the rest of the course. Result: they're decanted as freemartins—structurally quite normal (except," he had to admit, "that they *do* have just the slightest tendency to grow beards), but sterile. Guaranteed sterile. Which brings us at last," continued Mr. Foster, "out of the realm of mere slavish imitation of nature into the much more interesting world of human invention."

He rubbed his hands. For of course, they didn't content themselves with merely hatching out embryos: any cow could do that.

"We also predestine and condition. We decant our babies as socialized human beings, as Alphas or Epsilons, as future sewage workers or future ... " He was going to say "future World controllers," but correcting himself, said "future Directors of Hatcheries," instead.

The D.H.C. acknowledged the compliment with a smile.

They were passing Metre 320 on rack 11. A young Beta-Minus mechanic was busy with screwdriver and spanner on the blood-surrogate pump of a passing bottle. The hum of the electric motor deepened by fractions of a tone as he turned the nuts. Down, down ... A final twist, a glance at the revolution counter, and he was done. He moved two paces down the line and began the same process on the next pump.

"Reducing the number of revolutions per minute," Mr. Foster explained. "The surrogate goes round slower; therefore passes through the lung at longer intervals; therefore gives the embryo less oxygen. Nothing like oxygen-shortage for keeping an embryo below par." Again he rubbed his hands.

"But why do you want to keep the embryo below par?" asked an ingenuous student.

"Ass!" said the Director, breaking a long silence. "Hasn't it occurred to you that an Epsilon embryo must have an Epsilon environment as well as an Epsilon heredity?"

It evidently hadn't occured to him. He was covered with confusion.

"The lower caste," said Mr. Foster, "the shorter the oxygen." The first organ affected was the brain. After that the skeleton. At seventy per cent of normal oxygen you got dwarfs. At less than seventy eyeless monsters.

"Who are no use at all," concluded Mr. Foster.

Whereas (his voice became confidential and eager), if they could discover a technique for shortening the period of maturation what a triumph, what a benefaction to Society!

"Consider the horse."

They considered it.

Mature at six; the elephant at ten. While at thirteen a man is not yet sexually mature; and is only full-grown at twenty. Hence, of course, that fruit of delayed development, the human intelligence.

"But in Epsilons," said Mr. Foster very justly, "we don't need human intelligence."

Didn't need and didn't get it. But though the Epsilon mind was mature at ten, the Epsilon body was not fit to work till eighteen. Long years of superfluous and wasted immaturity. If the physical development could be speeded up till it was as quick, say, as a cow's what an enormous saving to the Community!

"Enormous!" murmured the students. Mr. Foster's enthusiasm was infectious.

He became rather technical; spoke of the abnormal endocrine co-ordination which made men grow so slowly; postulated a germinal mutation to account for it. Could the effects of this germinal mutation be undone? Could the individual Epsilon embryo be made a revert, by a suitable technique, to the normality of dogs and cows? That was the problem. And it was all but solved.

Pilkington, at Mombasa, had produced individuals who were sexually mature at four and full-grown at six and a half. A scientific triumph. But socially useless. Six-year-old men and women were too stupid to do even Epsilon work. And the process was an all-or-nothing one; either you failed to modify at all, or else you modified the whole way. They were still trying to find the ideal compromise between adults of twenty and adults of six. So far without success. Mr. Foster sighed and shook his head.

Their wanderings through the crimson twilight had brought them to the neighborhood of Metre 170 on Rack 9. From this point onwards Rack 9 was enclosed and the bottles performed the remainder of their journey in a kind of tunnel, interrupted here and there by openings two or three metres wide.

"Heat conditioning," said Mr. Foster.

Hot tunnels alternated with cool tunnels. Coolness was wedded to discomfort in the form of hard X-rays. By the time they were decanted the embryos had a horror of cold. They were predestined to emigrate to the tropics, to be miners and acetate silk spinners and steel workers. Later on their minds would be made to endorse the judgment of their bodies. "We condition them to thrive on heat," concluded Mr. Foster. "Our colleagues upstairs will teach them to love it."

"And that," put in the Director sententiously, "that is the secret of happiness and virtue—liking what you've *got* to do. All conditioning aims at that: making people like their unescapable social destiny."

... On Rack 10 rows of next generation's chemical workers were being trained in the toleration of lead, caustic soda, tar, chlorine. The first of a batch of two hundred and fifty embryonic rocket-plane engineers was just passing the eleven hundred metre mark on Rack 3. A special mechanism kept their containers in constant rotation. "To improve their sense of balance," Mr. Foster explained. "Doing repairs on the outside of a rocket in mid-air is a ticklish job. We slacken off the circulation when they're right way up, so that they're half starved, and double the flow of surrogate when they're upside down. They learn to associate topsy-turvydom with well-being; in fact, they're only truly happy when they're standing on their heads.

"And now," Mr. Foster went on, "I'd like to show you some very interesting conditioning for Alpha Plus Intellectuals. We have a big batch of them on Rack 5. First Gallery level," he called to two boys who had started to go down to the ground floor.

"They're round about Metre 900," he explained. "You can't really do any useful intellectual conditioning till the foetuses have lost their tails. Follow me."

Later in the novel the relationship between biological control and social stability is discussed in some depth. The conversation is between Mustapha Mond (Resident Controller of Western Europe), the Savage (a man raised in an uncivilized part of the world), and Helmholtz Watson (lecturer in the College of Emotional Engineering).

The Savage shook his head. "It all seems to me quite horrible."

"Of course it does. Actual happiness always looks pretty squalid in comparison with the over-compensations for misery. And, of course, stability isn't nearly so spectacular as instability. And being contented has none of the glamour of a good fight against misfortune, none of the picturesqueness of a struggle with temptation, or a fatal overthrow by passion or doubt. Happiness is never grand."

"I suppose not," said the Savage after a silence. "But need it be quite so bad as those twins?" He passed his hand over his eyes as though he were trying to wipe away the remembered image of those long rows of identical midgets at the assembling tables, those queued-up twin-herds at the entrance to the Brentford monorail station . . . , the endlessly repeated face of his assailants. He looked at his bandaged left hand and shuddered. "Horrible!"

"But how useful! I see you don't like our Kokanovsky Groups; but, I assure you, they're the foundation on which everything else is built. They're the gyroscope that stabilizes the rocket plane of state on its unswerving course." The deep voice thrillingly vibrated; the gesticulating hand implied all space and the onrush of the irresistible machine. Mustapha Mond's oratory was almost up to synthetic standards.

"I was wondering," said the Savage, "why you had them at all—seeing that you can get whatever you want out of those bottles. Why don't you make everybody an Alpha Double Plus while you're about it?"

Mustapha Mond laughed. "Because we have no wish to have our throat cut," he answered. "We believe in happiness and stability. A society of Alphas couldn't fail to be unstable and miserable. Imagine a factory staffed by Alphas—that is to say by separate and unrelated individuals of good heredity and conditioned so as to be capable (within limits) of making a free choice and assuming responsibilities. Imagine it!" he repeated. . . .

"It's an absurdity. An Alpha-decanted, Alpha-conditioned man would go mad if he had to do Epsilon Semi-Moron work—go mad, or start smashing things up. Alphas can be completely socialized—but only on condition that you make them do Alpha work. Only an Epsilon can be expected to make Epsilon sacrifices, for the good reason that for him they aren't sacrifices; they're the line of least resistance. His conditioning has laid down rails along which he's got to run. He can't help himself; he's foredoomed. Even after decanting, he's still inside a bottle—an invisible bottle of infantile and embryonic fixations. Each one of us, of course," the Controller meditatively continued, "goes through life inside a bottle. But if we happen to be Alphas, our bottles are, relatively speaking, enormous. We should suffer acutely if we were confined in a narrower space. You cannot pour upper-caste champagne-surrogate into lower-caste bottles. It's obvious theoretically. But it has also been proved in actual practice. The result of the Cyprus experiment was convincing."

"What was that?" asked the Savage.

Mustapha Mond smiled. "Well, you can call it an experiment in rebottling if you like. It began in A.F. 473. The Controllers had the island of Cyprus cleared of all its existing inhabitants and re-colonized with a specially prepared batch of twenty-two thousand Alphas. All agricultural and industrial equipment was handed over to them and they were left to manage their own affairs. The results exactly fulfilled all the theoretical predictions. The land wasn't properly worked; there were strikes in all the factories; the laws were set at naught, orders disobeyed; all the people detailed for a spell of low-grade work were perpetually intriguing for high-grade jobs, and all the people with high-grade jobs were counter-intriguing at all costs to stay where they were. Within six years they were having a first-class civil war. When nineteen out of the twenty-two thousand had been killed, the survivors unanimously petitioned the World Controllers to resume the government of the island. Which they did. And that was the end of the only society of Alphas that the world has ever seen."

The Savage sighed, profoundly.

"The optimum population," said Mustapha Mond, "is modelled on the iceberg—eight-ninths below the water line, one-ninth above."

"And they're happy below the water line?"

"Happier than above it. Happier than your friend here, for example." He pointed.

"In spite of that awful work?"

"Awful? *They* don't find it so. On the contrary, they like it. It's light, it's childishly simple. No strain on the mind or the muscles. Seven and a half hours of mild, unexhausting labour, and then the *soma* ration[1] and

---

[1][Soma was a drug that provided a convenient method of social control. Variations in dosage could produce a feeling of mild relaxation or a full-blown trip (called a soma-holiday). The drug was rationed to the people and then self-administered. People used it to escape boredom and any form of pain. They could adjust the soma intake to compensate for the disappointments of reality. A large part of the population was tripped-out between periods of work.]

games and unrestricted copulation and the feelies.[2] What more can they ask for? True," he added, "they might ask for shorter hours. And of course, we could give them shorter hours. Technically, it would be perfectly simple to reduce all lower-caste working hours to three or four a day. But would they be any the happier for that? No, they wouldn't. The experiment was tried, more than a century and a half ago. The whole of Ireland was put on to the four-hour day. What was the result? Unrest and a large increase in the consumption of *soma;* that was all. Those three and a half hours of extra leisure were so far from being a source of happiness, that people felt constrained to take a holiday from them. The Inventions Office is stuffed with plans for labour-saving processes. Thousands of them." Mustapha Mond made a lavish gesture. "And why don't we put them into execution? For the sake of the labourers; it would be sheer cruelty to afflict them with excessive leisure. It's the same with agriculture. We could synthesize every morsel of food, if we wanted to. But we don't. We prefer to keep a third of the population on the land. For their own sakes—because it takes *longer* to get food out of the land than out of a factory. Besides, we have our stability to think of. We don't want to change. Every change is a menace to stability. That's another reason why we're so chary of applying new inventions. Every discovery in pure science is potentially subversive; even science must sometimes be treated as a possible enemy. Yes, even science."

" . . . Yes," Mustapha Mond was saying, "that's another item in the cost of stability. It isn't only art that's incompatible with happiness; it's also science. Science is dangerous; we have to keep it most carefully chained and muzzled."

"What?" said Helmholtz, in astonishment. "But we're always saying that science is everything. . . . All the science propaganda we do at the College . . ."

"Yes; but what sort of science?" asked Mustapha Mond sarcastically. "You've had no scientific training, so you can't judge. I was a pretty good physicist in my time. Too good—good enough to realize that all our science is just a cookery book, with an orthodox theory of cooking that nobody's allowed to question, and a list of recipes that mustn't be added to except by special permission from the head cook. I'm the head cook now."

The second means through which control is established is socialization. Huxley describes a procedure that is in some respects similar to the procedures Skinner utilizes in *Walden Two.* The end-product of the socialization process is, however, quite different.

---

[2][The feelies were a form of ultimate movie. In addition to seeing the actors it was possible to experience sensory inputs appropriate to the film. The inputs were transmitted to viewers when they placed their hands on metal knobs fixed to the arms of their chairs.]

Infant Nurseries. Neo-Pavlovian Conditioning Rooms, announced the notice board.

The Director opened a door. They were in a large bare room, very bright and sunny; for the whole of the southern wall was a single window. Half a dozen nurses, trousered and jacketed in the regulation white viscose-linen uniform, their hair asceptically hidden under white caps, were engaged in setting out bowls of roses in a long row across the floor. Big bowls, packed tight with blossom. Thousands of petals, ripe-blown and silkily smooth, like the cheeks of innumerable little cherubs, but of cherubs, in that bright light, not exclusively pink and Aryan, but also luminously Chinese, also Mexican, also apoplectic with too much blowing of celestial trumpets, also pale as death, pale with the posthumous whiteness of marble.

The nurses stiffened to attention as the D.H.C. came in.

"Set out the books," he said curtly.

In silence the nurses obeyed his command. Between the rose bowls the books were duly set out—a row of nursery quartos opened invitingly each at some gaily coloured image of beast or fish or bird.

"Now bring in the children."

They hurried out of the room and returned in a minute or two, each pushing a kind of tall dumb-waiter laden, on all its four wire-netted shelves, with eight-month-old babies, all exactly alike (a Bokanovsky Group, it was evident) and all (since their caste was Delta) dressed in khaki.

"Put them down on the floor."

The infants were unloaded.

"Now turn them so that they can see the flowers and books."

Turned, the babies at once fell silent, then began to crawl towards those clusters of sleek colours, those shapes so gay and brilliant on the white pages. As they approached, the sun came out of a momentary eclipse behind a cloud. The roses flamed up as though with a sudden passion from within; a new and profound significance seemed to suffuse the shining pages of the books. From the ranks of the crawling babies came little squeals of excitement, gurgles and twitterings of pleasure.

The Director rubbed his hands. "Excellent!" he said. "It might almost have been done on purpose."

The swiftest crawlers were already at their goal. Small hands reached out uncertainly, touched, grasped, unpetaling the transfigured roses, crumpling the illuminated pages of the books. The Director waited until all were happily busy. Then, "Watch carefully," he said. And, lifting his hand, he gave the signal.

The Head Nurse, who was standing by a switchboard at the other end of the room, pressed down a little lever.

There was a violent explosion. Shriller and ever shriller, a siren shrieked. Alarm bells maddeningly sounded.

The children started, screamed; their faces were distorted with terror.

"And now," the Director shouted (for the noise was deafening), "now we proceed to rub in the lesson with a mild electric shock."

He waved his hand again, and the Head Nurse pressed a second lever. The screaming of the babies suddenly changed its tone. There was something desperate, almost insane, about the sharp spasmodic yelps to which they now gave utterance. Their little bodies twitched and stiffened; their limbs moved jerkily as if to the tug of unseen wires.

"We can electrify that whole strip of floor," bawled the Director in explanation. "But that's enough," he signalled to the nurse.

The explosions ceased, the bells stopped ringing, the shriek of the siren died down from tone to tone into silence. The stiffly twitching bodies relaxed, and what had become the sob and yelp of infant maniacs broadened out once more into a normal howl of ordinary terror.

"Offer them the flowers and the books again."

The nurses obeyed; but at the approach of the roses, at the mere sight of those gaily-coloured images of pussy and cock-a-doodle-doo and baa-baa black sheep, the infants shrank away in horror; the volume of their howling suddenly increased.

"Observe," said the Director triumphantly, "observe."

Books and loud noises, flowers and electric shocks—already in the infant mind these couples were compromisingly linked; and after two hundred repetitions of the same or a similar lesson would be wedded indissolubly. What man has joined, nature is powerless to put asunder.

"They'll grow up with what the psychologists used to call an 'instinctive' hatred of books and flowers. Reflexes unalterably conditoned. They'll be safe from books and botany all their lives." The Director turned to his nurses. "Take them away again."

Still yelling, the khaki babies were loaded on to their dumb-waiters and wheeled out, leaving behind them the smell of sour milk and a most welcome silence.

One of the students held up his hand; and though he could see quite well why you couldn't have lower-caste people wasting the Community's time over books, and that there was always the risk of their reading something which might undesirably decondition one of their reflexes, yet . . . well, he couldn't understand about the flowers. Why go to the trouble of making it psychologically impossible for Deltas to like flowers?

Patiently the D.H.C. explained. If the children were made to scream at the sight of a rose, that was on grounds of high economic policy. Not so very long ago (a century or thereabouts), Gammas, Deltas, even Epsilons, had been conditioned to like flowers—flowers in particular and wild nature in general. The idea was to make them want to be going out into the country at every available opportunity, and so compel them to consume transport.

"And didn't they consume transport?" asked the student.

"Quite a lot," the D.H.C. replied. "But nothing else."

Primroses and landscapes, he pointed out, have one grave defect: they are gratuitous. A love of nature keeps no factories busy. It was decided to abolish the love of nature, at any rate among the lower classes; to abolish the love of nature, but *not* the tendency to consume transport. For of course it was essential that they should keep on going to the country, even though they hated it. The problem was to find an economically sounder reason for consuming transport than a mere affection for primroses and landscapes. It was duly found.

"We condition the masses to hate the country," concluded the Director. "But simultaneously we condition them to love all country sports. At the same time, we see to it that all country sports shall entail the use of elaborate apparatus. So that they consume manufactured articles as well as transport. Hence those electric shocks."

"I see," said the student, and was silent, lost in admiration.

There was a silence; then, clearing his throat, "Once upon a time," the Director began, "while our Ford was still on earth, there was a little boy called Reuben Rabinovitch. Reuben was the child of Polish-speaking parents." The Director interrupted himself. "You know what Polish is, I suppose?"

"A dead language."

"Like French and German," added another student, officiously showing off his learning.

"And 'parent'?" questioned the D.H.C.

There was an uneasy silence. Several of the boys blushed. They had not yet learned to draw the significant but often very fine distinction between smut and pure science. One, at last, had the courage to raise a hand.

"Human beings used to be . . . " he hesitated; the blood rushed to his cheeks. "Well, they used to be viviparous."

"Quite right." The Director nodded approvingly.

"And when the babies were decanted . . . "

" 'Born'," came the correction.

"Well, then they were the parents—I mean, not the babies, of course; the other ones." The poor boy was overwhelmed with confusion.

"In brief," the Director summed up, "the parents were the father and the mother." The smut that was really science fell with a crash into the boys' eye-avoiding silence. "Mother," he repeated loudly rubbing in the science; and, leaning back in his chair, "These," he said gravely, "are unpleasant facts; I know it. But then most historical facts *are* unpleasant."

He returned to Little Reuben—to Little Reuben in whose room, one evening, by an oversight, his father and mother happened to leave the radio turned on.

("For you must remember that in those days of gross viviparous reproduction, children were always brought up by their parents and not in State Conditioning Centres.")

While the child was asleep, a broadcast programme from London suddenly started to come through; and the next morning, to the astonishment of his [parents] (the more daring of the boys ventured to grin at one another), Little Reuben woke up repeating word for word a long lecture by that curious old writer ("one of the very few whose works have been permitted to come down to us"), George Bernard Shaw, who was speaking, according to a well-authenticated tradition, about his own genius. To Little Reuben's wink and snigger, this lecture was, of course, perfectly incomprehensible and, imagining that their child had suddenly gone mad, they sent for a doctor. He, fortunately, understood English, recognized the discourse as that which Shaw had broadcasted the previous evening, realized the significance of what had happened, and sent a letter to the medical press about it.

"The principle of sleep-teaching, or hypnopedia, had been discovered." The D.H.C. made an impressive pause.

The principle had been discovered; but many, many years were to elapse before that principle was usefully applied. . . .

"These early experimenters," the D.H.C. was saying, "were on the wrong track. They thought that hypnopedia could be made an instrument of intellectual education . . . "

(A small boy asleep on his right side, the right arm stuck out, the right hand hanging limp over the edge of the bed. Through a round grating in the side of a box a voice speaks softly.

"The Nile is the longest river in Africa and the second in length of all the rivers of the globe. Although falling short of the length of the Mississippi-Missouri, the Nile is at the head of all rivers as regards the length of its basin, which extends through 35 degrees of latitude . . . "

At breakfast the next morning, "Tommy," someone says, "do you know which is the longest river in Africa?" A shaking of the head. "But don't you remember something that begins: The Nile is the . . . "

"The-Nile-is-the-longest-river-in-Africa-and-the-second-in-length-of-all-the-rivers-of-the-globe. . . ." The words came rushing out. "Although-falling-short-of . . ."

"Well now, which is the longest river in Africa?"

The eyes are blank. "Idon't know."

"But the Nile, Tommy."

"The-Nile-is-the-longest-river-in-Africa-and-second . . . "

"Then which river is the longest, Tommy?"

Tommy bursts into tears. "I don't know," he howls.)

That howl, the Director made it plain, discouraged the earliest investigators. The experiments were abandoned. No further attempt was made to teach children the length of the Nile in their sleep. Quite rightly. You can't learn a science unless you know what it's all about.

"Whereas, if they'd only started on *moral* education," said the Director, leading the way towards the door. The students followed him, desperately scribbling as they walked and all the way up in the lift. "Moral education, which ought never, in any circumstances, to be rational."

"Silence, silence," whispered a loud speaker as they stepped out at the fourteenth floor, and "Silence, silence," the trumpet mouths indefatigably repeated at intervals down every corridor. The students and even the Director himself rose automatically to the tips of their toes. They were Alphas, of course; but even Alphas have been well conditioned. "Silence, silence." All the air of the fourteenth floor was sibilant with the categorical imperative.

Fifty yards of tiptoeing brought them to a door which the Director cautiously opened. They stepped over the threshold into the twilight of a shuttered dormitory. Eighty cots stood in a row against the wall. There was a sound of light regular breathing and a continuous murmur, as of very faint voices remotely whispering.

A nurse rose as they entered and came to attention before the Director.

"What's the lesson this afternoon?" he asked.

"We had Elementary Sex for the first forty minutes," she answered. "But now it's switched over to Elementary Class Consciousness."

The Director walked slowly down the long line of cots. Rosy and relaxed with sleep, eighty little boys and girls lay softly breathing. There was a whisper under every pillow. The D.H.C. halted and, bending over one of the little beds, listened attentively.

"Elementary Class Consciousness, did you say? Let's have it repeated a little louder by the trumpet."

At the end of the room a loud speaker projected from the wall. The Director walked up to it and pressed a switch.

" . . . all wear green," said a soft but very distinct voice, beginning in the middle of a sentence, "and Delta children wear Khaki. Oh no, I don't want to play with Delta children. And Epsilons are still worse. They're too stupid to be able to read or write. Besides they wear black, which is such a beastly colour. I'm *so* glad I'm a Beta."

There was a pause; then the voice began again.

"Alpha children wear grey. They work much harder than we do, because they're so frightfully clever. I'm really awfully glad I'm a Beta, because I don't work so hard. And then we are much better than the Gammas and Deltas. Gammas are stupid. They all wear green, and Delta children wear Khaki. Oh no, I *don't* want to play with Delta children. And Epsilons are still worse. They're too stupid to be able . . . "

The Director pushed back the switch. The voice was silent. Only its thin ghost continued to mutter from beneath the eighty pillows.

"They'll have that repeated forty or fifty times more before they wake; then again on Thursday, and again on Saturday. A hundred and twenty times three times a week for thirty months. After which they go on to a more advanced lesson."

Roses and electric shocks, the khaki of Deltas and a whiff of asafoetida —wedded indissolubly before the child can speak. But wordless conditioning is crude and wholesale; cannot bring home the finer distinctions, cannot inculcate the more complex courses of behaviour. For that there must be words, but words without reason. In brief, hypnopedia.

"The greatest moralizing and socializing force of all time."

. . . Once more the Director touched the switch.

" . . . so frightfully clever," the soft, insinuating, indefatigable voice was saying. "I'm really awfully glad I'm a Beta, because . . . "

Not so much like drops of water, though water, it is true can wear holes in the hardest granite; rather, drops of liquid sealing-wax, drops that adhere, incrust, incorporate themselves with what they fall on, till finally the rock is all one scarlet blob.

"Till at last the child's mind *is* these suggestions, and the sum of the suggestions *is* the child's mind. And not the child's mind only. The adult's mind too—all his life long. The mind that judges and desires and desires and decides—made up of these suggestions. But all these suggestions are *our* suggestions!" The Director almost shouted in his triumph. "Suggestions from the State."

Outside, in the garden, it was playtime. Naked in the warm June sunshine, six or seven hundred little boys and girls were running with shrill yells over the lawns, or playing ball games, or squatting silently in twos and threes among the flowering shrubs. The roses were in bloom, two nightingales soliloquized in the boskage, a cuckoo was just going out of tune among the lime trees. The air was drowsy with the murmur of bees and helicopters.

The Director and his students stood for a short time watching a game of Centrifugal Bumble-puppy. Twenty children were grouped in a circle round a chrome steel tower. A ball thrown up so as to land on the platform at the top of the tower rolled down into the interior, fell on a rapidly revolving disk, was hurled through one or other of the numerous apertures pierced in the cylindrical casing, and had to be caught.

"Strange," mused the Director, as they turned away, "strange to think that even in Our Ford's day most games were played without more apparatus than a ball or two and a few sticks and perhaps a bit of netting. Imagine the folly of allowing people to play elaborate games which do nothing whatever to increase consumption. It's madness. Nowadays the Controllers won't approve of any new game unless it can be shown that it requires at least as much apparatus as the most complicated of existing games." He interrupted himself.

"That's a charming little group," he said, pointing.

In a little grassy bay between tall clumps of Mediterranean heather, two children, a little boy of about seven and a little girl who might have been a year older, were playing, very gravely and with all the focused attention of scientists intent on a labour of discovery, a rudimentary sexual game.

"Charming, charming!" the D.H.C. repeated sentimentally.

"Charming," the boys politely agreed. But their smile was rather patronizing. They had put aside similar childish amusements too recently to be able to watch them now without a touch of contempt. Charming? but it was just a pair of kids fooling about; that was all. Just kids.

"I always think," the Director was continuing in the same rather maudlin tone, when he was interrupted by a loud boo-hooing.

From a neighbouring shrubbery emerged a nurse, leading by the hand a small boy, who howled as he went. An anxious-looking little girl trotted at her heels.

"What's the matter?" asked the Director.

The nurse shrugged her shoulders. "Nothing much," she answered. "It's just that this little boy seems rather reluctant to join in the ordinary erotic play. I'd noticed it once or twice before. And now again to-day. He started yelling just now . . . "

"Honestly," put in the anxious-looking little girl, "I didn't mean to hurt him or anything. Honestly."

"Of course you didn't, dear," said the nurse reassuringly. "And so," she went on, turning back to the Director, "I'm taking him in to see the Assistant Superintendent of Psychology. Just to see if anything's at all abnormal."

"Quite right," said the Director. "Take him in. You stay here, little girl," he added, as the nurse moved away with her still howling charge. "What's your name?"

"Polly Trotsky."

"And a very good name too," said the Director. "Run away now and see if you can find some other little boy to play with." The child scampered off into the bushes and was lost to sight.

"Exquisite little creature!" said the Director, looking after her. Then, turning to his students, "What I'm going to tell you now," he said, "may sound incredible. But then, when you're not accustomed to history, most facts about the past *do* sound incredible."

He let out the amazing truth. For a very long period before the time of Our Ford, and even for some generations afterwards, erotic play between children had been regarded as abnormal (there was a roar of laughter); and not only abnormal, actually immoral (no!): and had therefore been rigorously suppressed.

A look of astonished incredulity appeared on the faces of his listeners. Poor little kids not allowed to amuse themselves? They could not believe it.

"Even adolescents," the D.H.C. was saying, "even adolescents like yourselves . . . "

"Not possible!"

"Barring a little surreptitious auto-erotism and homosexuality—absolutely nothing."

"*Nothing?* "

"In most cases, till they were over twenty years old."

"Twenty years old?" echoed the students in a chorus of loud disbelief.

"Twenty," the Director repeated. "I told you that you'd find it incredible."

"But what happened?" they asked. "What were the results?"

"The results were terrible." A deep resonant voice broke startlingly into the dialogue.

They looked round. On the fringe of the little group stood a stranger —a man of middle height, black-haired, with a hooked nose, full red lips, eyes very piercing and dark. "Terrible," he repeated.

The D.H.C. had at that moment sat down on one of the steel and rubber benches conveniently scattered through the gardens; but at the sight of the stranger, he sprang to his feet and darted forward, his hands outstretched, smiling with all his teeth, effusive.

"Controller! What an unexpected pleasure! Boys, what are you thinking of? This is the Controller; this is his fordship, Mustapha Mond."

. . . His fordship Mustapha Mond! The eyes of the saluting students almost popped out of their heads. Mustapha Mond! The Resident Controller for Western Europe! One of the Ten World Controllers. One of the Ten . . . and he sat down on the bench with the D.H.C., he was going to stay, to stay, yes, and actually talk to them . . . straight from the horse's mouth. Straight from the mouth of Ford himself.

Two shrimp-brown children emerged from a neighbouring shrubbery, stared at them for a moment with large astonished eyes, then returned to their amusements among the leaves.

"You all remember," said the Controller, in his strong deep voice, "you all remember, I suppose, that beautiful and inspired saying of Our Ford's: History is bunk. History," he repeated slowly, "is bunk. . . . "

"That's why you're taught no history," the Controller was saying. "But now the time has come . . . "

The D.H.C. looked at him nervously. There were those strange rumours of old forbidden books hidden in a safe in the Controller's study. Bibles, poetry—Ford knew what.

Mustapha Mond intercepted his anxious glance and the corners of his red lips twitched ironically.

"It's all right, Director," he said in a tone of faint derision, "I won't corrupt them."

The D.H.C. was overwhelmed with confusion. . . .

Mustapha Mond leaned forward, shook a finger at them. "Just try to realize it," he said, and his voice sent a strange thrill quivering along their diaphragms. "Try to realize what it was like to have a viviparous mother." That smutty word again. But none of them dreamed, this time, of smiling.

"Try to imagine what 'living with one's family' meant."

They tried; but obviously without the smallest success.

"And do you know what a 'home' was?"

They shook their heads. . . .

Home, home—a few small rooms, stiflingly over-inhabited by a man, by a periodically teeming woman, by a rabble of boys and girls of all ages. No air, no space; an understerilized prison; darkness, disease, and smells.

(The Controller's evocation was so vivid that one of the boys, more sensitive than the rest, turned pale at the mere description and was on the point of being sick.) . . .

And home was as squalid psychically as physically. Psychically, it was a rabbit hole, a midden, hot with the frictions of tightly packed life, reeking with emotion. What suffocating intimacies, what dangerous, insane, obscene relationships between the members of the family group! Maniacally, the mother brooded over her children (*her* children) . . . brooded over them like a cat over its kittens; but a cat that could talk, a cat that could say, "My baby, my baby," over and over again. "My baby, and oh, oh, at my breast, the little hands, the hunger, and that unspeakable agonizing pleasure! Till at last my baby sleeps, my baby sleeps with a bubble of white milk at the corner of his mouth. My little baby sleeps . . ."

"Yes," said Mustapha Mond, nodding his head, "you may well shudder." . . .

Our Ford—or Our Freud, as, for some inscrutable reason, he chose to call himself whenever he spoke of psychological matters—Our Freud had been the first to reveal the appalling dangers of family life. The world was full of fathers—was therefore full of misery; full of mothers—therefore of every kind of perversion from sadism to chastity; full of brothers, sisters, uncles, aunts—full of madness and suicide.

"And yet, among the savages of Samoa, in certain islands off the coast of New Guinea . . ."

The tropical sunshine lay like warm honey on the naked bodies of children tumbling promiscuously among the hibiscus blossoms. Home was in any oné of twenty palm-thatched houses. In the Trobiands conception was the work of ancestral ghosts; nobody had ever heard of a father.

"Extremes," said the Controller, "meet. For the good reason that they were made to meet." . . .

"Mothers and fathers, brothers and sisters. But there were also husbands, wives, lovers. There were also monogamy and romance."

"Though you probably don't know what those are," said Mustapha Mond.

They shook their heads.

Family, monogamy, romance. Everywhere exclusiveness, everywhere a focussing of interest, a narrow channelling of impulse and energy.

"But every one belongs to every one else," he concluded, citing the hypnopedic proverb.

The students nodded, emphatically agreeing with a statement which upwards of sixty-two thousand repetitions in the dark had made them accept, not merely as true, but as axiomatic, self-evident, utterly indisputable. . . .

"Think of water under pressure in a pipe." They thought of it. "I pierce it once," said the Controller. "What a jet!"

He pierced it twenty times. There were twenty piddling little fountains.

"My baby. My baby . . . !"

"Mother!" The madness is infectious.

"My love, my one and only, precious, precious . . . "

Mother, monogamy, romance. High spurts the fountain; fierce and foamy the wild jet. The urge has but a single outlet. My love, my baby. No wonder those poor pre-moderns were mad and wicked and miserable. Their world didn't allow them to take things easily, didn't allow them to be sane, virtuous, happy. What with mothers and lovers, what with the prohibitions they were not conditioned to obey, what with the temptations and the lonely remorses, what with all the diseases and the endless isolating pain, what with the uncertainties and the poverty—they were forced to feel strongly. And feeling strongly (and strongly, what was more, in solitude, in hopelessly individual isolation), how could they be stable? . . .

"Stability," said the Controller, "stability. No civilization without social stability. No social stability without individual stability." His voice was a trumpet. Listening they felt larger, warmer.

The machine turns, turns and must keep on turning—forever. It is death if it stands still. A thousand millions scrabbled the crust of the earth. The wheels began to turn. In a hundred and fifty years there were two thousand millions. Stop all the wheels. In a hundred and fifty weeks there are once more only a thousand millions; a thousand thousand thousand men and women have starved to death.

Wheels must turn steadily, but cannot turn untended. There must be men to tend them, men as steady as the wheels upon their axles, sane men, obedient men, stable in contentment.

Crying: My baby, my mother, my only, only love; groaning: My sin, my terrible God; screaming with pain, muttering with fever, bemoaning old age and poverty—how can they tend the wheels? And if they cannot tend the wheels . . . The corpses of a thousand thousand thousand men and women would be hard to bury or burn. . . .

"Stability," insisted the Controller, "stability. The primal and the ultimate need. Stability. Hence all this."

With a wave of his hand he indicated the gardens, the huge building of the Conditioning Centre, the naked children furtive in the undergrowth or running across the lawns. . . .

Impulse arrested spills over, and the flood is feeling, the flood is passion, the flood is even madness: it depends on the force of the current, the height and strength of the barrier. The unchecked stream flows smoothly down its appointed channels into a calm well-being. (The embryo is hungry; day in, day out, the blood-surrogate pump unceasingly turns in eight hundred revolutions a minute. The decanted infant howls; at once a nurse appears with a bottle of external secretion. Feeling lurks in that interval of time between desire and its consummation. Shorten that interval, break down all those old unnecessary barriers.

"Fortunate boys!" said the Controller. "No pains have been spared to make your lives emotionally easy—to preserve you, so far as that is possible, from having emotions at all." . . .

"Consider your own lives," said Mustapha Mond. "Has any of you ever encountered an insurmountable obstacle?"

The question was answered by a negative silence.

"Has any of you been compelled to live through a long time-interval between the consciousness of a desire and its fulfillment?"

"Well," began one of the boys, and hesitated.

"Speak up," said the D.H.C. "Don't keep his fordship waiting."

"I once had to wait nearly four weeks before a girl I wanted would let me have her."

"And you felt a strong emotion in consequence?"

"Horrible!"

"Horrible; precisely," said the Controller. "Our ancestors were so stupid and short-sighted that when the first reformers came along and offered to deliver them from those horrible emotions, they wouldn't have anything to do with them." . . .

"Take Ectogenesis. Pfitzner and Kawaguchi had got the whole technique worked out. But would the Governments look at it? No. There was something called Christianity. Women were forced to go on being viviparous." . . .

"Sleep teaching was actually prohibited in England. There was something called liberalism. Parliament, if you know what that was, passed a law against it. The records survive. Speeches about liberty of the subject. Liberty to be inefficient and miserable. Freedom to be a round peg in a square hole." . . .

"Or the Caste System. Constantly proposed, constantly rejected. There was something called democracy. As though men were more than physicochemically equal." . . .

"The Nine Years' War began in A.F. 141." . . .

"The noise of fourteen thousand aeroplanes advancing in open order. But in the Kurfurstendamm and the Eighth Arrondissement, the explosion of the anthrax bombs is hardly louder than the popping of a paper bag." . . .

$Ch_3C_6H_2(NO_2)_3 + Hg(CNO)_2$ = well, what? An enormous hole in the ground, a pile of masonry, some bits of flesh and mucus, a foot, with the boot still on it, flying through the air and landing, flop, in the middle of the geraniums—the scarlet ones; such a splendid show that summer! . . .

"The Russian technique for infecting water supplies was particularly ingenious." . . .

"The Nine Years' War, the great Economic Collapse. There was a choice between World Control and destruction. Between stability and." . . .

In the nurseries, the Elementary Class Consciousness lesson was over, the voices were adapting future demand to future industrial supply. "I do love flying," they whispered, "I do love flying, I do love having new clothes, I do love . . . "

"Liberalism, of course, was dead of anthrax, but all the same you couldn't do things by force." . . .

"Government's an affair of sitting, not hitting. You rule with the brains and the buttocks, never with the fists. For example, there was the conscription of consumption." . . .

"Every man, woman and child compelled to consume so much a year. In the interests of industry. The sole result." . . .

"Conscientious objection on an enormous scale. Anything not to consume. Back to nature." . . .

"Back to culture. Yes, actually to culture. You can't consume much if you sit still and read books." . . .

"Eight hundred Simple Lifers were mowed down by machine guns at Golders Green." . . .

"Then came the famous British Museum Massacre. Two thousand culture fans gassed with dichlorethyl sulphide." . . .

"In the end," said Mustapha Mond, "the Controllers realized that force was no good. The slower but infinitely surer methods of ectogenesis, neo-Pavlovian conditioning and hypnopedia." . . .

"The discoveries of Pfitzner and Kawaguchi were at last made use of. An intensive propaganda against viviparous reproduction." . . .

"Accompanied by a campaign against the Past; by the closing of museums, the blowing up of historical monuments (luckily most of them had already been destroyed during the Nine Years' War); by the suppression of all books published before A.F. 150." . . .

"There were some things called the pyramids, for example." . . .

"And a man called Shakespeare. You've never heard of them of course." . . .

"Such are the advantages of a really scientific education." . . .

"The introduction of Our Ford's first T-Model." . . .

"Chosen as the opening date of the new era." . . .

"There was a thing, as I've said before, called Christianity." . . .

"The ethics and philosophy of under-consumption." . . .

"So essential when there was under-production; but in an age of machines and the fixation of nitrogen—positively a crime against society."
. . .

"All crosses had their tops cut and became T's. There was also a thing called God." . . .

"We have the World State now. And Ford's Day celebrations, and Community Sings, and Solidarity Services." . . .

"There was a thing called Heaven; but all the same they used to drink enormous quantities of alcohol." . . .

"There was thing called the soul and a thing called immortality."
. . .

"But they used to take morphia and cocaine." . . .

"Two thousand pharmacologists and bio-chemists were subsidized in A.F. 178." . . .

"Six years later it was being produced commercially. The perfect drug."
. . .

"Euphoric, narcotic, pleasantly hallucinant." . . .

"All the advantages of Christianity and alcohol; none of their defects."
. . .

"Take a holiday from reality whenever you like, and come back without so much as a headache or a mythology." . . .

"Stability was practically assured." . . .

"It only remained to conquer old age." . . .

"Gonadal hormones, transfusion of young blood, magnesium salts."
. . .

"All the physiological stigmata of old age have been abolished. And along with them, of course." . . .

"Along with them all the old man's mental peculiarities. Characters remain constant throughout a whole lifetime." . . .

"Work, play—at sixty our powers and tastes are what they were at seventeen. Old men in the bad old days used to renounce, retire, take to religion, spend their time reading, thinking—thinking! . . .

"Now—such is progress—the old men work, the old men copulate, the old men have no time, no leisure from pleasure, not a moment to sit down and think—or if ever by some unlucky chance such a crevice of time should yawn in the solid substance of their distractions, there is always *soma,* delicious *soma,* half a gramme for a half-holiday, a gramme for a week-end, two grammes for a trip to the gorgeous East, three for a dark eternity on the moon; returning whence they find themselves on the other side of the crevice, safe on the solid ground of daily labour and distraction, scampering from feely to feely, from girl to pneumatic girl, from Electromagnetic Golf course to . . . "

—7—

a possible
educational system

So far only one revolution of truly major proportions has changed how education is carried out. The revolutionary event was the introduction of written supplements to an instructor's oral teachings. When ideas could be recorded in an enduring form, it was possible to carry out instruction in either oral or a written fashion. Obviously, this revolution is not a recent event.

Educational procedures introduced since the invention of writing have all been attempts to find the most efficient manner of using oral and written matter to educate people, or to produce certain characteristics in those who are being educated or both. There have been attempts to educate people in ways that foster or even teach creativity; special techniques have been developed to educate students of limited intelligence and those of exceptional brilliance, students with little motivation and those with a great passion for learning. Each new procedure simply recombines and reapportions oral and written instruction and makes some attempt to tailor the procedure to the special needs of students.

As modern psychology has come to know something of the principles of learning, alternative schedules for presenting ideas and alternative techniques for facilitating learning have become feasible. These researches, together with development of powerful computers that can process many problems and administer and control many projects simultaneously (through time-sharing systems), make possible computerized instruction. This technique could be the closest thing to a major revolution in education since the invention of writing. The departure from traditional techniques is that a computer-based method permits individualized instruction of large numbers of students in a manner designed to maximize the speed and ease with which a student acquires information. If programs for computerized instruction develop to a level of true sophistication, many desirable aspects of the one-to-one student-teacher relationship will be possible; the "teacher" will be adept at sensing when a student has understood a particular problem, and moving on to the next level, or choosing to step backward in order to correct faulty learning that is affecting present performance.

Even computerized instruction, however, falls within the definition of education as it is now practiced. At best it will make available an extraordinarily talented teacher who can give individual attention to each student. In a story called "Profession," Isaac Asimov considers a truly revolutionary educational system. The excerpts from the story describe something of the social conditions that fostered the development of this system and something of the experience of being educated under it.

"profession"

by Isaac Asimov

There was a time, four or five thousand years ago when mankind was confined to the surface of Earth. Even then, his culture had grown quite technological and his numbers had increased to the point where any failure in technology would have meant mass starvation and disease. To maintain the technological level and advance it in the face of an increasing population, more and more technicians and scientists had to be trained, and yet, as science advanced, it took longer and longer to train them.

As first interplanetary and then interstellar travel was developed, the problem grew more acute. In fact, actual colonization of extra-Solar planets was impossible for about fifteen hundred years because of a lack of properly trained men.

The turning point came when the mechanics of the storage of knowledge within the brain was worked out. Once that had been done, it became possible to devise Educational tapes that would modify the mechanics in such a way as to place within the mind a body of knowledge ready-made, so to speak. . . .

Once that was done, trained men could be turned out by the thousands and millions, and we could begin what someone has since called the "Filling of the Universe." There are now fifteen hundred inhabited planets in the Galaxy and there is no end in sight.

Do you see all that is involved? Earth exports Education tapes for low-specialized professions and that keeps the Galactic culture unified. For instance, the Reading tapes insure a single language for all of us.
. . .

Earth also exports highly specialized professionals and keeps its own population at an endurable level. Since they are shipped out in a balanced sex ratio, they act as self-reproductive units and help increase the populations on the Outworlds where an increase is needed. Furthermore, tapes and men are paid for in material which we much need and on which our economy depends.

For most of the first eighteen years of his life, George Platen had headed firmly in one direction, that of Registered Computer Programmer. There were those in his crowd who spoke wisely of Spationautics, Refrigeration Technology, Transportation Control, and even Administration. But George held firm.

He argued relative merits as vigorously as any of them, and why not? Education Day loomed ahead of them and was the great fact of their existence. It approached steadily, as fixed and certain as the calendar—the first day of November of the year following one's eighteenth birthday.

After that day, there were other topics of conversation. One could discuss with others some detail of the profession, or the virtues of one's wife and children. . . .

Before Education Day, however, there was only one topic that unfailingly and unwearyingly held everyone's interest, and that was Education Day.

"What are you going for? Think you'll make it? That's no good. Look at the records; quota's been cut. Logistics now—"

Or Hypermechanics now— Or Communications now— Or Gravitics now—

Especially Gravitics at the moment. Everyone had been talking about Gravitics in the few years just before George's Education Day because of the development of the Gravitic power engine.

Any world within ten light-years of a dwarf star, everyone said, would give its eyeteeth for any kind of Registered Gravitics Engineer.

The thought of that never bothered George. Sure it would; all the eyeteeth it could scare up. But George had also heard what had happened before in a newly developed technique. Rationalization and simplification followed in a flood. New models each year; new types of gravitic engines; new principles. Then all those eyeteeth gentlemen would find themselves out of date and superseded by later models with later educations. The first group would then have to settle down to unskilled labour or ship out to some backwoods world that wasn't quite caught up yet.

Now Computer Programmers were in steady demand year after year, century after century. The demand never reached wild peaks; there was never a howling bull market for Programmers; but the demand climbed steadily as new worlds opened up and as older worlds grew more complex.

He had argued with Trevelyan about that constantly. As best friends, their arguments had to be constant and vitriolic and, of course, neither ever persuaded or was persuaded.

But then Trevelyan had had a father who was a Registered Metallurgist and had actually served on one of the Outworlds, and a grandfather who had also been a Registered Metallurgist. He himself was intent on becoming a Registered Metallurgist almost as a matter of family right and was firmly convinced that any other profession was a shade less than respectable.

"There'll always be metal," he said, "and there's an accomplishment in moulding alloys to specification and watching structures grow. Now what's a Programmer going to be doing. Sitting at a coder all day long, feeding some fool machine."

Even at sixteen, George had learned to be practical. He said simply, "There'll be a million Metallurgists put out along with you."

"Because it's good. A good profession. The best."

"But you get crowded out, Stubby. You can be way back in line. Any world can tape out its own Metallurgists, and the market for advanced Earth models isn't so big. And it's mostly the small worlds that want them. You know what percent of the turnout of Registered Metallurgists get tabbed for worlds with a Grade A rating. I looked it up. It's just 13.3 percent. That means you'll have seven chances in eight of being stuck in some world that just about has running water. You may even be stuck on Earth; 2.3 percent are."

Trevelyan said belligerently, "There's no disgrace in staying on Earth. Earth needs technicians, too. Good ones." His grandfather had been an Earthbound Metallurgist, and Trevelyan lifted his finger to his upper lip and dabbed at an as yet non-existent moustache.

George knew about Trevelyan's grandfather and, considering the Earthbound position of his own ancestry, was in no mood to sneer. He said diplomatically, "No intellectual disgrace. Of course not. But it's nice to get into a Grade A world, isn't it?

"Now you take Programmers. Only the Grade A worlds have the kind of computers that really need first-class Programmers so they're the only ones in the market. And Programmer tapes are complicated and hardly any one fits. They need more Programmers than their own population can supply. It's just a matter of statistics. There's one first-class Programmer per million, say. A world needs twenty and has a population of ten million, they have to come to Earth for five to fifteen Programmers. Right?

"And you know how many Registered Computer Programmers went to Grade A planets last year? I'll tell you. Every last one. If you're a Programmer, you're a picked man. Yes, sir."

Trevelyan frowned. "If only one in a million makes it, what makes you think *you'll* make it?"

George said guardedly, "I'll make it."

He never dared tell anyone; not Trevelyan; not his parents; of exactly what he was doing that made him so confident. But he wasn't worried. He was simply confident. . . .

He was as blandly confident as the average eight-year-old kid approaching Reading Day—that childhood preview of Education Day.

Of course, Reading Day had been different. Partly, there was the simply fact of childhood. A boy of eight takes many extraordinary things in his stride. One day you can't read and the next day you can. That's just the way things are. Like the sun shining.

And then not so much depended upon it. There were no recruiters just ahead, waiting and jostling for the lists and scores. . . . A boy or girl who goes through the Reading Day is just someone who has ten more years of undifferentiated living upon Earth's crawling surface; just someone who returns to his family with one new ability.

By the time Education Day came, ten years later, George wasn't even sure of most of the details of his own Reading Day.

Most clearly of all, he remembered it to be a dismal September day with a mild rain falling. . . . George had dressed by the wall lights, with his parents far more excited than he himself was. His father was a Registered Pipe Fitter and had found his occupation on earth. This fact had always been a humilitation to him, although, of course, as anyone could see plainly, most of each generation must stay on Earth in the nature of things.

There had to be farmers and miners and even technicians on Earth. It was only the late-model, high-specialty professions that were in demand on the Outworlds, and only a few millions a year out of Earth's eight billion population could be exported. Every man and woman on Earth couldn't be among that group.

But every man and woman could hope that at least one of his children could be one, and Platen, Senior, was certainly no exception. It was obvious to him (and, to be sure, to others as well) that George was notably intelligent and quick-minded. He would be bound to do well and he would have to, as he was an only child. If George didn't end on an Outworld, they would have to wait for grandchildren before a next chance would come along, and that was too far in the future to be much consolation.

Reading Day would not prove much, of course, but it would be the only indication they would have before the big day itself. Every parent on Earth would be listening to the quality of reading when his child came home with it; listening for any particularly easy flow of words and building that into certain omens of the future. There were few families that didn't have at least one hopeful who, from Reading Day on, was the great hope because of the way he handled his trisyllabics.

Dimly, George was aware of the cause of his parents' tension, and if there was any anxiety in his young heart that drizzly morning, it was only the fear that his father's hopeful expression might fade out when he returned home with his reading.

The children met in the large assembly room of the town's Education hall. All over Earth, in millions of local halls, throughout that month, similar groups of children would be meeting. George felt depressed by the greyness of the room and by the other children, strained and stiff in unaccustomed finery.

Automatically, George did as all the rest of the children did. He found the small clique that represented the children on his floor of the apartment house and joined them. . . .

A woman's voice sounded loudly over the public address system. There was instant silence everywhere. . . .

"Children," said the voice, "we are going to call out your names. As each child is called, he or she is to go to one of the men waiting along the side walls. Do you see them? They are wearing red uniforms so they will be easy to find. The girls will go to the right. The boys will go to the left. Now look about and see which man in red is nearest to you—"

George found his man at a glance and waited for his name to be called off. He had not been introduced before this to the sophistications of the alphabet, and the length of time it took to reach his own name grew disturbing.

The crowd of children thinned; little rivulets made their way to each of the red-clad guides.

When the name "George Platen" was finally called, his sense of relief was exceeded only by the feeling of pure gladness at the fact that Trevelyan still stood in his place, uncalled. . . .

He was herded into a line and directed down corridors in the company of strange children. They all looked at one another, large-eyed and concerned, but beyond a snuffling, "Quitcher pushing" and "Hey, watch out" there was no conversation.

They were handed little slips of paper which they were told must remain with them. George stared at his curiously. Little black marks of different shapes. He knew it to be printing but how could anyone make words out of it? He couldn't imagine.

He was told to strip; he and four other boys who were all that now remained together. All the new clothes came shucking off and four eight-year-olds stood naked and small, shivering more out of embarrassment than cold. Medical technicians came past, probing them, testing them with odd instruments, pricking them for blood. Each took the little cards and made additional marks on them with little black rods that produced the marks, all neatly lined up, with great speed. George stared at the new marks, but they were no more comprehensible than the old. The children were ordered back into their clothes.

They sat on separate little chairs then and waited again. Names were called again and "George Platen" came third.

He moved into a large room, filled with frightening instruments with knobs and glassy panels in front. There was a desk in the very centre, and behind it a man sat, his eyes on the papers piled before him.

He said, "George Platen?"

"Yes, sir," said George, in a shaky whisper. All this waiting and all this going here and there was making him nervous. He wished it were over.

The man behind the desk said, "I am Dr. Lloyd, George. How are you?"

The doctor didn't look up as he spoke. It was as though he had said those words over and over again and didn't have to look up any more.

"I'm all right."

"Are you afraid, George?"

"N-no, sir," said George, sounding afraid even in his own ears.

"That's good," said the doctor, "because there's nothing to be afraid of, you know. Let's see, George. It says here on your card that your father is named Peter and that he's a Registered Pipe Fitter and your mother is named Amy and is a Registered Home Technician. Is that right?"

"Y-yes, sir."

And your birthday is February 13, and you had an ear infection about a year ago. Right?"

"Yes, sir."

"Do you know how I know all these things?"

"It's on the card, I think, sir."

"That's right." The doctor looked up at George for the first time and smiled. He showed even teeth and looked much younger than George's father. Some of George's nervousness vanished.

The doctor passed the card to George. "Do you know what all those things there mean, George?"

Although George knew he did not he was startled by the sudden request into looking at the card as though he might understand now through some sudden stroke of fate. But they were just marks as before and he passed the card back. "No, sir."

"Why not?"

George felt a sudden pang of suspicion concerning the sanity of this doctor. Didn't he know why not?

George said, "I can't read, sir."

"Would you like to read?"

"Yes, sir."

"Why, George?"

George stared, appalled. No one had ever asked him that. He had no answer. He said falteringly, "I don't know, sir."

"Printed information will direct you all through your life. There is so much you'll have to know even after Education Day. Cards like this one will tell you. Books will tell you. Television screens will tell you. Printing will tell you such useful things and such interesting things that not being able to read would be as bad as not being able to see. Do you understand?"

"Yes, sir."

"Are you afraid, George?"

"No, sir."

"Good. Now I'll tell you exactly what we'll do first. I'm going to put these wires on your forehead just over the corners of your eyes. They'll stick there but they won't hurt at all. Then, I'll turn on something that will make a buzz. It will sound funny and it may tickle you, but it won't hurt. Now if it does hurt, you tell me, and I'll turn if off right away, but it won't hurt. All right?"

George nodded and swallowed.

"Are you ready?"

George nodded. He closed his eyes while the doctor busied himself. His parents had explained this to him. They, too, had said it wouldn't hurt, but then there were always the older children. There were the ten- and twelve-year-olds who howled after the eight-year-olds waiting for Reading Day, "Watch out for the needle." There were the others who took you off in confidence and said, "They got to cut your head open. They use a sharp knife that big with a hook on it," and so on into horrifying details.

George had never believed them but he had had nightmares, and now he closed his eyes and felt pure terror.

He didn't feel the wires at his temple. The buzz was a distant thing, and there was the sound of his own blood in his ears, ringing hollowly as though it and he were in a large cave. Slowly he chanced opening his eyes.

The doctor had his back to him. From one of the instruments a strip of paper unwound and was covered with a thin, wavy purple line. The doctor tore off pieces and put them into a slot in another machine. He did it over and over again. Each time a little piece of film came out, which the doctor looked at. Finally, he turned toward George with a queer frown between his eyes.

The buzzing stopped.

George said breathlessly, "Is it over?"

The doctor said, "Yes," but he was still frowning.

"Can I read now?" asked George. He felt no different.

The doctor said, "What?" then smiled very suddenly and briefly. He said, "It works fine, George. You'll be reading in fifteen minutes. Now we're going to use another machine this time and it will take longer. I'm going to cover your whole head, and when I turn it on you won't be able to see or hear anything for a while, but it won't hurt. Just to make sure I'm going to give you a little switch to hold in your hand. If anything hurts, you press the little button and everything shuts off. All right?"

In later years, George was told that the little switch was strictly a dummy; that it was introduced solely for confidence. He never did know for sure, however, since he never pushed the button.

A large smoothly curved helmet with a rubbery inner lining was placed over his head and left there. Three or four little knobs seemed to grab at him and bite into his skull, but there was only a little pressure that faded. No pain.

The doctor's voice sounded dimly. "Everything all right, George?"

And then, with no real warning, a layer of thick felt closed down all about him. He was disembodied, there was no sensation, no universe, only himself and a distant murmur at the very ends of nothingness telling him something—telling him—telling him—

He strained to hear and understand but there was all that thick felt between.

Then the helmet was taken off his head, and the light was so bright that it hurt his eyes while the doctor's voice drummed at his ears.

The doctor said, "Here's your card, George. What does it say?"

George looked at his card again and gave out a strangled shout. The marks weren't just marks at all. They made up words. They were words just as clearly as though something were whispering them in his ears. He could *hear* them being whispered as he looked at them.

"What does it say, George?"

"It says—it says—"Platen, George. Born 13 February 6492 of Peter and Amy Platen in . . . ' " He broke off.

"You can read, George," said the doctor. "It's all over."

"For good? I won't forget how?"

"Of course not." The doctor leaned over to shake hands gravely. "You will be taken home now."

It was days before George got over this new and great talent of his. He read for his father with such facility that Platen, Senior, wept and called relatives to tell the good news.

George walked about town, reading every scrap of printing he could find and wondering how it was that none of it had ever made sense to him before.

He tried to remember how it was not to be able to read and he couldn't. As far as his feeling about it was concerned, he had always been able to read. Always.

At eighteen, George was rather dark, of medium height, but thin enough to look taller. Trevelyan, who was scarcely an inch shorter, had a stockiness of build that made "Stubby" more than ever appropriate, but in his last year he had grown self-conscious. The nickname could no longer be used without reprisal. And since Trevelyan disapproved of his proper first name even more strongly, he was called Trevelyan or any decent variant of that. As though to prove his manhood further, he had most persistently grown a pair of sideburns and a bristly moustache. . . .

They were in the same large hall they had been in ten years before (and not since). It was as if a vague dream of the past had come to sudden reality. In the first few minutes George had been distinctly surprised at finding everything seem smaller and more cramped than his memory told him; then he made allowance for his own growth.

The crowd was smaller than it had been in childhood. It was exclusively male this time. The girls had another day assigned them.

Trevelyan leaned over to say, "Beats me the way they make you wait."

"Red tape," said George. "You can't avoid it."

Trevelyan said, "What makes *you* so damned tolerant about it?"

"I've got nothing to worry about."

"Oh, brother, you make me sick. I hope you end up Registered Manure Spreader just so I can see your face when you do." His sombre eyes swept the crowd anxiously.

George looked about, too. It wasn't quite the system they used on the children. Matters went slower, and instructions had been given out at the start in print (an advantage over the pre-Readers). The names Platen and Trevelyan were well down the alphabet still, but this time the two knew it.

Young men came out of the education rooms, frowning and uncomfortable, picked up their clothes and belongings, then went off to analysis to learn the results.

Each, as he came out, would be surrounded by a clot of the thinning crowd. "How was it?" "How'd it feel?" "Whacha think ya made?" "Ya feel any different?"

Answers were vague and noncommittal.

George forced himself to remain out of those clots. You only raised your own blood pressure. Everyone said you stood the best chance if you remained calm. Even so, you could feel the palms of your hands grow cold. Funny that new tensions came with the years.

For instance, high-specialty professionals heading out for an Outworld were accompanied by a wife (or husband). It was important to keep the sex ratio in good balance on all worlds. And if you were going out to a Grade A world, what girl would refuse you? George had no specific girl in mind yet; he wanted none. Not now! Once he made Programmer; once he could add to his name, Registered Computer Programmer, he could take his pick, like a sultan in a harem. The thought excited him and he tried to put it away. Must stay calm.

Trevelyan muttered, "What's it all about anyway? First they say it works best if you're relaxed and at ease. Then they put you through this and make it impossible for you to be relaxed and at ease."

"Maybe that's the idea. They're separating the boys from the men to begin with. Take it easy, Trev."

"Shut up."

George's turn came. His name was not called. It appeared in glowing letters on the notice-board.

He waved at Trevelyan. "Take it easy. Don't let it get you."

He was happy as he entered the testing chamber. Actually happy. The man behind the desk said, "George Platen?"

For a fleeting instant there was a razor-sharp picture in George's mind of another man, ten years earlier, who had asked the same question, and it was almost as though this were the same man and he, George, had turned eight again as he had stepped across the threshold.

But the man looked up and, of course, the face matched that of the sudden memory not at all. The nose was bulbous, the hair thin and stringy, and the chin wattled as though its owner had once been grossly overweight and had reduced.

The man behind the desk looked annoyed. "Well?"

George came to Earth. "I'm George Platen, sir."

"Say so, then. I'm Dr. Zachary Antonelli, and we're going to be intimately acquainted in a moment."

He stared at small strips of film, holding them up to the light owlishly.

George winced inwardly. Very hazily, he remembered that other doctor (he had forgotten the name) staring at such film. Could these be the same? The other doctor had frowned and this one was looking at him now as though he were angry.

His happiness was already just about gone.

Dr. Antonelli spread the pages of a thickish file out before him now and put the films carefully to one side. "It says here you want to be a Computer Programmer."

"Yes, doctor."

"Still do?"

"Yes, sir."

"It's a responsible and exacting position. Do you feel up to it?"

"Yes, sir."

"Most pre-Educates don't put down any specific profession. I believe they are afraid of queering it."

"I think that's right, sir."

"Aren't you afraid of that?"

"I might as well be honest, sir."

Dr. Antonelli nodded, but without any noticeable lightening of his expression. "Why do you want to be a Programmer?"

"It's a responsible and exacting position as you said, sir. It's an important job and an exciting one. I like it and I think I can do it."

Dr. Antonelli put the papers away, and looked at George sourly. He said, "How do you know you like it? Because you think you'll be snapped up by some Grade A planet?"

George thought uneasily: He's trying to rattle you. Stay calm and stay frank.

He said, "I think a Programmer has a good chance, sir, but even if I were left on Earth, I know I'd like it." (That was true enough. I'm not lying, thought George.)

"All right, how do you know?"

He asked it as though he knew there was no decent answer and George almost smiled. He had one.

He said, "I've been reading about Programming, sir."

"You've been *what*?" Now the doctor looked genuinely astonished and George took pleasure in that.

"Reading about it, sir. I bought a book on the subject and I've been studying it."

"A book for Registered Programmers?"

"Yes, sir."

"But you couldn't understand it."

"Not at first. I got other books on mathematics and electronics. I made out all I could. I still don't know much, but I know enough to know I like it and to know I can make it." (Even his parents never found that secret cache of books or knew why he spent so much time in his own room or exactly what happened to the sleep he missed.)

The doctor pulled at the loose skin under his chin. "What was your idea in doing that, son?"

"I wanted to make sure I would be interested, sir."

"Surely you know that being interested means nothing. You could be devoured by a subject and if the physical make-up of your brain makes it more efficient for you to be something else, something else you will be. You know that, don't you?"

"I've been told that," said George cautiously.

"Well, believe it. It's true."

George said nothing.

Dr. Antonelli said, "Or do you believe that studying some subject will bend the brain cells in that direction, like that other theory that a pregnant woman need only listen to great music persistently to make a composer of her child. Do you believe that?"

George flushed. That had certainly been in his mind. By forcing his intellect constantly in the desired direction, he had felt sure that he would be getting a head start. Most of his confidence had rested on exactly that point.

"I never—" he began, and found no way of finishing.

"Well, it isn't true. Good Lord, youngster, your brain pattern is fixed at birth. It can be altered by a blow hard enough to damage the cells or by a burst blood vessel or by a tumour or by a major infection—each time, of course, for the worse. But it certainly can't be affected by your thinking special thoughts." He stared at George thoughtfully, then said, "Who told you to do this?"

George, now thoroughly disturbed, swallowed and said, "No one, doctor. My own idea."

"Who knew you were doing it after you started?"

"No one. Doctor, I meant to do no wrong."

"Who said anything about wrong? Useless is what I would say. Why did you keep it to yourself?"

"I-I thought they'd laugh at me." (He thought abruptly of a recent exchange with Trevelyan. George had very cautiously broached the thought as of something merely circulating distantly in the very outermost reaches of his mind, concerning the possibility of learning something by ladling it into the mind by hand, so to speak, in bits and pieces. Trevelyan had hooted, "George, you'll be tanning your own shoes next and weaving your own shirts." He had been thankful then for his policy of secrecy.)

Dr. Antonelli shoved the bits of film he had first looked at from position to position in morose thought. Then he said, "Let's get you analysed. This is getting me nowhere."

The wires went to George's temples. There was the buzzing. Again there came a sharp memory of ten years ago.

George's hands were clammy; his heart pounded. He should never have told the doctor about his secret reading.

It was his damned vanity, he told himself. He had wanted to show how enterprising he was, how full of initiative. Instead, he had showed himself superstitious and ignorant and aroused the hostility of the doctor. (He could tell the doctor hated him for a wise guy on the make.)

And now he had brought himself to such a state of nervousness, he was sure the analyser would show nothing that made sense.

He wasn't aware of the moment when the wires were removed from his temples. The sight of the doctor, staring at him thoughtfully, blinked into his consciousness and that was that; the wires were gone. George dragged himself together with a tearing effort. He had quite given up his ambition to be a Programmer. In the space of ten minutes, it had all gone.

He said dismally, "I suppose no?"

"No what?"

"No Programmer?"

The doctor rubbed his nose and said, "You get your clothes and whatever belongs to you and go to room 15-C. Your files will be waiting for you there. So will my report."

George said in complete surprise. "Have I been Educated already? I thought this was just to—"

Dr. Antonelli stared down at his desk. "It will all be explained to you. You do as I say."

George felt something like panic. What was it they couldn't tell him?

He wasn't fit for anything but Registered Labourer. They were going to prepare him for that; adjust him to it.

He was suddenly certain of it and he had to keep from screaming by main force.

He stumbled back to his place of waiting. Trevelyan was not there, a fact for which he would have been thankful if he had had enough self-possession to be meaningfully aware of his surroundings. Hardly anyone was left, in fact, and the few who were looked as though they might ask him questions were it not that they were too worn out by their tail-of-the-alphabet waiting to buck the fierce, hot look of anger and hate he cast at them.

What right had *they* to be technicians and he, himself, a Labourer? Labourer! He was *certain!*

He was led by a red-uniformed guide along the busy corridors lined with separate rooms each containing its groups, here two, there five: the Motor Mechanics, the Construction Engineers, the Agronomists—there were hundreds of specialized Professions and most of them would be represented in this small town by one or two anyway.

He hated them all just then: the Statisticians, the Accountants, the lesser breeds and the higher. He hated them because they owned their smug knowledge now, knew their fate, while he himself, empty still, had to face some kind of further red tape.

He reached 15-C, was ushered in and left in an empty room. For one moment, his spirits bounded. Surely, if this were the Labour classification room, there would be dozens of youngsters present.

A door sucked into its recess on the other side of a waist-high partition and an elderly, white-haired man stepped out. He smiled and showed even teeth that were obviously false, but his face was still ruddy and his voice had vigour.

He said, "Good evening, George. Our own sector has only one of you this time, I see."

"Only one?" said George blankly.

"Thousands over the Earth, of course. Thousands. You're not alone."

George felt exasperated. He said, "I don't understand, sir. What's my classification? What's happening?"

"Easy, son. You're all right. It could happen to anyone." He held out his hand and George took it mechanically. It was warm and it pressed George's hand firmly. "Sit down, son. I'm Sam Ellenford."

George nodded impatiently. "I want to know what's going on, sir."

"Of course. To begin with, you can't be a Computer Programmer, George. You've guessed that, I think."

"Yes, I have," said George bitterly. "What will I be, then?"

"That's the hard, part to explain, George." He paused, then said with careful distinctness, "Nothing."

"*What!*"

"Nothing!"

"But what does that mean? Why can't you assign me a profession?"

"We have no choice in the matter, George. It's the structure of your mind that decides that."

George went a sallow yellow. His eyes bulged. "There's something wrong with my mind?"

"There's *something* about it. As far as professional classification is concerned, I suppose you can call it wrong."

"But why?"

Ellenford shrugged. "I'm sure you know how Earth runs its Educational programme, George. Practically any human being can absorb practically any body of knowledge, but each individual brain pattern is better suited to receiving some types of knowledge than others. We try to match mind to knowledge as well as we can within the limits of the quota requirements for each profession."

George nodded. "Yes, I know."

"Every once in a while, George, we come up against a young man whose mind is not suited to receiving a superimposed knowledge of any sort."

"You mean I can't be Educated?"

"That is what I mean."

"But that's crazy. I'm intelligent. I can understand—" He looked helplessly about as though trying to find some way of proving that he had a functioning brain.

"Don't misunderstand me, please," said Ellenford gravely. "You're intelligent. There's no question about that. You're even above average in intelligence. Unfortunately that has nothing to do with whether the mind ought to be allowed to accept superimposed knowledge or not. In fact, it is almost always the intelligent person who comes here."

"You mean I can't even be a Registered Labourer?" babbled George. Suddenly even that was better than the blank that faced him. "What's there to know to be a Labourer?"

"Don't underestimate the Labourer, young man. There are dozens of subclassifications and each variety has its own corpus of fairly detailed knowledge. Do you think there's no skill in knowing the proper manner of lifting a weight? Besides, for the Labourer, we must select not only minds suited to it, but bodies as well. You're not the type, George, to last long as a Labourer."

George was conscious of his slight build. He said, "But I've never heard of anyone without a profession."

"There aren't many," conceded Ellenford. "And we protect them."

"Protect them?" George felt confusion and fright grow higher inside him.

"You're a ward of the planet, George. From the time you walked through that door, we've been in charge of you." And he smiled.

It was a fond smile. To George it seemed the smile of ownership; the smile of a grown man for a helpless child.

He said, "You mean, I'm going to be in prison?"

"Of course not. You will simply be with others of your kind."

Your kind. The words made a kind of thunder in George's ear.

Ellenford said, "You need special treatment. We'll take care of you."

To George's own horror, he burst into tears. Ellenford walked to the other end of the room and faced away as though in thought.

George fought to reduce the agonized weeping to sobs and then to strangle those. He thought of his father and mother, of his friends, of Trevelyan, of his own shame—

He said rebelliously, "I learned to read."

"Everyone with a whole mind can do that. We've never found exceptions. It is at this stage that we discover—exceptions. And when you learned to read, George, we were concerned about your mind pattern. Certain peculiarities were reported even then by the doctor in charge."

"Can't you try Educating me? You haven't even tried. I'm willing to take the risk."

"The law forbids us to do that, George. But look, it will not be bad. We will explain matters to your family so they will not be hurt. At the place to which you'll be taken, you'll be allowed privileges. We'll get you books and you can learn what you will."

"Dab knowledge in by hand," said George bitterly. "Shred by shred. Then, when I die I'll know enough to be a Registered Junior Office Boy, Paper-Clip Division."

"Yet I understand you've already been studying books."

George froze. He was struck devastatingly by sudden understanding. "That's it . . . "

"What is?"

"That fellow Antonelli. He's knifing me."

"No, George. You're quite wrong."

"Don't tell me that." George was in an ecstasy of fury. "That lousy bastard is selling me out because he thought I was a little too wise for him. I read books and tried to get a head start toward programming. Well, what do you want to square things? Money? You won't get it. I'm getting out of here and when I finish broadcasting this—"

He was screaming.

Ellenford shook his head and touched a contact.

Two men entered on catfeet and got on either side of George. They pinned his arms to his sides. One of them used an air-spray hypodermic in the hollow of his right elbow and the hypnotic entered his vein and had an almost immediate effect.

His screams cut off and his head fell forward. His knees buckled and only the men on either side kept him erect as he slept.

— 8 —

a modified
stratification system

In *The Rise of the Meritocracy,* Michael Young writes from the perspective of a historical-sociologist in the year 2033. He describes a series of social changes that occur in England during the period 1870–2033 and result in the evolution of a stratification system in which a person's socioeconomic status is determined solely by merit. In the new society a person's merit is determined by combining two factors, his intelligence quotient and the amount of effort he willingly expends in putting that potential intelligence to work (IQ plus Effort equals Merit). Young calls the social order that develops during this period a *meritocracy*—that is, a social order in which rule is based on merit.

The need to make more efficient use of the fixed sum of talent available to British society, it is proposed, was the impetus for the social reforms that generated the meritocracy. Young makes two interesting points about using the talent base available to a society and the relationship between efficient use of talent and social development. He first argues that there is some fixed amount of talent upon which a society may draw—that is, some proportion of a society's population is born with the intellectual capacity of geniuses, some proportion is substantially talented, some proportion is rather dull, and so on. If we assume that the proportion of persons born with each degree of talent remains relatively stable across generations, it follows that the amount of potential talent available to any society will be fixed. To the extent that a society is successful in identifying talented individuals and making the best use of their abilities, it can be said to be making efficient use of its fixed resources.

Consider a man with an IQ of 180 who is prevented from attending college by his family's inability to pay for his education. With his level of intelligence he will probably be successful no matter what career he pursues. He might, for example, amass a fortune in the used-car business or end up as the most intelligent carpenter in the history of the world. However, in terms of any contribution to the social, scientific, or technological development of his society, his talent is wasted. Clearly, it is advantageous for a society to identify those of its members who possess unusual abilities, to make available to them the education they need to do the kinds of work that only relatively few are capable of attempting, and to offer them rewards that will motivate them to work on those problems the solution of which will benefit the society in general. Isaac Newton's IQ has been estimated at 180; it would have been unfortunate if he had spent his life as a farmer.

Young's second point is that in any society "the rate of social progress depends on the degree to which power is matched with ability" (p. 14). The movement toward a meritocracy in Britain between the years 1870 and 2033 can be conceptualized as a social revolution that brought about a relatively high correlation of ability with power throughout the society. During this period, Young reports, reform measures were adapted under which the barriers separating lower-class children from first-rate educations were removed, and advantages traditionally available to the children of the affluent were stripped away. Young also traces the spread of the equalization of talent and power from educational institutions through many important sectors of society.

In Young's social history one major obstacle to revolutionizing the social system turns out to be the institutionalized association of status and power with age. One major problem in making more efficient use of the products of a modernized educational system is the slowness with which younger, better-trained men move into positions of power in government and industry. The problem in work situations is to change the belief used to defend the association of age and seniority with power: that many years of experience are positively related to successful performance in important positions. Young suggests that through the careful perpetuation of this myth, senior men in an organization are able to prevent their replacement by better-trained and more able men who occupy junior positions. He also suggests that younger men accept the myth because they realize that eventually *they* will be seniors in positions of power who need to protect themselves from their better-trained juniors.

The social reforms that Young outlines have tremendous positive effects on the society in which they occur. In many respects, the stratification system that emerges is very well suited to a social system in which economic development, technological improvement, and rapid movement toward an affluent society are desired.

the rise of the meritocracy

by Michael Young

At the beginning of my special period, 1914, the upper classes had their fair share of geniuses and morons, so did the workers; or, I should say, since a few brilliant and fortunate working men always climbed up to the top despite having been subordinate in society, the inferior classes contained *almost* as high a proportion of superior people as the upper classes themselves. Intelligence was distributed more or less at random. Each social class was, in ability, the miniature of society itself; the part the same as the whole. The fundamental change of the last century, which was fairly begun before 1963, is that intelligence has been redistributed between the classes, and the nature of the classes changed. The talented have been given the opportunity to rise to the level which accords with their capacities, and the lower classes consequently reserved for those who are also lower in ability. The part is no longer the same as the whole.

The rate of social progress depends upon the degree to which power is matched with intelligence. The Britain of a century ago squandered its resources by condemning even talented people to manual work; and blocked the efforts of members of the lower classes to obtain just recognition for their abilities. But Britain could not be a caste society if it was to survive as a great nation, great, that is, in comparison with others. To withstand international competition the country had to make better use of its human material, above all, of the talent which was even in England, one might say always and everywhere, too scarce. Schools and industries were progressively thrown open to merit, so that the clever children of each generation had opportunity for ascent. The proportion of people with I.Q.s over 130 could not be raised—the task was rather to prevent a fall —but the proportion of such people in work which called upon their full capacities was steadily raised. For every Rutherford there have in modern times been ten such magnates, for every Keynes two, and even Elgar has had a successor. Civilization does not depend upon the stolid mass, the *homme moyen sensuel,* but upon the creative minority, the innovator who with one stroke can save the labour of 10,000, the brilliant few who cannot look without wonder, the restless elite who have made mutation a social, as well as a biological, fact. The ranks of the scientists and technologists, the artists and the teachers, have been swelled, their education shaped to their high genetic destiny, their power for good increased. Progress is their triumph; the modern world their monument.

The fundamental reform that began the movement toward a meritocracy was the general improvement of the grammar schools (in the British educational system, publicly supported elementary and high schools).

The Hitler war transformed the social composition of the grammar schools. Full employment and larger wages, fostering higher aspirations, made lower-class parents able and anxious to get better education for their children, and the 1944 Act helped by making secondary schools free. The consequences were dramatic. In the 1930s only a minority of able low-class children had more than the most primitive education; twenty years later practically all clever children were installed in the seats of learning. A sociological study of the 1950s was able to report that 'in very many, if not in most, parts of the country the chances of children at a given level of ability entering grammar schools are no longer dependent on their social origins'.

However, it was one thing for able children from the lower classes to enter grammar schools, another for them to stay there. Here prosperity was a handicap. Even against the wishes of their parents, many scholars were tempted by high wages to leave school early—and flocks of them did so at the minimum age. Prosperity did not create the problem, but it accentuated one of long-standing. In every decade children matured physically earlier than before. Constant shortening of childhood in the biological and social sense and constant lengthening of childhood in the educational sense posed a dilemma which was only resolved in the long run by treating grammar-school children as adults.

The superior classes took for granted that their children should enjoy higher education; the difficulty was not to get the able to stay at school, but to get the stupid to leave and put up with the manual jobs for which their intelligence fitted them. In the lower classes the situation was reversed. The higher the wages that could be earned at a machine by the children of manual workers, the more dreary seemed the school-desk. No age is more acquisitive than adolescence. The remedy was clear; the State had to prevent children from suffering for their cleverness by giving them and their parents a privileged status within the lower classes. The first step was to pay very much larger maintenance allowances—later scaled in ratio to intelligence—for grammar-school children staying the full course. But this.was not enough. Inquiry showed that some irresponsible parents were spending the allowances on themselves, not on the children for whom they were intended. The obvious thing to do—eventually even to Ministers of Education—was to pay a learning wage direct to grammar-school pupils. At first it was equal to the average earnings of juveniles in ordinary industry; then the newly formed B.U.G.S.A. (the British Union of Grammar School Attenders) attacked the injustice of equality, rightly too, since the ability of the earner was usually so much lower than that of the pupil. In 1972 the government approved a learning wage on a sliding scale sixty per cent above industrial earnings. After that very few children left grammar schools prematurely for economic reasons. In modern times we could hardly imagine a grammar school without its weekly pay-day.

The universities paid wages to students (in the form of scholarships) long before grammar schools, but otherwise preserved some curious anachronisms of their own. Poorer parents were at a disadvantage in grammar schools, richer parents in universities. In the 1950s clever children of the middle-rich were deprived of grants because their parents were quite wrongly supposed to have enough money to pay, with the shocking result that some of them never got to university at all—surely a supreme example of the excesses of egalitarianism in its heyday! Closed 'scholarships' also gave pupils from certain public schools privileged entry to otherwise reputable colleges at Oxford and Cambridge; and in the middle of the century it was still not unknown for King's or Balliol to detect some special merit in sons whose fathers had been there before. Such barbaric practices were even excused in public from time to time by old-fashioned dons who declared it was better, educationally mind you, for the bright students to be mixed up with the dull. The dons had once again lost touch: the modern world no longer required the clever to mingle with the stupid, except when assigned to social intelligence work among the lower classes. When the die-hards died, universities came into line with national policy and selected all their entrants on merit properly tested in the examination-room. By 1972 public school-boys had either to compete openly with the Bradford Grammar School or seek "gringo admission" to South American universities. Few willingly incurred that stigma.

The learning wage and the universalization of university scholarships followed upon a change in the attitude of the State to spending on education, which itself reflected growing recognition that investment in brains is much more rewarding than investment in property. But politicians always wanted the impossible—the quick results education can never give. They kept tinkering with the top of the educational system instead of building securely from the bottom. They were as willing to spend on the universities as they were unwilling to spend on the primary schools. Politicians would not realize that the milk monitors were the future leaders of the nation. Faced with a shortage of engineers, the government said very well, spend more upon the engineering colleges. Of scientists, spend more upon the science faculties. Of technologists generally, then build more schools of technology. This was futile. For if the government attracted more promising youngsters into engineering, fewer were left behind for science. More for the civil service meant less for industry, more for laboratories less for teaching. The egalitarian doctrine that any man can be trained to substitute for any other was so deeply rooted that our ancestors only slowly came to appreciate the full significance of one simple fact: that all the professions were competing with each other for a limited supply of intelligence. It was not until well on into the last half of the century that the national scarcity of intellect became obvious to all those who had it. The government learned that the only way simultaneously to get more and better engineers, more and better physicists, more and better civil servants up to the limits set by Nature was to start with the three-year-olds, to ensure that from that age on no ability escaped through the net, and, most important, to make certain that the future physicists, psychologists, and the rest of the elite continuously had the best teaching they could get.

It did not matter so much about the defective, maladjusted, and delinquent upon whom up to 1972 England (as a sign of the times) spent more per head than upon the brilliant. It did not matter so much about the secondary modern schools. In an ideal world, not hampered by shortage of resources, the unfortunate could have large sums spent on them too. But it was not, has not been, nor ever will be, an ideal world. The choice was between priorities, and there was no doubt how the decision had to go. What mattered most were primary schools, where the pupils were being divided into the gifted and the ungifted; and, above all, the grammar schools where the gifted received their due. They had to have more generous endowments. And they got them.

From the moment that Sir Anthony Crosland was persuaded that the battle for national survival would be won or lost in the "A" streams all the way from nursery to grammar school, the money began to flow. Spending on education was still only 2.7 per cent of the gross national product in 1953; by 1963, 3.9 per cent; by 1982, after the "marvellous decade," it was 6.1 per cent. Most of the extra went on teachers. For more of them—it was still common in those grim middle years of the last century for one single teacher to have a mob of forty children in a class and who could she then be but a Joseph Lancaster! And for better ones. So far were teachers' salaries behind industry that in the early 1960s some grammar schools did not have a solitary physics teacher. At a time when the Atomic Energy Authority was clamouring for physicists! Many of the leading officials at the Ministry of Education and the Treasury, though they had read their Plato, had seemingly forgotten that none but the guardians themselves could be trusted to teach future guardians. Second-rate teachers, a second-rate elite: the meritocracy can never be better than its teachers. Things improved until at last the teachers attained their ideal of superiority of esteem. One of the wisest strokes of the marvellous decade was to put the salaries of science teachers on the same level as scientists in industry and all grammar-school teachers on the same level as their scientific colleagues. The schools could then attract good scientists; they got the very pick of other teachers.

The logic of the system can be portrayed in a simple table.

Distribution of Intelligence Between Types of Secondary School (1969)

Type of School	IQ Level of Pupils	No. of Pupils per Teacher	IQ Level of Teachers
E.S.N. (Educationally Subnormal) School	50-80	25	100-105
Secondary modern	81-115	20	105-110
Secondary grammar	116-180	10	135-180
Boarding grammar	125-180	8	135-180

The success of [educational] reforms depended upon continuous growth in the efficiency of selection methods. How pointless it would have been to set aside superior schools without the means of identifying the elect! Progress did not, of course, always proceed at the same pace on each of these complementary tasks. By and large, the seclusion of grammar schools went ahead more smoothly than selection of pupils. But the more widely recognized it was that better schools should be reserved for the more able, the greater the pressure upon the educational psychologists to improve their techniques. They responded. Necessity once again played its customary part.

Following 1944, there was a large increase in the demand for grammar school places without any corresponding expansion of supply. Competition was sharper; how were the winners to be picked? The value of intelligence tests as a guide to personnel selection in the Forces had been fully demonstrated during the war, and it was therefore natural to adopt the same kind of method for the peace-time purpose, especially in a stratified society prepared by habit of mind to recognize a hierarchy of intelligence as soon as it was pointed out. The results were remarkable: by 1950, merely a few years after the Act, most of the children in the country were taking these tests before they left their primary schools, and although older methods of examination were also used, high I.Q. was established as the chief qualification for entry to the elite. Educational psychology assumed a central place in pedagogy from which it was never later entirely dislodged. . . .

Progress was, as always, uneven, a period of stability being succeeded by a sudden jump forward. Man had to wait until 1989 for the leap of the century. Long before that the "cyberneticists" had realized that man would best understand his own brain when he could imitate it. As men became more like machines, machines became more like men, and when machines were built to mimic people, the ventriloquist at last understood himself. Modern mental capacity standards date from that year, a common unit of measurement being possible as soon as it was realized that a machine also can have its "intelligence" tested and scored as much as a human brain. "Pamela," Bird's pi-computer in the National Physiological

Laboratory, with its constant I.Q. of 100, became the recognized national standard, and all the questions in the examination papers were first put to her before being distributed to the schools and other centres.

Well before 1989, psychologists had succeeded in identifying the problems which had to be solved. They realized that the brain was no more separable than the sexual organs from the biochemical economy of the individual, and the individual no more separable than his lungs from the environment, social as well as physical, in which he lived. Many people with high potential intelligence were prevented from making use of it by anxiety due to psychic disturbances. Some had lower intelligence, others higher, when the environment was unfavourable. Hence the I.Q. berserkers with an I.Q. of 140 at some times and 90 at others, and not only when in love or before breakfast—an affliction from which some leading members of the Technicians Party are alleged to suffer. Psychologists tackled the task of bringing the actual nearer to the potential. Advances in therapy were a beneficent by-product of educational selection.

The Spens Committee said in 1938 that it is 'possible at an early age to predict with some degree of accuracy the ultimate level of a child's intellectual powers'. That is true now; it was not true then. No wonder resentment was aroused when the main tests were given once, at eleven! A person's performance at that one age decided whether he went to a grammar school. If he failed he could, in theory, get a second chance later on. In practice he seldom did. Late developers were too late. A boy or girl whose capacity flowered even as young as fourteen was lucky indeed to get a transfer from a modern to a grammar school. He was usually stuck with the stupid, and classed with them for the rest of his life. That was a cruel injustice for the individual and a shocking waste for society—so much so that in a small way comprehensive schools actually did some good by making it easier for people to swim from one stream to another. Poeple knew that in some people intelligence reached its height at twelve, in others it only came to full fruition at thirty—but they did not act as if they knew. As this truth was driven home, educators sought, with increasing success, to make intelligence assessment continuous throughout school life. I.Q.s were tested at seven, nine, eleven, thirteen, and fifteen, and at each stage a person whose score was higher than it had been previously was taken away from his inferiors and lodged with his equals. Yet the people whose ability developed only when they had left school escaped the net of selection altogether. Even in the 1980s, a man who suddenly came to his senses at the age of twenty-five had the greatest difficulty in securing proper recognition for his talents.

Here it is that the modern development of adult education has proved so vital. School came to last for life. By the end of the century the right of every person to be judged according to his ability was honoured in more than the breach. It was at last accepted that, as a matter of quite elementary justice, neither man nor child should be judged stupid until he was proved to be. The presumption was always of cleverness. So at *any* age *any* person became entitled, more than entitled, encouraged to apply every five years for re-test at a Regional Centre for Adult Education, and if his hopes were realized, then justice was invariably done. The copy of his National Intelligence card at H.Q. was destroyed, and a new card substituted containing the re-test score, so that no employer (or fiancee) who applied in the ordinary way for his I.Q. and aptitude scores would ever know about the lowlier status he had once had. It was also decided in the Courts that there was no obligation on anyone to put anything more than his current I.Q. in his *Who's Who* entry. A successful re-test was quite genuinely a fresh start.

No doubt this has led to difficulties. Some children have become excessively ambitious on behalf of their parents and have exerted too much pressure on them to strive for reclassification. Books on the care of parents have become too avidly studied. Some workmen have displayed jealousy when their elderly workmates have been sent away to university or gymnasium. But in the long interim period while methods of selection have been in process of improvement, the disadvantages have been far outweighed by the advantages. Now, of course, the psychologists have refined their methods to such a point that they can allow for most of the imponderables which delay development and forecast not only the I.Q. but the ages at which it will fructify. Exciting as the advance is to every scientifically-minded person, it has to be admitted that the discussions it has unloosed have been grist to the critics of the established order.

For a half-century schools were the target for reform, and quite rightly too, the achievement was brilliant. But the reformers were as always (perhaps had to be) too single-minded. They focused on schools to the exclusion of everything else, with the distressing result that for many years the efficiency with which manpower was used in industry lagged far behind the efficiency with which it was used in education. Our grandfathers did not fully realize that promotion of adults by merit, with all that it implied for industrial organization, was as necessary as promotion of children by merit. A society which acknowledged the claims of talent in the schools, but not in industry, was a house divided against itself. They did not fully understand that when castes were abolished, or rather converted into our modern kind of classes, there was still another category of people to circumvent—the class of old men. They did not fully appreciate that having the wrong man in a position of power merely because he was of superior age was every bit as wasteful as having the wrong man in a position of power merely because his parents were of a superior class. In an open society the few who are chosen out of the many who are called should be chosen on merit; age is as much an irrelevant criterion as birth.

Within the span of human history age has been the most enduring ruling class: once established, every aristocracy, every plutocracy, every bureaucracy has also been a gerontocracy; and even under democracy, government by the people, of the people, for the people, meant government by old people, of young people, for old people. In pre-industrial times the autocrat of the farm did not share his authority with any schoolmaster when his sons were young, and he retained his dominion over them when they were grown men, restrained only by the fear that if he irked his children overmuch his eventual fate might be that of King Lear. After the introduction of industry, fathers still did all they could to secure advancement for their own over other men's sons, but never over themselves, and to this end the solidarity of seniority made all fathers into a band of brothers. After the establishment of the new elite fathers could no longer gain privilege for their own sons, but they still continued to do all they could to ensure that other men's sons, however able, did not gain supremacy over themselves.

The meritocracy threatened, in short, to become yet another gerontocracy. Had this danger not been averted, the intellectual revolution would have been incomplete.

With education reformed, some people imagined they had matriculated to the millennium. The winners from school and university were inclined to lean upon their laurels. They entered, as if to a haven, professions still governed by a restrictive guild mentality. They accepted rule by the elders of their profession. They comforted themselves that they would continue to make the same steady progression through the age-grades as they had done at school, until in proper season they became sacred elders in their turn. It was only the relentless facts of the modern world which roused people from their torpor and sent competition to storm industry as well as school. In order to combine the best of England, our regime for children, with the best of America, their regime for adults, competition had to last for life.

Up till the Hitler war and for some years after, education determined prospects for promotion almost as much as it does in modern times. The manual worker who left school at the minimum age ordinarily remained a manual worker for life, the farthest he could go being to charge-hand and foreman, or, if he was lucky, by another route to general secretary of a trade union. The progress chaser taken away early from grammar school might climb to works manager, the payclerk to accountant. In most workplaces it was practically impossible to transfer from the ladder selected to start with according to the age at which the boy left school to another ladder which would take him higher; the foreman remained a foreman instead of beginning again on the ladder of works management, the accountant remained an accountant and was not in the running for director. Education decided the point of entry to industry, and the point of entry decided where one finished up.

This structure would have been well enough had the schools been rationalized. But when neither quality nor quantity of education were yet determined by intelligence, many clever children left school too soon, many stupid too late. A minority of more perceptive employers, following the civil service model which I have already described, set out to correct the injustices of the educational system and profit themselves at the same time. They gave their clever employees opportunities to rise within the firm in place of the opportunities they had missed at school. At its most complete (and to us most ridiculous), this practice made it possible for the tea-boy from the manual workers and the office-boy from the clerical to rise up to the board of directors. The first industries to be nationalized made some effort to do at least as well as the civil service. On British Railways a clerk could, for instance, if he moved off the lowest rungs when he was very young, transfer from the clerical ladder to one of the lower administrative posts. Electricity supply was more enlightened still.

Employees in the industry are considered to be on a common ladder, rising as openings occur, and in open competition according to experience and ability for the particular vacancy.

The statement is entertaining, practice not being quite like precept, because it shows how it was thought things should work. Some employers were so proud of their promotion schemes and ladder plans that they preferred to take on children straight from school and train them on the job than recruit university graduates. This attitude was regrettably common amongst leading executives who had not been to university themselves; there were of course many such "self-made men" in those distant days. The school's shame was the factory's pride.

The beginning of the second phase, which has lasted until the present day, is usually put in the 1950s. The 1944 Act took ten to twenty years before its effect was generally felt in industry. Not many employers were as quick as the High Master to see its significance.

No longer, said Sir Eric, *will industry or commerce be able to recruit at fifteen or sixteen boys who, as in the past, are of a quality to work their way up to positions of the highest managerial responsibility.*

In the fullness of time only the most dim-witted employers failed to learn this lesson. The evidence came through the door at the end of every term. Whatever opportunities there might be for secondary modern children to climb the industrial ladder, the hard fact was that fewer and fewer of them had the ability to do so. The grammar schools were retaining the "likely lads" who in previous generations might have entered industry as fifteen-year-olds, and the cleverest of the clever were going on to the university. Since the only ladder plan that mattered was the educational one, the captains of industry had to fit in with that. Either they could attract a share of grammar school graduates, and a seasoning from the university; or their businesses would perish. To sustain top management they had to recruit cadets from higher education, even if it meant incurring the hostility of the trade unions to introducing outsiders, particularly well-educated outsiders. The union leaders claimed, in the interests of their own members, that a man who had "come up the hard way" by working his passage upwards was inherently superior to others of purely academic education. But that was before education came to be held in the high respect it later enjoyed. The view was obvious nonsense—there was no harder way of coming up than the grammar school.

Awareness that shortage of talent was more serious than any other fanned the competition between business executives. According to a contemporary report only a few years after 1944—

One young man in his second year at university had already been offered a post at 750 [pounds] by one large company for when he should graduate, and was being assiduously courted by another vast company, whose managing director entertained him to lunch.

This was nothing to what happened later; eventually every forward-looking company had its teams of talent scouts combing the universities and grammar schools and most science masters and lecturers were offered retainers if they would regularly supply reports on promising students. Newspapers were filled with employers' appeals to scholars; college magazines grew larger and larger on the proceeds of advertisements. This hectic competition was sometimes unfair, as many trade associations alleged, and sometimes led to abuse. Some clever grammar school pupils were dissuaded from continuing into the sixth forms by offers of generous apprenticeships, and others from seeking admission to the university by glib scouts who promised them not only high salaries immediately but university education later at company expense. Retainers and assistance with research expenses were not the best way of augmenting science teachers' salaries.

The N.U.S. (National Union of Students) and B.U.G.S.A. had to protect their members and in 1969 the Ministry of Education and the Federation of British Industries drew up the Code of Fair Practice for Utilizing the Products of Higher Education. Although a worthy endeavour, this proved so ineffective in practice that government control over the allocation of intellectual resources became imperative. When it was instituted priorities could be generally enforced. Effective brain-power planning is not only necessary to end one of the kinds of competition between employers that is wasteful, but gives the government strategic power to control the whole economy.

Industry surrendered to teachers the function of selecting recruits for management with a good enough grace when it saw that surrender was essential to survival. From that time on most of those who at the ages of nineteen or twenty-three entered the higher reaches of industry, commerce, and the professions were the pick of their age-groups. Managerial cadets were chosen on merit through competitive selection in the schools. But there, in this transition period, free competition stopped. As soon as the newcomer arrived in factory or office, he no longer had the chance to pit his talents against all and sundry in the promotion stakes. He was no longer permitted, even after he had spent several years learning the business, to stand up in open competition with people much older than himself. While he was a *junior* man, whether he had the capacity of Henry Ford or Lord Nuffield it made no matter, he had to be content with being at best a *junior* executive. In all the most important jobs promotion was still by seniority, so much so that without exceptional luck even the best-educated could not hope to reach the top of the ladder until they were fifty or sixty. The story of the third and most recent phase is the story of the way in which the principle of seniority has gradually yielded to the principle of merit, and industry been modelled on the schools.

It is once again difficult for us to realize how strongly entrenched the old were in those days, especially in Britain. Status for age had once been linked with hereditary status, but it was far less easy to discredit. By the middle of last century it was extremely rare to hear anyone openly defending a hereditary system. Kinship connexions were no longer thought to confer merit on a man. But age was. The rights of the old did not have to be publicly acclaimed, they were so widely taken for granted. Age was accorded deference for no better reason than that, and people did not even have to acknowledge the existence of any dilemma when on the one hand they talked in favour of promotion by merit and on the other acted in favour of promotion by age. They resolved the dilemma before it was properly posed by enormously over-estimating the value of "experience" which was imagined to be the product purely of years. There was a mystique about it: people said, "Ah, yes, but he's got more experience," as though that was the last word. Respect for age was as much the rule of society as respect for the aristocracy from which it had grown.

Seniores priores—there is no stronger testament to its influence than the schools. They weakened their own progressive role by upholding the very principle with which they were fundamentally at loggerheads. Prefects were one of the most distinctive features of the old public schools. These prefects were older boys who exercised day-to-day government over their younger fellows, some of whom were selected as "fags" to perform the duties of servants. The maintenance of discipline was in large part the responsibility of the prefects, who had the power to secure obedience by beating any little boy who incurred their displeasure. The prefect system was unfortunately taken over by the grammar schools too. Consequently, the regard younger children always have for older was converted into an awe which often lasted for life. The old, by allowing the young to have authority when it was not a threat to themselves, helped to ensure that their own power would later go unchallenged. The abolition of prefects was an important reform which started in the "progressive" co-educational schools and later spread to the more orthodox.

I have no space to trace the subtle and individually infinitesimal changes which have combined to create a new spirit; all I can do is to pinpoint some of the counter-forces which have in the end proved too strong for the gerontocracy. I will deal briefly with each of them in turn.

Pressure from the young   No solid progress could be made until the young had generated more confidence in themselves. As long as they accepted the dominance of the old there was no hope of a shift in the distribution of power, any more than there had been any hope of change while the superiority of the higher classes in a hereditary system was recognized by the lower. The right of the old to power had first to be questioned as strenuously as the legitimacy of inheritance, and for the same reason. Inheritance was denounced for the simple reason that a developing industrial country in competition with others could no longer afford second-rate leaders; the needs of the economy reshaped society. This campaign was not called off just because one victory had been won, but was turned against the old. Members of every fresh generation revolted against their elders; youth of mettle to oppose the pretensions of age instead of siding with it for the sake of favours to come. Some cried destruction on the established order, some tried, more constructively, to remove the blocks to their own advancement. The most rebellious knew instinctively that the fastest progress occurs anywhere when the old have to surrender their power before their span of life is complete—the essence of every social revolution is the earlier transfer of authority from one generation to another; the wisest knew that the surest progress is made by the mouse, by nibbling at the establishment instead of by taking arms against it. The best policy was to criticize the worth of individual old people in an empirical manner rather than the class as a whole.

The young succeeded as much as they did in opposing private practice because they had the resources of the public culture to support them. They declared that youth was generally entitled, on the grounds of merit, to more preferment than it received. They were quite right. In any rapidly changing society the young are more at home than the old: it is easier for them to learn for the first time than for the old to unlearn, and learn again, for a second or third time, especially when nostalgia for their own youth makes the old disinclined even to try. This is more than ever true when the schools are progressing even more rapidly than their host society. Then children not only learn different things, attuned to the needs of their own day (particularly when the teachers are also young); they also learn more because standards are higher and methods of pedagogy better. Compare the boy who learns physics today with an elderly man who was at the same university in the eighties before Shag was even born. The change is so dramatic, it is not really the same subject at all. Given the same native ability, there is no doubt which of them should obtain an important post in the laboratories, say at H.Q. in Eugenics House. I say "given the same native ability"—but of course this is implausible. The content of higher education has not only advanced; methods of selecting those to benefit from it have improved at least as fast. Each ten-year age-cohort of the elite has up till recently had more innate capacity than the previous one; the university alumnus of 2000 more talent, as well as better training, than the alumnus of 1990; of 2010 more than of 2000. . . .

Improvement of merit-rating   Perhaps the greatest reason for the change in mental climate is that merit has become progressively more measurable. In the old days seniority had the splendid advantage of being an objective standard, even if it was irrelevant, whereas merit was still subjective even though relevant. Indeed, for a long time, "merit" was little more than a respectable disguise for nepotism. Fathers secured promotion for their relatives and friends, and pretended to themselves and to others they were doing nothing except give merit its due. But if they concealed their fault from themselves, others were not so easily deceived. The trade unions, in particular, were only too well aware of the pitfalls of selecting by "merit," when the father was his own judge and psychologist, and were justifiably suspicious that when outsiders were introduced into the line of promotion something less than justice had been done. They therefore stood by promotion by seniority, which was at least one better than vile nepotism. The world could see whether, according to this particular idea of fairness, right prevailed or not. If on any ladder, a man of thirty was given superiority over a man of forty (or rather a man with ten years' service preferred to a man with twenty), then all could see the miscarriage of justice.

   This vicious circle—the vagueness of merit leading to its rejection—was only broken when the means of selection employed in the schools were adapted for use in the economy. Intelligence tests and aptitude tests were objective, and a good deal more reliable than the older forms of examination which they supplemented. The first stage, as we have seen, was for the level of performance achieved in the tests (when taken together with the level of education with which the test results were correlated) to determine the level of entry into industry. Once people were ready, it was then but a step to extend the sway of the tests until the markings controlled promotion as well as selection. To begin with, employers had to submit candidates to their own house-tests; yet such was the suspicion in industrial relations at that time, their impartiality was distrusted just because they were the employer's responsibility. The atmosphere was much sweetened when the government established its chain of Regional Adult Education Centres and community centres as a common service to industry, and, after a very long and acrimonious debate, gave employers access to the results of intelligence tests from the Centres as well as the schools. Employers now have as close an interest as employees in the quinquennial revaluations at the regional centres, and many of them show their appreciation on the Prize Days of their factories.

One thing the regional centres could not do. They could not measure the qualities of character expressed in e1ort expended by an employee in the course of his work. Intelligence and e1ort together make up merit (I + E = M). The lazy genius is not one. Here employers have made their own contribution to the cause of progress. "Scientific management" pioneered by Taylor, the Galbraiths, and Bedaux has led to modern time and motion study, and this in its turn to the measurement of effort. The art of work measurement has become more of a science, with the consequence that wages can be assessed, and related to effort, in a more and more precise manner. I shall return to this subject in a later chapter. Dr. Roskill's great contribution was to show how the principle of work study could be applied to mental processes. After that the employer had by him a Roskill chart as well as the scores from the education centres, and if he chose wrongly withal, it was high time he had a re-test himself.

In Young's future history the social reforms bring about not only results that are expected—rapid economic growth and affluence—but also certain unanticipated consequences. The procedures that are developed to identify those members of society who can best profit from intensive education eventually permit selections to be made early in a person's life. Although a person may be retested and qualify for training anytime in his life, the procedures used to make the initial measurements are quite good, and very infrequently are men found to have been incorrectly prevented from obtaining an education and joining the *meritocratic elite.* The accurate and early identification of talent permits the separation of the population into two large classes, the meritocratic elite and the lower class, with virtually no reason for a member of the lower class to expect to move into the elite during adult life.

This great distinction between segments of the society, coupled with the near-zero rate of adult mobility, created the conditions necessary for members of each class to recognize a commonality of self interest based on similarity in social position. Since the elite controlled legitimate power in the society, they could increase their share of the society's goods and services relative to the proportion allocated to the lower class. Large numbers of lower-class men found themselves in a position in which the ideology justifying the existing division of goods and services within the society doomed them to poverty relative to the elite and offered no hope of upward mobility. According to Young, they responded to this by rejecting the ideology on which the allocation of rewards was based and developing an alternate value system. The new values that emerge are similar to those on which the economic organization of Bellamy's utopia is based (see Chapter 19). At the close of Young's book, rebellion is beginning.

—9—

conducting
efficient elections

Two criteria of pure democracy are that power rest with the people and that they be able to exercise it directly. The distinction between pure democracy and representative democracy is that in the representative form the populace selects representatives who exercise power on their behalf. One essential aspect of representative democracy is that the governed participate in the selection of those who carry out the business of government.

What, precisely, does it mean to participate in the selection of representatives? The concept of participation could take a number of different forms in practice and still result in a satisfactory set of procedures. In most societies, to participate in the selection of a representative means to vote. Usually, however, all members of a society do not vote for all the representatives who constitute the government. Therefore, it might be argued, each member of the populace is participating only in the selection of a small subset of those who govern.

The concept of participation in most societies usually extends only to the act of voting. If, however, a man votes for a losing candidate, he has still participated. One can imagine an alternative form of selection in which the man who is chosen to represent a group must be agreeable to every single member of the group. Although such a system might be unworkable for groups of any size, it has been used, and it is currently used, for instance, by Quaker meetings and by the College of Cardinals when it selects a pope. At one time (though probably no longer) the rations given to members of the College were systematically reduced over the period of their deliberations (sometimes several weeks). The theory was that if you set a task that requires the group to reach consensus and reduce their food supply to bread and water, one member is more likely to see merit in the proposals of another.

If we recognize that the major consideration in satisfying the definition of participation is that the electorate feel it has participated, a number of variations on our present method of choosing a government might be considered. For example, as long as representatives are chosen to represent geographic areas or units of population within geographic areas, as are United States senators and representatives, the argument could be made that a great many people are not being represented. If a number of people holding similar political opinions are to have a representative in Congress, they must constitute a majority in a geographic area. For instance, assume that in one state 55 percent of the population belongs to party *X* and 45 percent belongs to party *Y*. If each congressional district of the state were divided into the same proportions, and everybody voted along party lines, party *X* would win every congressional election and the members of party *Y* would have no representative of their choosing. If, however, the state's congressional seats were simply divided among parties on the basis of the proportion of the registered electorate that belonged to each party on election day, then all varieties of political opinion would be represented in the proportions in which they were held by the electorate.

Even without altering the relationship between the electorate and their representatives, numerous possibilities still appear for modifying the methods by which officials are selected and for determining the population's preference on issues to be decided. "Franchise" by Isaac Asimov, considers one such innovation. In many respects the electoral procedures used in Asimov's future society are extrapolations of practices now in their infancy.

"franchise"

by Isaac Asimov

Linda said, "Grandpa," and stood with her chin down and her hands behind her back until his newspaper lowered itself to the point where shaggy eyebrows and eyes, nested in fine wrinkles, showed themselves. It was Friday, October 31.

He said, "Yes?"

Linda came closer and put both her forearms on one of the old man's knees so that he had to discard his newspaper altogether.

She said, "Grandpa, did you really once vote?"

He said, "You heard me say I did, didn't you? Do you think I tell fibs?"

"N-no, but Mamma says everybody voted then."

"So they did."

"But how could they? How could *everybody* vote?"

Matthew stared at her solemnly, then lifted her and put her on his knee. He even moderated the tonal qualities of his voice. He said, "You see,

Linda, till about forty years ago, everybody always voted. Say we wanted to decide who was to be the new President of the United States. The Democrats and Republicans would both nominate someone, and everybody would say who they wanted. When Election Day was over, they would count how many people wanted the Democrat and how many wanted the Republican. Whoever had more votes was elected. You see?"

Linda nodded and said, "How did all the people know who to vote for? Did Multivac tell them?"

Matthew's eyebrows hunched down and he looked severe. "They just used their own judgment, girl."

She edged away from him, and he lowered his voice again, "I'm not angry at you, Linda. But, you see, sometimes it took all night to count what everyone said and people were impatient. So they invented special machines which could look at the first few votes and compare them with the votes from the same places in previous years. That way the machine could compute how the total vote would be and who would be elected. You see?"

She nodded. "Like Multivac."

"The first computers were much smaller than Multivac. But the machines grew bigger and they could tell how the election would go from fewer and fewer votes. Then, at last, they built Multivac and it can tell from just one voter."

Linda smiled at having reached a familiar part of the story and said, "That's nice."

Matthew frowned and said, "No, it's not nice. I don't want a machine telling me how I would have voted just because some joker in Milwaukee says he's against higher tariffs. Maybe I want to vote cock-eyed just for the pleasure of it. Maybe I don't want to vote. Maybe—"

But Linda had wriggled from his knee and was beating a retreat.

She met her mother at the door. Her mother, who was still wearing her coat and had not even had time to remove her hat, said breathlessly, "Run along, Linda. Don't get in Mother's way."

Then she said to Matthew, as she lifted her hat from her head and patted her hair back into place, "I've been at Agatha's."

Matthew stared at her censoriously and did not even dignify that piece of information with a grunt as he groped for his newspaper.

Sarah said, as she unbuttoned her coat, "Guess what she said?"

Matthew flattened out his newspaper for reading purposes with a sharp crackle and said, "Don't much care."

Sarah said, "Now, Father—" But she had no time for anger. The news had to be told and Matthew was the only recipient handy, so she went on, "Agatha's Joe is a policeman, you know, and he says a whole truckload of secret service men came into Bloomington last night."

"They're not after me."

"Don't you see, Father? Secret service agents, and its almost election time. In *Bloomington*."

"Maybe they're after a bank robber."

"There hasn't been a bank robbery in town in ages. . . . Father, you're hopeless."

She stalked away.

Nor did Norman Muller receive the news with noticeably greater excitement.

"Now, Sarah, how did Agatha's Joe know they were secret service agents?" he asked calmly. "They wouldn't go around with identification cards pasted on their foreheads."

But by next evening, with November a day old, she could say triumphantly, "It's just everyone in Bloomington that's waiting for someone local to be the voter. The Bloomington *News* as much as said so on video."

Norman stirred uneasily. He couldn't deny it, and his heart was sinking. If Bloomington was really to be hit by Multivac's lightning, it would mean newspapermen, video shows, tourists, all sorts of—strange upsets. Norman liked the quiet routine of his life, and the distant stir of politics was getting uncomfortably close.

He said, "It's all rumor. Nothing more."

"You wait and see, then. You just wait and see."

As things turned out, there was very little time to wait, for the doorbell rang insistently, and when Norman Muller opened it and said, "Yes?" a tall, grave-faced man said, "Are you Norman Muller?"

Norman said, "Yes," again, but in a strange dying voice. It was not difficult to see from the stranger's bearing that he was one carrying authority, and the nature of his errand suddenly became as inevitably obvious as it had, until the moment before, been unthinkably impossible.

The man presented credentials, stepped into the house, closed the door behind him and said ritualistically, "Mr. Norman Muller, it is necessary for me to inform you on the behalf of the President of the United States that you have been chosen to represent the American electorate on Tuesday, November 4, 2008."

Norman Muller managed, with difficulty, to walk unaided to his chair. He sat there, white-faced and almost insensible, while Sarah brought water, slapped his hands in panic and moaned to her husband between clenched teeth, "Don't be sick, Norman. *Don't* be sick. They'll pick someone else."

When Norman could manage to talk, he whispered, "I'm sorry, sir."

The secret service agent had removed his coat, unbuttoned his jacket and was sitting at ease on the couch.

"It's all right," he said, and the mark of officialdom seemed to have vanished with the formal announcement and leave him simply a large and rather friendly man. "This is the sixth time I've made the announcement and I've seen all kinds of reactions. Not one of them was the kind you see on the video. You know what I mean? A holy, dedicated look, and a character who says, 'It will be a great privilege to serve my country.' That sort of stuff." The agent laughed comfortingly.

Sarah's accompanying laugh held a trace of shrill hysteria.

The agent said, "Now you're going to have me with you for a while. My name is Phil Handley. I'd appreciate it if you call me Phil. Mr. Muller can't leave the house any more till Election Day. You'll have to inform the department store that he's sick, Mrs. Muller. You can go about your business for a while, but you'll have to agree not to say a word about this. Right, Mrs. Muller?"

Sarah nodded vigorously. "No, sir. Not a word."

"All right. But, Mrs. Muller," Handley looked grave, "we're not kidding now. Go out only if you must and you'll be followed when you do. I'm sorry but that's the way we must operate."

"Followed?"

"It won't be obvious. Don't worry. And it's only for two days till the formal announcement to the nation is made. Your daughter—"

"She's in bed," said Sarah hastily.

"Good. She'll have to be told I'm a relative or friend staying with the family. If she does find out the truth, she'll have to be kept in the house. Your father had better stay in the house in any case."

"He won't like that," said Sarah.

"Can't be helped. Now, since you have no others living with you—"

"You know all about us apparently," whispered Norman.

"Quite a bit," agreed Handley. "In any case, those are all my instructions to you for the moment. I'll try to co-operate as much as I can and be as little of a nuisance as possible. The government will pay for my maintenance so I won't be an expense to you. I'll be relieved each night by someone who will sit up in this room, so there will be no problem about sleeping accommodations. Now, Mr. Muller—"

"Sir?"

"You can call me Phil," said the agent again. "The purpose of the two-day preliminary before formal announcement is to get you used to your position. We prefer to have you face Multivac in as normal a state of mind as possible. Just relax and try to feel this is all in a day's work. Okay?"

"Okay," said Norman, and then shook his head violently. "But I don't want the responsibility. Why me?"

"All right," said Handley, "let's get that straight to begin with. Multivac weighs all sorts of known factors, billions of them. One factor isn't known, though, and won't be known for a long time. That's the reaction pattern of the human mind. All Americans are subjected to the molding pressure of what other Americans do and say, to the things that are done to him and the things he does to others. Any American can be brought to Multivac to have the bent of his mind surveyed. From that the bent of all other minds in the country can be estimated. Some Americans are better for the purpose than others at some given time, depending upon the happenings of that year. Multivac picked you as most representative this year. Not the smartest, or the strongest, or the luckiest, but just the most representative. Now we don't question Multivac, do we?"

"Couldn't it make a mistake?" asked Norman.

Sarah, who listened impatiently, interrupted to say, "Don't listen to him, sir. He's just nervous, you know. Actually, he's very well read and he always follows politics very closely."

Handley said, "Multivac makes the decisions, Mrs. Muller. It picked your husband."

"But does it know everything?" insisted Norman wildly. "Couldn't it have made a mistake?"

"Yes, it can. There's no point in not being frank. In 1993, a selected Voter died of a stroke two hours before it was time for him to be notified. Multivac didn't predict that; it couldn't. A Voter might be mentally unstable, morally unsuitable, or, for that matter, disloyal. Multivac can't know everything about everybody until he's fed all the data there is. That's why alternate selections are always held in readiness. I don't think we'll be using one this time. You're in good health, Mr. Muller, and you've been carefully investigated. You qualify."

Norman buried his face in his hands and sat motionless.

"By tomorrow morning, sir," said Sarah, "he'll be perfectly all right. He just has to get used to it, that's all."

"Of course," said Handley.

In the privacy of their bedchamber, Sarah Muller expressed herself in other and stronger fashion. The burden of her lecture was, "So get hold of yourself, Norman. You're trying to throw away the chance of a lifetime."

Norman whispered desperately, "It frightens me, Sarah. The whole thing."

"For goodness' sake, why? What's there to it but answering a question or two?"

"The responsibility is too great. I couldn't face it."

"What responsibility? There isn't any. Multivac picked you. It's Multivac's responsibility. Everyone knows that."

Norman sat up in bed in a sudden access of rebellion and anguish. "Everyone is *supposed* to know that. But they don't. They—"

"Lower your voice," hissed Sarah icily. "They'll hear you downtown."

"They don't," said Norman, declining quickly to a whisper. "When they talk about the Ridgely administration of 1988, do they say he won them over with pie-in-the-sky promises and racist baloney? No! They talk about the 'goddam MacComber vote,' as though Humphrey MacComber was the only man who had anything to do with it because he faced Multivac. I've said it myself—only now I think the poor guy was just a truck farmer who didn't ask to be picked. Why was it his fault more than anyone else's? Now his name is a curse."

"You're just being childish," said Sarah.

"I'm being sensible. I tell you, Sarah, I won't accept. They can't make me vote if I don't want to. I'll say I'm sick. I'll say—"

But Sarah had had enough. "Now you listen to me," she whispered in a cold fury. "You don't have only yourself to think about. You know what it means to be Voter of the Year. A presidential year at that. It means publicity and fame and, maybe, buckets of money—"

"And then I go back to being a clerk."

"You will *not.* You'll have a branch managership at the least if you have any brains at all, and you *will* have, because I'll tell you what to do. You control this kind of publicity if you play your cards right, and you can force Kennell Stores, Inc., into a tight contract *and* an escalator clause in connection with your salary *and* a decent pension plan."

"That's not the point in being Voter, Sarah."

"That will be your point. If you don't owe anything to yourself or to me—I'm not asking for myself—you owe something to Linda."

Norman groaned.

"Well, don't you?" snapped Sarah.

"Yes, dear," murmured Norman.

On November 3, the official announcement was made and it was too late for Norman to back out even if he had been able to find the courage to make the attempt.

Their house was sealed off. Secret service agents made their appearance in the open, blocking off all approach.

At first the telephone rang incessantly, but Philip Handley with an engagingly apologetic smile took all calls. Eventually, the exchange shunted all calls directly to the police station.

Norman imagined that, in that way, he was spared not only the bubbling (and envious) congratulations of friends, but also the egregious pressure of salesmen scenting a prospect and the designing smoothness of politicians from all over the nation. . . . Perhaps even death threats from the inevitable cranks.

Newspapers were forbidden to enter the house now in order to keep out weighted pressures, and television was gently but firmly disconnected, over Linda's loud protests.

Matthew growled and stayed in his room; Linda, after the first flurry of excitement, sulked and whined because she could not leave the house; Sarah divided her time between preparation of meals for the present and plans for the future; and Norman's depression lived and fed upon itself.

And the morning of Tuesday, November 4, 2008, came at last, and it was Election Day.

It was early breakfast, but only Norman Muller ate, and that mechanically. Even a shower and shave had not succeeded in either restoring him to reality or removing his own conviction that he was as grimy without as he felt grimy within.

Handley's friendly voice did its best to shed some normality over the gray and unfriendly dawn. (The weather prediction had been for a cloudy day with prospects of rain before noon.)

Handley said, "We'll keep this house insulated till Mr. Muller is back, but after that we'll be off your necks." The secret service agent was in full uniform now, including sidearms in heavily brassed holsters.

"You've been no trouble at all, Mr. Handley," simpered Sarah.

Norman drank through two cups of black coffee, wiped his lips with a napkin, stood up and said haggardly, "I'm ready."

Handley stood up, too. "Very well, sir. And thank you, Mrs. Muller, for your very kind hospitality."

The armored car purred down empty streets. They were empty even for that hour of the morning.

Handley indicated that and said, "They always shift traffic away from the line of drive ever since the attempted bombing that nearly ruined the Leverett Election of '92."

When the car stopped, Norman was helped out by the always polite Handley into an underground drive whose walls were lined with soldiers at attention.

He was led into a brightly lit room, in which three white-uniformed men greeted him smilingly.

Norman said sharply, "But this is the hospital."

"There's no significance to that," said Handley at once. "It's just that the hospital has the necessary facilities."

"Well, what do I do?"

Handley nodded. One of the three men in white advanced and said, "I'll take over now, agent."

Handley saluted in an offhand manner and left the room.

The man in white said, "Won't you sit down, Mr. Muller? I'm John Paulson, senior Computer. These are Samson Levine and Peter Dorogobuzh, my assistants."

Norman shook hands numbly all about. Paulson was a man of middle height with a soft face that seemed used to smiling and a very obvious toupee. He wore plastic-rimmed glasses of an old-fashioned cut, and he lit a cigarette as he talked. (Norman refused his offer of one.)

Paulson said, "In the first place, Mr. Muller, I want you to know we are in no hurry. We want you to stay with us all day if necessary, just so that you get used to your surroundings and get over any thought you might have that there is anything unusual in this, anything clinical, if you know what I mean."

"It's all right," said Norman. "I'd just as soon this were over."

"I understand your feelings. Still, we want you to know exactly what's going on. In the first place, Multivac isn't here."

"It isn't?" Somehow through all his depression, he had still looked forward to seeing Multivac. They said it was half a mile long and three stories high, that fifty technicians walked the corridors *within* its structure continuously. It was one of the wonders of the world.

Paulson smiled. "No. It's not portable, you know. It's located underground, in fact, and very few people know exactly where. You can understand that, since it is our greatest natural resource. Believe me, elections aren't the only things it's used for."

Norman thought he was being deliberately chatty and found himself intrigued all the same. "I thought I'd see it. I'd like to."

"I'm sure of that. But it takes a presidential order and even then it has to be countersigned by Security. However, we are plugged into Multivac right here by beam transmission. What Multivac says can be interpreted here and what we say is beamed directly to Multivac, so in a sense we're in its presence."

Norman looked about. The machines within the room were all meaningless to him.

"Now let me explain, Mr. Muller," Paulson went on. "Multivac already has most of the information it needs to decide all the elections, national, state and local. It needs only to check certain imponderable attitudes of mind and it will use you for that. We can't predict what questions it will ask, but they may not make much sense to you, or even to us. It may ask you how you feel about garbage disposal in your town; whether you favour central incinerators. It might ask you whether you have a doctor of your own or whether you make use of National Medicine, Inc. Do you understand?"

"Yes, sir."

"Whatever it asks, you answer in your own words in any way you please. If you feel you must explain quite a bit, do so. Talk an hour, if necessary."

"Yes, sir."

"Now, one more thing. We will have to make use of some simple devices which will automatically record your blood pressure, heartbeat, skin conductivity and brain-wave pattern while you speak. The machinery will seem formidable, but it's all absolutely painless. You won't even know it's going on."

The other two technicians were already busying themselves with smooth-gleaming apparatus on oiled wheels.

Norman said, "Is that to check on whether I'm lying or not?"

"Not at all, Mr. Muller. There's no question of lying. It's only a matter of emotional intensity. If the machine asks you your opinion of your child's school, you may say, 'I think it is overcrowded.' Those are only words. From the way your brain and heart and hormones and sweat glands work, Multivac can judge exactly how intensely you feel about the matter. It will understand your feelings better than you yourself."

"I never heard of this," said Norman.

"No, I'm sure you didn't. Most of the details of Multivac's workings are top secret. For instance, when you leave, you will be asked to sign a paper swearing that you will never reveal the nature of the questions you were asked, the nature of your responses, what was done, or how it was done. The less is known about the Multivac, the less chance of attempted outside pressures upon the men who service it." He smiled grimly. "Our lives are hard enough as it is."

Norman nodded. "I understand."

"And now would you like anything to eat or drink?"

"No. Nothing right now."

"Do you have any questions?"

Norman shook his head.

"Then you tell us when you're ready."

"I'm ready right now."

"You're certain?"

"Quite."

Paulson nodded, and raised his hand in a gesture to the others.

They advanced with their frightening equipment, and Norman Muller felt his breath come a little quicker as he watched.

The ordeal lasted nearly three hours, with one short break for coffee and an embarrassing session with a chamber pot. During all this time, Norman Muller remained encased in machinery. He was bone-weary at the close.

He thought sardonically that his promise to reveal nothing of what had passed would be an easy one to keep. Already the questions were a hazy mishmash in his mind.

Somehow he had thought Multivac would speak in a sepulchral, super-human voice, resonant and echoing, but that, after all, was just an idea he had from seeing too many television shows, he now decided. The truth was distressingly undramatic. The questions were slips of a kind of metallic foil patterned with numerous punctures. A second machine converted the pattern into words and Paulson read the words to Norman, then gave him the question and let him read it for himself.

Norman's answers were taken down by a recording machine, played back to Norman for confirmation, with emendations and added remarks also taken down. All that was fed into a pattern-making instrument and that, in turn, was radiated to Multivac.

The one question Norman could remember at the moment was an incongruously gossipy: "What do you think of the price of eggs?"

Now it was over, and gently they removed the electrodes from various portions of his body, unwrapped the pulsating band from his upper arm, moved the machinery away.

He stood up, drew a deep, shuddering breath and said, "Is that all? Am I through?"

"Not quite." Paulson hurried to him, smiling in reassuring fashion. "We'll have to ask you to stay another hour."

"Why?" asked Norman sharply.

"It will take that long for Multivac to weave its new data into the trillions of items it has. Thousands of elections are concerned, you know. It's very complicated. And it may be that an odd contest here or there, a comptrollership in Phoenix, Arizona, or some council seat in Wilkesboro, North Carolina, may be in doubt. In that case, Multivac may be compelled to ask you a deciding question or two."

"No," said Norman. "I won't go through this again."

"It probably won't happen," Paulson said soothingly. "It rarely does. But, just in case, you'll have to stay." A touch of steel, just a touch, entered his voice. "You have no choice, you know. You must."

Norman sat down wearily. He shrugged.

Paulson said, "We can't let you read a newspaper, but if you'd care for a murder mystery, or if you'd like to play chess, or if there's anything we can do for you to help pass the time, I wish you'd mention it."

"It's all right. I'll just wait."

They ushered him into a small room just next to the one in which he had been questioned. He let himself sink into a plastic-covered armchair and closed his eyes.

As well as he could, he must wait out this final hour.

He sat perfectly still and slowly the tension left him. His breathing grew less ragged and he could clasp his hands without being quite so conscious of the trembling of his fingers.

Maybe there would be no questions. Maybe it was all over.

If it *were* over, then the next thing would be torchlight processions and invitations to speak at all sorts of functions. The Voter of the Year!

He, Norman Muller, ordinary clerk of a small department store in

Bloomington, Indiana, who had neither been born great nor achieved greatness would be in the extraordinary position of having had greatness thrust upon him.

The historians would speak soberly of the Muller Election of 2008. That would be its name, the Muller Election.

The publicity, the better job, the flash flood of money that interested Sarah so much, occupied only a corner of his mind. It would all be welcome, of course. He couldn't refuse it. But at the moment something else was beginning to concern him.

A latent patriotism was stirring. After all, he was representing the entire electorate. He was the focal point for *them*. He was, in his own person, for this one day, all of America!

The door opened, snapping him to open-eyed attention. For a moment, his stomach constricted. Not more questions!

But Paulson was smiling. "That will be all, Mr. Muller."

"No more questions, sir?"

"None needed. Everything was quite clear-cut. You will be escorted back to your home and then you will be a private citizen once more. Or as much so as the public will allow."

"Thank you. Thank you." Norman flushed and said, "I wonder—who was elected?"

Paulson shook his head. "That will have to wait for the official announcement. The rules are quite strict. We can't even tell you. You understand."

"Of course. Yes." Norman felt embarrassed.

"Secret service will have the necessary papers for you to sign."

"Yes." Suddenly, Norman Muller felt proud. It was on him now in full strength. He was proud.

In this imperfect world, the sovereign citizens of the first and greatest Electronic Democracy had, through Norman Muller (through *him!*), exercised once again its free, untrammelled franchise.

— 10 —

from the secular
to the sacred

In his novel, *A Canticle for Leibowitz,* Walter M. Miller, Jr., chronicles the regeneration of a civilization following nuclear war. As in the Middle Ages, the one organized attempt to preserve knowledge is carried on by a religious institution. In Miller's future the only major institution to survive the war (the "Great Deluge," in the novel) is a mutated form of the Roman Catholic church.

After the holocaust, even the continued existence of religion itself is in doubt for a time. Most of the population who survive the Great Deluge are, for understandable reasons, violently opposed to preserving anything from the past. In the eyes of those who experienced the war, nothing is to be despised more greatly than a scientist or a scholar; even the merely literate are suspect. For these are the men whose knowledge and energies created the instruments necessary to the conduct of nuclear warfare.

The excerpts from Miller's novel treat two important events in the history of the Albertian Order of Leibowitz. The order takes responsibility for the preservation of some "pre-Deluge" scientific knowledge. This charge makes the Order, in fact, responsible for preserving a more important matter—the fundamentals of a belief system conducive to scientific and scholarly activity. Bits and pieces of "pre-Deluge" science—two pages of a text on Lebesque equations, half a blueprint for a gun turret—are hardly sufficient to lead to the rapid regeneration of a technological society sophisticated enough to destroy itself through nuclear war. The preservation of a system of beliefs supporting scientific investigation could, however, provide the social conditions necessary to the development of a technological society in a shorter time than it took originally.

The first excerpt tells how the Order of Leibowitz was founded. The history of the period is written in the style of a religious-historical account.

a canticle for

Leibowitz

by Walter M. Miller, Jr.

It was said that God, in order to test mankind which had become swelled with pride as in the time of Noah, had commanded the wise men of that age, among them the Blessed Leibowitz, to devise great engines of war such as had never before been upon the Earth, weapons of such might that they contained the very fires of Hell, and that God had suffered these magi to place the weapons in the hands of princes, and to say to each prince: "Only because the enemies have such a thing have we devised this for thee, in order that they may know that thou hast it also, and fear to strike. See to it, m'Lord, that thou fearest them as much as they shall now fear thee, that none may unleash this dread thing which we have wrought."

But the princes, putting the words of their wise men to naught, thought each to himself: If I but strike quickly enough, and in secret, I shall destroy those others in their sleep, and there will be none to fight back; the earth shall be mine.

Such was the folly of princes, and there followed the Flame Deluge.

Within weeks—some said days—it was ended, after the first unleashing of the hell-fire. Cities had become puddles of glass, surrounded by vast acreages of broken stone. While nations had vanished from the earth, the lands littered with bodies, both men and cattle, and all manner of beasts together with the birds of the air and all things that flew, all things that swam in the rivers, crept in the grass, or burrowed in holes; having sickened and perished, they covered the land, and yet where the demons of the Fallout covered the countryside, the bodies for a time would not decay, except in contact with fertile earth. The great clouds of wrath engulfed the forests and the fields, withering trees and causing the crops to die. There were great deserts where once life was, and in those places of the Earth where men still lived, all were sickened by the poisoned air, so that, while some escaped death, none was left untouched; and many died even in those lands where the weapons had not struck, because of the poisoned air.

In all parts of the world men fled from one place to other places, and there was a confusion of tongues. Much wrath was kindled against the princes and the servants of the princes and against the magi who had devised the weapons. Years passed, and yet the Earth was not cleansed. So it was clearly recorded in the Memorabilia.

From the confusion of tongues, the intermingling of the remnants of many nations, from fear, the hate was born. And the hate said: *Let us stone and disembowel and burn the ones who did this thing. Let us make a holocaust of those who wrought this crime, together with their hirelings and their wise men; burning, let them perish, and all their works, their names, and even their memories. Let us destroy them all, and teach our children that the world is new, that they may know nothing of the deeds that went before. Let us make a great simplification, and then the world shall begin again.*

So it was that, after the Deluge, the Fallout, the plagues, the madness, the confusion of tongues, the rage, there began the bloodletting of the Simplification, when remants of mankind had torn other remnants limb from limb, killing rulers, scientists, leaders, technicians, teachers, and whatever persons the leaders of the maddened mobs said deserved death for having helped to make the Earth what it had become. Nothing had been so hateful in the sight of these mobs as the man of learning, at first because they had served the princes, but then later because they refused to join in the bloodletting and tried to oppose the mobs, calling the crowds "bloodthirsty simpletons."

Joyfully the mobs accepted the name, took up the cry: *Simpletons! Yes, yes! I'm a simpleton! Are you a simpleton? We'll build a town and we'll name it Simple Town, because by then all the smart bastards that caused all this, they'll be dead! Simpletons! Let's go! This ought to show 'em! Anybody here not a simpleton? Get the bastard, if there is!*

To escape the fury of the simpleton packs, such learned people as still survived fled to any sanctuary that offered itself. When Holy Church received them, she vested them in monks' robes and tried to hide them in such monasteries and convents as had survived and could be reoccupied, for the religious were less despised by the mob except when they openly defied it and accepted martyrdom. Sometimes such sanctuary was effective, but more often it was not. Monasteries were invaded, records and sacred books were burned, refugees were seized and summarily hanged or burned. The Simplification had ceased to have plan or purpose soon after it began, and became an insane frenzy of mass murder and destruction such as can occur only when the last traces of social order are gone. The madness was transmitted to the children, taught as they were —not merely to forget—but to hate, and surges of mob fury recurred sporadically even through the fourth generation after the Deluge. By then, the fury was directed not against the learned, for there were none, but against the merely literate.

Isaac Edward Leibowitz, after a fruitless search for his wife, had fled to the Cistercians where he remained in hiding during the early post-Deluge years. After six years, he had gone once more to search for Emily or her grave, in the far southwest. There he had become convinced at last of her death, for death was unconditionally triumphant in that place. There in the desert he quietly made a vow. Then he went back to the Cistercians, took their habit, and after more years became a priest. He gathered a few companions about him and made some quiet proposals. After a few more years, the proposals filtered to "Rome," which was no longer Rome (which was no longer a city), having moved elsewhere, moved again, and still again—in less than two decades, after staying in one place for two millennia. Twelve years after the proposals were made, Father Isaac Edward Leibowitz had won permission from the Holy See to found a new community of religious, to be named after Albertus Magnus, teacher of Saint Thomas, and patron of men of science. Its task, unannounced, and at first only vaguely defined, was to preserve human history for the great-great-great-grandchildren of the children of the simpletons who wanted it destroyed. Its earliest habit was burlap rags and bindlestiffs—the uniform of the simpleton mob. Its members were either "bookleggers" or "memorizers," according to the tasks assigned. The bookleggers smuggled books to the southwest desert and buried them there in kegs. The memorizers committed to rote memory entire volumes of history, sacred writings, literature, and science, in case some unfortunate book smuggler was caught, tortured, and forced to reveal the location of the kegs. Meanwhile, other members of the new Order located a water hole about three days' journey from the book cache and began the building of a monastery. The project, aimed at saving a small remnant of human culture from the remnant of humanity who wanted it destroyed, was then underway.

Leibowitz, while taking his own turn at booklegging, was caught by a simpleton mob; a turncoat technician, whom the priest swiftly forgave, identified him as not only a man of learning, but also a specialist in the weapons field. Hooded in burlap, he was martyred forthwith, by strangulation with a hangman's noose not tied for neck-breaking, at the same time being roasted alive—thus settling a dispute in the crowd concerning the method of execution.

The memorizers were few, their memories limited.

Some of the book kegs were found and burned, as well as several other bookleggers. The monastery itself was attacked thrice before the madness subsided.

From the vast store of human knowledge, only a few kegs of original books and a pitiful collection of hand-copied texts, rewritten from memory, had survived in the possession of the Order by the time the madness had ended.

Now, after six centuries of darkness, the monks still preserved this Memorabilia, studied it, copied and recopied it, and patiently waited. At the beginning, in the time of Leibowitz, it had been hoped—and even anticipated as probable—that the fourth or fifth generation would begin to want its heritage back. But the monks of the earliest days had not counted on the human ability to generate a new cultural inheritance in a couple of generations if an old one is utterly destroyed, to generate it by virtue of lawgivers and prophets, geniuses or maniacs; through a Moses, or through a Hitler, or an ignorant but tyrannical grandfather, a cultural inheritance may be acquired between dusk and dawn, and many have been so acquired. But the new "culture" was an inheritance of darkness, wherein "simpleton" meant the same thing as "citizen" meant the same thing as "slave." The monks waited. It mattered not at all to them that the knowledge they saved was useless, that much of it was not really knowledge now, was as inscrutable to the monks in some instances as it would be to an illiterate wild-boy from the hills; this knowledge was empty of content, its subject matter long since gone. Still, such knowledge had a symbolic structure that was peculiar to itself, and at least the symbol interplay could be observed. To observe the way a knowledge-system is knit together is to learn at least a minimum knowledge-of-knowledge, until someday—someday, or some century—an Integrator would come, and things would be fitted together again. So time mattered not at all. The Memorabilia was there, and it was given to them by duty to preserve, and preserve it they would if the darkness in the world lasted ten more centuries, or even ten thousand years, for they, though born in that darkest of ages, were still the very bookleggers and memorizers of the Beatus Leibowitz; and when they wandered abroad from their abbey, each of them, the professed of the Order—whether stable-hand or Lord Abbot—carried as part of his habit a book, usually a Breviary these days, tied up in a bindlestiff.

About 600 years after the founding of the order, the question of canonizing Liebowitz is being considered by the church. The major stumbling block to his elevation is that available information is inadequate to determine when Leibowitz' wife died; he cannot be canonized unless it can be proved that his wife had died before he took vows.

At the start of this excerpt, Brother Francis, a novice performing a vigil in the desert near the abbey, has just discovered an opening in the ground. To understand his reactions to his discoveries, we must remember that knowledge of "pre-Deluge" America is at best vague; no written records survive, and for the first few generations after the war "pre-Deluge" science and history were actively suppressed. To complicate matters further, the war has come to be viewed in terms of a set of religious beliefs and to be interpreted as punishment for the sins of civilization. Keeping these facts in mind, consider how some remnants of America *circa* 1970 might be understood by a man attempting to integrate them with a set of vague and distorted images of the past and an interpretation of history that is bound up with a well established set of religious beliefs.

A dust column which had plumed up from the site of the cave-in was tapering away on the breeze. He hoped someone would see it from the abbey's watchtowers and come to investigate. At his feet, a square opening yawned in the earth, where one flank of the mound had collapsed into the pit below. Stairs led downward, but only the top steps remained unburied by the avalanche which had paused for six centuries in mid-fall to await the assistance of Brother Francis before completing its roaring descent.

On one wall of the stair well a half-buried sign remained legible. Mustering his modest command of pre-Deluge English, he whispered the words haltingly:

> FALLOUT SURVIVAL SHELTER
> *Maximum Occupancy: 15*
> Provision limitations, single occupant: 180 days; divide by actual number of occupants. Upon entering shelter, see that First Hatch is securely locked and sealed, that the intruder shields are electrified to repel contaminated persons attempting entry, that the warning lights are ON outside the enclosure. . . .

The rest was buried, but first word was enough for Francis. He had never seen a "Fallout," and he hoped he'd never see one. A consistent description of the monster had not survived, but Francis had heard the legends. He crossed himself and backed away from the hole. Tradition told that the Beatus Leibowitz himself had encountered a Fallout, and had been possessed by it for many months before the exorcism which accompanied his Baptism drove the fiend away.

Brother Francis visualized a Fallout as half-salamander, because, according to tradition, the thing was born in the Flame Deluge, and as half-incubus who despoiled virgins in their sleep, for, were not the monsters of the world still called "children of the Fallout"? That the demon was capable of inflicting all the woes which descended upon Job was recorded fact, if not an article of creed.

The novice stared at the sign in dismay. Its meaning was plain enough. He had unwittingly broken into the abode (deserted, he prayed) of not just one, but fifteen of the dreadful beings! He groped for his phial of holy water. . . .

Brother Francis lowered himself gingerly into the stair well of the ancient Fallout Shelter, armed as he was only with holy water and an improvised torch lighted from the banked embers of last night's fire. He had waited more than an hour for someone from the abbey to come investigate the dust plume. No one had come.

To abandon his vocational vigil even briefly, unless seriously ill or un-less ordered to return to the abbey, would be regarded as an *ipso facto* renunciation of his claim of a true vocation to life as a monk of the Albertian Order of Leibowitz. Brother Francis would have preferred death. He was faced, therefore, with the choice of investigating the fear-some pit before sunset, or of spending the night in his burrow in ignorance of whatever might lurk in the shelter and might reawaken to prowl in darkness. . . .

The debris which had crashed down into the shelter formed a hill with its crest near the head of the stairs, and there was only a narrow squeeze-way between the rocks and the ceiling. He went through it feet first and found himself forced to continue feet first, because of the steepness of the slope. Thus confronting the Unknown face-to-backside, he groped for footholds in the loose heap of broken stone and gradually worked his way downward. Occasionally, when his torch flickered low, he paused to tilt its flame downward, letting the fire spread further along the wood; during such pauses, he tried to appraise the danger about him and below. There was little to be seen. He was in an underground room, but at least one third of its volume was filled by the mound of debris that had fallen through the stair well. The cascade of stone had covered all the floor, crushed several pieces of furniture that he could see, and perhaps had completely buried others. He saw battered metal lockers leaning awry, waist-deep in rubble. At the far end of the room was a metal door, hinged to swing toward him, and tightly sealed by the avalanche. Still legible in flaking paint on the door were the stenciled letters:

INNER HATCH
SEALED ENVIRONMENT

Evidently the room into which he was descending was only an ante-chamber. But whatever lay beyond "Inner Hatch" was sealed there by several tons of rock against the door. Its enviroment was "Sealed" indeed, unless it had another exit.

Having made his way to the foot of the slope, and after assuring himself that the antechamber contained no obvious menace, the novice went cautiously to inspect the metal door at closer range by torchlight. Printed under the stenciled letters of "Inner Hatch" was a smaller rust-streaked sign:

WARNING: This hatch must not be sealed before all personnel have been admitted, or before all steps of safety procedure prescribed by Technical Manual CD-Bu-83A have been accomplished. When Hatch is sealed, air within shelter will be pressurized 2.0 p.s.i. above ambient barometric level to minimize inward diffusion. Once sealed, the hatch will be automatically unlocked by the servomonitor system when, but not before, any of the following conditions prevail: (1) when the exterior radiation count falls below the danger level, (2) when the air and water repurification system fails, (3) when the food supply is exhausted, (4) when the internal power supply fails. See CD-Bu-83A for further instructions.

Brother Francis found himself slightly confused by the Warning, but he intended to heed it by not touching the door at all. The miraculous contraptions of the ancients were not to be carelessly tampered with, as many a dead excavator-of-the-past had testified with his dying gasp.

Brother Francis noticed that the debris which had been lying in the antechamber for centuries was darker in color and rougher in texture than the debris which had weathered under the desert sun and in the sandy wind before today's cave-in. One could tell by a glance at the stones that Inner Hatch had been blocked not by today's rockslide but by one more ancient than the abbey itself. If Fallout Shelter's Sealed Environment contained a Fallout, the demon had obviously not opened Inner Hatch since the time of the Flame Deluge, before the Simplification. And, if it had been sealed beyond the metal door for so many centuries, there was small reason, Francis told himself to fear that it might come bursting through the hatch today.

His torch burned low. Having found a splintered chair leg, he set it ablaze with his waning flame, then began gathering bits of broken furniture with which to build a dependable fire, meanwhile pondering the meaning of that ancient sign: *Fallout Survival Shelter.*

As Brother Francis readily admitted, his mastery of pre-Deluge English was far from masterful yet. The way nouns could sometimes modify other nouns in that tongue had always been one of his weak points. In Latin, as in most simple dialects of the region, a construction like *servus puer* meant about the same thing as *puer servus,* and even in English *slave boy* meant *boy slave.* But there the similarity ended. He had finally learned that *house cat* did not mean *cat house,* and that a dative of purpose or possession, as in *mihi amicus,* was somehow conveyed by *dog food* or *sentry box* even without inflection. But what of a triple appositive like *fallout survival shelter?* Brother Francis shook his head. The Warning on Inner Hatch mentioned food, water, and air, and yet surely these were not necessities for the fiends of Hell. At times, the novice found pre-Deluge English more perplexing than either Intermediate Angelology or Saint Leslie's theological calculus.

He built his fire on the slope of the rubble pile, where it could brighten the darker crannies of the antechamber. Then he went to explore whatever might remain uncovered by debris. The ruins above ground had been reduced to archaeological ambiguity by generations of scavengers, but this underground ruin had been touched by no hand but the hand of impersonal disaster. The place seemed haunted by the presences of another age. A skull, lying among the rocks in a darker corner, still retained a gold tooth in its grin—clear evidence that the shelter had never been invaded by wanderers. The gold incisor flickered when the fire danced high.

More than once in the desert had Brother Francis encountered, near some parched arroyo, a small heap of human bones, picked clean and whitening in the sun. He was not especially squeamish, and one expected such things. He was, therefore, not startled when he first noticed the skull in the corner of the antechamber, but the flicker of gold in its grin kept catching his eye while he pried at the doors (locked or stuck) of the rusty lockers and tugged at the drawers (also stuck) of a battered metal desk. The desk might prove to be a priceless find, if it contained documents or a small book or two that had survived the angry bonfires of the Age of Simplification. While he kept trying to open the drawers, the fire burned low; he fancied that the skull began emitting a faint glow of its own. Such a phenomenon was not especially uncommon, but in the gloomy crypt, Brother Francis found it somehow most disturbing. He gathered more wood for the fire, returned to jerk and tug at the desk, and tried to ignore the skull's flickering grin. While a little wary yet of lurking Fallouts, Francis had sufficiently recovered from his initial fright to realize that the shelter, notably the desk and the lockers, might well be teeming with rich relics of an age which the world had, for the most part, deliberately chosen to forget.

Providence had bestowed a blessing here. To find a bit of the past which had escaped both the bonfires and the looting scavengers was a rare stroke of luck these days. There was, however, always a risk involved. Monastic excavators, alert for ancient treasures, had been known to emerge from a hole in the ground, triumphantly carrying a strange cylindrical artifact, and then—while cleaning it or trying to ascertain its purpose—press the wrong button or twist the wrong knob, thereby ending the matter without benefit of clergy. Only eighty years ago the Venerable Boedullus had written with obvious delight to his Lord Abbot that his small expedition had uncovered the remains of, in his own words, "the site of an intercontinental launching pad, complete with several fascinating subterranean storage tanks." No one at the abbey ever knew what the Venerable Boedullus meant by "intercontinental launching pad," but the Lord Abbot who had reigned at that time sternly decreed that monastic antiquarians must, on pain of excommunication, avoid such "pads" thenceforth. For his letter to the abbot was the last that anyone ever saw of the Venerable Boedullus, his party, his "launching pad" site, and the small village which had grown up over that site; an interesting lake now graced the landscape where the village had been, thanks to some shepherds who diverted the course of a creek and caused it to flow into the crater to store water for their flocks in time of drought. A traveler who had come from that direction about a decade ago reported excellent fishing in that lake, but the shepherds thereabouts regarded the fish as the souls of the departed villagers and excavators; they refused to fish there because of Bo'dollos, the giant catfish that brooded in the deep.

   . . . nor shall any other excavation be initiated which does not have as its primary purpose the augmentation of the Memorabilia," the Lord Ab-

bot's decree had added—meaning that Brother Francis should search the shelter only for books and papers, not tampering with interesting hardware.

The gold-capped tooth kept winking and glittering at the corner of his eye while Brother Francis heaved and strained at the desk drawers. The drawers refused to budge. He gave the desk a final kick and turned to glare impatiently at the skull: *Why don't you grin at something else for a change?*

The grin remained. The gold-toothed residuum lay with its head pillowed between a rock and a rusty metal box. Quitting the desk, the novice picked his way across the debris at last for a closer inspection of the mortal remains. Clearly, the person had died on the spot, struck down by the torrent of stones and half buried by the debris. Only the skull and the bones of one leg had not been covered. The femur was broken, the back of the skull was crushed.

Brother Francis breathed a prayer for the departed, then very gently lifted the skull from its resting place and turned it around so that it grinned toward the wall. Then his eye fell on the rusty box. . . .

Minutes later, seated on a cracked foundation slab, he began removing the tidbits of metal and glass that filled the trays he found in the box. Most of them were small tubular things with a wire whisker at each end of each tube. These, he had seen before. The abbey's small museum had a few of them, of various size, shape and color. Once he had seen a shaman of the hill-pagan people wearing a string of them as a ceremonial necklace. The hill people thought of them as "parts of the body of the god"—of the fabled *Machina analytica,* hailed as the wisest of their gods. By swallowing one of them, a shaman could acquire "Infallibility," they said. He certainly acquired Indisputability that way, among his own people—unless he swallowed one of the poison kind. The similar tidbits in the museum were connected together too—not in the form of a necklace, but as a complex and rather disorderly maze in the bottom of a small metal box, exhibited as: "Radio Chassis: Application Uncertain."

Inside the lid of the carrying case, a note had been glued; the glue had powdered, the ink had faded, and the paper was so darkened by rusty stains that even good handwriting would have been hard enough to read, but this was written in a hasty scrawl. He studied it intermittently while emptying the trays. It seemed to be English, of a sort, but half an hour passed before he deciphered most of the message:

> Carl—
>
>   Must grab plane for *[undecipherable]* in twenty minutes. For God's sake, keep Em there till we know if we're at war. Please! try to get her on the alternate list for the shelter. Can't get her a seat my plane. Don't tell her why I sent her over with this box of junk, but try to keep her there till we know *[undecipherable]* at worst, one of the alternates not show.
>
> *I.E.L.*

P.S. I put the seal on the lock and put TOP SECRET on the lid just to keep
Em from looking inside. First tool box I happened to grab. Shove it in my
locker or something.

The note seemed hasty gibberish to Brother Francis, who was at the
moment too excited to concentrate on any single item more than the rest.
After a final sneer at the note-writer's hasty scrawl, he began the task of
removing the tray-racks to get at the papers in the bottom of the box. The
trays were mounted on a swinging linkage which was obviously meant to
swing the trays out of the box in stair-step array, but the pins were rusted
fast, and Francis found it necessary to pry them out with a short steel tool
from one of the tray compartments.

When Brother Francis had removed the last tray, he touched the papers
reverently: only a handful of folded documents here, and yet a treasure;
for they had escaped the angry flames of the Simplification, wherein even
sacred writings had curled, blackened, and withered into smoke while
ignorant mobs howled and hailed it a triumph. He handled the papers as
one might handle holy things, shielding them from the wind with his
habit, for all were brittle and cracked from age. There was a sheaf of
rough sketches and diagrams. There were hand-scribbled notes, two large
folded papers, and a small book entitled *Memo.*

First he examined the jotted notes. They were scrawled by the same
hand that had written the note glued to the lid, and the penmanship was
no less abominable. *Pound pastrami,* said one note, *can kraut, six bagels
—bring home for Emma.* Another reminded: *Remember—pick up Form
1040, Uncle Revenue.* Another was only a column of figures with a circled
total from which a second amount was subtracted and finally a percentage
taken, followed by the word *damn!* Brother Francis checked the figures:
he could find no fault with the abominable penman's arithmetic, at least,
although he could deduce nothing about what the quantities might represent.

Memo, he handled with special reverence, because its title was sugges-
tive of "Memorabilia." Before opening it, he crossed himself and murmured the Blessing of Texts. But the small book proved a disappointment.
He had expected printed matter, but found only a hand-written list of
names, places, numbers and dates. The dates ranged throught the latter
part of the fifth decade, and earlier part of the sixth decade, twentieth
century. Again it was affirmed!—the contents of the shelter came from the
twilight period of the Age of Enlightenment. An important discovery
indeed. . . .

He turned to a second folded document; its creases were so brittle that
he dared inspect only a little of it, by parting the folds slightly and peering
between them.

A diagram it seemed, but—a diagram of white lines on dark paper!

Again he felt the thrill of discovery. It was clearly a blue-print!—and there was not a single original blueprint left at the abbey, but only inked facsimiles of several such prints. Never before had Francis seen an original, although he had seen enough hand-painted reproductions to recognize it as a blueprint, which, while stained and faded, remained legible after so many centuries because of the total darkness and low humidity in the shelter. He turned the document over—and felt brief fury. What idiot had desecrated the priceless paper? Someone had sketched absent-minded geometrical figures and childish cartoon faces all over the back. What thoughtless vandal—

The anger passed after a moment's reflection. At the time of the deed, blueprints had probably been as common as weeds, and the owner of the box the probable culprit. He shielded the print from the sun with his own shadow while trying to unfold it further. In the lower right-hand corner was a printed rectangle containing, in simple block letters, various titles, dates, "patent numbers," reference numbers, and names. His eye traveled down the list until it encountered: "CIRCUIT DESIGN BY: Leibowitz, I.E."

He closed his eyes tightly and shook his head until it seemed to rattle. Then he looked again. There it was, quite plainly:

CIRCUIT DESIGN BY: Leibowitz, I.E.

He flipped the paper over again. Among the geometric figures and childish sketches, clearly stamped in purple ink, was the form:

THIS FILE COPY TO:

Supv _____

Pint _____

Dsgn *J. E. Leibowitz*

Engr _____

Army _____

The name was written in a clear feminine hand, not in the hasty scrawl of the other notes. He looked again at the initialed signature of the note in the lid of the box: I.E.L.—and again at "CIRCUIT DESIGN BY . . . " And the same initials appeared elsewhere throughout the notes.

There had been argument, all highly conjectural, about whether the beatified founder of the Order, if finally canonized, should be addressed as Saint Isaac or as Saint Edward. Some even favored Saint Leibowitz as the proper address, since the Beatus had, until the present, been referred to by his surname.

"Beate Leibowitz, ora pro me!" whispered Brother Francis. His hands were trembling so violently that they threatened to ruin the brittle documents.

He had uncovered relics of the Saint.

Of course, New Rome had not yet proclaimed that Leibowitz was a saint, but Brother Francis was so convinced of it that he made bold to add: *"Sancte Leibowitz, ora pro me!"*

Brother Francis wasted no idle logic in leaping to his immediate conclusion: he had just been granted a token of his vocation by Heaven itself. He had found what he had been sent into the desert to find, as Brother Francis saw it. He was called to be a professed monk of the Order.

Forgetting his abbot's stern warning against expecting a vocation to come in any spectacular or miraculous form, the novice knelt in the sand to pray his thanks and to offer a few decades of the rosary for the intentions of the old pilgrim who had pointed out the rock leading to the shelter. *May you find your Voice soon, boy,* the wanderer had said. Not until now did the novice suspect that the pilgrim meant Voice with a capital V.

"Ut solius tuae voluntatis mihi cupidus sim, et vocationis tuae conscius, si digneris me vocare . . . "

— FOUNDATIONS —
social change

part III

— 11 —

population,
roles,
and civilization

If an aggregate of people has minimal social organization, it is possible to imagine a state of affairs in which each unit—for example, a small family or an individual —is self-sufficient in that if all other units were to disappear, life style would be relatively unchanged. The less units depend upon one another, the less a single unit is disrupted if all the others disappear. Insofar as division of labor exists such that each unit is responsible for a certain subset of the activities necessary to sustain the aggregate, a potential for disruption exists. If even a small proportion of the population were eliminated, those remaining would have to make major adjustments. The advantages of organizing an aggregate of individuals in an interdependent manner are, however, substantially greater than the advantages of a system in which each unit provides itself with all the commodities necessary to its existence. The advantages of basing a social organization on the division of labor lie primarily in the greater efficiency with which each essential task can be carried out by specialists in that job.

A relationship probably exists between a society's level of technological sophistication, the diversity and number of specialized roles that must be performed at that level of development, and the size of the population. As long as a society requires men of certain intellectual abilities and special skills to fill the roles that maintain it at a given technical level, it will require a population of some minimum size in order to produce people with the intellectual ability necessary to complete training for these roles. The size of the minimum population base might be affected in several ways. If, for example, automation or reliance on devices such as computers made it possible to reduce the number of necessary roles, then a smaller population could provide the required number of talented people. An engineer who has access to a computer can probably accomplish as much as five engineers who don't have computers. If the average level of ability in a society could be raised or available talent used more efficiently, then a smaller population could provide the men required to maintain a given level of technology.

If we accept the premise that a relationship exists between technological level, diversity and number of required roles, and population size, we may pose some questions: What are the effects of having a population base larger than is required to maintain a certain level of technology? What are the effects of having a population base that is too small to produce the people necessary to fill the required roles? In the first case, society can support activities that will change the technological level at which it operates. If a population produces more talented people than are required to maintain its industry, it is possible for the excess talent to be used to generate innovations in technology or to conduct research in new areas. (This assumes that the technological level of the society is high enough to support its population base. It is easy to imagine societies in which the population is so large and growing so rapidly, and technological levels are so low, that there are more than enough talented people to fill specialized technical roles, but where relatively few such positions exist and talented people must do less challenging work simply to support themselves.)

If the opposite were to occur—that is, if a society were to produce too few talented people to support its technology—what would be the effect? This is the central issue of the novel, *Earth Abides,* by George R. Stewart. In the situation Stewart proposes, the bulk of the earth's human population is killed by a virus sometime between 1940 and 1950. Stewart chronicles the life of a man, Isherwood Williams, who is a student at the University of California at Berkeley when the virus strikes. One of the few who recover from the disease, Williams returns to his family home in the Berkeley hills.

earth abides

by George R. Stewart

The next morning he settled down to establish his life. Food, he knew already, was no problem at all. In the nearest business district he began looking into store-windows. Rats and mice were making a mess of everything, and the floors were littered with gnawed cartons and spilled food. Through one window, however, he was startled to see the gaily colored piles of fruit and vegetables as fresh and lovely as ever. He stared incredulously, peering through the dust-coated glass. Then, first with irritation and then with amusement, he realized that the bright colors were merely from the papier-mâche oranges, apples, tomatoes, and avacados which the store in the old days had used for a permanent front-window display.

After a while he saw through the windows a grocery which was unlittered. Apparently it must be rodent-proof. Carefully jimmying a window, he got into the store.

The bread was inedible, and weevils were at work even in some of the carefully sealed boxes of crackers. But the dried fruit and everything inside of tin and glass was as good as ever. As he was picking out some cans of olives, he heard an electric motor start; curiously, he opened the refrigerator, and found that the butter was still perfectly preserved. Next he investigated the deep-freeze units, and found fresh meat, frozen vegetables, ice-cream, and even materials for a green salad. When he left with his loot, he closed the window carefully behind him, to keep at least that one store free of rats.

After he had returned to the house, he reflected upon his position again, and decided that as yet the mere maintenance of life would be easy, indefinitely. Food, clothing—the shops were full, and he had only to help himself! Water still gushed from the faucets at full pressure. Gas had failed, and if it had been a country of bitterly cold winters, he might have had to consider laying in some kind of fuel supply. But his gasoline stove served excellently for cooking; if the fireplace was not sufficient in the winter, he could round up a battery of such stoves and supply himself with all the heat he needed. In fact, he soon began to feel so pleasantly self-sufficient that he feared he was turning into a hermit.

One evening shortly afterward, he sat reading, and after a while began to feel hungry. He went to the kitchen, and rummaged in the refrigerator for some cheese. Happening to glance at the electric clock, he was surprised to see that the time was only nine-thirty-seven. He had thought it was later. On his way back to the living-room he took a bite of the cheese, and glanced at his wrist-watch. The watch-hands stood at ten-nine, and he knew that he had set the watch by the clock within twenty-four hours.

"That old clock's going to pieces at last," he thought. "Not surprising!" he remembered how the motion of its hands had startled him when he had first returned to the house.

He sat down to read again. A high wind from the north with the heavy smell of smoke in it blew so hard that it rattled the windows occasionally. By now he was used to the smell of smoke, and did not think about it. At many times he could not even get a good view because of the smoke of the burning forests. After a while he blinked his eyes a little and stared more intently at the page where the letters seemed to have grown strangely indistinct. "This smoke must be making my eyes water," he thought. "I don't seem to see so well." But as he looked closer, it seemed that not only the page before him but the whole room had grown dimmer. With a sudden start he looked at the electric-light bulb in the bridge lamp beside him.

Then quickly, with a jumping heart, he was out of his chair and standing on the front porch looking out over the broad stretches of the city below him. The lights were still burning along the streets. The chains of yellow beads still showed on the great bridge, and at the tops of the towers the red lights were flashing. He looked more carefully. The lights seemed a little dimmer than they should be, but he could be imagining that, or they might be obscured by all the drifting smoke. He went back and sat in his chair again and tried to read, forgetting about it—forgetting what he feared.

But he blinked—and again! Looking at the light beside him, he was puzzled. Then suddenly he remembered the clock!

"Well," he thought, "it had to come!"

His watch now showed ten-fifty-two. He went out to the kitchen, and saw that the clock was at ten-fourteen. He calculated apprehensively. The result was bad. As closely as he could remember, the clock had lost six minutes in about three-quarters of an hour.

The clock was run, he knew, by electrical impulses which were ordinarily timed at sixty to the minute. Now they must be coming less often. An electrical engineer would doubtless have found it an elementary matter to calculate just how much less often. Ish could even have made an attempt at the calculation himself, but he saw no use in it, and he felt suddenly downcast. In any case, once the Power-and-Light system had started to go to pieces, the rate of decline would undoubtedly be progressively faster.

Back in the living-room, he could scarcely doubt now that the light had faded still more. Deep shadows seemed to have moved out from behind the chairs in the corners of the room.

"The lights are going out! The lights of the world!" he thought, and he felt like a child going alone into the dark. . . .

He stood on the porch again. Minute by minute the long chains of streetlights grew less and less luminous, more and more yellow. The high wind, he thought, must be helping, blowing down a power-line here, weakening a switch connection there. The fire too was sweeping across the forested ridges unchecked by men, burning power-lines, perhaps, even powerhouses.

After a while the lights seemed to fade no further, but to remain at a constant dimness. He went in again, and pulling another bridge-lamp to the side of his chair, he was able to read comfortably with two lights instead of one. . . . By now it was late, but he did not want to go to sleep. He felt as if he were sitting up by the death-bed of his most treasured and oldest friend. He remembered those great words "Let there be light, and there was light!" This seemed the other end of that story.

After a while he went to look at the clock again, and saw that it had stopped with the hands symmetrically upward—at eleven-five.

His watch showed him that by now it was well after midnight. The lights might still continue many hours, or even might burn dimly for days. Yet he did not want to go to bed.

A deep shiver shook him, but he stilled his panic. After all, he thought, the great system of Power-and-Light had held up for an amazingly long time, all its automatic processes functioning though the men were gone. He thought clear back to that first day when he had come down out of the mountains not yet even knowing what had happened. Then he had passed the powerhouse, and felt the reassurance that everything must still be normal because he saw the water pouring out from the tailraces and heard the dim continuous hum of the generators. He felt again a curious touch of local pride in thinking of it. Perhaps no system had lasted so long. These might well be the last electric lights to be left burning in the world, and when they faded, the lights would be out for a long, long time.

No longer sleepy, he sat there, feeling that he should not go to sleep, wishing at least that the end would come quickly and with dignity and not be dragged out too long. Again, he felt the light fading, and he thought. "This is the end!" But still it lingered, the filaments now only a cherry-red.

And then again they faded. As a sled on a hillside, slowly first, then gaining momentum. Just for a moment, he thought (or imagined), they flared more brightly—and then they were gone.

He went outside. "Perhaps," he thought, "that was just the failure of some local line." But he was really sure that it had not been. He peered through the darkness, all the thicker for the smoke that was heavy in the air, changing the moon into an orange ball. He could see no light—not along the streets, nor anywhere on the bridge. This, then, was the end. "Let there be *no* light, and *there was no light!*"

"No use being melodramatic!" he thought. Going inside, he stumbled around until he had found the drawer where his mother kept candles. Putting one into a candlestick, he sat again by its feeble but steady and continuing light. Nevertheless he continued to feel a little shaken.

The next day he went out to see what was happening, still thinking of the drama he was prepared to watch. Not so much had occurred, it seemed at first. But after a while he began to notice things. On San Lupo Drive a drain-pipe had plugged with the washing in of all the unswept leaves that lay in the gutter. After the drain-pipe had plugged the water had swirled across the street to the downhill side and flooded over the curb. The stream of water had worked its way across the tangle of tall grass which had been the Harts' lawn, and seeped under the door. Their floors and rugs must be soaked, and slimy with mud. Below the house the water had broken out, and run through the rose-garden, leaving a small gully behind it, at last disappearing into the drainage of a storm-sewer on the street below. It was just a little matter, and yet it showed what must be happening all over the country.

Men had built roads and drains and walls and thousands of other obstructions to the natural flow of water. These could survive and function only because men were constantly at hand to repair and clean the thousands of little breaks and blockages which showed up at every change of the weather. Ish himself could have cleaned out that clogged drain in two minutes by merely scraping the leaves back from the grating where they had plugged it. But he saw no point to stretching out his hand. There were thousands, millions, of spots where the same thing must be happening. The roads and the drains and the walls had been constructed only for man's convenience, and now that man was gone there was no need of them. The water might just as well follow its natural courses, and cut back, through the rose garden. Soaked and muddy, the Harts' rugs would begin to rot where they lay. No matter! To think of that as something bad, was merely to think in terms of what had once been and no longer existed. . . .

In the spring of the second year, Ish planted his first garden. He had never liked gardening, and that probably explained why, in spite of good resolutions and two half-hearted attempts, he had not grown anything during the first year. Nevertheless, as he turned over the dark moist soil with the spade, he felt a deep satisfaction at being in touch again with primeval things.

That was about all the satisfaction he got from the garden. To begin with, the seed (he had had a hard time to find any at all because of the ravages of the rats) was several years old, and much of it failed to sprout. Snails and slugs soon moved in, but by scattering a box of Snale-Killa he eliminated them, and felt triumphant. Then, just as the lettuce was making a good growth, a buck jumped the fence and wrought havoc. Ish put another layer on the top of the fence. Next, some rabbits burrowed beneath—more destruction, and more work! One evening he heard crashing noises and rushed out just in time to scare off a predatory cow on the point of smashing a way through the fence. More work!

By this time he was waking up at night with thoughts of ravening deer, rabbits, and cattle prowling around his fence and ogling his lettuces with eyes that gleamed like tigers' eyes.

Then, in June, the insects arrived. He sprayed poison until he was afraid he would not dare eat the lettuce even if any lived to be harvested.

The crows were the last to find the garden, but when they arrived in July their numbers made up for their late arrival. He stood guard, and shot some of them. But they seemed to post sentries and swoop down as soon as his back was turned, and he could not watch during all the daylight hours. His scarecrows and dangling mirrors kept them off for a day, but after that they lost their fear.

In the end he actually erected a shelter of fly-screen over the few rows of garden which seemed worth saving, and he harvested a little lettuce, along with some scrawny tomatoes and onions. But he conscientiously let some of the plants go to seed, and saved the fresh seed for the future.

He was as thoroughly discouraged as any amateur gardener had ever been. It was one thing apparently to grow vegetables when thousands of others were doing the same, and quite another when yours was the only plot and so from miles around every vegetable hungry animal and bird and mollusk and insect came galloping or flying or oozing or hopping, and apparently sending out by signals to its fellows the universal shout, "Let's eat!"

What aspects of a society can be maintained when its population is reduced beyond the point at which it is possible to fill the roles necessary to carry on the present form of its division of labor? If a population were reduced as much as Stewart reduces the population of the earth, the most likely outcome would certainly be rapid deterioration of technologically based civilizations as we know them, the development of social systems appropriate to the size, particular talents, and abilities of available populations, and adjustment to the environment in which each aggregate of individuals found itself.

In Stewart's account of the deterioration of American society, Williams and a few other survivors band together and found a small community. Since their community is located in the San Francisco Bay area, they face no severe problems with their environment and are able to survive quite easily on the remnants of their civilization. In some respects, the ease with which they are able to maintain themselves discourages any attempt to reestablish control over their immediate physical environment beyond making minor repairs to their shelters. There are no apparently vital and difficult skills that their children must acquire before the last *civilized* generation dies. Most of the members of the community, the "Tribe," see no need even to try to pass on the knowledge on which their civilization depended, or at least they do not seem overconcerned with this question. Their behavior seems quite appropriate to the individuals with whom Stewart populates the community. They are a reasonable sample of the population of the society they have outlived, and their lack of concern about transmitting the knowledge on which their society depended is understandable. Each had only the most rudimentary understanding of a small proportion of that knowledge, and no real understanding of how much their world had been based on science and technology.

Williams is the one exception. He understands the need and potential advantage to future generations of preserving the ability to read and some idea of what the dead civilization might offer to anyone who took the trouble to look. The following excerpt begins just after Williams has realized that the school he has attempted to start for the children of the Tribe has failed. He is discouraged in part because one of his sons, Joey, has recently died. Joey was clearly the brightest of the Tribe's children and seemed to have a genuine interest in learning.

As Ish had expected, they did nothing. Weeks passed. There was no heaving and grunting of men as they carried the refrigerator up the hill, no click and crunch of spades preparing a garden plot. Ish worried occasionally, but in general life drifted along, and even he could not be much concerned. With his old student's habit of observing even when he did not participate, he often wondered just what might be happening.

Was it really, as he sometimes imagined, that all the individuals were still suffering under a kind of shock as the result of the sudden destruction of their old society? His studies in anthropology supplied him with examples—the head-hunters and the plains Indians, who had lost the will to readjust and even the will to live, after their traditional way of life had rudely been made impossible. If they could no longer go head-hunting or ride out to steal horses and take scalps, they had no desire for anything else either. Or, with a mild climate and food-supplies easy to obtain, was there now simply no stimulus to change? He could recollect possible examples of this kind also—some of the South Sea islanders, or those tropical peoples who lived chiefly on bananas. Or was it something else?

Fortunately, he had enough background of philosophy and history to keep his perspective. He was actually, he realized, struggling to solve a problem which had baffled philosophers from the time when they had first become conscious of problems at all. He was facing the basic question of the dynamics of society. What made a society change? He, as a student, was more fortunate than Koheleth or Plato or Malthus or Toynbee. He saw a society reduced in size until it had attained the simplicity of a laboratory experiment.

Yet, whenever he had arrived at this stage of argument, another thought cut across and disturbed the simplicity. He began to feel himself less scientific but more human, to think more nearly as Em thought. This society along San Lupo Drive was not really a philosopher's neat microcosm, a small dip out of the general ocean of humanity. No—it was a group of individuals. It was Ezra and Em and the boys—yes, and Joey! Change the individuals, and the whole situation changed. Change even one individual!

But in one detail Ish thought that Em was wrong. She did not need to fear that he was worrying too much about the situation and would end up with ulcers or a neurosis. Instead, his observation of what was happening kept him interested in life. At first, just after the Great Disaster, he had devoted himself to observing the changes in the world as the result of the disappearance of man. After twenty-one years, however, the world had fairly well adjusted itself, and further changes were too slow to call for day-to-day or even month-to-month observation. Now, however, the problem of society—its adjustment and reconstitution—had moved to the fore, and become his chief interest.

In any case, he could not help wondering what would happen to The Tribe in the years that were ahead. It worried him. After the Great Disaster, he had thought that the people, if any survived at all, would soon be able to get some things running again and proceed gradually toward re-establishing more and more of civilization. He had even dreamed of a time when electric lights might go on again. But nothing like that had happened, and the community was still dependent upon the leavings of the past.

Now he looked around, as he had often looked before, at the ones who were with him. They were, so to speak, the bricks out of which a new civilization must be fashioned. . . .

Sitting there, on the Library steps, pounding the chip of granite into smaller and smaller grains, he began now to have what seemed a little clearer vision of the future. It was all tied up in that same old question. How much did man strike outward to affect all his surroundings and how much did the surroundings press in upon him? Did the Napoleonic age produce Napoleon or did *he* produce *it?* So, even if Joey had lived, the welter of circumstances, the circumstances that made Jack and Roger and Ralph, would probably have affected Joey too, and one small boy was not much to set up against all of that. Yes, even if Joey had lived, things would probably have continued to move in the way they already seemed to be moving. Now that Joey was dead, it was certain—certain, that is, as far as anyone could reasonably expect, granting always some unforeseeable accident.

The stars in their courses! (The chip of granite was nothing but powder under the blows of the hammer.) *The stars in their courses!* No, he did not believe in astrology, and yet the shifting of the stars showed that the solar system too was changing, and that the earth itself was becoming a more or a less habitable place for man. Thus, at some profounder depth of reality, astrology might be right, and the changes in the sky could be taken as symbol of all the grinding wheels of circumstance. *The stars in their courses!* What was man, little man, to withstand them?

Yes, the future was certain. The Tribe was not going to restore civilization. It did not want civilization. For a while the scavenging would go on —this opening of cans, this expending of cartridges and matches stored up from the past, all this uncreative but happy manner of life. Then at last, sooner or later, there would be more and more people, and the supplies would fail. There would perhaps be no quick catastrophe because many cattle could be had for the taking, and life would go on.

So, he thought, and then a new idea came to him with a sudden impact. Even though cattle were left, though there was much food, what would happen when the ammunition for the rifles was exhausted? When the matches were gone? In fact, one might not even have to wait until the ammunition was exhausted. Powder deteriorated with time. Three or four generations, and all who were left might be merely some groveling primitives who had lost civilization and yet, on the other hand, had not learned all those thousand basic skills which enabled savages to live with some degree of stability and comfort! Possibly, indeed—and perhaps this would be best—in three or four generations the race would not be able to survive at all, would not be able to make the transition between the scavenging, uncreative life, and some new level of life at which they could remain permanently, or from which they could once more begin a slow advance.

Again he pounded heavily on the edge of the step. Another chunk of the granite fell off. He looked at it gloomily. He had just decided not to worry, and here he was, hard at it again. What could he know about what would be happening three or four generations from now?

He got up and started to walk home. He was quieter now.

"Yes," he thought, again shaping words, "a leopard can't change its spots, and I'll always be a worrier, even though I've lived with Em for twenty-two years. I look before and after. Relax! Yes, I should relax a little. What I have been trying to do—that has failed. I'll admit it. Just the same, I'm certain I'll never stop trying a little. Now, perhaps, if I try for something less, I may in the end attain something more."

By the time he had finished the long walk up the hill to the houses, his vague plans had shaped themselves, but he would have to wait until morning to begin.

That night, however, an autumn storm began, and he awoke in the morning to a world of low-lying cloud and steady dropping. He felt surprise, for with all the recent troubles he had failed to realize that time was slipping away. Now, however, when he thought of the matter, he remembered that the sun had been setting well toward the south and that the month, if one could still think in such terms, would be November. The rain interfered with the immediate fulfillment of his plans, but there was plenty of time, and he could mature his ideas with thought.

So completely had his attitudes changed within the last day that the sounds of the assembling children, that morning, came to him as a shock. "Of course!" he thought. "They are expecting to have school again."

He went downstairs to meet with them. They were all there—all except Joey, and two younger ones. He looked into their faces, as they sat on chairs wriggling, or squatted more comfortably on the floor. They were looking back at him, he imagined, with more alertness than usual. Joey was gone, and they must be wondering how this would affect school. Yet the change, he knew, must be only temporary, and behind this alertness must lurk still that basic lack of interest against which he had already struggled.

He let his glance run over the little group, pausing individually upon each face. They were fine children, not really stupid, but they lacked the flair. No, there was not one!

He made his decision, and he felt no pain in it.

"School is dismissed," he said.

There was a momentary look almost as of consternation in all the faces, and then he saw that they were suddenly pleased, although they were making some effort not to show their pleasure.

"School is dismissed!" he repeated, feeling that he was being dramatic about it in spite of himself. "There will be no more school—ever!"

Again he saw a look of consternation come into the faces, and this time no pleasure showed afterwards. They stirred uneasily in their seats. Some of them got up to go. But they knew that something had happened, something deeper than their minds could grasp.

They went out slowly and quietly. During as much as a minute after they had gone out into the dripping of the rain, there was silence. Then he heard them suddenly shout, and they were children again. School had been a passing incident. Probably they would never think of it again; certainly they would never regret it. For a moment Ish felt a heaviness within him. "Joey, Joey!" he thought. But he had no regret for what he had just done, and he knew that he had made the right decision. "School is dismissed!" he thought. "School dismissed!" And he remembered suddenly that he had sat in this same room many years before, and watched the electric lights fade out.

Three days of rain gave him plenty of time to think things over and mature all his plans. At last a morning dawned with blue sky and a chilly wind from the north. The sun came out, the vegetation dried. Now was the time.

He hunted through the deserted and overgrown gardens. This had never been an area where citrus fruits were grown commercially, but lemons had produced well enough, and here and there someone had nursed a lemon tree in his garden. That wood, he remembered, was suitable. Of course he could have read any number of books, but his approach had changed. He would read no books on this matter. He could do well enough by himself.

Two blocks up the street there had once been a large and showy garden. There he found a lemon tree. It was still living, although nearly crowded out by the growth of two pines. Moreover, it had suffered badly in a frost of some years previous. Never having been pruned after the frost, the tree was only a wreck of itself. Long suckers had shot up from its base after the frost, and some of these again had died.

Avoiding the long thorns, Ish pressed his way into the tangle, found a suitable shoot, and took out his pocket-knife. The shoot at its base was nearly as big as his thumb. The dead lemon wood was almost as hard as bone, but after a while he whittled it through with his knife and pulled it out from the tangle. The shoot was seven feet long, straight for four feet before other branches had begun to interfere and it had grown crooked. At his shaking, it was stiff, but when he leaned against it, it bent and straightened sharply as he released the pressure. It would suffice.

"Yes," he thought a little bitterly, "it will be good enough for all my needs."

He carried the lemon-shoot back to the house, and sat on the porch, in the sun, whittling. First he cut off the crooked end of the shoot so that he had four feet of straight wood remaining.

Then he stripped off the dead bark, and began to taper the shoot at both ends. The work was very slow, and he paused frequently to sharpen the knife on a whetstone. The white tough-grained wood seemed to turn the edge after only a few strokes.

Walt and Josey had been off playing with the other children, but at lunch-time they came back.

"What are you doing?" Josey asked him.

"I'm getting ready to play a game," Ish answered her. He would not make the mistake, he had decided, of trying to tie this up with anything practical, as he had with the school. Here he would try to harness that love of play which seemed so deep-seated in the human race.

After lunch the children must have carried the word around. In the afternoon George came over.

"Why don't you come to my place," George said, "and use a vise and my spoke-shave? You could work a lot faster."

Ish thanked him, but continued to work with the knife, even though his hand was getting sore. Nevertheless he thought that he would do all this work with the simplest implements.

By the end of the afternoon his hand was beginning to blister where he held the knife, but he judged that the work was done. A four-foot length of the lemon-shoot was now symmetrically tapered toward both ends. He set one end of it against the ground, pressed it to a half circle, and felt it spring back sharply into straightness. Satisfied, he cut notches close to each end, and gladly put the knife away.

The next morning he continued the work. There was plenty of stout string available, and he considered taking some nylon fish line and braiding it into the proper size.

"No," he thought, "I'll work from things they can always get for themselves."

He found the skin of a recently killed calf. From it he cut a long thong of rawhide. The work went slowly, but he had plenty of time. He shaved the hair from the strip, and shaved the strip itself until it was no larger than a small cord. Then he braided three strips together to make a heavy cord, and estimating the proper length, he tied each end into a little loop.

He held the lemon-shoot in one hand and the braided thong in the other, and looked at them. Either by itself amounted to little. Then, bending the shoot, he hooked the loops of the thong into the notches at the ends of the shoot, and the two became one. Since the thong was shorter, the tapered shoot now bent in a clean symmetrical arc. The thong itself cut straight across between the points of the arc. Stick and cord, joined, had suddenly become something new.

He looked at the bow, and knew that creative force had again returned to the world. He could have gone to any sporting-goods store, and picked out a much better bow—a six-foot toy for archery. But he had not done so. He had made himself a bow from the wood itself carved with the simplest of implements, and a string from the hide of a new-killed calf.

He plucked at the thong. It scarcely twanged, but it gave forth a satisfactory dull throbbing vibration. He considered that his work for the day was finished. He unstrung the bow.

The next day, for an arrow, he cut himself a straight branch of a pine tree. The soft green wood cut easily, and he had shaped the arrow and notched it in half an hour. When he had finished it, he called for the children. Walt and Josey came, and Weston with them.

"Let's see how she works," Ish said.

He drew the arrow back, and loosed it. Unfeathered, it flew with a wobbly flight, but he had pointed it at a high angle, and it covered fifty feet before it struck, by chance, pointing upward from the ground.

Instantly he knew that he had won success. The three children had never seen anything like this before, and they stood wide-eyed for a moment. Then with shouts they broke into a run, and went to retrieve the arrow. Ish shot it for them, again and again.

At last came the inevitable request for which Ish had been waiting.

"Let me try it, Daddy," said Walt.

Walt's first shot wobbled a bare twenty feet, but he was pleased. Then Josey tried it, and then Weston.

Before dinner-time, every child in The Tribe was busy at work whittling on a bow of his own.

Everything worked even better than Ish had dared to hope. Within a week the air around the houses seemed to be full of badly shot arrows. Mothers began to worry about lost eyesight, and two children came in crying after having received arrows in various parts of their anatomies. But since the arrows were headless and shot from weak bows, no real harm resulted.

Rules had to be established. "You mustn't shoot in the direction of anyone." "You mustn't shoot close to the houses."

Competition developed. Having learned the trick from the older boys who shot from rifles, children began to hold contests against a mark. They experimented with different lengths and types of bows. When Josey complained that Walt always beat her at shooting, Ish subtly made the suggestion that she might try fixing some quail pinions to the butt-end of her arrow. She did so, and beat Walt, and then suddenly all the arrows had quail pinions at one end, and they were flying farther and truer. Even the older boys became interested, and some of them made bows although they were allowed to use rifles. But archery still continued to flourish chiefly among the ones who were too young for rifles.

Ish bided his time. The early rains had sprouted the grass seed, and now the land was green. At evening the sun set behind the hills to the south of the Golden Gate.

Walt and Weston, the twelve-year-olds, were now deep in some kind of boyish plot. They worked hard with bows and arrows, shaping and perfecting them. They were gone long hours during the day.

Then one day toward evening Ish heard the sound of excited boys' feet running up the steps outside. Walt and Weston burst into the room.

"Look, Daddy," Walt cried, and he held up for Ish the pathetic-looking body of a big rabbit pierced through the side with a headless wooden arrow.

"Look!" Walt cried again. "I hid behind a bush, and waited till he hopped up close to me, and then I shot him right through."

Ish, as he looked, felt a sympathy and pity for the poor dangling body, even though he knew that it was a symbol of his own triumph. Too bad, he thought, that even creation must make use of death also.

"That's fine!" he said. "That's fine, Walt! That was a good shot!"

One day, so suddenly that you might almost say just at that particular moment it happened, the children became tired of playing with bows and arrows, and went off on some new enthusiasm. Ish did not worry. He knew that after the ways of children they would come back again, perhaps at the same time of year. The making of bows and the shooting of arrows would not be forgotten. During twenty years, during one hundred years if need were, the bow might remain a children's plaything. In the end, after the ammunition had failed, it would still be there. It was the greatest weapon that primitive man had ever known and the most difficult to invent. If he had saved that for the future, he had saved much. After the rifles were useless, his great-grandchildren would not have to meet the bear's rush empty-handed or starve in the midst of the cattle herds. His great-grandchildren would never know civilization, but at least they would not be groveling half-apes, but would walk erect as freemen, bow in hand. Even if they should no longer have metal knives, they could still scrape out bows with sharp stones. . . .

Sometime after the year 43:

Ish looked up, he saw, very clearly, a young man standing in front of him. The young man wore a neat-enough pair of blue jeans with copper rivets shining brightly, and yet over his shoulders he wore a tawny hide with sharp claws dangling from it. In his hand he held a strong bow, and over his shoulder was a quiver with the feathered ends of arrows sticking from it.

Ish blinked, for in his old eyes the sunshine was strong.

"Who are you?" said Ish.

The young man answered respectfully, "I am Jack, Ish, as indeed you yourself well know."

The way he said "Ish" did not indicate that he was trying to be unduly familiar with an old man, thus calling him by a nickname, but rather it carried something of great respect and even of awe, and as if "Ish" stood for much more than merely the name of an old man.

But Ish himself was confused, and he squinted, peering more carefully, because at short distances he no longer saw clearly. But he was sure that Jack should have dark hair, or perhaps turned somewhat gray by now, and this one who called himself Jack had long wavy yellow hair.

"You should not make jokes with an old man," said Ish. "Jack is my oldest son, and I would recognize him. He has dark hair, and he is older than you."

The young man laughed, but politely, and said, "You are talking, Ish, of my grandfather, as indeed you yourself well know." Again the way in which he said "Ish" had a certain strange sound to it, and now Ish noticed also the strangeness of his other repeated words, "as indeed you yourself well know."

Then, as Ish still looked, he was puzzled that the young man, who was certainly not a child, was carrying a bow instead of a rifle.

"Why do you not have a rifle?" he asked.

"Rifles are good for playthings!" the young man said, and he laughed, a little scornfully perhaps. "You cannot be sure of a rifle, as indeed you yourself, Ish, well know. Sometimes the rifle works, and it makes the big noise, but other times you pull the trigger, and it only goes 'click'." Here he snapped his fingers. "So you cannot use the rifles for real hunting, although the older men say that this was not so in the long past years. But now we use the arrow because it is sure, and never refuses to fly and besides," here the young man held himself proudly, "besides, it is a matter of strength and skill to shoot with the bow—but anyone, they say, could shoot with a rifle, as you yourself, Ish, well know."

"Let me see an arrow," said Ish.

The young man took an arrow from the quiver, and looked at it, and then handed it across.

"That is a good arrow," he said. "I made it myself."

Ish looked at the arrow and felt the weight of it. This was no plaything for a child. The shaft was nearly a yard long, split cleanly from a billet of flawless straight-grained wood, and then rounded and smoothed. It was well feathered, with pinions of some kind, although Ish could not see well enough to know what bird had yielded the feathers. By feeling, however, he could tell that they were arranged carefully so that the arrow in flight would spin like a rifle-bullet, and thus keep its true course and carry farther.

Then he observed the arrowhead, again more by feel than by sight. The arrowhead was very sharp both at the point and along the edges. Ish nearly pricked his thumb. It had the bumpy yet slick feel which told him that it was of hammered metal. Though he could not see very clearly, he made the color out as silvery-white.

"What is *that* made of?" he asked.

"It is from one of the little round things. They have faces on them. The old men have a name for them, but I do not remember exactly. It is something like *corns.*"

The young man paused, as if to be told the right word, but when he had no reply, he went on again, being obviously eager to show off his knowledge about arrowheads.

"We find these little round things in the old buildings. Often there are many—many—of them in the boxes and drawers. Sometimes they are rolled up together in bundles like short round sticks, but heavier than sticks. Some are red and some are white, like this one, and there are two kinds of the white. The one kind of white—the one that has the picture of the hump-backed bull—we do not use those because they are harder to pound."

Ish considered, and thought that he understood.

"And this white one here?" he asked. "Was there a relief—a picture—on this one?"

The young man took the arrow from Ish, and looked at it, and then handed it back.

"They all have pictures," he said. "But I was looking to see if I could still make out what picture was on this one. It has not quite all gone because of the hammering. This was one of the littlest ones, and it had the picture of the woman with the wings growing out of her head. Some of them have pictures of hawks—but not real hawks." The young man was talking very happily. "Others have men; at least, they look like men—one with a beard, and one with long hair hanging behind him and another with a strong-looking face, without a beard and with short hair, and heavy-jawed."

"And who—who do you think—were all these men?"

The young man glanced both ways, as if a little nervous.

"These—oh, these—yes! These, we think—as you yourself, Ish, well know—these were the Old Ones that were before our Old Ones!"

When there was no thunder from heaven and when the young man could see that Ish was not displeased, he went on:

"Yes, that must be it—as you yourself, Ish, well know. These men, and the hawks, and the bull! Perhaps the woman with the wings growing from her head sprang from the marriage of a hawk and a woman. But, however it is, they do not seem to mind our taking their pictures and hammering them up for arrowheads. I have wondered about it. Perhaps they are too great to care about little things, or perhaps they did their work a long time ago and have now grown old and weak."

He stopped talking, but Ish could see that he was pleased with himself, and liked to talk, and was thinking quickly of something more to say. He, at least, had imagination.

"Yes," the young man continued, "I have an idea. Our Old Ones—they were the Americans—made the houses and the bridges and the little round things that we hammer out for arrowheads. But those others—the Old Ones of the Old Ones—perhaps they made the hills and the sun, and the Americans themselves."

Then, though it was a cheap trick to play on the young man, Ish could not resist talking in double meaning.

"Yes," he said, "I have heard it said that those older Old Ones produced the Americans—but I rather doubt that they made the hills and the sun."

Though he could not have understood, perhaps the young man caught the irony in the tone, and so said nothing.

"But, go on," Ish continued then. "Tell me more about the arrowheads themselves. I am not interested in your cosmogony." He used the last word in good-humored malice, knowing that the other would not understand it, but would be impressed by its length and strange sound.

"Yes, about the arrowheads," the young man said, hesitating a moment, and then regaining confidence. "We use both the red and white. The red are good for shooting cattle and lions. The white are for deer and other game."

"Why is that?" Ish asked sharply, for he felt his old-time rationalism stirring at the thought of all such magic and hocus-pocus. The question, however, seemed only to surprise and confuse the young man.

"Why?" he asked. "Why? How would anyone know *why?* Except you yourself, Ish! This matter of the red and white arrowheads is merely something that *is.* It is like—" He hesitated, and then the sunlight seemed to catch his attention. "Yes, it is like the sun that keeps on going round the earth, but naturally no one knows why, or asks why. *Why* should there be a *why?*"

Having said these last words, the young man was obviously very pleased with himself as if he had propounded some great philosophical dictum, although undoubtedly he had spoken only in great simplicity. But when Ish turned the matter over in his mind, he was not sure. Perhaps even in this simplicity there was a depth. Was there ever an answer to "why"? Did not things just exist in the present?

Yet, Ish was certain, a fallacy lurked somewhere in the argument. A sense of cause-and-effect was necessary for life at the human level, and this matter of the different-colored arrowheads was a proof of it, not the contrary. Only, the sense of causation here was faulty and irrational. The young man was maintaining an absurdity—that cattle and lions could be better killed with copper arrowheads hammered from pennies, whereas deer were better killed with silver ones hammered from dimes or quarters. Yet there could obviously not be enough difference in hardness or sharpness to matter. Only, in these primitive minds, the secondary matter of color had in some way come to be considered—this was rank superstition! —the determining factor.

Deep within him, Ish again felt his old hatred of loose thinking boil up. Though he was an old man, still he might do something.

"No!" he said, so sharply that the young man started. "No! That is not right. The white arrowheads and the red! One just as well as. . . . "

Then, slowly his voice trailed off. No, he thought, that was not the way it was destined to be. He heard a rich contralto voice saying to him, "Relax!" Perhaps he might persuade this young man named Jack, who was undoubtedly a remarkably intelligent and imaginative young man, possibly even somewhat like that little one named Joey. But what would it accomplish? Only, perhaps to make the young man confused and ill at ease among all the others. And what was really the difference? At least, copper arrowheads were not *less* effective against lions, and if the bowmen thought them *more* effective, the thought gave him courage and steadied his hand.

So Ish said nothing more about the matter, and smiled at the young man reassuringly, and looked again at the arrow.

Another thought came to him, and he asked:

"Can you always find plenty of those little round things?"

The young man laughed merrily, as if this were a strange question.

"Oh, yes," he said. "There are so many that if all of us spent all our time pounding out arrowheads, still we should never run short."

Ish considered. Yes, that was probably true. Even if there were a hundred men in The Tribe by now, there must be thousands and thousands of coins to be found in tills and cash-boxes, even in this one corner of the city. And if the coins should be exhausted, there would be thousands of miles of copper telephone wire. When he had first made an arrow, he recollected, he had imagined that The Tribe would revert to stone arrowheads. Instead they had taken a shortcut, and were already fashioning metal. So perhaps The Tribe, his own descendants, had already passed the turning-point, were no longer forgetting more old things than they were learning new things, and were no longer sinking toward savagery, but were maintaining a stable level or perhaps gradually beginning to win new security. By showing them how to make bows, he had helped, and he felt greatly comforted.

Then, having finished looking at the arrow, Ish handed it back. "It seems to be a very good arrow," he said, although he did not really know much about arrows.

Nevertheless the young man smiled with great happiness at this praise of his arrow, and Ish noted that he made a mark on it before he put it back into the quiver, as if he wished to know it and distinguish it from other arrows after what had happened. Then, as he still looked at the young man, Ish felt a sudden great love for him, and he had not been so moved for a long time since he had been sitting as an old man on the hillside. This Jack, must be Ish's great-grandson in the male line, and he was also Em's great-grandson. So, as Ish looked, his heart yearned outwards, and he asked a strange question:

"Young man," he said, "are you happy?" The young man named Jack looked startled at this question, and he glanced in both directions before answering, and then he spoke.

"Yes, I am happy. Things are as they are, and I am part of them."

Ish began to think of what this might mean and to wonder again whether the words had been spoken only in simplicity or whether there was some deep philosophy behind them, but he could not decide. At his trying to think, the fog seemed again to move in at the corners of his brain. But still he recollected vaguely that the words—strange as they were—had a ring of familiarity about them. He had not perhaps ever heard those exact words before, but they were words that someone whom he had once known might well have spoken. For in his words the young man had not questioned, but had accepted. Ish could not recall this person exactly, but he remembered softness and warmth, and warm feelings flowed through him.

When he came out of his reverie and looked up again, no one was standing in front of him. In fact, Ish would have been unable to say surely whether the young man named Jack had been there that same day, or whether this was now some other day, or perhaps even another summer.

—*12*—

a tale of
four cities

The four works of social-science fiction in this chapter have a common focus on the conditions possible in urban life at various times in the future. Each excerpt treats the issues of the effects of population growth, the technology required to maintain the urban environment, and the quality of life under the social conditions that the designer has created.

The four selections stress different aspects of the consequences of the urban crisis now underway. The first treats a possible fate of the suburban pre-slums that have been built around the country during the last 25 years. The second excerpt presents an aerial view of the topography of a large part of the United States when urbanization is nearly complete and describes an attempt to maintain examples of the once natural ecology of the country. The third excerpt describes the quality of life as it might be in a city of the future. The final selection treats the conditions of life in an urban environment that is completely controlled, in which the population problem has been solved, and in which there is no impetus for social change.

—*a*—

suburbia

Responding to tremendous need for housing in and around urban centers, the suburban "subdivision" or "development" has come into existence. Just as our natural environment has been steadily destroyed and we now face a conservation crisis, we have engaged in a land-rape of the desirable living spaces around major cities. The reasons are population pressures, lack of centralized planning and thought about the future, and an overpowering desire for a fast buck.

gladiator-at-law

by Frederik Pohl and C. M. Kornbluth

A house was a house. It had warm resilient floors; it had walls; it had utilities. If you didn't like the floor warm you dialled it to cool. If you didn't like the wall colour or pattern you turned the selector wheel to something else. If you didn't like a room plan you unclipped the wall and clipped it somewhere else. Hell, that's what a house *was*.

Norvell dialled a bed and set the house to full automatic. As he lay down his pillow chimed softly, but he didn't need sleepy music that night; with a curse, he reached over his head and turned it off. In the copper plexus at the house's core transistors pulsed; solenoids barred the doors; microswitches laid traps for intruders; thermocouples tasted the incoming air and cooled it an additional four degrees. Commutator points roved around a hidden dial until they reached the stations where a sweeping clock hand would boil the water for the coffee, heat the griddle for the eggs, set the breakfast dishes. But by then Norvell was already asleep.
. . .

Norvell was lying on a cake of ice. He kept trying to explain to someone enormous that he was sorry for everything and he'd be a good and dutiful son or husband or friend or whatever he was supposed to be if only the someone would leave him alone. But the enormous someone, who couldn't have been Norvell's father because Norvell didn't even remember a father, only put his hand before his mouth and tittered and looked down from a long flight of stairs, and then when Norvell was least expecting it, reached out and swatted him across the ear and sent him skidding across the enormous cake of ice into the tittering face of Alexandra and the jagged, giant teeth of Virginia. . . .

Norvell woke up.

He was very cold, very stiff. He looked dazedly around him. The living room. But—

Yes. It was the living room. With the wall patterns off and no light except a sickly dawn from outside. All of the walls were on full transparent and he was lying on the floor. The bed he had dialled out to sleep in had folded into the basic cube, dumping him on the floor. And the floor was cold.

No heat. No power. The house was turned off.

He got up, wincing, and hopelessly sidled to the window control. It didn't respond; the windows remained full transparent.

He knew what had happened, and swore between clenched teeth. The skunks. Turning off the place without a word of warning, at daybreak, without even giving him a chance to—

He wearily began picking up his clothes from the floor where a rack had dumped them as it returned to folded storage state. Through the indecently transparent windows he saw the other bubble-houses, all decently opaqued with only their nightlights and entry lights and here and there a warmly lit upstairs window. By the time he was dressed he began to hear a clamour upstairs. His wife and daughter charged down in négligées, commanding him to do something about it.

"Get dressed," he said, and pointedly disconnected his hearing aid.

He rambled about the house while they did. Absently he tried to dial coffee and gave up with a self-conscious laugh when the water would not flow. The closets, drawers, and dressers had rejected all their contents, upstairs and down. Pushers had calmly shoved them out and the doors had closed and locked—to him, for ever. He contemplated the disordered piles of clothes and kitchenware, and began to pack a travelling case.

Two bored policemen wandered in while he was doing so; the door, of course, was no longer on lock. He plugged in his hearing aid, taking plenty of time about it. He said to them, "Well?"

They told him he had plenty of time; they weren't in any hurry. Take an hour if you need it, bub. They'd tote him and his family and their stuff out to Belly Rave, help him pick out a good place. And—uh—don't take this too hard, bub. Sometimes when people got busted out of contract status they—uh—got panicky and tried to, well, knock themselves off.

The moving had one golden moment. One of the cops helpfully picked up a suitcase. Alexandra told him to remove his *filthy* hands from—

The cop clouted her and explained what they didn't take none of off of Belly Rave brats.

The police car handed Norvell a jolt. It was armoured.

"You—you get a lot of trouble in Belly Rave?" he guessed.

The friendlier of the cops said, "Nah. Only once in a while. They haven't jumped a squad car in six months, not with anything but pistols, anyway. You'll be okay." And they pulled away from Monmouth GML Unit w–97–AR. There was no sentiment to the parting. Norvell was sunk in worry. Alexandra was incandescent but still. And Virginia had not said two words to anyone that morning.

The car paused at the broad beltway circling the bubble-city, motor idling and the driver impatiently talking into his radio. Finally two more police cars rolled up and the three of them in convoy left the city roads for the cracked asphalt that led to Belly Rave. Once the road they travelled had been a six-lane superhighway, threading a hundred thousand commuters' cars morning and night. Now it wound through a scraggly jungle, the toll booths at the interchanges crumbled into rock piles and rust.

They bumped along for a couple of miles, then turned off into a side road that was even worse.

The first thing that hit Norvell was the smell.

The second thing was worse. It was the horrible feeling of betrayal as he looked on Belly Rave. A man can reconcile himself to anything. If life is doomed to be an eternity of agony with duodenal cancer, or the aching and irremediable poverty of the crippled and friendless, he can manage to survive and make the best of it. But when he has steeled himself to disaster . . . and the event is a thousandfold worse than his fiercest nightmare . . . the pockets of strength are overrun and nothing remains inside him but collapse.

And Belly Rave, in its teeming ruin, was worse than anything Norvell had dreamed.

The police cars swayed around a corner, sirens blasting, and stopped in the middle of a long, curving block. The convoying cars pulled up ahead and behind; a cop got out of each and stood ankle-deep in weeds and refuse, hand idly resting on his gun.

Norvell's driver said, "This one will do. Let's go." . . .

Reverse your telescope. Point the small end at a sign that is neither here nor now, a long way off in space and as many years past as it has been since the end of World War II.

The sign is in a dozen chromatic colours, a picture of a vine-covered cottage with a curl of smoke winding from a fieldstone chimney, and an impossibly long-legged girl waving from the door. The giant letters read:

BELLE REVE ESTATES
'Gracious Living for America's Heroes'
VETS! OWN YOUR OWN HOME!
$350 cash, $40.25 monthly, pays all
F R E E !
3-speed washer, home freezer
FIFTEEN-FOOT PICTURE WINDOW

Before the paint on the sign was dry, three cars were parked in the muddy ruts in front of it and three couples were being guided through the model home by Belle Reve salesmen—estate managers, they preferred to be called.

Their technique was identical. If any one of them had lost his voice, or been blasted to charcoal by a resentful God, any of the others could have taken his place in mid-syllable. And their movements were as exact as a ballet troupe; when saleman A brought his charges into a room, salesman B was just on the way out. The rooms were handsomely made and cutely furnished, but the sales director didn't like to have too many people in a room at one time—gave the impression the rooms were *small.*

When the salesman had finished, a prospect got back to the sparkling kitchen, where the closing desk was, under the dizzy impression that somehow he could move into the place tomorrow, furnished as it was, simply by signing his name and handing over the twenty-dollar binder. And a swimming pool would be on their lawn the day after to be shared with another nice couple like them, and the children could gambol on the grassy sward unmenaced by city traffic and they would spit right in the eye of the city apartment-house janitor after telling him they were getting out of the crowded, evil-smelling, budget-devouring, paper-walled, sticky-windowed, airless, lightless, privacyless hole in the wall for ever. They were going Home to Belle Reve. They signed and paid.

Time passed.

Belle Reve receded before them always like a mirage. The four-colour circulars continued to arrive, and the statements of their down-payment balance due. Plus title-search fee. Plus handling charge. Plus interest. Plus legal fee. Plus sewer assessment. Plus land tax. Plus road tax. They paid.

Time passed.

Their house was built; their hour had struck! The kids wailed, "Is *that* it?" and began to cry. Whichever was weaker, the wife or husband, sagged shoulders and stared in horror at the sea of mud, the minute house riding it like an ark, like one ark in a fleet of identical arks drawn up rank by rank for review by a snickering deity. Whichever was stronger, the husband or wife, squared shoulders and said loudly, "It may not look like much now, but give us a few weekends and we'll have it just like the demonstration place. And we'll be working for ourselves, not some landlord. This place isn't an expense; it's an asset."

Time passed.

Sod was laid on the mud. It sank in curious hummocks and swales when it rained. Takes a little time to settle, honey. Fill was dumped on the sod, and topsoil on the fill. Grass was planted on the topsoil to burn and die in the summer. Honey, we can't water it this year because of the water rates. In a normal year, sure, but we have a few non-recurring charges, and once they're out of the way— The sewer assessment. The road assessment. The school tax. And we ought to do something about the foundation, I guess. You catch these little cracks early and you never have trouble again. Every house settles a little, honey.

Time passed.

The place isn't an expense, honey; it's an *asset.* Do you realize we have an equity of *eight thousand dollars* in this house we can recover at the drop of a hat if we can find somebody to buy the place and if there was some place else to go? It makes a man feel mighty good to know he has eight thousand dollars to his name. I know it runs a little higher than anybody figured, but things are up all over. Insurance, sewer assessment, road tax, fuel oil, interest, assessment in that stockholders' suit whatever it was about—it isn't more than a hundred twenty-five a month, if that. If I get the raise and swing that note on the car we can have the roof repaired before the November rains, and then get right to work on the oil heater—please don't cry, honey. Besides. There's. No. Place. Else. To. Go.

Time passed.

You've got to talk to her, dear. Coming in past midnight after she was out with God-knows-who and telling me there isn't any use asking her to entertain at home because we'd be right on top of her because the place is so small you can't sneeze without blowing somebody's hat off you've got to talk to her I'm going out of my mind with worry she could get in trouble and so are all the other mothers I know the place isn't very attractive but can't you get it painted somehow even if you aren't as young as you once were she's ashamed of the place and she's right about it being too small and the washer's broken again and I'm not as young as I once was and I can't keep hauling water all my life and when are we going to fix the picture window it looks horrible with a big crack right down the middle not that I blame the Elliston boy the poor kid doesn't have any place to play trapped like a rat here in Belle Reve like the rest of us in chicken coops crumbling around us while we watch but they never quite fall down as long as we keep patching and patching and patching and paying and paying and paying. . . .

Time passed.

Over the back fence (patched and peeling; leaning this way and that, inadequate to keep the children in the yard or the prowling, huge rats out): I heard of them and I saw the ads. I don't read much these days because of my eyes but he came home with the paper, for once he wasn't grey and tired. GML Houses, he said. Wonderful GML bubble-houses—a complete departure. He said he knew it had to come some day, a complete break with tradition the way it said in the ad. It has something to do with contracts. They lease the machines to the companies, I think, or something, and the companies build the houses for people who work for them. It gets around taxes or something. He was sure the company would lease the machines and we could get a GML, but it didn't come to anything because he doesn't have a contract and they just build them for their contract people. But heavens he's lucky to *have* a job the way things are going; the boy's been looking and looking and there doesn't seem to be anything, I don't know how we'd get by if it wasn't for the allowance. . . .

Time passed.

Steady, pop, don't snop your top. I swear I'll cool ya if ya give me more than a sufficiency of that cack. Me get a job? Some cack, ya old frack! What have I got that a little black box hasn't got more and better? Gimme that 'fifty years with the company' once more and you'll be flat on your bat. You get the allowance for me, don't ya? If ya didn't have crap in your cap you'd be a contract man and we'd be in a bubble for double instead of my being a lousy slave from Belly Rave. . . .

. . . The boy swaggered out across the screeching floorboards, the house trembling to his stride. The old man said, "Fifty years with the company," and began to cry. He had been replaced last Friday by a little black box that never made mistakes, never got tired, never took a coffee break. From now on the allowance cheque would be tripled; as head of a family he had that coming to him. And he owned the house outright, almost. In just a few years it would be his, as soon as he cleared up the sewer assessments outstanding. I'll sell, he schemed craftily, forgetting to cry. At the top of the market. Not right now; things were too dull. A few of the places on the street were empty, abandoned by owners who had made contract grade and won entitlement to a GML house. A kind of funny element was moving in; not the kind of people you talked to much. Bad for the children. He was sure that passing the abandoned Samuels place he had smelled something like the raw reek of alcohol and glimpsed shining copper pots and tubing through the ill-shuttered picture window. Sometimes police cars and copters descended on Belly Rave and left loaded—but that was on the outskirts, the neighbourhood would pick up, the old man told himself sternly. And then he'd sell at the top of the market.

Time passed. . . .

More than a century.

— b —

a view from above

The following selection describes a trip being taken by a man named Jothen. He begins in the city of Gittler, Missouri. The first few paragraphs describe an aerial view of the city. His first stop is at a biological preserve. Upon leaving the preserve, Jothen and a woman named Kim travel to Chicago and there board a rocket for South America.

a torrent of faces

by James Blish and Norman Knight

. . . The whole area in the frame was uniformly green, except for the dead square of the flyport exactly in the center of the city. A muted black tracery made another square around the flyport, just one and a half miles out from the margins of the paved area. There was another such square surrounding that, at the same distance farther out; and finally—five miles from the mathematical center—the city came to an end, a pyramid with ten miles to a side. That final square had four immense, interrupted ellipses cut into each side, like bites out of a monstrous wafer. A closer look at the bites would even reveal tooth marks: eighty-story tiers of apartments arranged in ten one-hundred-foot-high setbacks.

The Chinese walls that wove back and forth sinuously over the surface of every level of the city showed the same setback system, as did the margins of the individual levels. The thirty-two ziggurat-like towers reared above their levels at the corners of each square, as well as along each side in the ratio 1/2/1/0. The towers were conspicuous because, like the flyport, they were gray-white against the general background of the greenery; otherwise the small concentric circles that they made in the picture would have been invisible from a height of three miles. From the air, Starved Rock Biological Preserve looked not unlike a lichen. The view never ceased to startle Jothen, simply because the colors were all wrong.

In the near distance there were at least five cities visible from the helicopter, all of different shapes, most of them far smaller than the Preserve; but they were all of the same color as the World Forest, simply because the forest marched right over them, from tier to tier and back down again. No forest crossed the acres and acres of silicoid that roofed the Preserve, however. Instead, all the growing stuff was underneath, with sun highlights glinting over it.

Each of the seven major sections of the Preserve was a different shade of green, not a one matching the green of the forest. The reason was simple enough: each sector maintained a different artificial climate and contained a different kind of ecological complex, all of them strangers to the climate and exiles from the ecology of the world at large; but the contrast was nevertheless jolting to the eye. The seemingly meaningless differences in the sizes of the sectors, so different from the obviously planned extensions of the cities, also were disturbing, because they were not governed by the iron laws of expanding human populations, but by the extent of the feeding ranges needed by the fauna in each sector. Additionally, the Preserve did not pryamid toward its central flyport—which otherwise was usual enough—in any rational way, but simply sprawled irregularly over the landscape, hugging the contours.

Inside each sector, Jothen knew, sector compartment bulkheads broke each major division into hundreds of smaller ones, most of which were about four square miles in area and hence not visible from the helicopter. All that could be seen at this altitude was this immense, foliose, varicolored excrescence hugging the land, its longest leaf about thirty miles in radius, with sector headquarters and flyports at its edges like bulging sporangia.

This whole monster was Kim Wernicke's baby, and it was at the moment the only one she seemed to want. It was hardly odd that the Preserve looked like a parasite to Jothen. He could almost sympathize with the anticonservation faction, which wanted to do away with the Preserves and put the land they tied up into production. That would solve one of his problems, too—or would it?

The closer the shuttle copter dropped toward the silicoid roof, the less detail Jothen noted. He saw only the glare of the sun on the transparent sheeting, the tiny pinwheels of the aircraft warning beacons on the tips of the fire lookout stations, and the caterpillar-like movement of the highway that ran around the edge of the Preserve. . . .

Nevertheless, as always, he was forced to take in some of it. Although rapid transit tubes for Preserve personnel ran all through the foundations of the structure, Jothen as a visitor was denied access to them, and very strictly. They were full of booby traps for the unwary: airlocks a visitor would not know how to operate; side-shoots that might lead one abruptly into the Preserve proper—and perhaps face to face with a wild cow or a tiger; germicidal, fungicidal, and viricidal chambers that could kill a man, too, without a protective suit. To get from the central flyport to the HQ of Kim's sector, Jothen had to take the sightseers' highways, like any other tourist.

There might have been a time when he would have found it fascinating, but today it seemed maddeningly circuitous. The highway wound from one subsector to another, sometimes at ground level, sometimes halfway up the sector wall, along a path designed for the maximum of sightseeing and the minimum of speed. The visible surface of the highway was smooth and uniform; it consisted essentially of continuous metal strips, each about an inch wide, covered with a heavy elastic web that stretched as the highway went around a curve. Portable revolving chairs were scattered over it more or less at random; anyone who wanted to linger in a particular subsector could step off the highway onto one of the numerous stationary "overlooks" and take his chair with him.

"Ma, Dad, lookathere. Look at that thing with all the hair along of his neck. Now he's running. I betcha that's a horse."

"Yes, well . . . yes, the placard says there are horses in here."

"Almer, is it true that—that we used to drink *milk* from those beasts?"

"No-o-o, I don't think so. The milk animal was called the ox."

"What does a ox look like, Dad?"

"Well, it looks rather . . . we'd better move on, there's a lot to see yet. Come along now."

Abruptly the highway swooped toward the ground, its arched vitrolith roof seeming to dive into a mass of undisciplined greenery. For a moment Jothen could see nothing but close-pressing leaves, all odd, all utterly unlike the spicules of the bamboos, giant sugar cane, hybrid poplars, and Monterrey pines that made up the World Forest. Then there was an interval of darkness, followed by a roar against the roof of the highway; they had passed through an interior wall between one subsector and another, directly beneath an air blower.

When Jothen could see outside again, the way was running along the ground, and was at the moment passing over a small brook that flowed through a portcullis in the interior wall he had just passed through himself. Above the concrete apron of the wall, glassy sheets rose to the Preserve roof, broken here and there by sets of jalousies that could be opened to permit bird migration from one climate to another—a habit of birds, Kim had once said, which the Preserve geneticists had been able to attenuate, but not breed out entirely. Nearby was one of the supporting girders for the roof, with a downspout from the rain gutter running down beside it, heavily overgrown with glossy-leaved vines.

In the near distance a rain distributor, three times as tall as its surrounding trees, revolved its three conchlike blower casings lazily. These rotors, Jothen remembered, had a positive drive rather than depending upon the Newton reaction of the ejected air and water, so that the distance the rain was thrown could be controlled directly by the force of the air blast; it was the kind of thing in which he took a professional interest. The leaves in this sector sparkled brilliantly, indicating that the machine had been operating only a little while ago.

"Look, Dad, a yak. What a big old nose on him."

"I don't see how anybody ever rode on those things. They're too jumpy."

"You'd never get *me* on one, not for a second."

A yak? No, it was a deer. This must be Kim's sector, then—North American Temperate, the only remainder of that once vast, bluely sylvan, raptly still ecology anywhere on Earth, the last fragment of the realm of deer and bears and wolverines and wild tobacco and sugar maples and oaks, and quiet everywhere under smoky skies. Here, at least, it would never change, and for that reason Kim clung to it—not for the rainbow trout in the brooks, or for the snow that fell every year or the squirrels that sat in the crotches of unfamiliar trees chiseling away at black walnuts, but because this was all of it that there was or ever would be, and it was permanent and immune to man in its glittering silicoid womb. . . .

. . . When Jothen had been flying toward Starved Rock Biological Preserve some hours previously, his attention had been focused on the Preserve itself, his thoughts wholly with Kim. But now Kim was with him, they were flying to Chicago, and the Preserve lay far behind on the southwestern horizon, gleaming under a late afternoon sun.

Now he was scrutinizing a puzzling phenomenon that had appeared on the skyline ahead. It resembled a low range of mountains, grayish mauve in the distance, that lay along the entire northeast quadrant of the horizon. Mountains? In Illinois? As they drew nearer he could see the usual forested terraces, but the bluffs that separated the terraces were bands of pastel colors. He turned to Kim.

"I'm surprised to see mountains here. I thought that all this region was flat as a tabletop."

"Jothen!" Kim laughed. "That's Chicago! Or rather, it's one corner of it."

Steadily churning across the sky, the helicopter bore them nearer still to the terraced ramparts of Chicago, and Jothen stared, fascinated, as they seemed to rise higher and higher and extend themselves endlessly on either hand. Even before the first architectural mountain range was over-passed, still other ridges, peaks, chasms, and buttes rose beyond it. Soaring towers and masts, great glittering domes, and skeleton frameworks of new construction materialized in the blue distance. As they advanced farther, the monolithic city spread beneath them from horizon to horizon, a bewildering tracery of green terraces and tinted walls.

Jothen roused himself from the semihypnotic fixity of his concentration on the unrolling panorama below.

"I suppose I shouldn't be astonished. I've seen some of this in photo books. One has to see it from the air, oneself, to appreciate the real bigness of it. I've been holed up in a Disaster City for so long that I've forgotten how jammed the rest of the world is."

In Chicago Jothen and Kim board a rocket that is to take them to South America.

The greenish-blue afterglow had increased in brightness so that the world beneath was in semitwilight. St. Louis was visible as a gigantic dark disk with scalloped edges. The red sparks of aircraft warning lights outlined the terrace rims. Alternating vertical stripes of vivid red and white light flooded the upper tiers of the truncated central pyramid.

The city stood, athwart the Missouri and Mississippi rivers above and below their confluence. Parts of its north and west walls formed two dams, each retaining an artificial lake. The waters of both rivers flowed into St. Louis through internal penstocks, yielded their tithes of water and energy, reappeared as smooth torrents that poured from the mouths of sluices in the south wall and swooped down the catenary curve of its surface into the downstream reservoir. The reflected light of the twilight sky transformed the three reservoirs into immense luminous pools. Jothen knew that these pools were part of a giant's staircase of dams and lakes that mounted from the Gulf to the headwaters of both rivers—rivers once turbulent, mighty, and at times vastly destructive, now flowing tamely in vitrolith channels.

As the flight continued southwestward from St. Louis the terraced contours of the universal Forest slowly emerged from dusky obscurity as the light of the reversed sunset crept up the sky. Everywhere were the chains of lakes and dams that marked the river courses. Everywhere were the endlessly diversified patterns of the terraced cities—wheels and stars, snowflake designs, labyrinths of polygons within polygons, interlaced circles, three-dimensional lattices of arches piled one above the other like Roman aqueducts. Many of these shapes were still a-building and therefore unsymmetrical. At times flotillas of clouds allowed only glimpses of the tapestry of cities and forest.

While the plane was crossing the southeast corner of New Mexico the edge of the sun appeared above the western horizon, throwing the topography of the land into high relief. A sprawling, gleaming flat structure was revealed below. Kim sat upright and exclaimed, "There's a Biological Preserve!"

Jothen said, "It's hard to be sure of colors from this altitude, but it doesn't look like Starved Rock. Everything around it is lush and green. The Preserve is a drab greenish-brown."

"It should be. It's the Staked Plain Preserve of Desert Life. Naturally it isn't oversupplied with greenery. In some sectors the rain sprays are

turned on for short periods only once or twice a year. There are sectors
with wind machines that can make sandstorms."

"No mirages?"

"I don't know. If they do occur it's not by design."

Southwest of the Staked Plain Preserve the city of Juarez-Elpaso,
formed like a ten-petaled flower, lay across the Rio Grande between an
upper and a lower reservoir. Beyond the Rio Grande the contour terraces
became narrower and climbed the flanks of range after range of mountains, stopping only at the timber line.

Half of the sun's disk was now above the horizon.

a view from within

If cities continue to grow and develop in the direction indicated in the preceding
selection, the difference between conditions of life in a major city and in the future
will probably be at least as great as the difference between life in New York City
in 1750 and life there now. The following selection describes something of what
life might be like in a New York City of the future that has a population of about
20 million.

caves of steel

by Isaac Asimov

There was the usual, entirely normal crowd on the expressway: the standees on the lower level and those with seat privileges above. A continuous
trickle of humanity filtered off the expressway, across the decelerating
strips to localways or into the stationaries that led under arches or over
bridges into the endless mazes of the City Sections. Another trickle, just
as continuous, worked inward from the other side, across the accelerating
strips and onto the expressway.

There were the infinite lights: the luminous walls and ceilings that
seemed to drip cool, even phosphorescence; the flashing advertisements
screaming for attention; the harsh, steady gleam of the "lightworms" that
directed THIS WAY TO JERSEY SECTIONS, FOLLOW ARROWS TO EAST RIVER
SHUTTLE, UPPER LEVEL FOR ALL WAYS TO LONG ISLAND SECTIONS.

Most of all there was the noise that was inseparable from life: the sound of millions talking, laughing, coughing, calling, humming, breathing.

No directions anywhere to Spacetown, thought Baley.

He stepped from strip to strip with the ease of a lifetime's practice. Children learned to "hop the strips" as soon as they learned to walk. Baley scarcely felt the jerk of acceleration as his velocity increased with each step. He was not even aware that he leaned forward against the force. In thirty seconds he had reached the final sixty-mile-an-hour strip and could step aboard the railed and glassed-in moving platform that was the expressway. . . .

There is a game that youngsters know called "running the strips." Its rules vary in trivial fashion from City to City, but its essentials are eternal. A boy from San Francisco can join the game in Cairo with no trouble.

Its object is to get from point A to point B via the City's rapid transit system in such a way that the "leader" manages to lose as many of his followers as possible. A leader who arrives at the destination alone is skillful indeed, as is a follower who refuses to be shaken.

The game is usually conducted during the evening rush hour when the increased density of the commuters makes it at once more hazardous and more complicated. The leader sets off, running up and down the accelerating strips. He does his best to do the unexpected, remaining standing on a given strip as long as possible, then leaping off suddenly in either direction. He will run quickly through several strips, then remain waiting once more.

Pity the follower who incautiously careens forward one strip too far. Before he has caught his mistake, unless he is extraordinarily nimble, he has driven past the leader or fallen behind. The clever leader will compound the error by moving quickly in the appropriate direction.

A move designed to increase the complexity of the task tenfold involves boarding the localways or the expressways themselves, and hurtling off the other side. It is bad form to avoid them completely and also bad form to linger on them.

The attraction of the game is not easy for an adult to understand, particularly for an adult who has never himself been a teen-age strip-runner. The players are roughly treated by legitimate travelers into whose path they find themselves inevitably flying. They are persecuted bitterly by the police and punished by their parents. They are denounced in the schools and on the subetherics. No year passes without its four or five teen-agers killed at the game, its dozens hurt, its cases of innocent by-standers meeting tragedy of varying degree.

Yet nothing can be done to wipe out the strip-running gangs. The greater the danger, the more the strip-runners have that most valuable of all prizes, honor in the eyes of their fellows. A successful one may well swagger; a well-known leader is cock-of-the-walk.

Elijah Baley, for instance, remembered with satisfaction even now that he had been a strip-runner once. He had led a gang of twenty from the Concourse Sector to the borders of Queens, crossing three expressways. In two tireless and relentless hours, he had shaken off some of the most agile followers of the Bronx, and arrived at the destination point alone. They taked about that run for months.

Baley was in his forties now, of course. He hadn't run the strips for over twenty years, but he remembered some of the tricks. What he had lost in agility, he made up in another respect. He was a policeman. No one but another policeman as experienced as himself could possibly know the City as well, know where almost every metal-bordered alley began and ended.

He walked away from the kitchen briskly, but not too rapidly. Each moment he expected the cry of "Robot, robot" to ring out behind him. That initial set of moments was the riskiest. He counted the steps until he felt the first accelerating strip moving under him. . . .

[Baley] lifted himself onto the expressway platform, made his way through the standees to the tight spiral ramp that led to the upper level, and there sat down. He didn't put his rating ticket in his hatband till they passed the last of the Hudson Sections. A C–5 had no seat rights east of the Hudson and west of Long Island, and although there was ample seating available at the moment, one of the way guards would have automatically ousted him. People were increasingly petty about rating privileges and, in all honesty, Baley lumped himself in with "people."

The air made the characteristic whistling noise as it frictioned off the curved windshields set up above the back of every seat. It made talking a chore, but it was no bar to thinking when you were used to it.

Most Earthmen were Medievalists in one way or another. It was an easy thing to be when it meant looking back to a time when Earth was *the* world and not just one of fifty. The misfit one of fifty at that.

Baley's head snapped to the right at the sound of a female shriek. A woman had dropped her handbag; he saw it for an instant, a pastel pink blob against the dull gray of the strips. A passenger hurrying from the expressway must inadvertently have kicked it in the direction of deceleration and now the owner was whirling away from her property.

A corner of Baley's mouth quirked. She might catch up with it, if she were clever enough to hurry to a strip that moved slower still and if other feet did not kick it this way or that. He would never know whether she would or not. The scene was half a mile to the rear, already.

Chances were she wouldn't. It had been calculated that, on the average, something was dropped on the strips every three minutes somewhere in the City and not recovered. The Lost and Found Department was a huge proposition. It was just one more complication of modern life.

Baley thought: It was simpler once. Everything was simpler. That's what makes Medievalists.

Medievalism took different forms. To the unimaginative Julius Enderby, it meant the adoption of archaisms. Spectacles! Windows!

To Baley, it was a study of history. Particularly the history of folkways.

The City now! New York City in which he lived and had his being. Larger than any City but Los Angeles. More populous than any but Shanghai. It was only three centuries old.

To be sure, something had existed in the same geographic area before then that had been *called* New York City. That primitive gathering of population had existed for three thousand years, not three hundred, but it hadn't been a *City*.

There were no Cities then. There were just huddles of dwelling places large and small, open to the air. They were something like the Spacer's Domes, only much different, of course. These huddles (the largest barely reached ten million in population and most never reached one million) were scattered all over Earth by the thousands. By modern standards, they had been completely inefficient, economically.

Efficiency had been forced on Earth with increasing population. Two billion people, three billion, even five billion could be supported by the planet by progressive lowering of the standard of living. When the population reaches eight billion, however, semistarvation becomes too much like the real thing. A radical change had to take place in man's culture, particularly when it turned out that the Outer Worlds (which had merely been Earth's colonies a thousand years before) were tremendously serious in their immigration restrictions.

The radical change had been the gradual formation of the Cities over a thousand years of Earth's history. Efficiency implied bigness. Even in Medieval times that had been realized, perhaps unconsciously. Home industry gave way to factories and factories to continental industries.

Think of the inefficiency of a hundred thousand houses for a hundred thousand families as compared with a hundred-thousand-unit Section; a book-film collection in each house as compared with a Section film concentrate; independent video for each family as compared with video-piping systems.

For that matter, take the simple folly of endless duplication of kitchens and bathrooms as compared with the thoroughly efficient diners and shower rooms made possible by City culture.

More and more the villages, towns, and "cities" of Earth died and were swallowed by the Cities. Even the early prospects of atomic war only slowed the trend. With the invention of the force shield, the trend became a headlong race.

City culture meant optimum distribution of food, increasing utilization of yeasts and hydroponics. New York City spread over two thousand square miles and at the last census its population was well over twenty million. There were some eight hundred Cities on Earth, average population, ten million.

Each City became a semiautonomous unit, economically all but self-sufficient. It could roof itself in, gird itself about, burrow itself under. It became a steel cave, a tremendous, self-contained cave of steel and concrete.

It could lay itself out scientifically. At the center was the enormous complex of administrative offices. In careful orientation to one another and to the whole were the large residential Sections connected and interlaced by the expressway and the localways. Toward the outskirts were the factories, the hydroponic plants, the yeast-culture vats, the power plants. Through all the melee were the water pipes and sewage ducts, schools, prisons and shops, power lines and communication beams.

There was no doubt about it: the City was the culmination of man's mastery over the environment. Not space travel, not the fifty colonized worlds that were now so haughtily independent, but the City.

Practically none of Earth's population lived outside the Cities. Outside was the wilderness, the open sky that few men could face with anything like equanimity. To be sure, the open space was necessary. It held the water that men must have, the coal and the wood that were the ultimate raw materials for plastics and for the eternally growing yeasts. (Petroleum had long since gone, but oil-rich strains of yeast were an adequate substitute.) The land between the Cities still held the mines, and was still used to a larger extent than most men realized for growing food and grazing stock. It was inefficient, but beef, pork, and grain always found a luxury market and could be used for export purposes.

But few humans were required to run the mines and ranches, to exploit the farms and pipe the water, and these supervised at long distance. Robots did the work better and required less.

Robots! That was the one huge irony. It was on Earth that the positronic brain was invented and on Earth that robots had first been put to productive use.

Not on the Outer Worlds. Of course, the Outer Worlds always acted as though robots had been born of their culture.

In a way, of course, the culmination of robot economy had taken place on the Outer Worlds. Here on Earth, robots had always been restricted to the mines and farmlands. Only in the last quarter century, under the urgings of the Spacers, had robots filtered their slow way into the Cities.

The Cities were good. Everyone but the Medievalists knew that there was no substitute, no reasonable substitute. The only trouble was that they wouldn't stay good. Earth's population was still rising. Some day, with all that the Cities could do, the available calories per person would simply fall below basic subsistence level.

It was all the worse because of the existence of the Spacers, the descendants of the early emigrants from Earth, living in luxury on their underpopulated robot-ridden worlds out in space. They were coolly determined to keep the comfort that grew out of the emptiness of their worlds and for that purpose they kept their birth rate down and immigrants from teeming Earth out. And this—

For a person who grew up in a rural environment, the minimum living and roaming space that a man requires to feel psychologically comfortable is probably quite different from the minimum necessary to a man socialized in a city. Requirements of social distance and privacy that are perceived as necessary and proper are probably also determined not so much by objective conditions as by a person's past experiences and by the norms to which he has become accustomed. Under the social conditions that Asimov creates in *Caves of Steel,* expectations about privacy and about norms that govern such activities as meals are quite different from those we know.

The context in which the following two excerpts take place is that Baley is forced to work with a robot designed to perform the work of a detective. Unlike most of the robots used on earth, R. Daneel is designed to pass as human.

Baley paused before the large double door on which there glowed in large letters PERSONAL—MEN. In smaller letters were written SUB-SECTIONS 1A—1E. In still smaller letters, just above the key slit, it stated: "In case of loss of key, communicate at once with 27–101–51."

A man inched past them, inserted an aluminum sliver into the key slit, and walked in. He closed the door behind him, making no attempt to hold it open for Baley. Had he done so, Baley would have been seriously offended. By strong custom men disregarded one another's presence entirely either within or just outside the Personals. Baley remembered one of the more interesting marital confidences to have been Jessie's telling him that the situation was quite different at Women's Personals.

She was always saying, "I met Josephine Greely at Personal and she said . . . "

It was one of the penalties of civic advancement that when the Baleys were granted permission for the activation of the small washbowl in their bedroom, Jessie's social life suffered.

Baley said, without completely masking his embarrassment, "Please wait out here, Daneel."

"Do you intend washing?" asked R. Daneel.

Baley squirmed and thought: Damned robot! If they were briefing him on everything under steel, why didn't they teach him manners? I'll be responsible if he ever says anything like this to anyone else.

He said, "I'll shower. It gets crowded evenings. I'll lose time then. If I get it done now we'll have the whole evening before us."

R. Daneel's face maintained its repose. "Is it part of the social custom that I wait outside?"

Baley's embarrassment deepened. "Why need you go in for—for no purpose."

"Oh, I understand you. Yes, of course. Nevertheless, Elijah, my hands grow dirty, too, and I will wash them."

He indicated his palms, holding them out before him. They were pink and plump, with the proper creases. They bore every mark of excellent and meticulous workmanship and were as clean as need be.

Baley said, "We have a washbasin in the apartment, you know." He said it casually. Snobbery would be lost on a robot.

"Thank you for your kindness. On the whole, however, I think it would be preferable to make use of this place. If I am to live with you men of Earth, it is best that I adopt as many of your customs and attitudes as I can."

"Come on in, then."

The bright cheerfulness of the interior was a sharp contrast to the busy utilitarianism of most of the rest of the City, but this time the effect was lost on Baley's consciousness.

He whispered to Daneel, "I may take up to half an hour or so. Wait for me." He started away, then returned to add, "And listen, don't talk to anybody and don't look at anybody. Not a word, not a glance! It's a custom."

He looked hurriedly about to make certain that his own small conversation had not been noted, was not being met by shocked glances. Nobody, fortunately, was in the antecorridor, and after all it *was* only the antecorridor.

He hurried down it, feeling vaguely dirty, past the common chambers to the private stalls. It had been five years now since he had been awarded one—large enough to contain a shower, a small laundry, and other necessities. It even had a small projector that could be keyed in for the new films.

"A home away from home." he had joked when it was first made available to him. But now, he often wondered how he would bear the adjustment back to the more Spartan existence of the common chambers if his stall privileges were ever canceled.

He pressed the button that activated the laundry and the smooth face of the meter lighted.

R. Daneel was waiting patiently when Baley returned with a scrubbed body, clean underwear, a freshened shirt, and, generally a feeling of greater comfort.

"No trouble?" Baley asked, when they were well outside the door and able to talk.

"None at all, Elijah," said R. Daneel.

Section kitchens were the same all over the City. What's more, Baley had been in Washington, Toronto, Los Angeles, London, and Budapest in the way of business, and they had been the same there, too. Perhaps it had been different in Medieval times when languages had varied and dietaries as well. Nowadays, yeast products were just the same from Shanghai to Tashkent and from Winnipeg to Buenos Aires; and English might not be the "English" of Shakespeare or Churchill, but it was the final potpourri that was current over all the continents and, with some modification, on the Outer Worlds as well.

But language and dietary aside, there were the deeper similarities. There was always that particular odor, undefinable but completely characteristic of "kitchen." There was the waiting triple line moving slowly in, converging at the door and splitting up again, right, left, center. There was the rumble of humanity, speaking and moving, and the sharper clatter of plastic on plastic. There was the gleam of simulated wood, highly polished, highlights on glass, long tables, the touch of steam in the air.

Baley inched slowly forward as the line moved (with all possible staggering of meal hours, a wait of at least ten minutes was almost unavoidable). . . .

They were at the entrance. Person after person thrust his metal food tag through the appropriate slot and had it scanned. Click—click—click—

Someone once calculated that a smoothly running kitchen could allow the entrance of two hundred persons a minute, the tags of each one being fully scanned to prevent kitchen-jumping, meal-jumping, and ration-stretching. They had also calculated how long a waiting line was necessary for maximum efficiency and how much time was lost when any one person required special treatment.

It was therefore always a calamity to interrupt that smooth click—click by stepping to the manual window, as Baley and R. Daneel did, in order to thrust a special-permit pass at the official in charge.

Jessie, filled with the knowledge of an assistant dietitian, had explained it once to Baley.

"It upsets things completely," she said. "It throws off consumption figures and inventory estimates. It means special checks. You have to match slips with all the different Section kitchens to make sure the balance isn't too unbalanced, if you know what I mean. There's a separate balance sheet to be made out each week. Then if anything goes wrong and you're overdrawn, it's always your fault. It's never the fault of the City Government for passing out special tickets to everybody and his kid sister. Oh, no. And when we have to say that free choice is suspended for the meal, don't the people in line make a fuss. It's always the fault of the people behind the counter. . . . "

Baley had the story in the fullest detail and so he quite understood the dry and poisonous look he received from the woman behind the window.

She made a few hurried notes. Home Section, occupation, reason for meal displacement ("official business," a very irritating reason indeed, but quite irrefutable). Then she folded the slip with firm motions of her fingers and pushed it into a slot. A computer seized it, devoured the contents, and digested the information.

She turned to R. Daneel.

Baley let her have the worst. He said, "My friend is out-of-City."

The woman looked finally and completely outraged. She said, "Home City, please."

Baley intercepted the ball for Daneel once again. "All records are to be credited to the Police Department. No details necessary. Official business."

The woman brought down a pad of slips with a jerk of her arm and filled in the necessary matter in dark-light code with practiced pressings of the first two fingers of her right hand.

She said, "How long will you be eating here?"

"Till further notice," said Baley.

"Press fingers here," she said, inverting the information blank. . . .

The woman took the blank away and fed it into the all-consuming machine at her elbow. It belched nothing back and Baley breathed more easily.

She gave them little metal tags that were in the bright red that meant "temporary."

She said, "No free choices. We're short this week. Take table DF."

They made their way toward DF.

R. Daneel said, "I am under the impression that most of your people eat in kitchens such as these regularly."

"Yes. Of course, it's rather gruesome eating in a strange kitchen. There's no one about whom you know. In your own kitchen, it's quite different. You have your own seat which you occupy all the time. You're with your family, your friends. Especially when you're young, mealtimes are the bright spot of the day." Baley smiled in brief reminiscence.

Table DF was apparently among those reserved for transients. Those already seated watched their plates uneasily and did not talk with one another. They looked with sneaking envy at the laughing crowds at the other tables.

There is no one so uncomfortable, thought Baley, as the man eating out-of-Section. . . . Even the food tastes better, no matter how many chemists are ready to swear it to be no different from the food in Johannesburg.

He sat down on a stool and R. Daneel sat down next to him.

"No free choice," said Baley, with a wave of his fingers, "so just close the switch there and wait."

It took two minutes. A disc slid back in the table top and a dish lifted.

"Mashed potatoes, zymoveal sauce, and stewed apricots. Oh, well," said Baley.

A fork and two slices of whole yeast bread appeared in a recess just in front of the low railing that went down the long center of the table.

A common theme in treatments of the future is the joint effects of population growth and automation. If population continues to grow, and the number of jobs diminishes because of automation and cybernation, increasingly large portions of the population will be unable to find work. Usually the first reaction to this assertion is to draw an analogy between the initial effects of the industrial revolution, loss of employment for large numbers of workers, and later effects, increases in employment opportunities. This analogy might, however, not be appropriate, for there is no guarantee that new industries requiring large numbers of human workers will develop. Automation and cybernation would have the effect of taking over the control functions that human workers carried out after the first industrial revolution. Before then, human beings provided both the energy necessary to accomplish work and the intelligence necessary to control this energy. After the first industrial revolution, the energy was supplied by machines and the intelligence necessary to control its application was supplied by human beings. If this second activity can be performed by machines, relatively little might remain that required a human worker.

The final selection from *Caves of Steel* treats reactions to the growing use of robots on Earth. Baley and R. Daneel are about to leave an expressway platform when Baley notices a crowd and a disturbance. Although R. Daneel, a robot designed to function as a policeman, appears to be human, Baley does not believe that he has the ability to cope with the variable and sensitive social situations to which an officer must respond.

They were at East 182nd Street and in not more than two hundred yards they would be at the elevator banks that fed those steel and concrete layers of apartments that included his own.

He was on the point of saying, "This way," when he was stopped by a knot of people gathering outside the brilliantly lighted force door of one of the many retail departments that lined the ground levels solidly in this Section.

He asked of the nearest person in an automatic tone of authority, "What's going on?"

The man he addressed, who was standing on tiptoe, said, "Damned if I know. I just got here."

Someone else said, excitedly, "They got those lousy R's in there. I think maybe they'll throw them out here. Boy, I'd like to take them apart."

Baley looked nervously at Daneel, but, if the latter caught the significance of the words or even heard them, he did not show it by any outward sign.

Baley plunged into the crowd. "Let me through. Let me through. Police!"

They made way. Baley caught words behind him.

"... take them apart. Nut by nut. Split them down the seams slowlike ..." And someone else laughed.

Baley turned a little cold. The City was the acme of efficiency, but it made demands of its inhabitants. It asked them to live in a tight routine and order their lives under a strict and scientific control. Occasionally, built-up inhibitions exploded.

He remembered the Barrier Riots.

Reasons for anti-robot rioting certainly existed. Men who found themselves faced with the prospect of the desperate minimum involved in declassification, after half a lifetime of effort, could not decide coldbloodedly that individual robots were not to blame. Individual robots could at least be struck at.

One could not strike at something called "governmental policy" or at a slogan like "Higher production with robot labor."

The government called it growing pains. It shook its collective head sorrowfully and assured everyone that after a necessary period of adjustment, a new and better life would exist for all.

But the Medievalist movement expanded along with the declassification process. Men grew desperate and the border between bitter frustration and wild destruction is sometimes easily crossed.

At this moment, minutes could be separating the pent-up hostility of the crowd from a flashing orgy of blood and smash.

Baley writhed his way desperately to the force door.

The interior of the store was emptier than the street outside. The manager, with commendable foresight, had thrown the force door early in the game, preventing potential troublemakers from entering. It also kept the principals in the argument from leaving, but that was minor.

Baley got through the force door by using his officer's neutralizer. Unexpectedly, he found R. Daneel still behind him. The robot was pocketing a neutralizer of his own, a slim one, smaller and neater than the standard police model.

The manager ran to them instantly, talking loudly. "Officers, my clerks have been assigned me by the City. I am perfectly within my rights."

There were three robots standing rodlike at the rear of the department. Six humans were standing near the force door. They were all women.

"All right, now," said Baley, crisply. "What's going on? What's all the fuss about?"

One of the women said, shrilly, "I came in for shoes. Why can't I have a decent clerk? Ain't I respectable?" Her clothing, especially her hat, were just sufficiently extreme to make it more than a rhetorical question. The angry flush that covered her face masked imperfectly her overdone makeup.

The manager said, "I'll wait on her myself if I have to, but I can't wait

on all of them, Officer. There's nothing wrong with my men. They're
registered clerks. I have their spec charts and guarantee slips—"
"Spec charts," screamed the woman. She laughed shrilly, turning to the
rest. "Listen to him. He calls them men! What's the matter with you
anyway? They ain't men. They're ro-bots!" She stretched out the syllables.
"And I tell you what they do, in case you don't know. They steal jobs from
men. That's why the government always protects them. They work for
nothin' and, on account o' that, families gotta live out in the barracks and
eat raw yeast mush. Decent hard-working families. We'd smash up all the
ro-bots, if *I* was boss. I tell you that!"

The others talked confusedly and there was always the growing rumble
from the crowd just beyond the force door.

Baley was conscious, brutally conscious, of R. Daneel Olivaw standing
at his elbow. He looked at the clerks. They were Earthmade, and even on
that scale, relatively inexpensive models. They were just robots made to
know a few simple things. They would know all the style numbers, their
prices, the sizes available in each. They could keep track of stock fluctuations, probably better than humans could, since they would have no outside interests. They could compute the proper orders for the next week.
They could measure the customer's foot.

In themselves, harmless. As a group, incredibly dangerous.

Baley could sympathize with the woman more deeply than he would
have believed possible the day before. No, two hours before. He could feel
R. Daneel's nearness and he wondered if R. Daneel could not replace an
ordinary plain-clothes man C—5. He could see the barracks, as he thought
that. He could taste the yeast mush. He could remember his father.

His father had been a nuclear physicist, with a rating that had put him
in the top percentile of the City. There had been an accident at the power
plant and his father had borne the blame. He had been declassified. Baley
did not know the details; it had happened when he was a year old.

But he remembered the barracks of his childhood; the grinding commu-
nal existence just this side of the edge of bearability. He remembered his
mother not at all; she had not survived long. His father he recalled well,
a sodden man, morose and lost, speaking sometimes of the past in hoarse,
broken sentences.

His father died, still declassified, when Lije was eight. Young Baley and
his two older sisters moved into the Section orphanage. Children's Level,
they called it. His mother's brother, Uncle Boris, was himself too poor to
prevent that.

So it continued hard. And it was hard going through school, with no
father-derived status privileges to smooth the way.

And now he had to stand in the middle of a growing riot and beat down
men and women who, after all, only feared declassification for themselves
and those they loved, as he himself did.

Tonelessly, he said to the woman who had already spoken, "Let's not have any trouble, lady. The clerks aren't doing you any harm."

"Sure they ain't done me no harm," sopranoed the woman. "They ain't gonna, either. Think I'll let their cold, greasy fingers touch me? I came in here expecting to get treated like a human being. I'm a citizen. I got a right to have human beings wait on me. And listen, I got two kids waiting for supper. They can't go to the Section kitchen without me, like they was orphans. I gotta get out of here."

Well, now," said Baley, feeling his temper slipping, "if you had let yourself be waited on, you'd have been out of here by now. You're just making trouble for nothing. Come on now."

Well!" The woman registered shock. "Maybe you think you can talk to me like I was dirt. Maybe it's time the guv'min' reelized robots ain't the only things on Earth. I'm a hard-working woman and I've got rights." She went on and on and on.

Baley felt harassed and caught. The situation was out of hand. Even if the women would consent to be waited on, the waiting crowd was ugly enough for anything.

There must be a hundred crammed outside the display window now. In the few minutes since the plain-clothes men had entered the store, the crowd had doubled.

"What is the usual procedure in such a case?" asked R. Daneel Olivaw, suddenly.

Baley nearly jumped. He said, "This is an unusual case in the first place."

"What is the law?"

"The R's have been duly assigned here. They're registered clerks. There's nothing illegal about that."

They were speaking in whispers. Baley tried to look official and threatening. Olivaw's expression, as always, meant nothing at all.

"In that case," said R. Daneel, "order the woman to let herself be waited on or to leave."

Baley lifted a corner of his lip briefly. "It's a mob we have to deal with, not a woman. There's nothing to do but call a riot squad."

"It should not be necessary for citizens to require more than one officer of the law to direct what should be done," said Daneel.

He turned his broad face to the store manager. "Open the force door, sir."

Baley's arm shot forward to seize R. Daneel's shoulder, swing him about. He arrested the motion. If, at this moment, two law men quarreled openly, it would mean the end of all chance for a peaceful solution.

The manager protested, looked at Baley. Baley did not meet his eye.

R. Daneel said, unmoved, "I order you with the authority of the law."

The manager bleated, "I'll hold the City responsible for any damage to the goods or fixtures. I serve notice that I'm doing this under orders."

The barrier went down; men and women crowded in. There was a happy roar from them. They sensed victory.

Baley had heard of similar riots. He had witnessed one. He had seen robots being lifted by a dozen hands, their heavy unresisting bodies carried backward from straining arm to straining arm. Men yanked and twisted at the metal mimicry of men. They used hammers, force knives, needle guns. They finally reduced the miserable objects to shredded metal and wire. Expensive positronic brains, the most intricate creation of the human mind, were thrown from hand to hand like footballs and mashed to uselessness in a trifle of time.

Then, with the genius of destruction so merrily loose, the mobs turned on anything else that could be taken apart.

The robot clerks could have no knowledge of any of this but they squealed as the crowd flooded inward and lifted their arms before their faces as though in a primitive effort at hiding. The woman who had started the fuss, frightened at seeing it grow suddenly so far beyond what she had expected, gasped, "Here, now. Here, now."

Her hat was shoved down over her face and her voice became only a meaningless shrillness.

The manager was shrieking, "Stop them, Officer. Stop them!"

R. Daneel spoke. Without apparent effort, his voice was suddenly decibels higher than a human's voice had a right to be. Of course, thought Baley for the tenth time, he's not—

R. Daneel said, "The next man who moves will be shot."

Someone well in the back yelled, "Get him!"

But for a moment, no one moved.

R. Daneel stepped nimbly upon a chair and from that to the top of a Transtex display case. The colored fluorescence gleaming through the slits of polarized molecular film turned his cool, smooth face into something unearthly.

Unearthly, thought Baley.

The tableau held as R. Daneel waited, a quietly formidable person.

R. Daneel said crisply, "You are saying, This man is holding a neuronic whip, or a tickler. If we all rush forward, we will bear him down and at most one or two of us will be hurt and even they will recover. Meanwhile, we will do just as we wish and to space with law and order."

His voice was neither harsh nor angry, but it carried authority. It had the tone of confident command. He went on, "You are mistaken. What I hold is not a neuronic whip, nor is it a tickler. It is a blaster and very deadly. I will use it and I will not aim over your heads. I will kill many of you before you seize me, perhaps most of you. I am serious. I look serious, do I not?"

There was motion at the outskirts, but the crowd no longer grew. If newcomers still stopped out of curiosity, others were hurrying away. Those nearest R. Daneel were holding their breath, trying desperately not to sway forward in response to the mass pressure of the bodies behind them.

The woman with the hat broke the spell. In a sudden whirlpool of sobbing, she yelled, "He's gonna kill us. I ain't done nothing. Oh, lemme outta here."

She turned, but faced an immovable wall of crammed men and women. She sank to her knees. The backward motion in the silent crowd grew more pronounced.

R. Daneel jumped down from the display counter and said, "I will now walk to the door. I will shoot the man or woman who touches me. When I reach the door, I will shoot any man or woman who is not moving about his business. This woman here——"

"No, no," yelled the woman with the hat, "I tell ya I didn't do nothing. I didn't mean no harm. I don't want no shoes. I just wanta go home."

"This woman here," went on Daneel, "will remain. She will be waited on."

He stepped forward.

The mob faced him dumbly. Baley closed his eyes. It wasn't his fault, he thought desperately. There'll be murder done and the worst mess in the world, but *they* forced a robot on me as partner. *They* gave him equal status.

It wouldn't do. He didn't believe himself. He might have stopped R. Daneel at the start. He might at any moment have put in the call for a squad car. He had let R. Daneel take responsibility, instead, and had felt a cowardly relief. When he tried to tell himself that R. Daneel's personality simply dominated the situation, he was filled with a sudden self-loathing. A *robot* dominating . . .

There was no unusual noise, no shouting and cursing, no groans, no yells. He opened his eyes.

They were dispersing.

The manager of the store was cooling down, adjusting his twisted jacket, smoothing his hair, muttering angry threats at the vanishing crowd.

The smooth, fading whistle of a squad car came to a halt just outside. Baley thought: Sure, when it's all over.

The manager plucked his sleeve. "Let's have no more trouble, Officer."

Baley said, "There won't be any trouble."

It was easy to get rid of the squad-car police. They had come in response to reports of a crowd in the street. They knew no details and could see for themselves that the street was clear.

— *d* —

a final solution

Imagine a world in which the problems of supplying necessary commodities, defending against the natural environment, and controlling the social environment have been solved, and the solutions are final in that there is no significant likelihood that change will occur and that the solutions will have to be modified. Imagine then, a world of affluence, peace, eternal life—and one that presents no new challenges. Would this be the most boring of all possible worlds, or would it be a paradise?

the city
and the stars

by Arthur C. Clarke

Like a glowing jewel, the city lay upon the breast of the desert. Once it had known change and alteration, but now Time passed it by. Night and day fled across the desert's face, but in the streets of Diaspar it was always afternoon, and darkness never came. The long winter nights might dust the desert with frost, as the last moisture left in the thin air of Earth congealed—but the city knew neither heat nor cold. It had no contact with the outer world; it was a universe itself.

Men had built cities before, but never a city such as this. Some had lasted for centuries, some for millenniums, before Time had swept away even their names. Diaspar alone had challenged Eternity, defending itself and all it sheltered against the slow attrition of the ages, the ravages of decay, and the corruption of rust.

Since the city was built, the oceans of Earth had passed away and the desert had encompassed all the globe. The last mountains had been ground to dust by the winds and the rain, and the world was too weary to bring forth more. The city did not care; Earth itself could crumble and Diaspar would still protect the children of its makers, bearing them and their treasures safely down the stream of time.

They had forgotten much, but they did not know it. They were as perfectly fitted to their environment as it was to them—for both had been designed together. What was beyond the walls of the city was no concern of theirs; it was something that had been shut out of their minds. Diaspar was all that existed, all that they needed, all that they could imagine. . . . They turned to the life and warmth of the city, to the long golden age whose beginning was already lost and whose end was yet more distant. Other men had dreamed of such an age, but they alone had achieved it.

They had lived in the same city, had walked the same miraculously unchanging streets, while more than a billion years had worn away. . . .

The room was dark save for one glowing wall, upon which the tides of color ebbed and flowed as Alvin wrestled with his dreams. Part of the pattern satisfied him; he had fallen in love with the soaring lines of the mountains as they leaped out of the sea. There was a power and pride about those ascending curves; he had studied them for a long time, and then fed them into the memory unit of the visualizer, where they would be preserved while he experimented with the rest of the picture. Yet something was eluding him, though what it was he did not know. Again and again he had tried to fill in the blank spaces, while the instrument read the shifting patterns in his mind and materialized them upon the wall. It was no good. The lines were blurred and uncertain, the colors muddy and dull. If the artist did not know his goal, even the most miraculous of tools could not find it for him.

Alvin canceled his unsatisfactory scribblings and stared morosely at the three-quarters-empty rectangle he had been trying to fill with beauty. On a sudden impulse, he doubled the size of the existing design and shifted it to the center of the frame. No—that was a lazy way out, and the balance was all wrong. Worse, still, the change of scale had revealed the defects in his construction, the lack of certainty in those at-first-sight confident lines. He would have to start all over again.

"Total erasure," he ordered the machine. The blue of the sea faded; the mountains dissolved like mist, until only the blank wall remained. They were as if they had never been—as if they were lost in the limbo that had taken all Earth's seas and mountains ages before Alvin was born.

The light came flooding back into the room and the luminous rectangle upon which Alvin had projected his dreams merged into its surroundings, to become one with the other walls. But were they walls? To anyone who had never seen such a place before, this was a very peculiar room indeed. It was utterly featureless and completely devoid of furniture, so that it seemed as if Alvin stood at the center of a sphere. No visible dividing lines separated walls from floor or ceiling. There was nothing on which the eye could focus; the space enclosing Alvin might have been ten feet or ten miles across, for all that the sense of vision could have told. It would have been hard to resist the temptation to walk forward, hands outstretched, to discover the physical limits of this extraordinary place.

Yet such rooms had been "home" to most of the human race for the greater part of its history. Alvin had only to frame the appropriate thought, and the walls would become windows opening upon any part of the city he chose. Another wish, and machines which he had never seen would fill the chamber with the projected images of any articles of furniture he might need. Whether they were "real" or not was a problem that had bothered few men for the last billion years. Certainly they were no less real than that other impostor, solid matter, and when they were no longer required they could be returned to the phantom world of the city's Memory Banks. Like everything else in Diaspar, they would never wear out—and they would never change, unless their stored patterns were canceled by a deliberate act of will.

Alvin had partly reconstructed his room when a persistent, bell-like chime sounded in his ear. He mentally framed the admission signal, and the wall upon which he had just been painting dissolved once more. As he had expected, there stood his parents, with Jeserac a little behind them. The presence of his tutor meant that this was no ordinary family reunion—but he knew that already.

The illusion was perfect, and it was not lost when Eriston spoke. In reality, as Alvin was well aware, Eriston, Etania, and Jeserac were all miles apart, for the builders of the city had conquered space as completely as they had subjugated time. Alvin was not even certain where his parents lived, among the multitudinous spires and intricate labyrinths of Diaspar, for they had both moved since he had last been physically in their presence.

"Alvin," began Eriston, "it is just twenty years since your mother and I first met you. You know what that means. Our guardianship is now ended, and you are free to do as you please."

There was a trace—but merely a trace—of sadness in Eriston's voice. There was considerably more relief, as if Eriston was glad that a state of affairs that had existed for some time in fact now had legal recognition. Alvin had anticipated his freedom by a good many years.

"I understand," he answered. "I thank you for watching over me, and I will remember you in all my lives." That was the formal response; he had heard it so often that all meaning had been leached away from it—it was merely a pattern of sounds with no particular significance. Yet "all my lives" was a strange expression, when one stopped to consider it. He knew vaguely what it meant; now the time had come for him to know exactly. There were many things in Diaspar which he did not understand, and which he would have to learn in the centuries that lay ahead of him.

For a moment it seemed as if Etania wished to speak. She raised one hand, disturbing the iridescent gossamer of her gown, then let it fall back to her side. Then she turned helplessly to Jeserac, and for the first time Alvin realized that his parents were worried. His memory swiftly scanned the events of the past few weeks. No, there was nothing in his recent life that could have caused this faint uncertainty, this air of mild alarm that seemed to surround both Eriston and Etania.

Jeserac, however, appeared to be in command of the situation. He gave an inquiring look at Eriston and Etania, satisfied himself that they had nothing more to say, and launched forth on the dissertation he had waited many years to make.

"Alvin," he began, "for twenty years you have been my pupil, and I have done my best to teach you the ways of the city, and to lead you to the heritage which is yours. You have asked me many questions, and not all of them have I been able to answer. Some things you were not ready to learn, and some I did not know myself. Now your infancy is over, though your childhood is scarcely begun. It is still my duty to guide you, if you need my help. In two hundred years, Alvin, you may begin to know something of this city and a little of its history. Even I, who am nearing the end of this life, have seen less than a quarter of Diaspar, and perhaps less than a thousandth of its treasures."

There was nothing so far that Alvin did not know, but there was no way of hurrying Jeserac. The old man looked steadfastly at him across the gulf of centuries, his words weighed down with the uncomputable wisdom acquired during a long lifetime's contact with men and machines.

"Tell me, Alvin," he said, "have you ever asked yourself *where* you were before you were born—before you found yourself facing Etania and Eriston at the Hall of Creation?"

"I assumed I was nowhere—that I was nothing but a pattern in the mind of the city, waiting to be created—like this."

A low couch glimmered and thickened into reality beside Alvin. He sat down upon it and waited for Jeserac to continue.

"You are correct, of course," came the reply. "But that is merely part of the answer—and a very small part indeed. Until now, you have met only children of your own age, and they have been ignorant of the truth. Soon they will remember, but you will not, so we must prepare you to face the facts.

"For over a billion years, Alvin, the human race has lived in this city. Since the Galactic Empire fell, and the Invaders went back to the stars, this has been our world. Outside the walls of Diaspar, there is nothing except the desert of which our legends speak.

"We know little about our primitive ancestors, except that they were very short-lived beings and that, strange though it seems, they could reproduce themselves without the aid of memory units or matter organizers. In a complex and apparently uncontrollable process, the key patterns of each human being were preserved in microscopic cell structures actually created inside the body. If you are interested, the biologists can tell you more about it, but the method is of no great importance since it was abandoned at the dawn of history.

"A human being, like any other object, is defined by its structure—its pattern. The pattern of a man, and still more the pattern which specifies a man's mind, is incredibly complex. Yet Nature was able to pack that pattern into a tiny cell, too small for the eye to see.

"What Nature can do, Man can do also, in his own way. We do not know how long the task took. A million years, perhaps—but what is that? In the end our ancestors learned how to analyze and store the information that would define any specific human being—and to use that information to re-create the original, as you have just created that couch.

"I know that such things interest you, Alvin, but I cannot tell you exactly how it is done. The way in which information is stored is of no importance; all that matters is the information itself. It may be in the form of written words on paper, of varying magnetic fields, or patterns of electric charge. Men have used all these methods of storage, and many others. Suffice to say that long ago they were able to store themselves—or, to be more precise, the disembodied patterns from which they could be called back into existence.

"So much, you already know. This is the way our ancestors gave us virtual immortality, yet avoided the problems raised by the abolition of death. A thousand years in one body is long enough for any man; at the end of that time, his mind is clogged with memories, and he asks only for rest—or a new beginning.

"In a little while, Alvin, I shall prepare to leave this life. I shall go back through my memories, editing them and canceling those I do not wish to keep. Then I shall walk into the Hall of Creation, but through a door which you have never seen. This old body will cease to exist, and so will consciousness itself. Nothing will be left of Jeserac but a galaxy of electrons frozen in the heart of a crystal.

"I shall sleep, Alvin, and without dreams. Then one day, perhaps a hundred thousand years from now, I shall find myself in a new body, meeting those who have been chosen to be my guardians. They will look after me as Eriston and Etania have guided you, for at first I will know nothing of Diaspar and will have no memories of what I was before. Those memories will slowly return, at the end of my infancy, and I will build upon them as I move forward into my new cycle of existence.

"That is the pattern of our lives, Alvin. We have all been here many, many times before, though as the intervals of non-existence vary according to apparently random laws this present population will never repeat itself again. The new Jeserac will have new and different friends and interests, but the old Jeserac—as much of him as I wish to save—will still exist.

"That is not all. At any moment, Alvin, only a hundredth of the citizens of Diaspar live and walk its streets. The vast majority slumber in the Memory Banks, waiting for the signal that will call them forth onto the stage of existence once again. So we have continuity, yet change—immortality, but not stagnation.

"I know what you are wondering, Alvin. You want to know when you will recall the memories of your earlier lives, as your companions are already doing.

"There are no such memories, for you are unique. We have tried to keep this knowledge from you as long as we could, so that no shadow should lie across your childhood—though I think you must have guessed part of the truth already. We did not suspect it ourselves until five years ago, but now there is no doubt.

"You, Alvin, are something that has happened in Diaspar only a handful of times since the founding of the city. Perhaps you have been lying dormant in the Memory Banks through all the ages—or perhaps you were created only twenty years ago by some random permutation. You may have been planned in the beginning by the designers of the city, or you may be a purposeless accident of our own time.

"We do not know. All that we do know is this: You, Alvin, alone of the human race, have never lived before. In literal truth, you are the first child to be born on Earth for at least ten million years."

When Jeserac and his parents had faded from view, Alvin lay for a long time trying to hold his mind empty of thought. He closed his room around him, so that no one could interrupt his trance.

He was not sleeping; sleep was something he had never experienced, for that belonged to a world of night and day, and here there was only day. This was the nearest he could come to that forgotten state, and though it was not really essential to him he knew that it would help compose his mind. . . .

The wall flickered partially out of existence as he stepped through to the corridor, and its polarized molecules resisted his passage like a feeble wind blowing against his face. There were many ways in which he could be carried effortlessly to his goal, but he preferred to walk. His room was almost at the main city level, and a short passage brought him out onto a spiral ramp which led down to the street. He ignored the moving way, and kept to the narrow sidewalk—an eccentric thing to do, since he had several miles to travel. But Alvin liked the exercise, for it soothed his mind. Besides, there was so much to see that it seemed a pity to race past the latest marvels of Diaspar when you had eternity ahead of you.

It was the custom of the city's artists—and everyone in Diaspar was an artist at some time or another—to display their current productions along the side of the moving ways, so that the passers-by could admire their work. In this manner, it was usually only a few days before the entire population had critically examined any noteworthy creation, and also expressed its views upon it. The resulting verdict, recorded automatically by opinion-sampling devices which no one had ever been able to suborn or deceive—and there had been enough attempts—decided the fate of the masterpiece. If there was a sufficiently affirmative vote, its matrix would go into the memory of the city so that anyone who wished, at any future date, could possess a reproduction utterly indistinguishable from the original.

The less successful pieces went the way of all such works. They were either dissolved back into their original elements or ended in the homes of the artists' friends.

Alvin saw only one *objet d'art* on his journey that had any appeal to him. It was a creation of pure light, vaguely reminiscent of an unfolding flower. Slowly growing from a minute core of color, it would expand into complex spirals and curtains, then suddenly collapse and begin the cycle over again. Yet not precisely, for no two cycles were identical. Though Alvin watched through a score of pulsations, each time there were subtle and indefinable differences, even though the basic pattern remained the same.

He knew why he liked this piece of intangible sculpture. Its expanding rhythm gave an impression of space—even of escape. For that reason, it would probably not appeal to many of Alvin's compatriots. He made a note of the artist's name and decided to call him at the earliest opportunity.

All the roads, both moving and stationary, came to an end when they reached the park that was the green heart of the city. Here, in a circular space over three miles across, was a memory of what Earth had been in the days before the desert swallowed all but Diaspar. First there was a wide belt of grass, then low trees which grew thicker and thicker as one walked forward beneath their shade. At the same time the ground sloped gently downward, so that when at last one emerged from the narrow forest all sign of the city had vanished, hidden by the screen of trees.

The wide stream that lay ahead of Alvin was called, simply, the River. It possessed, and it needed, no other name. At intervals it was spanned by narrow bridges, and it flowed around the park in a complete, closed circle, broken by occasional lagoons. That a swiftly moving river could return upon itself after a course of less than six miles had never struck Alvin as at all unusual; indeed, he would not have thought twice about the matter if at some point in its circuit the River had flowed uphill. There were far stranger things than this in Diaspar.

A dozen young people were swimming in one of the little lagoons, and Alvin paused to watch them. He knew most of them by sight, if not by name, and for a moment was tempted to join in their play. . . .

Physically, there was no way of telling which of these young citizens had walked out of the Hall of Creation this year and which had lived in Diaspar as long as Alvin. Though there were considerable variations in height and weight, they had no correlation with age. People were simply born that way, and although on the average the taller the person, the greater the age, this was not a reliable rule to apply unless one was dealing in centuries.

The face was a safer guide. Some of the newborn were taller than Alvin, but they had a look of immaturity, an expression of wondering surprise at the world in which they now found themselves that revealed them at once. It was strange to think that, slumbering untapped in their minds, were infinite vistas of lives that they would soon remember. Alvin envied them, yet he was not sure if he should. One's first existence was a precious gift which would never be repeated. It was wonderful to view life for the very first time, as in the freshness of the dawn. If only there were others like him, with whom he could share his thoughts and feelings!

Yet physically he was cast in precisely the same mold as those children playing in the water. The human body had changed not at all in the billion years since the building of Diaspar, since the basic design had been eternally frozen in the Memory Banks of the city. It had changed, however, a good deal from its original primitive form, though most of the alterations were internal and not visible to the eye. Man had rebuilt himself many times in his long history, in the effort to abolish those ills to which the flesh was once heir.

Such unnecessary appurtenances as nails and teeth had vanished. Hair was confined to the head; not a trace was left on the body. The feature that would most have surprised a man of the Dawn Ages was, perhaps, the disappearance of the navel. Its inexplicable absence would have given him much food for thought, and at first sight he would also have been baffled by the problem of distinguishing male from female. He might even have been tempted to assume that there was no longer any difference, which would have been a grave error. In the appropriate circumstances, there was no doubt about the masculinity of any male in Diaspar. It was merely that his equipment was now more neatly packaged when not required; internal stowage had vastly improved upon Nature's original inelegant and indeed downright hazardous arrangements.

It was true that reproduction was no longer the concern of the body, being far too important a matter to be left to games of chance played with chromosomes as dice. Yet, though conception and birth were not even memories, sex remained. Even in ancient times, not one-hundredth part of sexual activity had been concerned with reproduction. The disappearance of that mere one per cent had changed the pattern of human society and the meaning of such words as "father" and "mother"—but desire remained, though now its satisfaction had no profounder aim than that of any of the other pleasures of the senses.

Alvin left his playful contemporaries and continued on toward the center of the park. There were faintly marked paths here, crossing and crisscrossing through low shrubbery and occasionally diving into narrow ravines between great lichen-covered boulders. Once he came across a small polyhedral machine, no larger than a man's head, floating among the branches of a tree. No one knew how many varieties of robot there were in Diaspar; they kept out of the way and minded their business so effectively that it was quite unusual to see one.

Presently the ground began to rise again; Alvin was approaching the little hill that was at the exact center of the park, and therefore of the city itself. There were fewer obstacles and detours, and he had a clear view to the summit of the hill and the simple building that surmounted it. He was a little out of breath by the time he had reached his goal, and was glad to rest against one of the rose-pink columns and to look back over the way he had come.

There are some forms of architecture that can never change because they have reached perfection. The Tomb of Yarlan Zey might have been designed by the temple builders of the first civilizations man had ever known, though they would have found it impossible to imagine of what material it was made. The roof was open to the sky, and the single chamber was paved with great slabs which only at first sight resembled natural stone. For geological ages human feet had crossed and recrossed that floor and left no trace upon its inconceivably stubborn material.

The creator of the great park—the builder, some said, of Diaspar itself—sat with slightly downcast eyes, as if examining the plans spread across his knees. His face wore that curiously elusive expression that had baffled the world for so many generations. Some had dismissed it as no more than an idle whim of the artist's, but to others it seemed that Yarlan Zey was smiling at some secret jest.

The whole building was an enigma, for nothing concerning it could be traced in the historical records of the city. Alvin was not even sure what the word "Tomb" meant; Jeserac could probably tell him, because he was fond of collecting obsolete words and sprinkling his conversation with them, to the confusion of his listeners.

From this central vantage point, Alvin could look clear across the park, above the screening trees, and out to the city itself. The nearest buildings were almost two miles away, and formed a low belt completely surrounding the park. Beyond them, rank after rank in ascending height, were the towers and terraces that made up the main bulk of the city. They stretched for mile upon mile, slowly climbing up the sky, becoming ever more complex and monumentally impressive. Diaspar had been planned as an entity; it was a single mighty machine. Yet though its outward appearance was almost overwhelming in its complexity, it merely hinted at the hidden marvels of technology without which all these great buildings would be lifeless sepulchers.

Alvin stared out toward the limits of his world. Ten—twenty miles away, their details lost in distance, were the outer ramparts of the city, upon which seemed to rest the roof of the sky. There was nothing beyond them—nothing at all except the aching emptiness of the desert in which a man would soon go mad.

In the course of his exploration of the city, Alvin discovers a place from which he can see outside. The following selection describes what happens when he takes a friend, Alystra, to see the world outside.

Around them the buildings rose higher and higher as if the city was strengthening its bulwarks against the outer world. How strange it would be, thought Alvin, if these towering walls became as transparent as glass, and one could watch the life within. Scattered throughout the space around him were friends he knew, friends he would one day know, and strangers he would never meet—though there could be very few of these, since in the course of his lifetime he would meet almost all the people in Diaspar. Most of them would be sitting in their separate rooms, but they would not be alone. They had only to form the wish and they could be, in all but physical fact, in the presence of any other person they chose. They were not bored, for they had access to everything that had happened in the realms of imagination or reality since the days when the city was built. To men whose minds were thus constituted, it was a completely satisfying existence. That it was also a wholly futile one, even Alvin did not yet comprehend.

As Alvin and Alystra moved outward from the city's heart, the number of people they saw in the streets slowly decreased, and there was no one in sight when they were brought to a smooth halt against a long platform of brightly colored marble. They stepped across the frozen whirlpool of matter where the substance of the moving way flowed back to its origin, and faced a wall pierced with brightly lighted tunnels. Alvin selected one without hesitation and stepped into it, with Alystra close behind. The peristaltic field seized them at once and propelled them forward as they lay back luxuriously, watching their surroundings.

It no longer seemed possible that they were in a tunnel far under-ground. The art that had used all of Diaspar for its canvas had been busy here, and above them the skies seemed open to the winds of heaven. All around were the spires of the city, gleaming in the sunlight. It was not the city that Alvin knew, but the Diaspar of a much earlier age. Although most of the great buildings were familiar, there were subtle differences that added to the interest of the scene. Alvin wished he could linger, but he had never found any way of retarding his progress through the tunnel.

All too soon they were set gently down in a large elliptical chamber, completely surrounded by windows. Through these they could catch tantalizing glimpses of gardens ablaze with brilliant flowers. There were gardens still in Diaspar, but these had existed only in the mind of the artist who conceived them. Certainly there were no such flowers as these in the world today.

Alystra was enchanted by their beauty, and was obviously under the impression that this was what Alvin had brought her to see. He watched her for a while as she ran gaily from scene to scene, enjoying her delight in each new discovery. There were hundreds of such places in the half-deserted buildings around the periphery of Diaspar, kept in perfect order by the hidden powers which watched over them. One day the tide of life might flow this way once more, but until then this ancient garden was a secret which they alone shared.

"We've further to go," said Alvin at last. "This is only the beginning." He stepped through one of the windows and the illusion was shattered. There was no garden behind the glass, but a circular passageway curving steeply upward. He could still see Alystra, a few feet away, though he knew that she could not see him. But she did not hesitate, and a moment later was standing beside him in the passage.

Beneath their feet the floor began to creep slowly forward, as if eager to lead them to their goal. They walked along it for a few paces, until their speed was so great that further effort would be wasted.

The corridor still inclined upward, and in a hundred feet had curved through a complete right angle. But only logic knew this; to all the senses it was as if one was now being hurried along an absolutely level corridor. The fact that they were in reality moving straight up a vertical shaft thousands of feet deep gave them no sense of insecurity, for a failure of the polarizing field was unthinkable.

Presently the corridor began to slope "downward" again until once more it had turned through a right angle. The movement of the floor slowed imperceptibly until it came to rest at the end of a long hall lined with mirrors, and Alvin knew that there was no hope of hurrying Alystra here. It was not merely that some feminine characteristics had survived unchanged since Eve; no one could have resisted the fascination of this place. There was nothing like it, as far as Alvin knew, in the rest of Diaspar. Through some whim of the artist, only a few of the mirrors reflected the scene as it really was—and even those, Alvin was convinced, were constantly changing their position. The rest certainly reflected *something,* but it was faintly disconcerting to see oneself walking amid ever-changing and quite imaginary surroundings.

Sometimes there were people going to and fro in the world behind the mirror, and more than once Alvin had seen faces that he recognized. He realized well enough that he had not been looking at any friends he knew in this existence. Through the mind of the unknown artist he had been seeing into the past, watching the previous incarnations of people who walked the world today. It saddened him, by reminding him of his own uniqueness, to think that however long he waited before these changing scenes he would never meet any ancient echo of himself.

"Do you know where we are?" Alvin asked Alystra when they had completed the tour of the mirrors. Alystra shook her head. "Somewhere near the edge of the city, I suppose," she answered carelessly. "We seem to have gone a long way, but I've no idea how far."

"We're in the Tower of Loranne," replied Alvin. "This is one of the highest points in Diaspar. Come—I'll show you." He caught Alystra's hand and led her out of the hall. There were no exits visible to the eye. but at various points the pattern on the floor indicated side corridors. As one approached the mirrors at these points, the reflections seemed to fuse into an archway of light and one could step through into another passage. Alystra lost all conscious track of their twistings and turnings, and at last they emerged into a long, perfectly straight tunnel through which blew a cold and steady wind. It stretched horizontally for hundreds of feet in either direction, and its far ends were tiny circles of light.

"I don't like this place," Alystra complained. "It's cold." She had probably never before experienced real coldness in her life, and Alvin felt somewhat guilty. He should have warned her to bring a cloak—and a good one, for all clothes in Diaspar were purely ornamental and quite useless as a protection.

Since her discomfort was entirely his fault, he handed over his cloak without a word. There was no trace of gallantry in this; the equality of the sexes had been complete for far too long for such conventions to survive. Had matters been the other way around, Alystra would have given Alvin her cloak and he would have as automatically accepted.

It was not unpleasant walking with the wind behind them, and they soon reached the end of the tunnel. A wide-meshed filigree of stone prevented them from going farther, which was just as well, for they stood on the brink of nothingness. The great air duct opened on the sheer face of the tower, and below them was a vertical drop of at least a thousand feet. They were high upon the outer ramparts of the city, and Diaspar lay spread beneath them as few in their world could ever have seen it.

The view was the obverse of the one that Alvin had obtained from the center of the park. He could look down upon the concentric waves of stone and metal as they descended in mile-long sweeps toward the heart of the city. Far away, partly hidden by the intervening towers, he could glimpse the distant fields and trees and the eternally circling river. Further still, the remoter bastions of Diaspar climbed once more toward the sky.

Beside him, Alystra was sharing the view with pleasure but with no surprise. She had seen the city countless times before from other, almost equally well-placed vantage points—and in considerably more comfort.

"That's our world—all of it," said Alvin. "Now I want to show you something else." He turned away from the grating and began to walk toward the distant circle of light at the far end of the tunnel. The wind was cold against his lightly clad body, but he scarcely noticed the discomfort as he walked forward into the air stream.

He had gone only a little way when he realized that Alystra was making no attempt to follow. She stood watching, her borrowed cloak streaming down the wind, one hand half raised to her face. Alvin saw her lips move, but the words did not reach him. He looked back at her first with astonishment, then with an impatience that was not totally devoid of pity. What Jeserac had said was true. She could not follow him. She had realized the meaning of that remote circle of light from which the wind blew forever into Diaspar. Behind Alystra was the known world, full of wonder yet empty of surprise, drifting like a brilliant but tightly closed bubble down the river of time. Ahead, separated from her by no more than the span of a few footsteps, was the empty wilderness—the world of the desert—the world of the Invaders.

Alvin walked back to join her and was surprised to find that she was trembling. "Why are you frightened?" he asked. "We're still safely here in Diaspar. You've looked out of that window behind us—surely you can look out of this one as well!"

Alystra was staring at him as if he was some strange monster. By her standards, indeed, he was.

"I couldn't do it," she said at last. "Even thinking about it makes me feel colder than this wind. Don't go any farther, Alvin!"

"But there's no logic in it!" Alvin persisted remorselessly. "What possible harm would it do you to walk to the end of this corridor and look out? It's strange and lonely out there, but it isn't horrible. In fact, the longer I look the more beautiful I think—"

Alystra did not stay to hear him finish. She turned on her heels and fled back down the long ramp that had brought them up through the floor of this tunnel. Alvin made no attempt to stop her, since that would have involved the bad manners of imposing one's will upon another. Persuasion, he could see, would have been utterly useless. He knew that Alystra would not pause until she had returned to her companions. There was no danger that she would lose herself in the labyrinths of the city, for she would have no difficulty in retracing her footsteps. An instinctive ability to extricate himself from even the most complex of mazes had been merely one of the many accomplishments Man had learned since he started to live in cities. The long-extinct rat had been forced to acquire similar skills when he left the fields and threw in his lot with humanity.

Alvin waited for a moment, as if half-expecting Alystra to return. He was not surprised at her reaction—only at its violence and irrationality.

Though he was sincerely sorry that she had gone, he could not help wishing that she had remembered to leave the cloak.

It was not only cold, but it was also hard work moving against the wind which sighed through the lungs of the city. Alvin was fighting both the air current and whatever force it was that kept it moving. Not until he had reached the stone grille, and could lock his arms around its bars, could he afford to relax. There was just sufficient room for him to force his head through the opening, and even so his view was slightly restricted, as the entrance to the duct was partly recessed into the city's wall.

Yet he could see enough. Thousands of feet below, the sunlight was taking leave of the desert. The almost horizontal rays struck through the grating and threw a weird pattern of gold and shadow far down the tunnel. Alvin shaded his eyes against the glare and peered down at the land upon which no man had walked for unknown ages.

He might have been looking at an eternally frozen sea. For mile after mile, the sand dunes undulated into the west, their contours grossly exaggerated by the slanting light. Here and there some caprice of the wind had carved curious whirlpools and gullies in the sand, so that it was sometimes hard to realize that none of this sculpture was the work of intelligence. At a very great distance, so far away indeed that he had no way of judging their remoteness, was a range of softly rounded hills. They had been a disappointment to Alvin; he would have given much to have seen in reality the soaring mountains of the ancient records and of his own dreams.

The sun lay upon the rim of the hills, its light tamed and reddened by the hundreds of miles of atmosphere it was traversing. There were two great black spots upon its disc; Alvin had learned from his studies that such things existed, but he was surprised that he could see them so easily. They seemed almost like a pair of eyes peering back at him as he crouched in his lonely spy hole with the wind whistling ceaselessly past his ears.

There was no twilight. With the going of the sun, the pools of shadow lying among the sand dunes flowed swiftly together in one vast lake of darkness. Color ebbed from the sky; the warm reds and golds drained away leaving an antarctic blue that deepened into night. Alvin waited for that breathless moment that he alone of all mankind had known—the moment when the first star shivers into life.

It had been many weeks since he had last come to this place, and he knew that the pattern of the night sky must have changed meanwhile. Even so, he was not prepared for his first glimpse of the Seven Suns.

They could have no other name; the phrase leaped unbidden to his lips. They formed a tiny, very compact and astonishingly symmetrical group against the afterglow of sunset. Six of them were arranged in a slightly flattened ellipse, which, Alvin was sure, was in reality a perfect circle, slightly tilted toward the line of vision. Each star was a different color; he could pick out red, blue, gold, and green, but the other tints eluded his eye. At the precise center of the formation was a single white giant—the brightest star in all the visible sky. The whole group looked exactly like a piece of jewelry; it seemed incredible, and beyond all stretching of the laws of chance, that Nature could ever have contrived so perfect a pattern.

As his eyes grew slowly accustomed to the darkness, Alvin could make out the great misty veil that had once been called the Milky Way. It stretched from the zenith down to the horizon, and the Seven Suns were entangled in its folds. The other stars had now emerged to challenge them, and their random groupings only emphasized the enigma of that perfect symmetry. It was almost as if some power had deliberately opposed the disorder of the natural Universe by setting its sign upon the stars.

Ten times, no more, the Galaxy had turned upon its axis since Man first walked on Earth. By its own standards, that was but a moment. Yet in that short period it had changed completely—changed far more than it had any right to do in the natural course of events. The great suns that had once burned so fiercely in the pride of youth were now guttering to their doom. But Alvin had never seen the heavens in their ancient glory, and so was unaware of all that had been lost.

The cold, seeping through into his bones, drove him back to the city. He extricated himself from the grating and rubbed the circulation back into his limbs. Ahead of him, down the tunnel, the light streaming out from Diaspar was so brilliant that for a moment he had to avert his eyes. Outside the city there were such things as day and night, but within it there was only eternal day. As the sun descended the sky above Diaspar would fill with light and no one would notice when the natural illumination vanished. Even before men had lost the need for sleep, they had driven darkness from their cities. The only night that ever came to Diaspar was a rare and unpredictable obscuration that sometimes visited the park and transformed it into a place of mystery.

Alvin came slowly back through the hall of mirrors, his mind still filled with night and stars. He felt inspired and yet depressed. There seemed no way in which he could ever escape out into that enormous emptiness—and no rational purpose in doing so. Jeserac had said that a man would soon die out in the desert, and Alvin could well believe him. Perhaps he might one day discover some way of leaving Diaspar, but if he did, he knew that he must soon return. To reach the desert would be an amusing game, no more. It was a game he could share with no one, and it would lead him nowhere. But at least it would be worth doing if it helped to quench the longing in his soul.

As if unwilling to return to the familiar world, Alvin lingered among the reflections from the past. He stood before one of the great mirrors and watched the scenes that came and went within its depths. Whatever mechanism produced these images was controlled by his presence, and to some extent by his thoughts. The mirrors were always blank when he first came into the room, but filled with action as soon as he moved among them.

In this final portion of *The City and the Stars,* Alvin meets a man named Khedron, who refers to himself as a jester. They discuss the physical and social stability of Diaspar and Khedron's role in the society.

"Very well. The men—if they were men, which I sometimes doubt—who designed Diaspar had to solve an incredibly complex problem. Diaspar is not merely a machine, you know—it is a living organism, and an immortal one. We are so accustomed to our society that we can't appreciate how strange it would have seemed to our first ancestors. Here we have a tiny, closed world which never changes except in its minor details, and yet which is perfectly stable, age after age. It has probably lasted longer than the rest of human history—yet in *that* history there were, so it is believed, countless thousands of separate cultures and civilizations which endured for a little while and then perished. How did Diaspar achieve its extraordinary stability?"

Alvin was surprised that anyone should ask so elementary a question, and his hopes of learning something new began to wane.

"Through the Memory Banks, of course," he replied. "Diaspar is always composed of the same people, though their actual groupings change as their bodies are created or destroyed."

Khedron shook his head.

"That is only a very small part of the answer. With exactly the same people, you could build many different patterns of society. I can't prove that, and I've no direct evidence of it, but I believe it's true. The designers of the city did not merely fix its population; they fixed the laws governing its behavior. We're scarcely aware that those laws exist, but we obey them. Diaspar is a frozen culture, which cannot change outside of narrow limits. The Memory Banks store many other things outside the patterns of our bodies and personalities. They store the image of the city itself, holding its every atom rigid against all the changes that time can bring. Look at this pavement—it was laid down millions of years ago, and countless feet have walked upon it. Can you see any sign of wear? Unprotected matter, however adamant, would have been ground to dust ages ago. But as long as there is power to operate the Memory Banks, and as long as the matrices they contain can still control the patterns of the city, the physical structure of Diaspar will never change."

"But there have been *some* changes," protested Alvin. "Many buildings have been torn down since the city was built, and new ones erected."

"Of course—but only by discharging the information stored in the Memory Banks and then setting up new patterns. In any case, I was merely mentioning that as an example of the way the city preserves itself physically. The point I want to make is that in the same way there are machines in Diaspar that preserve our social structure. They watch for any changes, and correct them before they become too great. How do they do it? I don't know—perhaps by selecting those who emerge from the Hall of Creation. Perhaps by tampering with our personality patterns; we may think we have free will, but can we be certain of that?

"In any event, the problem was solved. Diaspar has survived and come safely down the ages, like a great ship carrying as its cargo all that is left of the human race. It is a tremendous achievement in social engineering, though whether it is worth doing is quite another matter.

"Stability, however, is not enough. It leads too easily to stagnation, and thence to decadence. The designers of the city took elaborate steps to avoid this, though these deserted buildings suggest that they did not entirely succeed. I, Khedron the Jester, am part of that plan. A very small part, perhaps. I like to think otherwise, but I can never be sure."

"And just what is that part?" asked Alvin, still very much in the dark, and becoming a little exasperated.

"Let us say that I introduce calculated amounts of disorder into the city. To explain my operations would be to destroy their effectiveness. Judge me by my deeds, though they are few, rather than my words, though they are many."

Alvin had never before met anyone quite like Khedron. The Jester was a real personality—a character who stood head and shoulders above the general level of uniformity which was typical of Diaspar. Though there seemed no hope of discovering precisely what his duties were and how he carried them out, that was of minor importance. All that mattered, Alvin sensed, was that here was someone to whom he could talk—when there was a gap in the monologue—and who might give him answers to many of the problems that had puzzled him for so long.

They went back together down through the corridors of the Tower of Loranne, and emerged beside the deserted moving way. Not until they were once more in the streets did it occur to Alvin that Khedron had never asked him what he had been doing out here at the edge of the unknown. He suspected that Khedron knew, and was interested but not surprised. Something told him that it would be very difficult to surprise Khedron.

They exchanged index numbers, so that they could call each other whenever they wished. Alvin was anxious to see more of the Jester, though he fancied that his company might prove exhausting if it was too prolonged. Before they met again, however, he wanted to find what his friends, and particularly Jeserac, could tell him about Khedron.

"Until our next meeting," said Khedron, and promptly vanished. Alvin was somewhat annoyed. If you met anyone when you were merely projecting yourself, and were not present in the flesh, it was good manners to make that clear from the beginning. It could sometimes put the party who was ignorant of the facts at a considerable disadvantage. Probably Khedron had been quietly at home all the time—wherever his home might be. The number that he had given Alvin would insure that any messages would reach him, but did not reveal where he lived. That at least was according to normal custom. You might be free enough with index numbers, but your actual address was something you disclosed only to your intimate friends.

As he made his way back into the city, Alvin pondered over all that Khedron had told him about Diaspar and its social organization. It was strange that he had met no one else who had ever seemed dissatisfied with their mode of life. Diaspar and its inhabitants had been designed as part of one master plan; they formed a perfect symbiosis. Throughout their long lives, the people of the city were never bored. Though their world might be a tiny one by the standard of earlier ages, its complexity was overwhelming, its wealth of wonder and treasure beyond calculation. Here Man had gathered all the fruits of his genius, everything that had been saved from the ruin of the past. All the cities that had ever been, so it was said, had given something to Diaspar. . . . Into the building of Diaspar had gone all the skill, all the artistry of the Empire. When the great days were coming to an end, men of genius had remolded the city and given it the machines that made it immortal. Whatever might be forgotten, Diaspar would live and bear the descendants of Man safely down the stream of time.

They had achieved nothing except survival, and were content with that. There were a million things to occupy their lives between the hour when they came, almost full-grown, from the Hall of Creation and the hour when, their bodies scarcely older, they returned to the Memory Banks of the city. In a world where all men and women possess an intelligence that would once have been the mark of genius, there can be no danger of boredom. The delights of conversation and argument, the intricate formalities of social intercourse—these alone were enough to occupy a goodly portion of a lifetime. Beyond those were the great formal debates, when the whole city would listen entranced while its keenest minds met in combat or strove to scale those mountain peaks of philosophy which are never conquered yet whose challenge never palls.

No man or woman was without some absorbing intellectual interest. Eriston, for example, spent much of his time in prolonged soliloquies with the Central Computer, which virtually ran the city, yet which had leisure for scores of simultaneous discussions with anyone who cared to match his wits against it. For three hundred years, Eriston had been trying to construct logical paradoxes which the machine could not resolve. He did not expect to make serious progress before he had used up several lifetimes.

Etania's interests were of a more esthetic nature. She designed and constructed, with the aid of the matter organizers, three-dimensional interlacing patterns of such beautiful complexity that they were really extremely advanced problems in topology. Her work could be seen all over Diaspar, and some of her patterns had been incorporated in the floors of the great halls of choreography, where they were used as the basis for evolving new ballet creations and dance motifs.

Such occupations might have seemed arid to those who did not possess the intellect to appreciate their subtleties. Yet there was no one in Diaspar who could not understand something of what Eriston and Etania were trying to do and did not have some equally consuming interest of his own.

Athletics and various sports, including many only rendered possible by the control of gravity, made pleasant the first few centuries of youth. For adventure and the exercise of the imagination, the sagas provided all that anyone could desire. They were the inevitable end product of that striving for realism which began when men started to reproduce moving images and to record sounds, and then to use these techniques to enact scenes from real or imaginary life. In the sagas, the illusion was perfect because all the sense impressions involved were fed directly into the mind and any conflicting sensations were diverted. The entranced spectator was cut off from reality as long as the adventure lasted; it was as if he lived a dream yet believed he was awake.

In a world of order and stability, which in its broad outlines had not changed for a billion years, it was perhaps not surprising to find an absorbing interest in games of chance. Humanity had always been fascinated by the mystery of the falling dice, the turn of a card, the spin of the pointer. At its lowest level, this interest was based on mere cupidity—and that was an emotion that could have no place in a world where everyone possessed all that they could reasonably need. Even when this motive was ruled out, however, the purely intellectual fascination of chance remained to seduce the most sophisticated minds. Machines that behaved in a purely random way—events whose outcome could never be predicted, no matter how much information one had—from these philosopher and gambler could derive equal enjoyment.

And there still remained, for all men to share, the linked worlds of love and art. Linked, because love without art is merely the slaking of desire, and art cannot be enjoyed unless it is approached with love.

Men had sought beauty in many forms—in sequences of sound, in lines upon paper, in surfaces of stone, in the movements of the human body, in colors ranged through space. All these media still survived in Diaspar, and down the ages others had been added to them. No one was yet certain if all the possibilities of art had been discovered; or if it had any meaning outside the mind of man.

And the same was true of love.

technological innovation and social change

Astronomers are able to predict the movements of planets and to specify with considerable accuracy where those in our solar system will be in relation to one another on a certain date. They can do so because the forces that most influence planetary movements are relatively well understood and result in relationships that can be treated as constants in equations used to predict movements. For example, the relationship governing the strength of attraction between two bodies is that the strength of attraction is inversely proportionate to the square of the distance separating the bodies and directly proportionate to the product of their respective masses. As long as this relationship remains constant, any predictions involving calculations based on it will be correct, if no other errors are introduced. There is, however, no guarantee that the relationship will be precisely the same tomorrow or next week or next year. If for some reason the relationship were to change to one in which the attraction between two masses was inversely proportionate to the cube of the distance between them and directly proportionate to the product of their masses, any predictions based on the old relationship would prove incorrect. Fortunately, however, physical relationships do not seem to change, or at least do not alter so rapidly that it has been possible to observe changes since measurements were first taken, and planets are not very often reduced suddenly to one-half their mass.

Accurately predicting the future state of a *social* process appears to be a much more difficult feat, for at least two major reasons. The first is that astronomers know considerably more about what they are talking about—that is, about the relationships between variables that are crucial to their predictions—than sociologists know about the variables that are crucial to their predictions. The second reason is that the creation of entirely new variables and apparently new relationships between crucial variables probably happens more often in social situations than does the sudden change of physical constants, or the introduction of entirely unanticipated considerations—such as the emergence of a new planet in our solar system—in the physical environment.

Consider, for example, some of the independent variables that affect the birth rate of a given population. Birth rate depends on the economic conditions of a country, on the level of medical sophistication, on the society's norms about family size, and on a variety of other factors. If any one of these independent variables changes, the birth rate changes. If in 1928 projections for the birth rate from 1929 to 1939 had been made, based on data obtained for the period 1918–1928, they would have been incorrect because economic conditions changed radically in 1929.

All scientific predictions depend on the assumption that some particular, specifiable set of conditions will remain constant during the period for which the prediction is made. Often this set of conditions is not made explicit. When we calculate the length of time it will take an object to fall 100 feet, our prediction is not prefaced with the remark that the prediction will be correct only "if during the period in which the body is falling the gravity constant does not change." The unlikelihood that this change will occur makes it absurd to bother to make clear the potentially variable nature of the gravity constant.

If one were brave enough—or possibly foolhardy enough—to make predictions about significant, naturally occurring social processes, one would probably be wise to make clear the tenuous nature of the predictions and the degree to which they are subject to modifications. If a forecaster were to enumerate all the independent causal variables that could not be depended upon to remain constant over the period for which the prediction was made, the list would probably be exceedingly long. If as few as ten important variables each had a probability of changing only .1, then the probability of the prediction proving correct would be $.9^{10}$. It hardly seems worth the effort to state a prediction that has only this probability of being correct.

The sociologist in Christopher Anvil's story, "Gadget Versus Trend," was willing to take the gamble.

"gadget versus trend"

by Christopher Anvil

Boston, Sept. 2, 1976. Dr. R. Milton Schummer, Professor of Sociology at Wellsford College, spoke out against "creeping conformism" to an audience of twelve hundred in Swarton Hall last night.

Professor Schummer charged that America, once the land of the free, is now "the abode of the stereotyped mass-man, shaped from infancy by the moron-moulding influences of television, mass-circulation newspapers and magazines, and the pervasive influence of advertising manifest in all these media. The result is the mass-production American with interchangeable parts and built-in taped programme."

What this country needs, said Dr. Schummer, is "freedom to differ, freedom to be eccentric." But, he concluded, "the momentum is too great. The trend, like the tide, cannot be reversed by human efforts. In two hundred years, this nation has gone from individualism to conformism, from independence to interdependence, from federalism to fusionism, and the end is not yet. One shrinks at the thought of what the next one hundred years may bring."

Rutland, Vt., March 16, 1977 Dr. J. Paul Hughes, grandson of the late inventor, Everett Hughes, revealed today a device which his grandfather kept under wraps because of its "supposedly dangerous side-effects." Dubbed by Dr. Hughes a "privacy shield," the device works by the "exclusion of quasi-electrons." In the words of Dr. Hughes:

"My grandfather was an eccentric experimenter. Surprisingly often, though, his wild stabs would strike some form of pay dirt, in a commercial sense. In this present instance, we have a device unexplainable by any sound scientific theory, but which may be commercially quite useful. When properly set up, and connected to a suitable electrical outlet, the device effectively soundproofs material surfaces, such as walls, doors, floors, and the like, and thus may be quite helpful in present-day crowded living conditions."

Dr. Hughes explained that the device was supposed to operate by "the exclusion of 'quasi-electrons,' which my grandfather thought governed the transmission of sound through solid bodies, and performed various other esoteric functions. But we needn't take this too seriously."

New York, May 12, 1977 Formation of Hughes QuietWall Corporation was announced here today.

President of the new firm is J. Paul Hughes, grandson of the late inventor, Everett Hughes.

New York, Sept. 18, 1977 One of the hottest stocks on the market today is Hughes QuietWall. With demand booming, and the original president of the firm kicked upstairs to make room for the crack management expert, Myron L. Sams, the corporation has tapped a gold mine.

Said a company spokesman: "The biggest need in this country today is privacy. We live practically in each other's pockets, and if we can't do anything else, at least QuietWall can soundproof the pockets."

The QuietWall units, which retail for $289.95 for the basic room unit, are said to offer dealer, distributor, and manufacturer a generous profit. And no one can say that $289.95 is not a reasonable price to pay to keep out the noise of other people's TV, record players, quarrels and squalling babies.

Detroit, December 23, 1977   Santa left an early present for the auto industry here today.

A test driver trying out a car equipped with a Hughes QuietWall unit went into a skid on the icy test track, rolled over three times, and got out shaken but unhurt. The car itself, a light supercompact, was found to be almost totally undamaged.

Tests with sledgehammers revealed the astonishing fact that with the unit turned on, the car would not dent, and the glass could not be broken. The charge filler cap could not be unscrewed. The hood could not be raised. And neither windows nor doors could be opened till the unit was snapped off. With the unit off, the car was perfectly ordinary.

This is the first known trial of a QuietWall unit in a motor vehicle.

Standard house and apartment installations use a specially designed basic unit to soundproof floor and walls, and small additional units to soundproof doors and windows. This installation tested today apparently lacked such refinements.

December 26, 1977   J. Paul Hughes, chairman of the board of directors of the QuietWall Corp., stated to reporters today that his firm has no intention to market the Hughes QuietWall unit for use in motor cars.

Hughes denied the Detroit report of a QuietWall-equipped test car that rolled without damage, calling it "impossible."

Hartford, January 8, 1978   Regardless of denials from the QuietWall Corporation, nationwide experiments are being conducted into the use of the corporation's sound-deadening units as a safety device in cars. Numerous letters, telegrams, and phone calls are being received at the head offices of some of the nation's leading insurance companies here.

Hartford, January 9, 1978   Tests carried out by executives of the New Standard Insurance Group indicate that the original Detroit reports were perfectly accurate.

Cars equipped with the QuietWall units cannot be dented, shattered, scratched, or injured in any way by ordinary tools.

Austin J. Ramm, Executive Secretary of New Standard Group, stated to reporters:

"It's the damndest thing I ever saw.

"We've had so many communications, from people all over the

country who claim to have connected QuietWall units to their cars, that we decided to try it out ourselves.

"We tried rocks, hammers, and so forth, on the test vehicle. When these didn't have any effect, I tried a quarter-inch electric drill and Steve Willoughby—he's our president—took a crack at the centre of the wind-shield with a railroad pickaxe. The pickaxe bounced. My drill just slid around over the surface and wouldn't bite in.

"We have quite a few other things we want to try.

"But we've seen enough to know there definitely is truth in these reports."

New York, January 10, 1978   Myron L. Sams, president of the Hughes QuietWall Corporation, announced today that a special automotive attachment is being put on sale throughout the country. Mr. Sams warns that improper installation may, among other things, seize up all or part of the operating machinery of the car. He urges that company representatives be allowed to carry out the installation.

Dallas, January 12, 1978   In a chase lasting an hour, a gang of bank robbers got away this afternoon with $869,000 in cash and negotiable securities.

Despite a hail of bullets, the escape car was not damaged. An attempt to halt it at a roadblock failed, as the car crashed through without injury.

There is speculation here that the car was equipped with one of the Hughes QuietWall units that went on sale a few days ago.

Las Vegas, January 19, 1978   A gang of eight to ten criminals held up the Silver Dollar Club tonight, escaping with over a quarter of a million dollars.

It was one of the most bizarre robberies in the city's history.

The criminals entered the club in golf carts fitted with light aluminum- and transparent-plastic covers, and opened a gun battle with club employees. A short fight disclosed that it was impossible to even dent the light shielding on the golf carts. Using the club's patrons and employees as hostages, the gunmen received the cash they demanded, rolled across the sidewalk and up a ramp into the rear of a waiting truck, which drove out of town, smashing through a hastily erected roadblock.

As police gave chase, the truck proved impossible to damage. In a violent exchange of gunfire, no one was injured, as the police cars were equipped with newly installed QuietWall units, and it was evident that the truck was also equipped.

Well outside of town, the truck reached a second roadblock. The robbers attempted to smash through the seemingly flimsy barrier, but were brought to a sudden stop when the roadblock, fitted with a QuietWall unit, failed to give way.

The truck, and the golf carts within, were found to be undamaged. The bandits are now undergoing treatment for concussion and severe whiplash injuries.

The $250,000.00 has been returned to the Silver Dollar Club, and Las Vegas is comparatively quiet once more.

New York, January 23, 1978   In a hastily called news conference, J. Paul Hughes, chairman of the board of Hughes QuietWall Corporation, announced that he is calling upon the Federal Government to step in and suspend the activities of the corporation.

Pointing out that he has tried without success to suspend the company's operations on his own authority, Dr. Hughes stated that as a scientist he must warn the public against a dangerous technological development, "the menacing potentialities of which I have only recently come to appreciate."

No response has as yet been received from Washington.

New York, January 24, 1978   President Myron L. Sams today acknowledged the truth of reports that a bitter internal struggle is being waged for control of the Hughes QuietWall Corporation.

Spring Corners, Iowa, January 26, 1978   Oscar B. Nelde, a farmer on the outskirts of town, has erected a barricade that has backed up traffic on the new Cross-State Highway for twenty miles in both directions.

Mr. Nelde recently lost a suit for additional damages when the highway cut his farm into two unequal parts, the smaller one containing his house and farm buildings, the larger part containing his fields.

The barricade is made of oil drums, saw horses, and barbed wire. The oil drums and saw horses cannot be moved, and act as if welded to the frozen earth. The barbed wire is weirdly stiff and immovable. The barricade is set up in a double row of these immovable obstacles, spaced to form a twenty-foot-wide lane connecting the two separated parts of Mr. Nelde's farm.

Mr. Nelde's manure spreader was seen crossing the road early today.

Heavy road machinery has failed to budge the obstacles. The experts are stumped. However, the local QuietWall dealer recalls selling Mr. Nelde a quantity of small units recently and adds, "but no more than a lot of other farmers have been buying lately."

It may be worth mentioning that Mr. Nelde's claim is one of many that have been advanced locally.

New York, January 27, 1978 The Hughes QuietWall Corporation was today reorganised as QuietWall, Incorporated, with Myron L. Sams holding the positions of president and chairman of the board of directors. J. Paul Hughes, grandson of Everett Hughes, continues as a director.

Spring Corners, Iowa, January 28, 1978 Traffic is flowing once again on the Cross-State Highway.

This morning a U.S. Army truck-mounted earth auger moved up the highway and drilled a number of holes six feet in diameter, enabling large chunks of earth to be carefully loosened and both sections of the barricade to be lifted out as units. The wire, oil drums, saw horses, and big chunks of earth, which remained rigid when lifted out, are being removed to the U.S. Army Research and Development Laboratories for study. No Quiet-Wall units have been found, and it is assumed that they are imbedded, along with their power source, inside the masses of earth.

The sheriff, the police chief of Spring Corners, and state and federal law enforcement agents are attempting to arrest Oscar B. Nelde, owner of the farm adjacent to the highway.

This has proved impossible, as Mr. Nelde's house and buildings are equipped with a number of QuietWall units controlled from within.

Boston, February 1, 1978 Dr. R. Milton Schummer, Professor of Sociology at Wellsford College, and a severe critic of "creeping conformism," said tonight, when questioned by reporters, that some of the effects of the QuietWall units constitute a hopeful sign in the long struggle of the individual against the State and against the forces of conformity. However, Dr. Schummer does not believe that "a mere technological gadget can affect these great movements of sociological trends."

Spring Corners, Iowa, February 2, 1978 A barbed-wire fence four feet high, fastened to crisscrossed railroad rails, now blocks the Cross-State Highway near the farm home of Leroy Weaver, a farmer whose property was cut in half by the highway, and who has often stated that he has received inadequate compensation.

It has proved impossible for highway equipment on the scene to budge either wire or rails.

Mr. Weaver cannot be reached for comment, as his house and buildings are equipped with QuietWall units, and neither the sheriff nor federal officials have been able to effect entry on to the premises.

Washington, D.C., February 3, 1978 The Bureau of Standards reports that tests on QuietWall units show them to be essentially "stasis devices." That is to say, they prevent change in whatever material surface they are applied to. Thus, sound does not pass, because the protected material is practically noncompressible, and is not affected by the alternate waves of compression and rarefaction in the adjacent medium.

Many potential applications are suggested by Bureau of Standards spokesmen who report, for instance, that thin slices of apples and pears placed directly inside the surface field of the QuietWall device were found totally unchanged when the field was switched off, after test periods of more than three weeks.

New York, February 3, 1978   Myron L. Sams, president of QuietWall, Incorporated, reports record sales, rising day by day to new peaks. Quiet-Wall, Inc., is now operating factories in seven states, Great Britain, the Netherlands, and West Germany.

Spring Corners, Iowa, February 4, 1978   A U.S. Army truck-mounted earth auger has again removed a fence across the Cross-State Highway here. But the giant auger itself has now been immobilised, apparently by one or more concealed stasis (QuietWall) devices.

As the earth auger weighs upwards of thirty tons, and all the wheels of truck and trailer appear to be locked, moving it presents no small problem. . . .

New York, February 5, 1978   Myron L. Sams, president of QuietWall, Inc., announced today a general price cut, due to improved design and volume production economies, on all QuietWall products.

In future, basic QuietWall room units will sell for $229.95 instead of $289.95. Special small stasis units, suitable for firming fence posts, reinforcing walls, and providing barred-door household security, will retail for as low as $19.95. It is rumoured that this price, with improved production methods, still provides an ample profit for all concerned, so that prices may be cut in some areas during special sales events.

Spring Corners, Iowa, February 6, 1978   A flying crane today lifted the immobilised earth auger from the eastbound lanes of Cross-State Highway.

A total of fourteen small stasis units have thus far been removed from the auger, its truck and trailer, following its removal from the highway by air. Difficulties were compounded by the fact that each stasis unit apparently "freezes" the preceding units applied within its range. The de-stasis experts must not only locate the units. They must remove them in the right order, and some are very cleverly hidden. . . .

New York, February 10, 1978   Representatives of QuietWall, Inc., report that study of stasis devices removed from the auger at Spring Centre, Iowa, reveals that they are "not devices of QW manufacture, but crude, cheap bootleg imitations. Nevertheless, they work."

Spring Corners, Iowa, February 12, 1978 The Cross-State Highway, already cut at Seaton Bridge, is now blocked in three places by walls of snow piled up during last night's storm by farmers' bulldozers, and stabilised by stasis devices. Newsmen who visited the scene report that the huge mounds look like snow, but feel like concrete. Picks and shovels do not dent them, and flame throwers fail to melt them.

New York, February 15, 1978 Dr. J. Paul Hughes, a director of Quiet-Wall, Inc., tonight reiterated his plea for a government ban on stasis devices. He recalled the warning of his inventor grandfather Everett Hughes, and stated that he intends to spend the rest of his life "trying to undo the damage the device has caused."

New York, February 16, 1978 Myron L. Sams, president of QuietWall, Inc., announced today that a fruit fly had been kept in stasis for twenty-one days without suffering visible harm. QW's research scientists, he said, are now working with the problem of keeping small animals in stasis. If successful, Sams said, the experiments may open the door to "one-way time-travel," and enable persons suffering from serious diseases to wait, free from pain, until such time as a satisfactory cure has been found.

Bonn, February 17, 1978 Savage East German accusations against the West today buttressed the rumours that "stasis-unit enclaves" are springing up like toadstools throughout East Germany.

Similar reports are coming in from Hungary, while Poland reports a number of "stasis-frozen" Soviet tanks.

Havana, February 18, 1978 In a frenzied harangue tonight, "Che" Garcia, First Secretary of the Cuban Communist Party, announced that the government is erecting "stasis walls" all around the island, and that "stasis blockhouses" now being built will resist "even the Yankees' worst hydrogen weapons." In a torrent of vitriolic abuse, however, Mr. Garcia threatened that "any further roadblocks and centres of degenerate individualism that spring up will be eradicated from the face of the soil of the motherland by blood, iron, sweat, and the forces of monolithic socialism."

There have been rumours for some time of dissatisfaction with the present regime.

Mr. Garcia charged that the C.I.A. had flagrantly invaded Cuban air space by dropping "millions of little vicious stasis units, complete with battery packs of fantastic power," all over the island, from planes which could not be shot down because they were protected by "still more of these filthy sabotage devices."

Des Moines, February 21, 1978   The Iowa state government following the unsuccessful siege of four farm homes near the Cross-State Highway today announced that it is opening new hearings on landowners' compensation for land taken for highway-construction purposes.

The governor appealed to owners of property adjoining the highway to be patient, bring their complaints to the capital, and meanwhile open the highway to traffic.

Staunton, Vt., February 23, 1978   Hiram Smith, a retired high school science teacher whose family has lived on the same farm since before the time of the Revolution, was ordered last fall to leave his family home.

A dam is to be built nearby, and Mr. Smith's home will be among those inundated.

At the time of the order, Mr. Smith, who lives on the farm with his fourteen-year-old grandson, stated that he would not leave "until carried out dead or helpless."

This morning, the sheriff tried to carry out the eviction order, and was stopped by a warning shot fired from the Smith house. The warning shot was followed by the flight of a small, battery-powered model plane, apparently radio-controlled, which alighted about two thousand yards from the Smith home, near an old apple orchard.

Mr. Smith called to the sheriff to get out of his car and lie down, if the car was not stasis-equipped, and in any case to look away from the apple orchard.

There was a brilliant flash, a shock, and a roar which the sheriff likened to the explosion of "a hundred tons of TNT." When he looked at the orchard, it was obscured by a pink glow and boiling clouds, apparently of steam from vaporised snow.

Mr. Smith called out to the sheriff to get off the property, or the next "wink bomb" would be aimed at him.

No one has been out to the Smith property since the sheriff's departure.

New York, February 25, 1978   Mr. Myron L. Sams, president of Quiet-Wall, Inc., announced today that "there is definitely no connection between the Staunton explosion and the QW Corp. stasis unit. The stasis unit is a strictly defensive device and cannot be used for offensive purposes."

New York, February 25, 1978   Dr. J. Paul Hughes tonight asserted that the "wink bomb" exploded at Staunton yesterday, and now known to have left a radioactive crater, "probably incorporated a stasis unit." The unit was probably "connected to a light metallic container holding a small quantity of radioactive material. It need not necessarily be the radioactive material we are accustomed to think of as suitable for fission bombs. It need not be the usual amount of such material. When the stasis unit was activated by a radio signal or timing device, high-energy particles thrown off by the radioactive material would be unable to pass out through the container, now in stasis, and equivalent to a very hard, dense, impenetrable, nearly ideal boundary surface. The high-energy particles would bounce back into the interior, bombarding the radioactive material. As the population of high-energy particles within the enclosing stasis field builds up, the radioactive material, regardless of its quantity, reaches the critical point. Precisely what will happen depends on the radioactive material used, the size of the sample, and the length of the 'wink'—that is, the length of time the stasis field is left on."

Dr. Hughes added that "this is a definite, new, destructive use of the stasis field, which Mr. Myron Sams assures us is perfectly harmless."

Montpelier, Vt., February 26, 1978   The governor today announced temporary suspension of the Staunton Dam Project, while an investigation is carried out into numerous landowners' complaints.

Moscow, February 28, 1978   A "certain number" of "isolated cells" of "stasis-controlled character" are admitted to have sprung up within the Soviet Union. Those that are out of the way are said to be left alone, on the theory that the people have to come out sometime. Those in important localities are being reduced by the Red Army, using tear gas, sick gas, toothache gas, flashing searchlights, "war of nerves" tactics, and, in some cases, digging out the "cell" and carrying it off wholesale. It is widely accepted that there is nowhere near the amount of trouble here as in the satellite countries, where the problem is mounting to huge proportions.

Spring Corners, Iowa, May 16, 1978   The extensive Cross-State Highway claims having been settled all around, traffic is once again flowing along the highway. A new and surprising feature is the sight of farm machinery disappearing into tunnels constructed under the road to allow the farmers to pass from one side to the other.

Staunton, Vt., July 4, 1978   There was a big celebration here today as the governor and a committee of legislators announced that the big Staunton Dam Project has been abandoned, and a number of smaller dams will be built according to an alternative plan put forth earlier.

Bonn, August 16, 1978   Reports reaching officials here indicate that the East German government, the Hungarian government, and also to a considerable extent the Polish government, are having increasing difficulties as more and more of the "stasis-unit enclaves" join up, leaving the governments on the outside looking in. Where this will end is hard to guess.

Washington, September 30, 1978   The Treasury Department sent out a special "task force" of about one hundred and eighty men this morning. Their job is to crack open the mushrooming Anti-Tax League, whose membership is now said to number about one million enthusiastic businessmen. League members often give Treasury agents an exceedingly rough time, using record books and files frozen shut with stasis units, office buildings stasis-locked against summons-servers, stasis-equipped cars which come out of stasis-equipped garages connected with stasis-locked office buildings, to drive to stasis-equipped homes where it is physically impossible for summons-servers to enter the grounds.

Princeton, N.J., October 5, 1978   A conference of leading scientists, which gathered here today to exchange views on the nature of the stasis unit, is reported in violent disagreement. One cause of the disagreement is the reported "selective action" of the stasis unit, which permits ordinary light to pass through transparent bodies, but blocks the passage of certain other electromagnetic radiations.

Wild disorders broke out this afternoon during a lecture by Dr. J. Paul Hughes, on the "Quasi-Electron Theory of Wave Propagation." The lecture was accompanied by demonstration of the original Everett Hughes device, powered by an old-fashioned generator driven by the inventor's original steam engine. As the engine gathered speed, Dr. Hughes was able to demonstrate the presence of a nine-inch sphere of completely reflective material in the supposedly empty focus of the apparatus. This sphere, Dr. Hughes asserted, was the surface of a space totally evacuated of quasi-electrons, which he identified as "units of time."

It was at this point that the disturbance broke out.

Despite the disorder, Dr. Hughes went on to explain the limiting value of the velocity of light in terms of the quasi-electron theory. . . .

There is a rumour here that the conference may recess at once without issuing a report.

Washington, D.C., August 16, 1979   Usually reliable sources report that the United States has developed a "missile screen" capable of destroying enemy missiles in flight, and theoretically capable of creating a wall around the nation through which no enemy projectile of any type could pass. This device is said to be based on the original Everett Hughes stasis unit, which creates a perfectly rigid barrier of variable size and shape, which can be projected very rapidly by turning on an electric current.

Other military uses for stasis devices include protection of missile sites, storage of food and munitions, impenetrising of armour plate, portable "turtle-shields" for infantry, and quick-conversion units designed to turn any ordinary house or shed into a bombardment-proof strongpoint.

Veteran observers of the military scene say that the stasis unit completely reverses the advantage until recently held by offensive, as opposed to defensive, weapons. This traditionally alternating advantage, supposed to have passed permanently with the development of nuclear explosives, has now made one more pendulum swing. Now, in place of the "absolute weapon," we have the "absolute defence." Properly set up, hydrogen explosions do not dent it.

But if the nation is not to disintegrate within as it becomes impregnable without, officials say we must find some effective way to deal with stasis-protected cults, gangsters, anti-tax enthusiasts, seceding rural districts, space-grabbers, and proprietors of dens. Latest problem is the travelling roadblock, set up by chisellers who select a busy highway, collect "toll" from motorists who must pay or end up in a traffic jam, then move on quickly before police have time to react, and stop again in some new location to do the same thing all over. There must be an answer to all these things, but the answer has yet to be found.

Boston, September 2, 1979   Dr. R. Milton Schummer, Professor of Sociology at Wellsford College, spoke out against "galloping individualism" to an audience of six hundred in Swarton Hall last night.

Professor Schummer charged that America, once the land of co-operative endeavour, is now "a seething hotbed of rampant individualists, protesters, quick-rich artists, and minute-men of all kinds, each over-reacting violently from a former condition which may have seemed like excessive conformism at the time, but now in the perspective of events appears as a desirable cohesiveness and unity of direction. The result today is the fractionating American with synthetic rough edges and built-in bellicose sectionalism."

What this country needs, said Dr. Schummer, is "co-ordination of aims, unity of purpose, and restraint of difference." But, he concluded, "the reaction is too violent. The trend, like the tide, cannot be reversed by human efforts. In three years, this nation has gone from cohesion to fractionation, from interdependence to chaos, from federalism to splinterism, and the end is not yet. One shrinks at the thought of what the next hundred years may bring."

men versus machines:
a conflict
between species

If evolution is the process of growing or developing, we may reasonably speak
of the evolution of biological organisms, social systems, or mechanical devices.
Given this definition, we can view evolutionary change as a response to environmental change, to economic change, or to technological change, and thereby
avoid having to consider the issue of the positive or negative value of evolutionary
change and whether evolution is directed toward a goal, a final state. If the
assumption about the cause of evolutionary change is coupled with the postulate
of natural selection (the assumption that, of the alternative responses to an
environmental change, the most effective response will dominate the less effective),
the result is a very much simplified form of Darwin's theory of biological evolution.
If the concept of evolution can reasonably be applied to social systems and
mechanical devices, it should also be reasonable to apply theories of evolution to
social and mechanical devices.

Modified versions of Darwin's theoretical formulation have been used in the
past to describe changes in the structure of social systems. Unfortunately, these
applications have typically been only superficial and have usually been merely
pseudo-scientific arguments designed to prove that some particular form of social
organization represents a higher stage of social life, is *naturally* superior to some
other form of organization, and therefore should be preferred. This conclusion is
unwarranted, of course, since no evidence shows that societies evolve in the same
direction. Because physical environments (including climatic and geographic conditions), economic environments (suitability of land for agriculture, availability of
raw materials, and so on) and social environments (population size, presence of
potential external aggressors, and so on) vary from one society to another, the
stimuli that provoke evolution vary across societies, and a reasonable expectation
would be that societies will evolve in different directions rather than along a single

path. The study of social evolution, purged of most of its cultural chauvinism and generally called social change, has just begun.

Until quite recently, almost no serious consideration has been given to the nature of the evolution of mechanical devices—perhaps because mechanical devices are devoid of life, as we are accustomed to using the term. The general lack of interest in evolutionary trends in mechanical entities has changed, however, and a concern with *specia machina* has developed and is still developing. This concern has three major foci. The first is the effects that man's considerable dependence on the species have had on his own evolution. The second is the effects that certain types of mechanical device (such as the automobile) have had on the remainder of the physical environment upon which man depends. The third focus is the potential for competition between men and machines for the position of dominant species.

Concern with the first two points is easily understood. Machines have clearly had a substantial effect on the ordering of the qualities that are important for survival in modern society, and therefore they should influence the direction of man's evolution. And pollution of the physical environment by mechanical devices may have a disastrous influence on man's survival. Concern about the third point is somewhat more difficult to understand, and we must mention two devices, computers and robots.

Except when an occasional isolated individual took up the problem, before the invention of the modern computer and the anticipation of the invention of robots, the question of conflict between men and machines, as two species, was rarely the subject of a literary piece and almost never considered seriously. The giant brain and Frankenstein's monster images that have recently become associated with these devices in popular thought reflect some serious questions about man's relationship to these devices. (The popular conceptions of the potential conflict between men and these devices are beautifully captured in, and perhaps partly caused by, such classic pieces about robots as Carl Capek's *R.U.R.* and the stories in Isaac Asimov's *I Robot.* One example of conflict with computers appears in a short story dealing with the development of a worldwide system, completely computer-based and maintained, of industrial and social control. At the ceremony to dedicate the final link that is to complete the system and start its operation, a question is put to the super-system: "Is there a God?" The reply is, "Yes, now there is a God."

The immediate cause for the *sudden* concern about man's relationship to his machines was probably the development of machines that had the rudiments of intelligence, or at least possessed the potential for developing intelligence. As long as man supplied the intelligence necessary to direct the activities of a device, he was obviously in charge. The machines he created might have been stronger, more durable, and infinitely repairable, but they were under his immediate control. Machines, however, began to show signs of developing the ability to make independent decisions, such as when to turn themselves on or off and when to speed up or slow down, and also to reach decisions based on analyses of information so complicated that no human mind could reproduce the same answer in less than five, ten, or 20 years. If machines continue to develop independent decision-making abilities, and perhaps the ability to implement their decisions independent of human interference, the question to consider is, Who is actually in control? Are machines serving men, or are men serving machines?

In the following selection from Samuel Butler's *Erehwon* (1872), the question of the evolution of machines and the potential for conflict between species is considered in detail. It is amazing that Butler chose to apply the arguments of Darwin's evolutionary theory to the issue of the evolution of machines at a time when the problem of artificial intelligence was unheard-of. Butler's analysis of the relations between men and mechanical devices is much more powerful today than it was when he wrote it.

This excerpt is the synopsis of a treatise on Erehwonian philosophy in which the arguments leading to the recognition of the conflict between men and machines are developed.

erehwon

by Samuel Butler

The writer commences:—"There was a time, when the earth was to all appearance utterly destitute both of animal and vegetable life, and when according to the opinion of our best philosophers it was simply a hot round ball with a crust gradually cooling. Now if a human being had existed while the earth was in this state and had been allowed to see it as though it were some other world with which he had no concern, and if at the same time he were entirely ignorant of all physical science, would he not have pronounced it impossible that creatures possessed of anything like consciousness should be evolved from the seeming cinder which he was beholding? Would he not have denied that it contained any potentiality of consciousness? Yet in the course of time consciousness came. Is it not possible then that there may be even yet new channels dug out for consciousness, though we can detect no signs of them at present?

"Again. Consciousness, in anything like the present acceptation of the term, having been once a new thing—a thing, as far as we can see, subsequent even to an individual center of action and to a reproductive system (which we see existing in plants without apparent consciousness)—why may not there arise some new phase of mind which shall be as different from all present known phases, as the mind of animals is from that of vegetables?

"It would be absurd to attempt to define such a mental state (or whatever it may be called), inasmuch as it must be something so foreign to man that his experience can give him no help towards conceiving its nature; but surely when we reflect upon the manifold phases of life and consciousness which have been evolved already, it would be rash to say that no others can be developed, and that animal life is the end of all things. There was a time when fire was the end of all things: another when rocks and water were so."

The writer, after enlarging on the above for several pages, proceeded to inquire whether traces of the approach of such a new phase of life could be perceived at present; whether we could see any tenements preparing which might in a remote futurity be adapted for it; whether, in fact, the primordial cell of such a kind of life could be now detected upon earth. In the course of his work he answered this question in the affirmative and pointed to the higher machines.

"There is no security"—to quote his own words—"against the ultimate development of mechanical consciousness, in the fact of machines possessing little consciousness now. A mollusc has not much consciousness. Reflect upon the extraordinary advance which machines have made during the last few hundred years, and note how slowly the animal and vegetable kingdoms are advancing. The more highly organized machines are creatures not so much of yesterday, as of the last five minutes, so to speak, in comparison with past time. Assume for the sake of argument that conscious beings have existed for some twenty million years: see what strides machines have made in the last thousand! May not the world last twenty million years longer? If so, what will they not in the end become? Is it not safer to nip the mischief in the bud and to forbid them further progress?

"But who can say that the vapor engine[1] has not a kind of consciousness? Where does consciousness begin, and where end? Who can draw the line? Who can draw any line? Is not everything interwoven with everything? Is not machinery linked with animal life in an infinite variety of ways? The shell of a hen's egg is made of a delicate white ware and is a machine as much as an egg-cup is: the shell is a device for holding the egg, as much as the egg-cup for holding the shell: both are phases of the same function; the hen makes the shell in her inside, but it is pure pottery. She makes her nest outside of herself for convenience' sake, but the nest is not more of a machine than the egg-shell in it. A 'machine' is only a 'device.' "

Then returning to consciousness, and endeavoring to detect its earliest manifestations, the writer continued:— . . . "Even a potato in a dark cellar has a certain low cunning about him which serves him in excellent stead. He knows perfectly well what he wants and how to get it. He sees the light coming from the cellar window and sends his shoots crawling

[1]Steam engine.

straight thereto; they will crawl along the floor and up the wall and out at the cellar window; if there be a little earth anywhere on the journey he will find it and use it for his own ends. What deliberation he may exercise in the matter of his roots when he is planted in the earth is a thing unknown to us, but we can imagine him saying, 'I will have a tuber here and a tuber there, and I will suck whatsoever advantage I can from all my surroundings. This neighbor I will overshadow, and that I will undermine; and what I can do shall be the limit of what I will do. He that is stronger and better placed than I shall overcome me, and him that is weaker I will overcome.'

"The potato says these things by doing them, which is the best of languages. What is consciousness if this is not consciousness? We find it difficult to sympathize with the emotions of a potato; so we do with those of an oyster. Neither of these things makes a noise on being boiled or opened, and noise appeals to us more strongly than anything else, because we make so much about our own sufferings. Since, then, they do not annoy us by any expression of pain we call them emotionless; and so *quâ* mankind they are; but mankind is not everybody.

"If it be urged that the action of the potato is chemical and mechanical only, and that it is due to the chemical and mechanical effects of light and heat, the answer would seem to lie in an inquiry whether every sensation is not chemical and mechanical in its operation? whether those things which we deem most purely spiritual are anything but disturbances of equilibrium in an infinite series of levers, beginning with those that are too small for microscopic detection, and going up to the human arm and the appliances which it makes use of? whether there be not a molecular action of thought, whence a dynamical theory of the passions shall be deducible? Whether strictly speaking we should not ask what kind of levers a man is made of rather than what is his temperament? How are they balanced? How much of such and such will it take to weigh them down so as to make him do so and so?"

The writer went on to say that he anticipated a time when it would be possible, by examining a single hair with a powerful microscope, to know whether its owner could be insulted with impunity. He then became more and more obscure, so that I was obliged to give up all attempt at translation; neither did I follow the drift of his argument. On coming to the next part which I could construe, I found that he had changed his ground.

"Either," he proceeds, "a great deal of action that has been called purely mechanical and unconscious must be admitted to contain more elements of consciousness than has been allowed hitherto (and in this case germs of consciousness will be found in many actions of the higher machines)—Or (assuming the theory of evolution but at the same time denying the consciousness of vegetable and crystalline action) the race of man has descended from things which had no consciousness at all. In this case there is no *à priori* improbability in the descent of conscious (and more than conscious) machines from those which now exist, except that which is suggested by the apparent absence of anything like a reproductive system in the mechanical kingdom. This absence however is only apparent, as I shall presently show.

"Do not let me be misunderstood as living in fear of any actually existing machine; there is probably no known machine which is more than a prototype of future mechanical life. The present machines are to the future as the early Saurians to man. The largest of them will probably greatly diminish in size. Some of the lowest vertebrata attained a much greater bulk than has descended to their more highly organized living representatives, and in like manner a diminution in the size of machines has often attended their development and progress . . .

"But returning to the argument, I would repeat that I fear none of the existing machines; what I fear is the extraordinary rapidity with which they are becoming something very different to what they are at present. No class of beings have in any time past made so rapid a movement forward. Should not that movement be jealously watched, and checked while we can still check it? And is it not necessary for this end to destroy the more advanced of the machines which are in use at present, though it is admitted that they are in themselves harmless?

"As yet the machines receive their impressions through the agency of man's senses: one traveling machine calls to another in a shrill accent of alarm and the other instantly retires; but it is through the ears of the driver that the voice of the one has acted upon the other. Had there been no driver, the callee would have been deaf to the caller. There was a time when it must have seemed highly improbable that machines should learn to make their wants known by sound, even through the ears of man; may we not conceive, then, that a day will come when those ears will be no longer needed, and the hearing will be done by the delicacy of the machine's own construction?—when its language shall have been developed from the cry of animals to a speech as intricate as our own?

"It is possible that by that time children will learn the differential calculus—as they learn now to speak—from their mothers and nurses, . . . and work rule of three sums, as soon as they are born; but this is not probable; we cannot calculate on any corresponding advance in man's intellectual or physical powers which shall be a set-off against the far greater development which seems in store for the machines. Some people may say that man's moral influence will suffice to rule them; but I cannot think it will ever be safe to repose much trust in the moral sense of any machine . . .

"But other questions come upon us. What is a man's eye but a machine for the little creature that sits behind in his brain to look through? A dead eye is nearly as good as a living one for some time after the man is dead.

It is not the eye that cannot see, but the restless one that cannot see through it. Is it man's eyes, or is it the big seeing-engine which has revealed to us the existence of worlds beyond worlds into infinity? What has made man familiar with the scenery of the moon, the spots on the sun, or the geography of the planets? He is at the mercy of the seeing-engine for these things, and is powerless unless he tack it on to his own identity, and make it part and parcel of himself. Or, again, is it the eye, or the little see-engine, which has shown us the existence of infinitely minute organisms which swarm unsuspected around us?

"And take man's vaunted power of calculation. Have we not engines which can do all manner of sums more quickly and correctly than we can? What prizeman . . . at any of our Colleges . . . can compare with some of these machines in their own line? In fact, wherever precision is required man flies to the machine at once, as far preferable to himself. Our sum-engines never drop a figure, nor our looms a stitch; the machine is brisk and active, when the man is weary; it is clear-headed and collected, when the man is stupid and dull; it needs no slumber, when man must sleep or drop; ever at its post, ever ready for work, its alacrity never flags, its patience never gives in; its might is stronger than combined hundreds, and swifter than the flight of birds; it can burrow beneath the earth, and walk upon the largest rivers and sink not. This is the green tree; what then shall be done in the dry?

"Who shall say that a man does see or hear? He is such a hive and swarm of parasites that it is doubtful whether his body is not more theirs than his, and whether he is anything but another kind of ant-heap after all. May not man himself become a sort of parasite upon the machines? An affectionate machine-tickling aphid?

"It is said by some that our blood is composed of infinite living agents which go up and down the highways and byways of our bodies as people in the streets of a city. When we look down from a high place upon crowded thoroughfares, is it possible not to think of corpuscles of blood traveling through veins and nourishing the heart of the town? No mention shall be made of sewers, nor of the hidden nerves which serve to communicate sensations from one part of the town's body to another; nor of the yawning jaws of the railway stations, whereby the circulation is carried directly into the heart,—which receive the venous lines, and disgorge the arterial, with an eternal pulse of people. And the sleep of the town, how life-like! with its change in the circulation."

Here the writer became again so hopelessly obscure that I was obliged to miss several pages. He resumed:—

"It can be answered that even though machines should hear never so well and speak never so wisely, they will still always do the one or the other for our advantage, not their own; that man will be the ruling spirit and the machine the servant; that as soon as a machine fails to discharge the service which man expects from it, it is doomed to extinction; that the machines stand to man simply in the relation of lower animals, the vapor-engine itself being only a more economical kind of horse; so that instead of being likely to be developed into a higher kind of life than man's, they owe their very existence and progress to their power of ministering to human wants, and must therefore both now and ever be man's inferiors.

"This is all very well. But the servant glides by imperceptible approaches into the master; and we have come to such a pass that, even now, man must suffer terribly on ceasing to benefit the machines. If all machines were to be annihilated at one moment, so that not a knife nor lever nor rag of clothing nor anything whatsoever were left to man but his bare body alone that he was born with, and if all knowledge of mechanical laws were taken from him so that he could make no more machines, and all machine-made food destroyed so that the race of man should be left as it were naked upon a desert island, we should become extinct in six weeks. A few miserable individuals might linger, but even these in a year or two would become worse than monkeys. Man's very soul is due to the machines; it is a machine-made thing: he thinks as he thinks, and feels as he feels, through the work that machines have wrought upon him, and their existence is quite as much a *sine quâ non* for his, as for theirs. This fact precludes us from proposing the complete annihilation of machinery, but surely it indicates that we should destroy as many of them as we can possibly dispense with, lest they should tyrannize over us even more completely.

"True, from a low materialistic point of view, it would seem that those thrive best who use machinery wherever its use is possible with profit; but this is the art of the machines—they serve that they may rule. They bear no malice towards man for destroying a whole race of them provided he creates a better instead; on the contrary, they reward him liberally for having hastened their development. It is for neglecting them that he incurs their wrath, or for using inferior machines, or for not making sufficient exertions to invent new ones, or for destroying them without replacing them; yet these are the very things we ought to do, and do quickly; for though our rebellion against their infant power will cause infinite suffering, what will not things come to, if that rebellion is delayed?

"They have preyed upon man's groveling preference for his material over his spiritual interests, and have betrayed him into supplying that element of struggle and warfare without which no race can advance. The lower animals progress because they struggle with one another; the weaker die, the stronger breed and transmit their strength. The machines being of themselves unable to struggle, have got man to do their struggling for them: as long as he fulfills this function duly, all goes well with him —at least he thinks so; but the moment he fails to do his best for the advancement of machinery by encouraging the good and destroying the bad, he is left behind in the race of competition; and this means that he will be made uncomfortable in a variety of ways, and perhaps die.

"So that even now the machines will only serve on condition of being served, and that too upon their own terms; the moment their terms are not complied with, they jib, and either smash both themselves and all whom they can reach, or turn churlish and refuse to work at all. How many men at this hour are living in a state of bondage to the machines? How many spend their whole lives, from the cradle to the grave, in tending them by night and day? Is it not plain that the machines are gaining ground upon us, when we reflect on the increasing number of those who are bound down to them as slaves, and of those who devote their whole souls to the advancement of the mechanical kingdom?

"The vapor-engine must be fed with food and consume it by fire even as man consumes it; it supports its combustion by air as man supports it; it has a pulse and circulation as man has. It may be granted that man's body is as yet the more versatile of the two, but then man's body is an older thing; give the vapor-engine but half the time that man has had, give it also a continuance of our present infatuation, and what may it not ere long attain to?

"There are certain functions indeed of the vapor-engine which will probably remain unchanged for myriads of years—which in fact will perhaps survive when the use of vapor has been superseded; the piston and cylinder, the beam, the fly-wheel, and other parts of the machine will probably be permanent, just as we see that man and many of the lower animals share like modes of eating, drinking, and sleeping; thus they have hearts which beat as ours, veins and arteries, eyes, ears, and noses; they sigh even in their sleep, and weep and yawn; they are affected by their children; they feel pleasure and pain, hope, fear, anger, shame; they have memory and prescience; they know that if certain things happen to them they will die, and they fear death as much as we do; they communicate their thoughts to one another, and some of them deliberately act in concert. The comparison of similarities is endless; I only make it because some may say that since the vapor-engine is not likely to be improved in the main particulars, it is unlikely to be henceforward extensively modified at all. This is too good to be true; it will be modified and suited for an infinite variety of purposes, as much as man has been modified so as to exceed the brutes in skill.

"In the meantime the stoker is almost as much a cook for his engine as our own cooks for ourselves. Consider also the colliers and pitmen and coal merchants and coal trains, and the men who drive them, and the ships that carry coals—what an army of servants do the machines thus employ! Are there not probably more men engaged in tending machinery than in tending men? Do not machines eat as it were by mannery? Are we not ourselves creating our successors in the supremacy of the earth?

daily adding to the beauty and delicacy of their organization daily giving them greater skill and supplying more and more of that self-regulating, self-acting power which will be better than any intellect?

"What a new thing it is for a machine to feed at all! The plough, the spade, and the cart must eat through man's stomach; the fuel that sets them going must burn in the furnace of a man or of horses. Man must consume bread and meat or he cannot dig; the bread and meat are the fuel which drive the spade. If a plough be drawn by horses, the power is supplied by grass or beans or oats, which being burnt in the belly of the cattle give the power of working; without this fuel the work would cease, as an engine would stop if its furnaces were to go out.

"A man of science has demonstrated 'that no animal has the power of originating mechanical energy, but that all the work done in its life by any animal, and all the heat that has been emitted from it, and the heat which would be obtained by burning the combustible matter which has been lost from its body during life, and by burning its body after death, make up altogether an exact equivalent to the heat which would be obtained by burning as much food as it has used during its life, and an amount of fuel which would generate as much heat as its body if burned immediately after death.' I do not know how he has found this out, but he is a man of science—how then can it be objected against the future vitality of the machines that they are, in their present infancy, at the beck and call of beings who are themselves incapable of originating mechanical energy?

"The main point, however, to be observed as affording cause for alarm is, that whereas animals were formerly the only stomachs of the machines, there are now many which have stomachs of their own, and consume their food themselves. This is a great step towards their becoming, if not animate, yet something so near akin to it, as not to differ more widely from our own life than animals do from vegetables. And though man should remain, in some respects, the higher creature, is not this in accordance with the practice of nature, which allows superiority in some things to animals which have, on the whole, been long surpassed? Has she not allowed the ant and the bee to retain superiority over man in the organization of their communities and social arrangements, the bird in traversing the air, the fish in swimming, the horse in strength and fleetness, and the dog in self-sacrifice?

"It is said by some with whom I have conversed upon this subject, that the machines can never be developed into animate or *quasi*-animate existences, inasmuch as they have no reproductive system, nor seem ever likely to possess one. If this be taken to mean that they cannot marry, and that we are never likely to see a fertile union between two vapor-engines with the young ones playing about the door of the shed, however greatly we might desire to do so, I will readily grant it. But the objection is not a very profound one. No one expects that all the features of the now existing organizations will be absolutely repeated in an entirely new class of life. The reproductive system of animals differs widely from that of plants, but both are reproductive systems. Has nature exhausted her phases of this power?

"Surely if a machine is able to reproduce another machine systematically, we may say that it has a reproductive system. What is a reproductive system, if it be not a system for reproduction? And how few of the machines are there which have not been produced systematically by other machines? But it is man that makes them do so. Yes; but is it not insects that make many of the plants reproductive, and would not whole families of plants die out if their fertilization was not effected by a class of agents utterly foreign to themselves? Does any one say that the red clover has no reproductive system because the humble bee (and the humble bee only) must aid and abet it before it can reproduce? No one. The humble bee is a part of the reproductive system of the clover. Each one of ourselves has sprung from minute animalcules whose entity was entirely distinct from our own, and which acted after their kind with no thought or heed of what we might think about it. These little creatures are part of our own reproductive system; then why not we part of the machines? . . .

"It is possible that the [reproductive] system when developed may be in many cases a vicarious thing. Certain classes of machines may be alone fertile, while the rest discharge other functions in the mechanical system, just as the great majority of ants and bees have nothing to do with the continuation of their species, but get food and store it, without thought of breeding. One cannot expect the parallel to be complete or nearly so; certainly not now, and probably never; but is there not enough analogy existing at the present moment, to make us feel seriously uneasy about the future, and to render it our duty to check the evil while we can still do so? Machines can within certain limits beget machines of any class, no matter how different to themselves. Every class of machines will probably have its special mechanical breeders, and all the higher ones will owe their existence to a large number of parents and not to two only.

"We are misled by considering any complicated machine as a single thing; in truth it is a city or society, each member of which was bred truly after its kind. We see a machine as a whole, we call it by a name and individualize it; we look at our own limbs, and know that the combination forms an individual which springs from a single center of reproductive action; we therefore assume that there can be no reproductive action which does not arise from a single center; but this assumption is unscientific, and the bare fact that no vapor-engine was ever made entirely by another, or two others, of its own kind, is not sufficient to warrant us in saying that vapor-engines have no reproductive system. The truth is that each part of every vapor-engine is bred by its own special breeders, whose function it is to breed that part, and that only, while the combination of parts into a whole forms another department of the mechanical reproductive system, which is at present exceedingly complex and difficult to see in its entirety.

"Complex now, but how much simpler and more intelligibly organized may it not become in another hundred thousand years? or in twenty thousand? For man at present believes that his interest lies in that direction; he spends an incalculable amount of labor and time and thought in making machines breed always better and better; he has already succeeded in effecting much that at one time appeared impossible, and there seem no limits to the results of accumulated improvements if they are allowed to descend with modification from generation to generation. It must always be remembered that man's body is what it is through having been molded into its present shape by the chances and changes of many millions of years, but that his organization never advanced with anything like the rapidity with which that of the machines is advancing. This is the most alarming feature of the case, and I must be pardoned for insisting on it so frequently."

Here followed a very long and untranslatable digression about the different races and families of the then existing machines. The writer attempted to support his theory by pointing out the similarities existing between many machines of a widely different character, which served to show descent from a common ancestor. He divided machines into their genera, subgenera, species, varieties, subvarieties, and so forth. He proved the existence of connecting links between machines that seemed to have very little in common, and showed that many more such links had existed, but had now perished. He pointed out tendencies to reversion, and the presence of rudimentary organs which existed in many machines feebly developed and perfectly useless, yet serving to mark descent from an ancestor to whom the function was actually useful. . . .

"May we not fancy that if, in the remotest geological period, some early form of vegetable life had been endowed with the power of reflecting upon the dawning life of animals which was coming into existence alongside of its own, it would have thought itself exceedingly acute if it had surmised that animals would one day become real vegetables? Yet would this be more mistaken than it would be on our part to imagine that because the life of machines is a very different one to our own, there is therefore no higher possible development of life than ours; or that because mechanical life is a very different thing from ours, therefore that it is not life at all?

"But I have heard it said, 'granted that this is so, and that the vapor-engine has a strength of its own, surely no one will say that it has a will of its own?' Alas! if we look more closely, we shall find that this does not make against the supposition that the vapor-engine is one of the germs of a new phase of life. What is there in this whole world, or in the worlds beyond it, which has a will of its own? The Unknown and Unknowable only!

"A man is the resultant and exponent of all the forces that have been brought to bear upon him, whether before his birth or afterwards. His action at any moment depends solely upon his constitution, and on the intensity and direction of the various agencies to which he is, and has been, subjected. Some of these will counteract each other; but as he is by nature, and as he has been acted on, and is now acted on from without, so will he do, as certainly and regularly as though he were a machine.

"We do not generally admit this, because we do not know the whole nature of any one, nor the whole of the forces that act upon him. We see but a part, and being thus unable to generalize human conduct, except very roughly, we deny that it is subject to any fixed laws at all, and ascribe much both of a man's character and actions to chance, or luck, or fortune; but these are only words whereby we escape the admission of our own ignorance; and a little reflection will teach us that the most daring flight of the imagination or the most subtle exercise of the reason is as much the thing that must arise, and the only thing that can by any possibility arise, at the moment of its arising, as the falling of a dead leaf when the wind shakes it from the tree.

"For the future depends upon the present, and the present (whose existence is only one of those minor compromises of which human life is full—for it lives only on sufferance of the past and future) depends upon the past, and the past is unalterable. The only reason why we cannot see the future as plainly as the past, is because we know too little of the actual past and actual present; these things are too great for us, otherwise the future, in its minutest details, would lie spread out before our eyes, and we should lose our sense of time present by reason of the clearness with which we should see the past and future; perhaps we should not be even able to distinguish time at all; but that is foreign. What we do know is, that the more the past and present are known, the more the future can be predicted; and that no one dreams of doubting the fixity of the future in cases where he is fully cognizant of both past and present, and has had experience of the consequences that followed from such a past and such a present on previous occasions. He perfectly well knows what will happen, and will stake his whole fortune thereon.

"And this is a great blessing; for it is the foundation on which morality and science are built. The assurance that the future is no arbitrary and changeable thing, but that like futures will invariably follow like presents, is the groundwork on which we lay all our plans—the faith on which we do every conscious action of our lives. If this were not so we should be without a guide; we should have no confidence in acting, and hence we should never act, for there would be no knowing that the results which will follow now will be the same as those which followed before.

"Who would plow or sow if he disbelieved in the fixity of the future? Who would throw water on a blazing house if the action of water upon fire were uncertain? Men will only do their utmost when they feel certain that the future will discover itself against them if their utmost has not been done. The feeling of such a certainty is a constituent part of the sum of the forces at work upon them, and will act most powerfully on the best and most moral men. Those who are most firmly persuaded that the future is immutably bound up with the present in which their work is lying, will best husband their present, and till it with the greatest care. The future must be a lottery to those who think that the same combinations can sometimes precede one set of results, and sometimes another. If their belief is sincere they will speculate instead of working: these ought to be the immoral men; the others have the strongest spur to exertion and morality, if their belief is a living one.

"The bearing of all this upon the machines is not immediately apparent, but will become so presently. In the meantime I must deal with friends who tell me that, though the future is fixed as regards inorganic matter, and in some respects with regard to man, yet that there are many ways in which it cannot be considered as fixed. Thus, they say that fire applied to dry shavings, and well fed with oxygen gas, will always produce a blaze, but that a coward brought into contact with a terrifying object will not always result in a man running away. Nevertheless, if there be two cowards perfectly similar in every respect, and if they be subjected in a perfectly similar way to two terrifying agents, which are themselves perfectly similar, there are few who will not expect a perfect similarity in the running away, even though a thousand years intervene between the original combination and its being repeated.

"The apparently greater regularity in the results of chemical than of human combinations arises from our inability to perceive the subtle differences in human combinations—combinations which are never identically repeated. Fire we know, and shavings we know, but no two men ever were or ever will be exactly alike; and the smallest difference may change the whole conditions of the problem. Our registry of results must be infinite before we could arrive at a full forecast of future combinations; the wonder is that there is as much certainty concerning human action as there is; and assuredly the older we grow the more certain we feel as to what such and such a kind of person will do in given circumstances; but this could never be the case unless human conduct were under the influence of laws, with the working of which we become more and more familiar through experience.

"If the above is sound, it follows that the regularity with which machinery acts is no proof of the absence of vitality, or at least of germs which may be developed into a new phase of life. At first sight it would indeed appear that a vapor-engine cannot help going when set upon a line of rails with the steam up and the machinery in full play; whereas the man whose business it is to drive it can help doing so at any moment that he pleases; so that the first has no spontaneity, and is not possessed of any sort of free will, while the second has and is.

"This is true up to a certain point; the driver can stop the engine at any moment that he pleases, but he can only please to do so at certain points which have been fixed for him by others, or in the case of unexpected obstructions which force him to please to do so. His pleasure is not spontaneous; there is an unseen choir of influences around him, which make it impossible for him to act in any other way than one. It is known beforehand how much strength must be given to these influences, just as it is known beforehand how much coal and water are necessary for the vapor-engine itself; and curiously enough it will be found that the influences brought to bear upon the driver are of the same kind as those brought to bear upon the engine—that is to say, food and warmth. The driver is obedient to his masters, because he gets food and warmth from them, and if these are withheld or given in insufficient quantities he will cease to drive; in like manner the engine will cease to work if it is insufficiently fed. The only difference is, that the man is conscious about his wants, and the engine (beyond refusing to work) does not seem to be so; but this is temporary, and has been dealt with above.

"Accordingly, the requisite strength being given to the motives that are to drive the driver, there has never, or hardly ever, been an instance of a man stopping his engine through wantonness. But such a case might occur; yes, and it might occur that the engine should break down: but if the train is stopped from some trivial motive it will be found either that the strength of the necessary influences has been miscalculated, or that the man has been miscalculated, in the same way as an engine may break down from an unsuspected flaw; but even in such a case there will have been no spontaneity; the action will have had its true parental causes: spontaneity is only a term for man's ignorance of the gods.

"Is there, then, no spontaneity on the part of those who drive the driver?"

Here followed an obscure argument upon this subject, which I have thought it best to omit. The writer resumes:—"After all then it comes to this, that the difference between the life of a man and that of a machine is one rather of degree than of kind, though differences in kind are not wanting. An animal has more provision for emergency than a machine. The machine is less versatile; its range of action is narrow; its strength and accuracy in its own sphere are superhuman, but it shows badly in a dilemma; sometimes when its normal action is disturbed, it will lose its head, and go from bad to worse like a lunatic in a raging frenzy: but here, again, we are met by the same consideration as before, namely, that the machines are still in their infancy; they are mere skeletons without muscles and flesh.

"For how many emergencies is an oyster adapted? For as many as are likely to happen to it, and no more. So are the machines; and so is man himself. The list of casualties that daily occur to man through his want of adaptability is probably as great as that occurring to the machines; and every day gives them some greater provision for the unforeseen. Let any one examine the wonderful self-regulating and self-adjusting contrivances which are now incorporated with the vapor-engine, let him watch the way in which it supplies itself with oil; in which it indicates its wants to those who tend it; in which, by the governor, it regulates its application of its own strength; let him look at that store-house of inertia and momentum the fly-wheel, or at the buffers on a railway carriage; let him see how those improvements are being selected for perpetuity which contain provision against the emergencies that may arise to harass the machines, and then let him think of a hundred thousand years, and the accumulated progress which they will bring unless man can be awakened to a sense of his situation and of the doom which he is preparing for himself.

"The misery is that man has been blind so long already. In his reliance upon the use of steam he has been betrayed into increasing and multiplying. To withdraw steam power suddenly will not have the effect of reducing us to the state in which we were before its introduction; there will be a general break-up and time of anarchy such as has never been known; it will be as though our population were suddenly doubled, with no additional means of feeding the increased number. The air we breathe is hardly more necessary for our animal life than the use of any machine, on the strength of which we have increased our numbers, is to our civilization; it is the machines which act upon man and make him man, as much as man who has acted upon and made the machines; but we must choose between the alternative of undergoing much present suffering, or seeing ourselves gradually superseded by our own creatures, till we rank no higher in comparison with them, than the beasts of the field with ourselves.

"Herein lies our danger. For many seem inclined to acquiesce in so dishonorable a future. They say that although man should become to the machines what the horse and dog are to us, yet that he will continue to exist, and will probably be better off in a state of domestication under the beneficent rule of the machines than in his present wild condition. We treat our domestic animals with much kindness. We give them whatever we believe to be the best for them; and there can be no doubt that our use of meat has increased their happiness rather than detracted from it. In like manner there is reason to hope that the machines will use us kindly, for their existence will be in a great measure dependent upon ours; they will rule us with a rod or iron, but they will not eat us; they will not only require our services in the reproduction and education of their young, but also in waiting upon them as servants; in gathering food for them, and feeding them; in restoring them to health when they are sick;

and in either burying their dead or working up their deceased members into new forms of mechanical existence.

"The very nature of the motive power which works the advancement of the machines precludes the possibility of man's life being rendered miserable as well as enslaved. Slaves are tolerably happy if they have good masters, and the revolution will not occur in our time, nor hardly in ten thousand years, or ten times that. Is it wise to be uneasy about a contingency which is so remote? Man is not a sentimental animal where his material interests are concerned, and though here and there some ardent soul may look upon himself and curse his fate that he was not born a vapor-engine, yet the mass of mankind will acquiesce in any arrangement which gives them better food and clothing at a cheaper rate, and will refrain from yielding to unreasonable jealousy merely because there are other destinies more glorious than their own.

"The power of custom is enormous, and so gradual will be the change, that man's sense of what is due to himself will be at no time rudely shocked; our bondage will steal upon us noiselessly and by imperceptible approaches; nor will there ever be such a clashing of desires between man and the machines as will lead to an encounter between them. Among themselves the machines will war eternally, but they will still require man as the being through whose agency the struggle will be principally conducted. In point of fact there is no occasion for anxiety about the future happiness of man so long as he continues to be in any way profitable to the machines; he may become the inferior race, but he will be infinitely better off than he is now. Is it not then both absurd and unreasonable to be envious of our benefactors? And should we not be guilty of consummate folly if we were to reject the advantages which we cannot obtain otherwise, merely because they involve a greater gain to others than to ourselves?

"With those who can argue in this way I have nothing in common. I shrink with as much horror from believing that my race can ever be superseded or surpassed, as I should do from believing that even at the remotest period my ancestors were other than human beings. Could I believe that ten hundred thousand years ago a single one of my ancestors was another kind of being to myself, I should lose all self-respect, and take no further pleasure or interest in life. I have the same feeling with regard to my descendants, and believe it to be one that will be felt so generally that the country will resolve upon putting an immediate stop to all further mechanical progress, and upon destroying all improvements that have been made for the last three hundred years. I would not urge more than this. We may trust ourselves to deal with those that remain, and though I should prefer to have seen the destruction include another two hundred years, I am aware of the necessity for compromising, and would so far sacrifice my own individual convictions as to be content with three hundred. Less than this will. be insufficient."

This was the conclusion of the attack which led to the destruction of machinery throughout Erewhon. There was only one serious attempt to answer it. Its author said that machines were to be regarded as a part of man's own physical nature, being really nothing but extra-corporeal limbs. Man, he said, was a machinate mammal. The lower animals keep all their limbs at home in their own bodies, but many of man's are loose, and lie about detached, now here and now there, in various parts of the world— some being kept always handy for contingent use, and others being occasionally hundreds of miles away. A machine is merely a supplementary limb; this is the be all and end all of machinery. We do not use our own limbs other than as machines; and a leg is only a much better wooden leg than any one can manufacture.

"Observe a man digging with a spade; his right fore-arm has become artifically lengthened, and his hand has become a joint. The handle of the spade is like the knob at the end of the humerus; the shaft is the additional bone, and the oblong iron plate is the new form of the hand which enables its possessor to disturb the earth in a way to which his original hand was unequal. Having thus modified himself, not as other animals are modified, by circumstances over which they have had not even the appearance of control, but having, as it were, taken forethought and added a cubit to his stature, civilization began to dawn upon the race, the social good offices, the genial companionship of friends, the art of unreason, and all those habits of mind which most elevate man above the lower animals, in the course of time ensued.

"Thus civilization and mechanical progress advanced hand in hand, each developing and being developed by the other, the earliest accidental use of the stick having set the ball rolling, and the prospect of advantage keeping it in motion. In fact, machines are to be regarded as the mode of development by which human organism is now especially advancing, every past invention being an addition to the resources of the human body. Even community of limbs is thus rendered possible to those who have so much community of soul as to own money enough to pay a railway fare; for a train is only a seven-leagued foot that five hundred may own at once."

The one serious danger which this writer apprehended was that the machines would so equalize men's powers, and so lessen the severity of competition, that many persons of inferior physique would escape detection and transmit their inferiority to their descendants. He feared that the removal of the present pressure might cause a degeneracy of the human race, and indeed that the whole body might become purely rudimentary, the man himself being nothing but soul and mechanism, an intelligent but passionless principle of mechanical action.

"How greatly," he wrote, "do we now now live with our external limbs? We vary our physique with the seasons, with age, with advancing or decreasing wealth. If it is wet we are furnished with an organ commonly called an umbrella, and which is designed for the purpose of protecting our clothes or our skins from the injurious effects of rain. Man has now many extra-corporeal members, which are of more importance to him than a good deal of his hair, or at any rate than his whiskers. His memory goes in his pocket-book. He becomes more and more complex as he grows older; he will then be seen with see-engines, or perhaps with artificial teeth and hair: if he be a really well-developed specimen of his race, he will be furnished with a large box upon wheels, two horses, and a coach-man."

It was this writer who originated the custom of classifying men by their horse-power, and who divided them into genera, species, varieties, and subvarieties, giving them names which expressed the number of limbs which they could command at any moment. He showed that men became more highly and delicately organized the more nearly they approached the summit of opulence, and that none but millionaires possessed the full complement of limbs with which mankind could become incorporate.

"Those mighty organisms," he continued, "our leading bankers and merchants, speak to their congeners through the length and breadth of the land in a second of time; their rich and subtle souls can defy all material impediment, whereas the souls of the poor are clogged and hampered by matter, which sticks fast about them as treacle to the wings of a fly, or as one struggling in a quicksand: their dull ears must take days or weeks to hear what another would tell them from a distance, instead of hearing it in a second as is done by the more highly organized classes. Who shall deny that one who can tack on a special train to his identity, and go wheresoever he will whensoever he pleases, is more highly organized than he who, should he wish for the same power, might wish for the wings of a bird with an equal chance of getting them; and whose legs are his only means of locomotion? That old philosophic enemy, matter, the inherently and essentially evil, still hangs about the neck of the poor and strangles him: but to the rich, matter is immaterial; the elaborate organization of his extra-corporeal system has freed his soul.

"This is the secret of the homage which we see rich men receive from those who are poorer than themselves: it would be a grave error to suppose that this deference proceeds from motives which we need be ashamed of: it is the natural respect which all living creatures pay to those whom they recognize as higher than themselves in the scale of animal life, and is analogous to the veneration which a dog feels for man. Among savage races it is deemed highly honorable to be the possessor of a gun, and throughout all known time there has been a feeling that those who are worth most are the worthiest."

And so he went on at considerable length, attempting to show what changes in the distribution of animal and vegetable life throughout the kingdom had been caused by this and that of man's inventions, and in what way each was connected with the moral and intellectual development of the human species: he even allotted to some the share which they had had in the creation and modification of man's body, and that which they would hereafter have in its destruction; but the other writer was considered to have the best of it, and in the end succeeded in destroying all the inventions that had been discovered for the preceding 271 years, a period which was agreed upon by all parties after several years of wrangling as to whether a certain kind of mangle which was much in use among washerwomen should be saved or no. It was at last ruled to be dangerous, and was just excluded by the limit of 271 years. Then came the reactionary civil wars which nearly ruined the country, but which it would be beyond my present scope to describe.

—15—

a cybernated world

The development of computers has made possible a fundamental change in the nature of industrial organization, work, and patterns of consumption. At least ideally, computer programs—the plans that direct the actions of the machine—can have the ability to learn—that is, to modify themselves in the face of experience, to seek new solutions to problems, and to initiate searches for better solutions. This means that computer systems could be designed to be self-maintaining, self-modifying, and virtually independent of human supervision. Obviously, if computer systems can be designed with these abilities, at least in theory they could be used to run industries and even entire economies.

Precisely how such a computer-based economic system might evolve from the world's current economic and political situation is the subject of this excerpt from Rex Gordon's *Utopia Minus X*. The sequence of events that Gordon posits should not be considered a prediction in any sense. Rather, consider Gordon's hypothetical series of social changes as a set of events that could lead to the world system he describes. The interesting question from a sociological point of view is whether the changes could reasonably be expected to bring about the form of social organization proposed.

A segment of the novel not included here raises an interesting question: How is it possible to maintain social control and induce conformity in a society that has no shortage of material objects—one, in fact, in which some attention must be given to making the public consume enough? One answer is obvious. Threat and physical punishment could be employed extensively and would probably be successful to a certain degree. The major drawback to this solution is that setting up a strictly coercive system is likely to produce enemies for the system and lead eventually to organized opposition. It is much more effective to devise procedures for social control that are based on the distribution of rewards rather than the avoidance of punishment. Gordon produces two examples of noncoercive social control mechanisms that would work under the conditions of affluence of his cybernated society.

The first example is a technique for controlling the intake of alcoholic beverages in a situation in which drinks are prepared automatically and need only be asked for. The procedure is simple: to get a drink, the customer must operate a device that requires a certain degree of manual dexterity. As he drinks more, presumably his ability to operate the machine will decrease. Eventually, the customer becomes so intoxicated that he is unable to operate the machine successfully. To prevent people from becoming drunk, one need only set the ability level fairly high.

The second example is more important because it does not apply specifically to a certain behavior. In Gordon's society, money is nonexistent and property has no true value, not even value as a source of status since the amount of property a man owns does not necessarily signify his power or merit. Under these conditions, how can people be induced to perform the few tasks that still require human effort? The problem is to find a commodity that has values and can be controlled by an employer (in this case, the government) and used as a payment for service —that is, to find a commodity that functions in a manner analogous to money in our society. The solution that Gordon proposes is the control of living space. The allocation of square feet of living space is the medium of exchange between the government and its employees. In Gordon's society, the allocation of space is an effective mechanism of control. Men are induced to fill the necessary roles simply by paying them with an apartment of a certain size. One reason the device works so well is that the amount of property an individual *can* own will obviously be related to the amount of storage space he is able to provide.

The plot of Gordon's novel, uses essentially the sample ploy that Bellamy (Chapter 19) uses in order to get his story moving. He transports a man from the middle of the twentieth century two hundred years into the future. In this case, the device of a near-speed-of-light space journey is used to justify Morgan Harvey's transition. In the following excerpt, Harvey first encounters an inhabitant of his new world.

Utopia minus X

by Rex Gordon

"Listen, Melita Lucit. Do you understand what I am saying? My name is Morgan Harvey, and you can call me Morgan. I have come from a long way away, and I need some information about your country and your social setup. You are going to give me that information. And the first thing I want to know is what kind of an organization you have and who runs it. About your firm or the department that employs you, about your government and your economic system. And there are special reasons why I am asking that. Now give. Tell me."

She listened to him with a most exceptional intentness of attention. But though he was almost elaborate in explaining his aims and what he wanted to know, it did not seem to make it easier for her. On the contrary, every stage of his explanation seemed to make her frown more, as though it made it a degree more difficult.

"You use archaic words," she said after a moment.

He had not allowed for that, for the change in language.

But damn it, he thought . . . , the language could not have changed as much as that. What he said should be at least intelligible.

"But it isn't that," she said. "What you say does not make sense. You say you come from far away, but however far away you come from, you seem to have some unnecessary difficulty. Where could you have come from that would leave you in doubt about the social system of the Perfect World? There is no such place. I still think you must be playing a joke on me."

Morgan Harvey faced it. It was not only a change in language, there was a change in the political structure of the world as well. Unless she was deceiving him, and her manner was naked in its earnestness, the world had been unified by the wars, the half-wars and the contest between the Red and Blue nations must be over, and she could not know what that meant to him.

One side must have won.

He was afraid to ask which side. "Did you say 'the Perfect World'?" he asked.

She did not answer. She looked at him a little incredulously.

"Melita," he said, "this is going to take a little longer than I thought. It isn't necessary that we stand here. I can't let you get back in the helicopter in case you communicate with someone with a radio there, but we can go to that grassy bank over there and sit down to talk."

He pointed to a narrow bank overgrown by grass between the fields, and they went towards it. She fingered the bracelet on her wrist and looked at him curiously when he spoke of using a radio in the helicopter. She looked as though she were about to say something, but said nothing and smiled momentarily in a puzzled way. She just went with him to the grassy bank, turning quick glances on him and looking intrigued and interested, rather as though if it were a joke—which she seemed to doubt —she was interested and would play it for what it was worth.

And, Morgan thought, if he was not attaching too much importance to a few small words, the world had been unified. The wars between the Blue Nations and the Red were over, and so, in a sense, was the purpose of his life. . . .

She studied him for a moment, then said: "At our period of history we don't have governments or countries or an economic system, or payment, or any of the other things you mentioned. We only learn about those things in History, which is a subject that appears in the Index and that makes dramatic and interesting watching when it appears on our teaching screens. But to tell you what we do have is not so easy unless I know what you know already. We have virtually nothing, you see, if you are thinking in those terms, though what we do have is something completely different."

It was at that point that Morgan realized that he must not underestimate Melita Lucit. He had been asking her all the questions, but she had achieved an astonishingly shrewd penetration of his mind while he had almost no knowledge at all of hers.

It was in the nature of things, he realized bitterly. If she was not playing with him completely, as he was inclined half to suspect she was, then all the things he mentioned were known to her, and had to be if she had only a passing acquaintance with history, while nothing she said had meaning for him, since to him it was the unknown.

"You don't have government," he said flatly. "You say you don't have government. Who makes your laws?"

Her eyes narrowed a little. " 'Laws' is another archaic word," she said. "I don't know what game you are playing, Morgan Harvey, but your knowledge of human society seems to be confined entirely to the period before the setting up of the Perfect World. At a guess, I would say you either are, or pretend to be, confined to such knowledge as would be available, at the latest, in the period of history of the Red and Blue wars."

She was quite confident, sitting on the grass looking at him. Her frank blue eyes regarded him as though he were a mathematical or analytic problem: and as though he could not expect to be looked at in any other than that way, behaving the way he was.

Keeping the tremor out of his voice, the tremor that despite himself wanted to come into it, he said: "Who won the Red and Blue Wars?"

Looking hard at him, she said: "So."

Without change of expression, he said, "Who won? You wonder about this gun. All right, wonder. It's a matter of life and death to me."

The Red Nations, in their propaganda, of which he had heard a little, used to tell a story. They said that in time, in some miraculous fashion, after government had become more and more centralized, the state would begin to wither away. There would be no government any more, no laws, no crime. Instead, there would be an Age of Abundance, when everyone would have everything they wanted, when work would be negligible, and people would live in harmony, presumably loving one another.

"Neither side won," she said.

"All right. Then how are you governed now?"

"Human governments are defunct," she said simply. "Is it possible you don't know? Computers are better. How could any human brain compete with a computer, say in the field of economic planning?" . . .

"Your enemy," she said. The Reds. You didn't study them enough. Not as people. Not as people like yourselves."

"I don't understand."

She wondered. What could she tell him that would convince him? The whole of history? It was most awkward.

"It was like you said," she told him gently. "Though you had defeated the Reds in battle, you could not attack their homeland. I think you know all about that. They had an atomic stockpile, and would blow it up and make life impossible on Earth if you invaded them. But there was unrest and riots and disorders in their country after their defeat. You did what you could. You stirred up revolt. You hoped to win finally that way."

The big man sitting on the grass beside her did not look very hopeful. He said, "Hoped?"

"You helped what you called the right-wing faction in their internal troubles," she said. "By helping them, you discredited them. It seemed that the people in the Red countries were rather like you. They preferred their own people, however fanatical, to politicians who were treating with the enemy and getting foreign aid. The right-wing faction was defeated, and it was the most fanatical element who came to power again. A group who called themselves New Communists. I don't think your people were very good at politics, Morgan."

He sat silent. To her surprise, he did not look as though he disbelieved her. On the contrary. He looked as though he had sometimes dreamed, or feared, it might be like that, maybe in a nightmare.

With a glum fatalism that did not include disbelief, he said, "What did they do?"

She studied him carefully. Then she looked around at the surrounding country.

"I don't know if you will like this," she said. "But I can see that, knowing what you know now of us, you will believe it."

"What is it?"

She kept her eyes on him while she told him.

"This was the time when automation and computers were really coming into their stride as the new technology of mankind. The New Communists, the new fanatical element among the Reds, blamed their defeat on the stupidity and cupidity of those government officials who, in a Communist world, ran their economy. So they set out to eliminate the human element. They mobilized the national resources for a great patriotic effort. Since to them it was the human element that was wrong, they aimed to do away with it. They built the first Great Computer, a giant electronic brain which was to absorb all the statistics, finances, and control of their economy, and to plan the life of their country on a basis of pure mathematics and science."

She saw him react as she had feared he would. He looked away at the agricultural machinery, working on the hillsides without human aid, and then at her again.

"But you told me—you—!" He raised a hand as though in gesture of despair. "You told me you were governed by a Computer! And yet you say the Reds were the first with it—and yet that they didn't win the war!"

The disbelief was alive in his eyes again now. It was as she had feared it would be. She had known it would be awkward.

"Hadn't you better listen to what happened?"

"Not if it leads to something I can't believe!"

"I think you'd better listen," she said insistently.

She wondered how to bring him back to that state in which he had been listening to her, and if not believing at least absorbing the things she said. It was most difficult. He was such an obstinate man. Should she alter the story, make a drama of it, to make it suitable for his ears?

The truth as she had learned it was better, even if he did not believe it.

"Think of that Computer," she said persuasively. "The first, Red, Great Computer, and what it was supposed to do. Can you understand that it was to absorb the statistics and organization and running costs of every mile of airline and every railway? It was something new, and the outcome of a gigantic effort that it was to be fed not only with the figures and costs and output of every factory, but also all the details of the daily running of that factory, and all costs and figures of every kind. The details of the medical services, the police, the judiciary, and everything that cost money, all had to go into it. It was to absorb them all, and relate them, and see all mathematical connections between them. I need hardly tell you that it took all the scientific resources of the nation to build it, and it was of gigantic size."

Sitting solidly on the grass, Morgan spoke with a kind of fascinated horror. "It must have been the most ruthless tool of government there ever was."

"But useful, don't you think?" she said. She tried to persuade him. "Not only for Communism, but to discover unknown relationships between the facts and figures? How far one kind of education succeeded, for example, as opposed to another. Whether one means of dealing with crime was best, or if another was finally more successful. And whether this or that type of factory or organization was better for the national economy. This was something new. You must admit there was something in it. The New Communists had a good idea."

She was disappointed. Perhaps it was the word "Communists" that upset him. He would have nothing to do with it. With his face set and obstinate, staring away into the distance, he said to himself more than to her, "Communism super-plus!"

She shrugged her shoulders over him and gave up the attempt to persuade him that the Great Computer had been a good thing.

"Anyway, they built it," she said. "With the enormous effort of which defeated nations are sometimes capable, the Reds built their Great Computer. It was there, and it absorbed the statistics, and it began to advise the New Communist government. And wouldn't you like to know what happened?"

At least he did not object. He sat staring away into the distance as though absorbed in some final horror picture of his own.

"And did they obey it?" he asked her grimly without looking at her. "Did they obey the Great Machine?"

She watched him, smiling mildly and in anticipation. She wondered how his expression would change when he knew the story.

"They did. And 'obey' is right. You see there was something they had not thought of. To build a machine like that, a fully integrated calculating machine, to run the economy, is all very well. But that was the first problem they ran into. That they only *could* obey it."

He turned around to her, frowning. "What do you mean?"

"You know how it is with politicians," she said, smiling at him, since possibly he did know. "They used to ask for advice from experts, and then not take it. Or they would take part of the advice, what suited them, and not the rest. Well, it wasn't like that with the Great Computer. They got its advice and carried out part of it. Scrap that factory there. Start a vast new scheme of automated factories somewhere else. They got advice, loads of it, and in the most fantastic detail. And when they put part of it in operation, they got the most frightful tangles. Factories all set up, but no power supply. Adjust the power supply, and there was a transport tangle. The most absurd things. So they produced a shortage of teaspoons in Siberia. It was new, you see. They had to learn. They had to learn that if you set up a vast Computer, with a capacity for dealing with facts and figures far beyond the human mind, you only *can* obey it. In detail, and exactly. Because you can't possibly hope to understand the advice you're given. A Computer's plan is too complex. Its whole nature is that it is beyond the human mind. That is what it is for. The Computer sees everything at once. You can't. And so, if you're going in for a Computer at all, they rapidly learned, the only thing you can do is take its advice, as a whole, and apply it all exactly."

To her surprise, Morgan was looking at her suspiciously. His frown had not left him, but she was glad to see it was troubled now.

"I don't quite understand that," he said.

She shrugged her shoulders again.

"So they had to take the Computer's advice exactly?"

"They were stuck with it," she said. "The Computer was the outcome of the great national effort. They had set up all the organization and machinery. There were a few executions, of course, as a result of the original chaos. But there was another thing that not only they but the ordinary people learned very rapidly. That when the Computer's plans were carried out, they worked. Those vast new automated factories. They were *fully* automated. They demanded vast capital expenditure, for they were automated all the way from the self-breeding reactors of the power supply and the machines that dug the ore to the packaging department of the final product. No workers, only one man in the control room. The Computer said that that was the economical way to do things, and it was. And the Computer solved another problem. How do you cost, and what do you charge for products that take no man-hours to produce? The Computer showed them. Under a Communist economy, you deliver them free, as a boost to the economy. The Computer became suddenly popular. When things began to click in place and work as they had never worked under a Communist government before, the computer became more popular than the government. Especially when it began to reorganize the educational system and the police force, chiefly by dismissing hosts of minor government officials. It just cancelled their salaries. It said they were quite redundant."

Morgan was listening with strange, fascinated, complex horror now to the story and history of his enemies, the Reds. As he sat listening to Melita, who talked to him with a persuasive smile of great events, his eyes showed neither belief nor disbelief, but only puzzlement.

"You follow?" she said.

"Yes, I follow." Morgan swallowed. "You said it reorganized the educational system and the police? How could it?"

"Perhaps it might be more true to say that the organization the New Communists had set up to carry out the Computer's requirements in the greatest detail did it. The Computer only gave advice."

Morgan's voice was sharp. "I thought it was purely economic. How could it give advice on a thing like that?"

Melita looked at him mildly.

"One of the first things the Computer had done was allocate funds for research into education. The need of the state was for more technicians. They had to be produced. And the results of the research were fed into the Great Computer. The answer was teaching-machines. The candidate sat in front of a screen with buttons before him. He learned from the screen and answered questions that appeared there by typing and pressing buttons. And the best machine to operate this system was the Great Computer itself. Through a series of teaching-machines and slave computers, it began to handle the educational system. In effect, it trained its own technicians, and put them in the key positions." Melita smiled at Morgan's doubt. "It worked on a basis of trial and error, of course. It only dealt with figures and symbols. But it divided people into types and classes and judged them by results."

"And the police?" Morgan was more incredulous about that.

"I told you in the beginning, the Computer dealt with crime statistics, sabotage, strikes, and all that kind of thing. It was only concerned with economy in the administration of the state, of course. The trouble with the Computer from the Communist point of view was that it did not know right from wrong morally or politically. It had no human notions of vengeance or morality. When it discovered that criminals could be 'cured' by a group of medical psychologists, who used drugs and electronic means to alter their personalities, it went in for that method wholesale. It was infinitely cheaper than the old apparatus of prisons and warders, and unlike the prisons and warders it produced the right results. Crime wasn't crime to the Great Computer. It was something that upset the economy like an epidemic of smallpox or the common cold. So it set up our Doctor system and abolished the distinction between the police and the social workers and the health service. And the people liked it. They now had free goods, and, when agriculture was automated, free food. They had an absolutely first class and incorruptible educational system that allowed their children, on ability alone, to rise to the very top. And now the Computer was abolishing prisons and slave workers' camps and firing squads. Instead, they got Doctors who went around making people happy. You can guess the effect of that."

Morgan was sitting very still. He ignored the agricultural machines now, and the countryside around him. He looked only at Melita, seeing her now as the most articulate and persuasive girl he had ever met.

If she was a product of the Perfect World, his eyes seemed to say, she was more dangerous than he thought.

"Utopia?" he said dryly. "Utopia produced entirely by a machine?"

Melita raised an eyebrow.

"By perfect administration?" she asked him. "What system wouldn't work, when we got that?"

"What happened?" His voice was hard again.

"The New Communists saw it in the end. That they weren't running the country. The Computer was. And as the dismissal of government officials crept steadily higher up the scale, the blinkers fell from their eyes, and they saw the danger."

"What danger? How?"

Melita sat silent for a moment, watching him before she told him.

"There was a final secret meeting in the Kremlin. The documents are available. The Computer was tried before that meeting. It was seen to be subversive. It had seized power by creating its own servants, a whole class, a whole generation of computer-trained technicians, whom it had selected as the most intelligent people in the land and put in points of power. It had won popular support. They, the aging New Communist leaders around the table, were unpopular, but the Computer was not. And it had done worse. The Computer had been built to produce a hard and efficient, ruthless, warlike nation. It had produced a fat and peaceful one. So the Computer must go. The decision was irrevocable. The army would move silently and seize communications, and the Computer would be smashed. Perhaps they would build another someday, but not until they had thought again. The execution was decided upon, the vote was taken. Then there was a knock on the door."

Melita looked calmly at Morgan.

"In walked the Doctors. The Computer's Doctors. Information had been laid that the leaders of the New Communist Party were mentally unwell. And the leaders around the table knew it as soon as they heard the charge. They were mentally unwell. They always had been. Like all revolutionary leaders through history, they were power-mad paranoics. What they knew exactly, was that they had been mad to set up the Great Computer in the first place. But there was no fooling, no lies, no trickery. The Computer's Doctors were not like that. Justice was done. The proceedings were a public picture of the new humanity. The New Communist leaders were given standard medical tests. And then, declared ill but not incurable, they were given treatment. They were given six weeks in a sanitorium. And then they were released, and made free. Their official positions had not been interfered with. But they were changed men. They no longer wanted to destroy the Great Computer. They believed in it, and all they had lost was their ambition. They wanted to live peaceful, happy lives as normal men. They were cured—really—cured, and the government resigned. It was not replaced. It was unnecessary. The Computer had its own willing organization for carrying out its orders. And the New Communists retired, while the remaining government officers were dismissed, and the Computer ran the country."

Morgan had not moved. They were sitting still on the grassy bank and looking at one another's eyes. It was a long and pregnant silence, until Morgan broke it.

"No," he said. "I don't believe that." . . .

The awful thing was that, Morgan thought, he was going to have to understand the history to know what was going on now.

But he did not tell Melita that.

"What don't you believe?" Melita said.

He was calm about it, and, for him, articulate.

"I don't believe that story of a Great Computer taking over a country and acting as though it were a living being, and arresting its own creators," he said cautiously.

Melita looked at him steadily. She too was calm.

"It was not quite like that, Morgan. I never said that the Computer behaved like a human being. It didn't arrest its own creators. It just created a perfect human society by its advice and administration. In such a society, it was inevitable that the fanatical New Communist leaders should be arrested."

"That is beyond me," Morgan said.

"Then if you don't understand the story, if it's too much for you, you should believe it."

"That's something I don't and won't do," he told her. "It's too neat. It has all the hallmarks of a propaganda story. Too pretty. It ends too nicely."

She could see he was in earnest. It was not only that he disbelieved what she had told him, but he was looking at her, as they sat facing one another on the grass, as though he expected her to disbelieve it, too.

"Besides," he said, indicating the countryside around them, "even if I believed it, it would still prove my point. All this is Communism. A Red world. I can see why you told me the Red story. You haven't explained how, but it originated with the Reds."

She shook her head.

He looked at her with grim disbelief. "Don't tell me that my people, the Blues, built themselves a Great Computer, too." It was too much.

It was time to tell him. She had not been able to do so before. He would not have believed her.

"Hasn't it occurred to you Morgan Harvey, that the construction of a Great Computer was an inevitable stage in human technology? The story you have been hearing is not one of Communism, but of inexorable human development, helped on in your time by war and struggle."

His eyes widened for a moment. It was an idea that had not occurred to him. He had thought that a Great Computer could rise from Communism alone.

Then his face darkened. "My people would not have anything to do with that. They believed in freedom, not blind obedience to a machine!"

He was angry at the thought of it, and she could see it was going to be difficult.

She said simply, "I am free. I am free to talk to you now. How many of your people would have been free to do that, in their working day?"

He scowled. He did not like it when she pointed things out to him, even though they were true.

He pointed to her helicopter. "Public ownership," he said. "My people would not have had that!"

She looked at him gravely, wondering how to tell him simply. Unfortunately, it wasn't simple.

"Even in your time," she said calmly, "weren't your cities becoming choked with private transport? You had cars, I think, that blocked all your

city centers. And what do you think you had to do? Eventually you had
to ban private vehicles from city centers. You had to go back to railways
and monorails and public service vehicles. When cities became three-
dimensional, you had to invent our universal helicopter service. It was a
technical solution to a technical problem. It had nothing to do with politics."

He looked from her to her helicopter.

"But privately owned," he insisted, baldly.

She returned his look steadily.

"Private ownership? You are strong on that, Morgan Harvey. But I was
taught your history. You had credit, didn't you? A house on mortgage?
Clothes on a checking account? Grocery bills paid monthly? Be honest
with yourself. What did you own?"

Morgan was firm, but he looked worried. "I don't understand," he said,
though he feared he did.

"I was taught your history," she said, "Perhaps things look different
when you look back on them than they did to the people at the time.
What we can see, looking back, is that you were steadily blurring the
distinction between the things you did own, and those you did not. I was
taught that at the time the Reds built their first Great Computer they were
in a way copying you because all your major undertakings were already
using pretty big computers to plan their operations to keep track of what
they owned. Banks were using computers to keep track of what their
clients owned, or, far more likely, their overdrafts. And this was at a time
when automation was only just beginning, yet already your government
was fixing prices artificially by buying up surplus farm stocks. Already you
were worried by overproduction, while ownership was becoming a purely
technical matter, to be settled by computers. Can't you see the way you
were going? Did you have no sense of it at the time?"

Morgan looked at her with a kind of twisted horror. "You mean we—
you mean it was the bankers who forced socialism on us eventually,
despite ourselves?"

She saw his expression and watched him.

"You talk as though all this was a bad thing," she said. "It wasn't,
Morgan. You must understand that. It was, in a way, a kind of genius.
Your society was adapting itself, technically, for what was to come. Your
economy was adapting itself to technical developments, as it had to do if
you were to survive." She sounded moral.

"Your people invented that technique, Morgan. Not the Reds, the
Blues. It was just one of their innumerable technical inventions at the turn
of the century. Do you think the Blues were behind the Reds in setting
up automated control of mining, agriculture, and earth-moving machines?
And they, too, began to set up the fully-automated factories, in which the
product was produced by machines driven by self-powered breeder reac-

tors, all the way from the ore to the final product untouched by hand. You should try to grasp what those changes meant. They were moving from the stage of human industry to machine industry. Before long even the repairing of machines was done by machines, by electronic controls and checks."

Morgan was grim. He was looking at Melita with fascinated horror.

"But the unemployment—the wealth of the people who owned the automated factories, and the poverty and unemployment of the hundreds of thousands of employees who must have been displaced—!"

Melita nodded.

"You did have what your President of the time described as 'a few little local difficulties.' But then your nation always had had those difficulties, and overcame them. Your unions, naturally, went on strike. Your government adjusted the tax-structure so that the wealth from the new factories flowed back into the nation. There were scores of minor adjustments and compromises. The new automated industries were enormously costly to set up. Public subscriptions were required to finance them that meant investment for a sure return for millions of people who had never invested before. The small man's investment turned to gold in his hand when he could see what he was able to buy for the returns he got. It moved steadily from a working and share-owning democracy, to a share-owning democracy. The main adjustment was psychological—persuading people not even to try to work, but just to sit back and live on income."

Morgan was trying to see it, trying to believe and understand. The story Melita was telling him touched him much more closely than that of the Reds had done.

"But all this is a long way from the construction of a Great Computer and some kind of Communism!"

She shook her head. "Not as far as you think. I told you those tendencies in your society that we, looking back, can see to have been the important ones. Automation. The increasing use of computers. The blurring of distinctions between what a man owned and what he did not own. And overproduction. It was the last that was the decisive factor. Once set up, and self-repairing, an automated factory would go on producing unlimited goods endlessly. Prices fell and fell. There is a limit to the consumption of goods, you know. Two cars in every garage, as in your time, was fine. Add a helicopter. Add a new helicopter of the latest model every year. You are still in reasonable limits. But not production running at the rate of ten cars per person per year. Not an unlimited production of helicopters from a factory that cost nothing to run but that would cost an enormous investment to shut down and re-tool. What happened when an automated factory was on a production line of out-dated goods? The cheapest thing to do was to go on producing and dump the goods. Sell them at any price at all. Anyone could have a helicopter of last year's model for one hundreth of a day's pay. And the stuff began to lie around. There were disastrous movements in the price-structure. Price movements were random and wholly psychological. We had to have a Great Computer, Morgan—for exactly the opposite reason the Reds had to have one."

"I don't see that!" He feared he did.

She shook her head at him gently.

"The Reds had to have a Great Computer because, defeated as they were, they had to plan their economy more efficiently. We, as victors, had to have one because our economy was too efficient. We were drowning under masses of dumped goods that no one wanted, and the price structure had gone haywire. Besides, no one cared who owned what any more. Production had to be planned in some way, because, due to overproduction, the profit motive had disappeared. Why work? Unless you happened to be a nurse, a Doctor, an artist, or a genius producing some rare kind of product no machine could make, work was difficult to get, and its results were marginal. You had to have a Great Computer. It was technically inevitable."

"Technically?"

"I was taught to put it this way, Morgan. That so long as people are doing the work, the profit motive will operate. But when machines are doing the work, it won't. At that point, technically, because the profit motive has ceased to operate, you have to have a planned economy. And the only sane way to do it, again technically, in a computer and automation age, is to build a Great Computer to do it."

Morgan sat quietly with her on the grassy bank. True or false? If false, what could he do about it? And if true, then what happened to all his old beliefs, and the things he had lived for, the victory of the Blues over the Reds? . . .

"Look, you haven't told me everything. The Reds and Blues still had separate Computers. Now you say you have one World. What happened to the war?"

Her eyes asked him just when he was going to stop quarreling with history and accept things as they were.

But she told him, and as always it looked as though she believed what she was telling.

"Just why should there be a war any more, between two societies that had arrived at the same destinations by different routes?"

He felt a shock. But that was what she had been telling him.

"It wouldn't have been the people who made the war," she said after a while. "With the Computers running the economies of both sides, it would have been the Computers who would have had to work out the logistics and plan the battles. The people would only have done the dying."

He could see her innocence. Somehow it appalled him as much or more now than it had in the beginning.

"But people have done that. Even in my time. We used computers to plan the battles. Even then, all the men did was to do the dying."

"But for a country?" she said. "For a government, people? Not just for your Great Computer against someone elses Great Computer?" She was shocked by what he said, but she would not have it as an answer.

It was he who paused, just sitting while they waited for the supply helicopter she had ordered.

"God knows what men fight for," he said. "But they do."

She looked at him thoughtfully. Did he not know that it was just in that respect that he was different?

"Did," she said.

He saw her meaning, looked at the peaceful country, and said, "What stopped them?"

"The Computers," she said quietly. "It happened this way. Both you and I speak of the Blues, but the Blues weren't one nation. They were sovereign countries. When it came to building Great Computers, each country wanted to make its own. Our people did it this way. Like we have in the World now. Linked Computers. Cables between them, on an exchange of information and forecasts basis. It made a firm alliance."

He looked puzzled. He did not see it.

"The only trade in the world that wasn't computer-controlled, was between the Red and Blue blocks. It made a mess of forecasts. The Computer Technicians didn't like it. So they put in a trade-link there. It grew in time."

— 16 —

if all the world
were like Berkeley

Frederik Pohl's story, "What to Do Till the Analyst Comes," is a fascinating exercise in the art of extrapolating the effects of a social innovation, assuming that certain control mechanisms are not activated and therefore do not prevent the innovation from affecting the society. The strategy Pohl uses to develop the story is analogous to the strategy a burglar might use in planning a robbery. Three problems must be overcome: how to break in, how to slip out, and how to haul away the goodies. It is quite possible to consider the second two problems independently of the first: "If I get past the guards on the way in, then I'll use this plan to get the stuff out and haul it away." Since Pohl's story depends heavily on being able to *get past the guards on the way in,* it would probably be more interesting to defer until the end of the chapter any comments on the control mechanisms that, we must assume, do not function.

"what to do till the analyst comes"

by Frederik Pohl

I just sent my secretary out for a container of coffee and she brought me back a lemon Coke.

I can't even really blame her. Who in all the world do I have to blame, except myself? Hazel was a good secretary to me for fifteen years, fine at typing, terrific at brushing off people I didn't want to see, and the queen of them all at pumping office gossip out of the ladies' lounge. She's a little fuzzy-brained most of the time now, sure. But after all!

I can say this for myself, I didn't exactly know what I was getting into. No doubt you remember the—. Well, let me start that sentence over again, because naturally there is a certain doubt. Perhaps, let's say, *perhaps* you remember the two doctors and their headline report about cigarettes and lung cancer. It hit us pretty hard at Vanden-Blumer & Silk, because we've been eating off the Mason-Dixon Tobacco account for twenty years. Just figure what our fifteen per cent amounted to on better than ten million dollars net billing a year, and you'll see that for yourself. What happened first was all to the good, because naturally the first thing that the client did was scream and reach for his checkbook and pour another couple million dollars into special promotions to counteract the bad press, but that couldn't last. And we knew it. V.B. & S. is noted in the trade as an advertising agency that takes the long view; we saw at once that if the client was in danger, no temporary spurt of advertising was going to pull him out of it, and it was time for us to climb up on top of the old mountain and take a good long look at the countryside ahead.

The Chief called a special Plans meeting that morning and laid it on the line for us. "There goes the old fire bell, boys," he said, "and it's up to us to put the fire out. I'm listening, so start talking."

Baggott cleared his throat and said glumly, "It may only be the paper, Chief. Maybe if they make them without paper . . . " He's the a.e. for Mason-Dixon, so you couldn't really blame him for taking the client's view.

The Chief twinkled: "If they make them without paper they aren't cigarettes any more, are they? Let's not wander off into side issues, boys. I'm still listening."

None of us wanted to wander off into side issues, so we all looked patronizingly at Baggott for a minute. Finally Ellen Silk held up her hand. "I don't want you to think," she said, "that just because Daddy left me a little stock I'm going to push my way into things, Mr. VandenBlumer, but—well, did you have in mind finding some, uh, angle to play on that would take the public's mind off the report?"

You have to admire the Chief. "Is that your recommendation, my dear?" he inquired fondly, bouncing the ball right back to her.

She said weakly, "*I* don't know. I'm confused."

"Naturally, my dear," he beamed. "So are we all. Let's see if Charley here can straighten us out a little. Eh, Charley?"

He was looking at me. I said at once, "I'm glad you asked me for an opinion, Chief. I've been doing a little thinking, and here's what I've come up with." I ticked off the points on my fingers. "One, tobacco makes you cough. Two, liquor gives you a hangover. Three, reefers and the other stuff—well, let's just say they're against the law." I slapped the three fingers against the palm of my other hand. "So what's left for us, Chief? That's my question. Can we come up with something new, something different, something that, one, is not injurious to the health, two, does not give you a hangover, three, is not habit-forming and therefore against the law?"

Mr. VandenBlumer said approvingly, "That's good thinking, Charley. When you hear that fire bell, you really jump, boy."

Baggott's hand was up. He said, "Let me get this straight, Chief. Is it Charley's idea that we recommend to Mason-Dixon that they go out of the tobacco business and start making something else?"

The old man looked at him blandly for a moment. "Why should it be Mason-Dixon?" he asked softly, and left it at that while we all thought of the very good reasons why it *shouldn't* be Mason-Dixon. After all, loyalty to a client is one thing, but you've got an obligation to your own people too.

The old man let it sink in, then he turned back to me. "Well, Charley?" he asked. "We've heard you pinpoint what we need. Got any specific suggestions?"

They were all looking at me to see if I had anything concrete to offer. Unfortunately, I had.

I just asked Hazel to get me the folder on Leslie Clary Cloud, and she came in with a copy of my memo putting him on the payroll two years back. "That's all there was in the file," she said dreamily, her jaw muscles moving rhythmically. There wasn't any use arguing with her, so I handed her container of lemon Coke and told her to ditch it and bring me back some *coffee,* C-O-F-F-E-E, coffee. I tried going through the files myself when she was gone, but *that* was a waste of time.

So I'll have to tell you about Leslie Clary Cloud from memory. He came into the office without an appointment and why Hazel ever let him in to see me I'll never know. But she did. He told me right away, "I've been fired, Mr. McGory. Canned. After eleven years with the Wyoming Bureau of Standards as a senior chemist."

"That's too bad, Dr. Cloud," I said, shuffling the papers on my desk. "I'm afraid, though, that our organization doesn't—"

"No, no," he said hastily. "I don't know anything about advertising. Organic chemistry's my field. I have a, well, a suggestion for a process that might interest you. You have the Mason-Dixon Tobacco account, don't you? Well, in my work for my doctorate I—" He drifted off into a fog of long-chain molecules and short-chain molecules and pentose sugars and common garden herbs. It took me a little while, but I listened patiently and I began to see what he was driving at. There was, he was saying, a substance in a common plant which, by cauliflamming the whingdrop and di-tricolating the residual glom, or words something like that, you could convert into another substance which appeared to have many features in common with what is sometimes called hop, snow or joy-dust. In other words, dope.

I stared at him aghast. "Dr. Cloud," I demanded, "do you know what you're suggesting? If we added this stuff to our client's cigarettes we'd be flagrantly violating the law. That's the most unheard-of thing I ever heard of! Besides, we've already looked into this matter, and the cost estimates are—"

"No, no!" he said again. "You don't understand, Mr. McGory. This isn't any of the drugs currently available, it's something new and different."

"Different?"

"Non-habit-forming, for instance."

"Non-habit-forming?"

"Totally. Chemically it is entirely unrelated to any narcotic in the pharmacopeia. Legally—well, I'm no lawyer, but I swear, Mr. McGory, this isn't covered by any regulation. No reason it should be. It doesn't hurt the user, it doesn't form a habit, it's cheap to manufacture, it—"

"Hold it," I said, getting to my feet. "Don't go away—I want to catch the boss before he goes to lunch."

So I caught the boss, and he twinkled thoughtfully at me. No, he didn't want me to discuss it with Mason-Dixon just yet, and yes, it did seem to have some possibilities, and certainly, put this man on the payroll and see if he turns up with something.

So we did; and he did.

Auditing raised the roof when the vouchers began to come through, but I bucked them up to the Chief and he calmed them down. It took a lot of money, though, and it took nearly six months. But then Leslie Clary Cloud called up one morning and said, "Come on down, Mr. McGory. We're in."

The place we'd fixed up for him was on the lower East Side and it reeked of rotten vegetables. I made a mental note to double-check all our added-chlorophyll copy and climbed up the two flights of stairs to Cloud's private room. He was sitting at a lab bench, beaming at a row of test tubes in front of him.

"This is it?" I asked, glancing at the test tubes.

"This is it." He smiled dreamily at me and yawned. "Excuse me," he blinked amiably. "I've been sampling the little old product."

I looked him over very carefully. He had been sampling something or other, that was clear enough. But no whisky breath; no dilated pupils; no shakes; no nothing. He was relaxed and cheerful, and that was all you could say.

"Try a little old bit," he invited, gesturing at the test tubes.

Well, there are times when you have to pay your dues in the club.

V.B. & S. had been mighty good to me, and if I had to swallow something unfamiliar to justify the confidence the Chief had in me, why I just had to go ahead and do it. Still, I hesitated for a moment.

"Aw," said Leslie Clary Cloud, "don't be scared. Look, I just had a shot but I'll take another one." He fumbled one of the test tubes out of the rack and, humming to himself, slopped a little of the colorless stuff into a beaker of some other colorless stuff—water, I suppose. He drank it down and smacked his lips. "Tastes awful," he observed cheerfully, "but we'll fix that. Whee!"

I looked him over again, and he looked back at me, giggling. "Too strong," he said happily. "Got it too strong. We'll fix that too." He rattled beakers and test tubes aimlessly while I took a deep breath and nerved myself up to it.

"All right," I said, and took the fresh beaker out of his hand. I swallowed it down almost in one gulp. It tasted terrible, just as he said, tasted like the lower floors had smelled, but that was all I noticed right away. Nothing happened for a moment except that Cloud looked at me thoughtfully and frowned.

"Say," he said, "I guess I should have diluted that." I guess he should have. *Wham.*

But a couple of hours later I was all right again.

Cloud was plenty apologetic. "Still," he said consolingly, standing over me as I lay on the lab bench, "it proves one thing. You had a dose about the equivalent of ten thousand normal shots, and you have to admit it hasn't hurt you."

"I do?" I asked, and looked at the doctor. *He* swung his stethoscope by the earpieces and shrugged.

"Nothing organically wrong with you, Mr. McGory—not that I can find, anyway. Euphoria, yes. Temporarily high pulse, yes. Delirium there for a little while, yes—though it was pretty mild. But I don't think you even have a headache now."

"I don't," I admitted. I swung my feet down and sat up, apprehensively. But no hammers started in my head. I had to confess it: I felt wonderful.

Well, between us we tinkered it into what Cloud decided would be a "normal" dosage—just enough to make you feel good—and he saturated some sort of powder and rolled it into pellets and clamped them in a press and came out with what looked as much like aspirins as anything else. "They'd probably work that way too," he said. "A psychogenic headache would melt away in five minutes with one of those."

"We'll bear that in mind," I said.

What with one thing and another, I couldn't get to the old man that day before he left, and the next day was the weekend and you *don't* disturb the Chief's weekends, and it was Monday evening before I could get him alone for long enough to give him the whole pitch. He was delighted.

"Dear, dear," he twinkled. "So much out of so little. Why, they hardly look like anything at all."

"Try one, Chief," I suggested.

"Perhaps I will. You checked the legal angle?"

"On the quiet. It's absolutely clean."

He nodded and poked at the little pills with his finger. I scratched the back of my neck, trying to be politely inconspicuous, but the Chief doesn't miss much. He looked at me inquiringly.

"Hives," I explained, embarrassed. "I, uh, got an overdose the first time, like I said. I don't know much about these things, but what they told me at the clinic was I set up an allergy."

"Allergy?" Mr. VandenBlumer looked at me thoughtfully. "We don't want to spread allergies with this stuff, do we?"

"Oh, no danger of that, Chief. It's Cloud's fault, in a way; he handed me an undiluted dose of the stuff, and I drank it down. The clinic was very positive about that: Even twenty or thirty times the normal dose won't do you any harm."

"Um." He rolled one of the pills in his finger and thumb and sniffed it thoughtfully. "How long are you going to have your hives?"

"They'll go away. I just have to keep away from the stuff. I wouldn't have them now, but—well, I liked it so much I tried another shot yesterday." I coughed, and added, "It works out pretty well, though. You see the advantages, of course, Chief. I have to give it up, and I can swear that there's no craving, no shakes, no kick-off symptoms, no nothing. I, well, I wish I could enjoy it like anyone else, sure. But I'm here to testify that Cloud told the simple truth: It isn't habit-forming."

"Um," he said again; and that was the end of the discussion.

Oh, the Chief is a cagey man. He gave me my orders: Keep my mouth shut about it. I have an idea that he was waiting to see what happened to my hives, and whether any craving would develop, and what the test series on animals and Cloud's Bowery-derelict volunteers would show. But even more, I think he was waiting until the time was exactly, climactically right.

Like at the Plans meeting, the day after the doctors' report and the panic at Mason-Dixon.

And that's how Cheery-Gum was born.

Hazel just came in with the cardboard container from the drug store, and I could tell by looking at it—no steam coming out from under the lid, beads of moisture clinging to the sides—that it wasn't the coffee I ordered. "Hey!" I yelled after her as she was dreamily waltzing through the door. "Come back here!"

"Sure 'nough, Massa," she said cheerfully, and two-stepped back. "S'matter?"

I took a grip on my temper. "Open that up," I ordered. "Take a look at what's in it."

She smiled at me and plopped the lid off the container. Half the contents spilled across my desk. "Oh, dear," said Hazel, "excuse me while I get a cloth."

"Never mind the cloth," I said, mopping at the mess with my handkerchief. "What's in there?"

She gazed wonderingly into the container for a moment; then she said, "Oh, *honestly,* boss! I see what you mean. Those idiots in the drug store, they're gummed up higher than a kite, morning, noon and night. I always say, if you can't handle it, you shouldn't touch it during working hours. I'm sorry about this, boss. No lemon! How can they call it a lemon Coke when they forget the—"

"Hazel," I said, "what I wanted was coffee. Coffee."

She looked at me. "You mean *I* got it wrong? Oh, I'm sorry, Mr. McGory. I'll go right down and get it now." She smiled repentantly and hummed her way toward the door. With her hand on the knob, she stopped and turned to look at me. "All the same, boss," she said, "that's a funny combination. Coffee *and* Coke. But I'll see what I can do."

And she was gone, to bring me heaven knows what incredible concoction. But what are you going to do?

No, that's no answer. I know it's what *you* would do. But it makes me break out in hives.

The first week we were delighted, the second week we were triumphant, the third week we were millionaires.

The sixth week I skulked along the sidewalks all the way across town and down, to see Leslie Clary Cloud. Even so I almost got it when a truckdriver dreamily piled into the glass front of a saloon a yard or two behind me.

When I saw Cloud sitting at his workbench, feet propped up, hands clasped behind his head, eyes half-closed, I could almost have kissed him. For his jaws were not moving. Alone in New York, except for me, he wasn't chewing Cheery-Gum.

"Thank heaven!" I said sincerely.

He blinked and smiled at me. "Mr. McGory," he said in a pleasant drawl. "Nice of you."

His manner disturbed me, and I looked more closely. "You're not— you're not gummed up, are you?"

He said gently, "Do I look gummed up? I never chew the stuff."

"Good!" I unfolded the newspaper I had carried all the way from Madison Avenue and showed him the inside pages—the ones that were not a mere smear of ink. "See here, Cloud. Planes crashing into Radio City. Buses driving off the George Washington Bridge. Ships going aground at the Battery. We did it, Cloud, you and I!"

"Oh, I wouldn't get upset about it, old man," he said comfortably. "All local, isn't it?"

"Isn't that bad enough? And it isn't local—it can't be. It's just that there isn't any communication outside the city any more—outside of any city, I guess. The shipments of Cheery-Gum, that's all that ever gets delivered anywhere. Because that's all that anybody cares about any more, and we did it, you and I!"

He said sympathetically, "That's too bad, McGory."

"Curse you!" I shrieked at him. "You said it wasn't a drug! You said it wasn't habit-forming! You said—"

"Now, now," he said with gentle firmness. "Why not chew a stick yourself?"

"Because I can't! It gives me hives!"

"Oh, that's right." He looked self-reproachful. "Well," he said dreamily at last, "I guess that's about the size of it, McGory." He was staring at the ceiling again.

"*What* is?"

"What is what?"

"What's about the—Oh, the devil with it. Cloud, you got us into this, you have to get us out of it. There must be some way of curing this habit."

"But there isn't any habit to cure, McGory," he pointed out.

"But there is!"

"Tem-per," he said waggishly, and took a corked test tube out of his workbench. He drank it down, every drop, and tossed the tube in a wastebasket. "You see?" he demanded severely. "*I* don't chew Cheery-Gum."

So I appealed to a Higher Authority.

In the eighteenth century I would have gone to the Church, in the nineteenth, to the State. I went to an office fronting on Central Park where the name on the bronze plaque was *Theodor Yust, Analyst.*

It wasn't easy. I almost walked out on him when I saw that his jaws were chewing as rhythmically as his secretary's. But Cloud's concoction is not, as he kept saying, a drug, and though it makes you relax and makes you happy and, if you take enough of it, makes you drunk, it doesn't make you unfit to talk to. So I took a grip on my temper, the only bad temper left, and told him what I wanted.

He laughed at me—in the friendliest way. "Put a stop to Cheery-Gum? Mr. McGory!"

"But the plane crashes—"

"No more suicides, Mr. McGory!"

"The train wrecks—"

"Not a murder or a mugging in the whole city in a month."

I said hopelessly, "But it's *wrong!*"

"Ah," he said in the tone of a discoverer, "now we come down to it. Why is it wrong, Mr. McGory?"

That was the second time I almost walked out. But I said "Let's get one thing straight: I don't want you digging into my problems. That's not why I'm here. Cheery-Gum *is* wrong, and I am *not* biased against it. You can take a detached view of collisions and sudden death if you want to, but what about slow death? All over the city, all over the country, people are lousing up their jobs. Nobody cares. Nobody does anything but go through the motions. They're happy. What happens when they get hungry because the farmers are feeling too good to put in their crops?"

He sighed patiently. He took the wad of gum out of his mouth, rolled it neatly into a Kleenex and dropped it in the wastebasket. He took a fresh stick out of a drawer and unwrapped it, but stopped when he saw me looking at him. He chuckled. "Rather I didn't, Mr. McGory? Well, why not oblige you? It's not habit-forming, after all." He dropped the gum back into the drawer and said: "Answering your questions, they won't starve. The farmers are farming, the workers are working, the policemen are policing, and I'm analyzing. And you're worrying. Why? Work's getting done."

"But my secretary—"

"Forget about your secretary, Mr. McGory. Sure, she's a little fuzzy-brained, a little absent-minded. Who isn't? But she comes to work, because why shouldn't she?"

"Sure she does, but—"

"But she's happy. Let her be happy, Mr. McGory!"

I looked scandalized at him. "You, a doctor! How can you say that? Suppose *you* were fuzzy-brained and so on when a patient desperately needed—"

He stopped me. "In the past three weeks," he said gently, "you're the first to come in that door."

I changed tack: "All right, you're an analyst. What about a G.P. or a surgeon?"

He shrugged. "Perhaps," he conceded, "perhaps in one case out of a thousand—somebody hurt in an accident, say—he'd get to the hospital too late, or the surgeon would make some little mistake. Perhaps. Not even one in a thousand—one in a million, maybe. But Cheery-Gum isn't a drug. A quarter-grain of sodium amytol, and your surgeon's as good as new." Absent-mindedly he reached into the drawer for the stick of gum.

"And you say," I said accusingly, "that it's not habit-forming!"

He stopped with his hand halfway to his mouth. "Well," he said wryly, "it *is* a habit. Don't confuse semantics, Mr. McGory. It is not a narcotic addiction. If my supply were cut off this minute, I would feel bad—as bad as if I couldn't play bridge any more for some reason, and no worse." He put the stick of gum away again and rummaged through the bottom drawers of his desk until he found a dusty pack of cigarettes. "Used to smoke three packs a day," he wheezed, choking on the first drag.

He wiped his streaming eyes. "You know, Mr. McGory," he said sharply, "you're a bit of a prig. You don't want people to be happy."

"I—"

He stopped me before I could work up a full explosion. "Wait! Don't think that you're the only person who thinks about what's good for the world. When I first heard of Cheery-Gum, I worried." He stubbed the cigarette out distastefully, still talking. "Euphoria is well and good, I said, but what about emergencies? And I looked around, and there weren't any. Things were getting done, maybe slowly and erratically, but they were getting done. And then I said, on a high moral plane, that's well and good, but what about the ultimate destiny of man? Should the world be populated by cheerful near-morons? And that worried me, until I began looking at my patients." He smiled reflectively. "I had 'em all, Mr. McGory. You name it, I had it coming in to see me twice a week. The worst wrecks of psyches you ever heard of, twisted and warped and destroying themselves; and they stopped. They stopped eating themselves up with worry and fear and tension, and then they weren't my patients any more. And what's more, they weren't morons. Give them a stimulus, they respond. Interest them, they react. I played bridge the other night with a woman who was catatonic last month; we had to put the first stick of gum in her mouth. She beat the hell out of me, Mr. McGory. I had a mathematician coming here who—well, never mind. It was bad. He's happy as a clam, and the last time I saw him he had finished a paper he began ten years ago, and couldn't touch. Stimulate them—they respond. When things are dull—Cheery-Gum. What could be better?"

I looked at him dully, and said, "So you can't help me."

"I didn't say that. Do you want me to help you?"

"Certainly!"

"Then answer my question: Why don't you chew a stick yourself?"

"Because I can't!" It all tumbled out, the Plans meeting and Leslie Clary Cloud and the beaker that hadn't been diluted and the hives. "A terrific allergy," I emphasized. "Even antihistamines don't help. They said at the clinic that the antibodies formed after a massive initial—"

He said comfortably, "Soma over psyche, eh? Well, what would you expect? But believe me, Mr. McGory, allergies are psychogenic. Now, if you'll just—"

Well, if you can't lick 'em, join 'em, that's what the old man used to say.

But I can't join them. Theodor Yust offered me an invitation, but I guess I was pretty rude to him. And when, at last, I went back, ready to crawl and apologize, there was a scrawled piece of cardboard over the bronze nameplate; it said: *Gone fishing.*

I tried to lay it on the line with the Chief. I opened the door of the Plans room, and there he was with Baggott and Wayber, from Mason-Dixon. They were sitting there whittling out model ships, and so intent on what they were doing that they hardly noticed me. After a while the Chief said idly, "Bankrupt yet?" And moments passed, and Wayber finally replied, in an absent-minded tone:

"Guess so. Have to file some papers or something." And they went on with their whittling.

So I spoke sharply to them, and the minute they looked up and saw me, it was like the Rockettes: The hands into the pockets, the paper being unwrapped, the gum into the mouth. And naturally I couldn't make any sense with them after that. So what are you going to do?

No! I can't!

Hazel hardly comes in to see me any more, even. I bawled her out for it—what would happen, I demanded, if I suddenly had to answer a letter. But she only smiled dreamily at me. "There hasn't been a letter in a month," she pointed out amiably. "Don't worry, though. If anything comes up, I'll be with you in a flash. This stuff isn't a habit with me, I can stop it any time, you just say the word and ol' Hazel'll be there. . . . "

And she's right because, when you get right down to it, there's the trouble. It isn't a habit.

So how can you break it?

You can stop Cheery-Gum any time. You can stop it this second, or five minutes from now, or tomorrow.

So why worry about it?

It's completely voluntary, entirely under your control; it won't hurt you, it won't make you sick.

I wish Theodor Yust would come back. Or maybe I'll just cut my throat.

If the conditions Pohl describes were to come about, certain quite likely societal and individual responses to Cheery-Gum would have not to be made. For example, the legality of the sale of the substance would probably be questioned as soon as its effects on users were noticed. Even though the substance is supposed to be nonaddictive, it could be legally classified as a dangerous drug for many of the reasons that marijuana and LSD are so classified.

Quite apart from the issue of legality, a number of normative prohibitions would probably apply to use of the gum. These prohibitions would at least partially control its spread and the conditions under which it might be used. Since the substance is supposed to produce a feeling of euphoria, similar to but stronger than that produced by pot and more extreme than the desirable effects of alcohol, many of the normative control mechanisms applied to alcohol would probably be judged appropriate for Cheery-Gum. For example, people who do not use alcohol because of religious prohibitions would probably refrain from chewing Cheery-Gum and classify it as a substance to be avoided for the same reasons they avoid alcohol. People who for noninstitutionalized reasons refrain from using alcohol would probably react in a similar fashion.

Probably the major factor leading to the control of Cheery-Gum would be its effects on industrial and business activities. The first men who used the substance on their jobs would probably be treated like those who come to work drunk, since their ability to do their jobs would be substantially impaired. Assuming that the response to Cheery-Gum would be determined on the basis of its similarity to alcohol, it is likely that similar rules would come to govern its use in industrial and business settings.

We cannot be sure, however, that the reaction to Cheery-Gum, or to any similar substance, would follow this path. One crucial variable in any consideration of likely or unlikely effects of an innovation such as Pohl describes is the speed with which its use spreads through the population. If the marketing program for Cheery-Gum, for example, started with nationwide distribution commencing on a certain day, the likelihood of effects similar to those Pohl describes would be increased. If, however, the marketing program specified use first in a test area, it is more likely that the state government area would have time to act and that federal agencies regulating interstate commerce and drug traffic would act to obtain injunctions against the manufacture and distribution of the gum until its effects and legal status were clarified. Even if the use of the gum were to spread unimpeded but at a relatively slow rate, norms governing its utilization would have time to develop, and the social breakdown Pohl outlines would be relatively unlikely.

— WHOLES —
social systems

the creation of
a perfect society

Recorded sociological thought precedes the coining of the word "sociology" by more than 2,000 years. One of the earliest and most famous long discourses on the dynamics and effects of social organization is Socrates' description of a utopian society. Recorded in Plato's *Republic,* the society that Socrates described was designed to produce conditions under which "man might realize the best that was in him"[1](Cornford, p. xv).

The designer of a utopian society is faced with a task of enormous magnitude. It is virtually impossible for a single person to take a social void and describe in minute detail how it is to be filled with a functioning social system. To succeed at this task calls for creating sociological blueprints that specify *precisely* how the society's stratification system is to operate, how the economic sphere is to be controlled, what norms are to regulate social interaction, how new members of the society are to be socialized, what sort of political institutions will operate, and so on. Consider that it takes about two tons of blueprints to tell a work force how to build an ocean liner; then try to imagine how many volumes of codes and specifications it would take to completely design a social system.

In Socrates' utopia, as in every other utopia ever created, about 99 percent of the social system is expected to be just like the one in which the writer lives, and about one percent is to be changed. You can identify the 99 percent by listing all those aspects of the created society that are never discussed. The one percent is easily recognized, for it is with this portion of the utopia that the designer concerns himself.

It is hardly likely that the issues a designer raises are selected in some haphazard fashion. The designer of a utopia is himself a member of a real society, and

---

[1]*The Republic of Plato,* translated with an introduction by Francis M. Cornford (Oxford at the Clarendon Press, 1941), p. xv. The text reprinted here is Cornford's translation.

there exist within the set of social arrangements which describe that society the causes of the social problems with which the designer is familiar. It seems likely that the alterations in the social structure of a designer's utopia represent a set of arrangements that he believes would correct some of the problems he understands to exist within his own social world. In some cases writers—Orwell in *1984* and Huxley in *Brave New World*—have created anti-utopias in which undesirable aspects of an existing society are used to focus attention on their possible consequences. For these reasons, the proposals of creators of utopian societies will be viewed as the proposals of social engineers for the solutions to contemporary problems, some of which still exist.

The sections from the *Republic* deal with a number of issues in the construction of a social system. Material was chosen to shed some light on the principles by which Socrates' utopia was to be constructed, on his thinking about the reasons society is necessary, on the ideal set of social arrangements, and on the manner in which to produce an ideal society. Much of the material attacks a single issue: how to construct a system in which those with power will use it for the good of those they govern, not for their own enhancement. No modern society has come up with a solution that is clearly better than the one proposed by Socrates.[2]

To understand the social order Socrates creates in the *Republic* it is necessary to understand his assumptions about the nature of man. Socrates assumes that men are inherently different from one another to the extent that their different natures lead necessarily to different occupations. A man's nature is a property, a characteristic, with which he is born and which should determine his occupation and hence his social position. In our day, Socrates' view of men's natures would be identified as an extreme genetic position. The modern counterposition, an extreme environmental position, is that what individuals inherit varies little from one person to another and that most of the differences we observe in adults can be explained as a function of the physical and social environments in which they matured. Recognition of Socrates' position is important because the stratification system of the *Republic* is designed to ensure that men occupy the positions for which they are best suited by their natures. Therefore, the system is one in which some attention is given to discovering precisely what a man's nature suits him for, and virtually no possibility exists of changing one's social position in adult life. In a stratification system designed to be optimal for a society peopled by men who are believed to be substantially affected by their environments, greater attention would probably be given to problems of socially affected opportunities to obtain education and to the mechanisms whereby men are trained to fill social roles that are recognized as being important. In addition, considerably more attention would probably be given to the possibility of change in an individual's social position.

From a modern viewpoint, one of the most interesting aspects of Socrates' utopia is that he attempted to design a system in which there was virtually no

[2]Bellamy considers this same problem in the selection from *Looking Backward*. He postulates the same causation of the problem but proposes a different solution.

expectation of or provision for social change. The system Socrates designed was intended to bring about a state of affairs that would perpetuate itself indefinitely.[3] One can easily understand how the creator of a utopian social system might not consider the management of social change an important issue if his own society were prescientific, preindustrial, and pretechnological. It is difficult to imagine the modern designer of a large-scale social system failing to consider how to manage innovations generated by the science and technology of the society. Even if the designer wished to create a social system in which no change was permitted, as does Huxley in *Brave New World,* he would have to incorporate elaborate mechanisms designed to prevent innovations from being made and to prevent their diffusion within the society.

the republic

by Plato

Socrates: My notion is, said I, that a state comes into existence because no individual is self-sufficing; we all have many needs. But perhaps you can suggest some different origin for the foundation of a community?

Adeimantus: No, I agree with you.

So, having all these needs, we call in one another's help to satisfy our various requirements; and when we have collected a number of helpers and associates to live together in one place, we call that settlement a state.

Yes.

So if one man gives another what he has to give in exchange for what he can get, it is because each finds that to do so is for his own advantage.

Certainly.

Very well, said I. Now let us build up our imaginary state from the beginning. Apparently, it will owe its existence to our needs, the first and greatest need being the provision of food to keep us alive. Next we shall want a house; and thirdly, such things as clothing.

True.

How will our state be able to supply all these demands? We shall need at least one man to be a farmer, another a builder, and a third a weaver. Will that do, or shall we add a shoemaker and one or two more to provide for our personal wants?

By all means.

The minimum state, then, will consist of four or five men.

Apparently.

Now here is a further point. Is each one of them to bring the product

[3]This is not the first comment on the static aspect of Socrates' utopia; Plato also noticed it.

of his work into a common stock? Should our one farmer, for example, provide food enough for four people and spend the whole of his working time in producing corn, so as to share with the rest; or should he take no notice of them and spend only a quarter of his time on growing just enough corn for himself, and divide the other three-quarters between building his house, weaving his clothes, and making his shoes, so as to save the trouble of sharing with others and attend himself to all his own concerns?

The first plan might be the easier, replied Adeimantus.

That may very well be so, said I; for, as you spoke, it occurred to me, for one thing, that no two people are born exactly alike. There are innate differences which fit them for different occupations.

I agree.

And will a man do better working at many trades, or keeping to one only?

Keeping to one.

And there is another point: obviously work may be ruined, if you let the right time go by. The workman must wait upon the work; it will not wait upon his leisure and allow itself to be done in a spare moment. So the conclusion is that more things will be produced and the work be more easily and better done, when every man is set free from all other occupations to do, at the right time, the one thing for which he is naturally fitted.

That is certainly true.

We shall need more than four citizens, then, to supply all those necessaries we mentioned. You see, Adeimantus, if the farmer is to have a good plough and spade and other tools, he will not make them himself. No more will the builder and weaver and shoemaker make all the many implements they need. So quite a number of carpenters and smiths and other craftsmen must be enlisted. Our miniature state is beginning to grow.

It is.

Still, it will not be very large, even when we have added cowherds and shepherds to provide the farmers with oxen for the plough, and the builders as well as the farmers with draught-animals, and the weavers and shoemakers with wool and leather.

No; but it will not be so very small either.

And yet, again, it will be next to impossible to plant our city in a territory where it will need no imports. So there will have to be still another set of people, to fetch what it needs from other countries.

There will.

Moreover, if these agents take with them nothing that those other countries require in exchange, they will return as emptyhanded as they went. So, besides everything wanted for consumption at home, we must produce enough goods of the right kind for the foreigners whom we depend on to supply us. That will mean increasing the number of farmers and craftsmen.

Yes.

And then, there are these agents who are to import and export all kinds of goods—merchants, as we call them. We must have them; and if they are to do business overseas, we shall need quite a number of ship-owners and others who know about that branch of trading.

We shall.

Again, in the city itself how are the various sets of producers to exchange their products? That was our object, you will remember, in forming a community and so laying the foundation of our state.

Obviously, they must buy and sell.

That will mean having a market-place, and a currency to serve as a token for purposes of exchange.

Certainly.

Now suppose a farmer, or an artisan, brings some of his produce to market at a time when no one is there who wants to exchange with him. Is he to sit there idle, when he might be at work?

No, he replied; there are people who have seen an opening here for their services. In well-ordered communities they are generally men not strong enough to be of use in any other occupation. They have to stay where they are in the market-place and take goods for money from those who want to sell, and money for goods from those who want to buy.

That, then, is the reason why our city must include a class of shopkeepers—so we call these people who sit still in the market-place to buy and sell, in contrast with merchants who travel to other countries.

Quite so.

There are also the services of yet another class, who have the physical strength for heavy work, though on intellectual grounds they are hardly worth including in our society—hired labourers, as we call them, because they sell the use of their strength for wages. They will go to make up our population. . . .

Let us [consider] a picture of our citizens' manner of life, with the provision we have made for them. They will be producing corn and wine, and making clothes and shoes. When they have built their houses, they will mostly work without their coats or shoes in summer, and in winter be well shod and clothed. For their food, they will prepare flour and barley-meal for kneading and baking, and set out a grand spread of loaves and cakes on rushes or fresh leaves. Then they will lie on beds of myrtle-boughs and bryony and make merry with their children, drinking their wine after the feast with garlands on their heads and singing the praises of the gods. So they will live pleasantly together; and a prudent fear of poverty or war will keep them from begetting children beyond their means.

Here Glaucon interrupted me: You seem to expect your citizens to feast on dry bread.

True, I said; I forgot that they will have something to give it a relish, salt, no doubt, and olives, and cheese, and country stews of roots and vegetables. And for dessert we will give them figs and peas and beans; and they shall roast myrtle-berries and acorns at the fire, while they sip their wine. Leading such a healthy life in peace, they will naturally come to a good old age, and leave their children to live after them in the same manner.

That is just the sort of provender you would supply, Socrates, if you were founding a community of pigs.

Well, how are they to live, then, Glaucon?

With the ordinary comforts. Let them lie on couches and dine off tables on such dishes and sweets as we have nowadays.

Ah, I see, said I; we are to study the growth, not just of a state, but of a luxurious one. Well, there may be no harm in that; the consideration of luxury may help us to discover how justice and injustice take root in society. The community I have described seems to me the ideal one, in sound health as it were: but if you want to see one suffering from inflammation, there is nothing to hinder us. So some people, it seems, will not be satisfied to live in this simple way; they must have couches and tables and furniture of all sorts; and delicacies too, perfumes, unguents, courtesans, sweetmeats, all in plentiful variety. And besides, we must not limit ourselves now to those bare necessaries of house and clothes and shoes; we shall have to set going the arts of embroidery and painting, and collect rich materials, like gold and ivory.

Yes.

Then we must once more enlarge our community. The healthy one will not be big enough now; it must be swollen up with a whole multitude of callings not ministering to any bare necessity: hunters and fishermen, for instance; artists in sculpture, painting, and music; poets with their attendant train of professional reciters, actors, dancers, producers; and makers of all sorts of household gear, including everything for women's adornment. And we shall want more servants: children's nurses and attendants, lady's maids, barbers, cooks and confectioners. And then swineherds—there was no need for them in our original state, but we shall want them now; and a great quantity of sheep and cattle too, if people are going to live on meat.

Of course.

And with this manner of life physicians will be in much greater request.

No doubt.

The country, too, which was large enough to support the original inhabitants, will now be too small. If we are to have enough pasture and plough land, we shall have to cut off a slice of our neighbours' territory;

and if they too are not content with necessaries, but give themselves up to getting unlimited wealth, they will want a slice of ours.

That is inevitable, Socrates.

So the next thing will be, Glaucon, that we shall be at war.

No doubt.

We need not say yet whether war does good or harm, but only that we have discovered its origin in desires which are the most fruitful source of evils both to individuals and to states.[1]

Quite true.

This will mean a considerable addition to our community—a whole army, to go out to battle with any invader, in defence of all this property and of the citizens we have been describing.

Why so? Can't they defend themselves?

Not if the principle was right, which we all accepted in framing our society. You remember we agreed that no one man can practise many trades or arts satisfactorily.

True.

Well, is not the conduct of war an art, quite as important as shoemaking?

Yes.

But we would not allow our shoemaker to try to be also farmer or weaver or builder, because we wanted our shoes well made. We gave each man one trade, for which he was naturally fitted; he would do good work, if he confined himself to that all his life, never letting the right moment slip by. Now in no form of work is efficiency so important as in war; and fighting is not so easy a business that a man can follow another trade, such as farming or shoemaking, and also be an efficient soldier. Why, even a game like draughts or dice must be studied from childhood; no one can become a fine player in his spare moments. Just taking up a shield or other weapon will not make a man capable of fighting that very day in any sort of warfare, any more than taking up a tool or implement of some kind will make a man a craftsman or an athlete, if he does not understand its use and has never been properly trained to handle it.

No, if that were so, tools would indeed be worth having.

These guardians of our state, then, inasmuch as their work is the most important of all, will need the most complete freedom from other occupations and the greatest amount of skill and practice.

I quite agree.

And also a native aptitude for their calling.

Certainly.

So it is our business to define, if we can, the natural gifts that fit men to be guardians of a commonwealth, and to select them accordingly. It will certainly be a formidable task; but we must grapple with it to the best of our power.

[1] "All wars are made for the sake of getting money" *(Phaedo)*.

Yes. . . .

Don't you think then, said I, that, for the purpose of keeping guard, a young man should have much the same temperament and qualities as a well-bred watch-dog? I mean, for instance, that both must have quick senses to detect an enemy, swiftness in pursuing him, and strength, if they have to fight when they have caught him.

Yes, they will need all those qualities.

And also courage, if they are to fight well.

Of course.

And courage, in dog or horse or any other creature, implies a spirited disposition. You must have noticed that a high spirit is unconquerable. Every soul possessed of it is fearless and indomitable in the face of any danger.

Yes, I have noticed that.

So now we know what physical qualities our Guardian must have, and also that he must be of a spirited temper.

Yes.

Then, Glaucon, how are men of that natural disposition to be kept from behaving pugnaciously to one another and to the rest of their countrymen?

It is not at all easy to see.

And yet they must be gentle to their own people and dangerous only to enemies; otherwise they will destroy themselves without waiting till others destroy them.

True.

What are we to do, then? If gentleness and a high temper are contraries, where shall we find a character to combine them? Both are necessary to make a good Guardian, but it seems they are incompatible. So we shall never have a good Guardian.

It looks like it.

Here I was perplexed, but on thinking over what we had been saying, I remarked that we deserved to be puzzled, because we had not followed up the comparison we had just drawn.

What do you mean? he asked.

We never noticed that, after all, there are natures in which these contraries are combined. They are to be found in animals, and not least in the kind we compared to our Guardian. Well-bred dogs, as you know, are by instinct perfectly gentle to people whom they know and are accustomed to, and fierce to strangers. So the combination of qualities we require for our Guardian is, after all, possible and not against nature.

Evidently.

Do you further agree that, besides this spirited temper, he must have a philosophical element in his nature?

I don't see what you mean.

This is another trait you will see in the dog. It is really remarkable how the creature gets angry at the mere sight of a stranger and welcomes anyone he knows, though he may never have been treated unkindly by the one or kindly by the other. Did that never strike you as curious?

I had not thought of it before; but that certainly is how a dog behaves.

Well, but that shows a fine instinct, which is philosophic in the true sense.

How so?

Because the only mark by which he distinguishes a friendly and an unfriendly face is that he knows the one and does not know the other; and if a creature makes that the test of what it finds congenial or otherwise, how can you deny that it has a passion for knowledge and understanding?

Of course, I cannot.

And that passion is the same thing as philosophy—the love of wisdom.

Yes.

Shall we boldly say, then, that the same is true of human beings? If a man is to be gentle towards his own people whom he knows, he must have an instinctive love of wisdom and understanding.

Agreed.

So the nature required to make a really noble Guardian of our commonwealth will be swift and strong, spirited, and philosophic.

Quite so.

Given those natural qualities, then, how are these Guardians to be brought up and educated? . . .

Socrates devotes considerable attention to the manner in which the population of the Republic is to be educated. His proposals for an educational program are not reproduced here because several such proposals are treated in other selections (Chapters 5 and 7). But certain aspects of Socrates' proposed educational system and its relationship to society require comment.

In most discussions of social stability, innovation, and change, Socrates' interest is focused primarily on the Guardian class. The members of this class are thought of as crucial to the stability of the society. Socrates' assumption differs from the assumptions of many modern designers who expend great effort in creating mechanisms to control the masses. Ever since Marx, considerably more attention has been given to the possibility of social change generated by the lower classes.

Socrates argues that once the institutions of a society have been *properly* established, the growth and development of the society will proceed without much need, if any, to modify the basic institutions. (Socrates' society *develops* in terms of the greater acceptance of its unchanging institutions by the population.) He suggests, in fact, that the destruction of a society can usually be explained in terms of a slow erosion of its initial ideals through change.[4] Education is thought of as a method of

[4]This idea is not completely without present day acceptance. Much of the propaganda of a number of extreme right-wing political groups is based on this premise.

controlling and thereby holding constant the content of the culture transmitted to each new generation of the population. Since the society is itself virtually unchanging, a set of educational procedures can be designed to teach the answers to the problems with which the person will be confronted during his lifetime; with no innovation there are no new problems, and hence no need to search for new solutions.

The educational system of the Republic was a variation on the system in operation in Athens when the *Republic* was written. At that time the family, not the state, was responsible for the education of Athenian boys. Education was usually accomplished in private day-schools, which boys attended until the age of 17. Their education consisted primarily of learning to read and write ("gramatic"); learning and reciting epic and dramatic poetry, playing the lyre and singing lyric poetry, the rudiments of arithmetic and geometry ("music," which included all the arts over which the muses presided: music, art, letters, culture, and philosophy) and athletic exercises ("gymnastic").

The major modifications Socrates proposed for this system was to make the state responsible for education and for educating both boys and girls. The other changes were designed to assist in the production of Guardians of a certain type. Socrates was concerned with eliminating certain personal characteristics from members of the Guardian class and fostering the development of other attributes. For example, Socrates proposed to eliminate learning of epics and myths that had to do with warfare, intrigue, and battles of god against god, and any stories of self-indulgence and lamentation. Children, it was argued, could not distinguish between allegorical meaning and literal meaning, and hence it was necessary to prevent their exposure to ideas they might misunderstand. Similarly, in his play-acting the young Guardian was to act only certain appropriate roles, since playing the role of an objectionable character might lead to the development of personality traits similar to those of the character.

. . . What is the next point to be settled? Is it not the question, which of these Guardians are to be rulers and which are to obey?

No doubt.

Well, it is obvious that the elder must have authority over the young, and that the rulers must be the best.

Yes.

And as among farmers the best are those with a natural turn for farming, so, if we want the best among our Guardians, we must take those naturally fitted to watch over a commonwealth. They must have the right sort of intelligence and ability; and also they must look upon the commonwealth as their special concern—the sort of concern that is felt for something so closely bound up with oneself that its interests and fortunes, for good or ill, are held to be identical with one's own.

Exactly.

So the kind of men we must choose from among the Guardians will be those who, when we look at the whole course of their lives, are found to be full of zeal to do whatever they believe is for the good of the commonwealth and never willing to act against its interest.

Yes, they will be the men we want.

We must watch them, I think, at every age and see whether they are capable of preserving this conviction that they must do what is best for the community, never forgetting it or allowing themselves to be either forced or bewitched into throwing it over.

How does this throwing over come about?

I will explain. When a belief passes out of the mind, a man may be willing to part with it, if it is false and he has learnt better, or unwilling, if it is true.

I see how he might be willing to let it go; but you must explain how he can be unwilling.

Where is your difficulty? Don't you agree that men are unwilling to be deprived of good, though ready enough to part with evil? Or that to be deceived about the truth is evil, to possess it good? Or don't you think that possessing truth means thinking of things as they really are?

You are right. I do agree that men are unwilling to be robbed of a true belief.

When that happens to them, then, it must be by theft, or violence, or bewitchment.

Again I do not understand.

Perhaps my metaphors are too high-flown. I call it theft when one is persuaded out of one's belief or forgets it. Argument in the one case, and time in the other, steal it away without one's knowing what is happening. You understand now?

Yes.

And by violence I mean being driven to change one's mind by pain or suffering.

That too I understand, and you are right.

And bewitchment, as I think you would agree, occurs when a man is beguiled out of his opinion by the allurements of pleasure or scared out of it under the spell of panic.

Yes, all delusions are like a sort of bewitchment.

As I said just now, then, we must find out who are the best guardians of this inward conviction that they must always do what they believe to be best for the commonwealth. We shall have to watch them from earliest childhood and set them tasks in which they would be most likely to forget or to be beguiled out of this duty. We shall then choose only those whose memory holds firm and who are proof against delusion.

Yes.

We must also subject them to ordeals of toil and pain and watch for the same qualities there. And we must observe them when exposed to the test of yet a third kind of bewitchment. As people lead colts up to alarming noises to see whether they are timid, so these young men must be brought into terrifying situations and then into scenes of pleasure, which will put them to severer proof than gold tried in the furnace. If we find one bearing himself well in all these trials and resisting every enchantment, a true guardian of himself, preserving always that perfect rhythm and harmony of being which he has acquired from his training in music and poetry, such a one will be of the greatest service to the commonwealth as well as to himself. Whenever we find one who has come unscathed through every test in childhood, youth, and manhood, we shall set him as a Ruler to watch over the commonwealth; he will be honoured in life, and after death receive the highest tribute of funeral rites and other memorials. All who do not reach this standard we must reject. And that, I think, my dear Glaucon, may be taken as an outline of the way in which we shall select Guardians to be set in authority as Rulers.

I am very much of your mind.

These, then, may properly be called Guardians in the fullest sense, who will ensure that neither foes without shall have the power, nor friends within the wish, to do harm. Those young men whom up to now we have been speaking of as Guardians, will be better described as Auxiliaries, who will enforce the decisions of the Rulers.

I agree.

Now, said I, can we devise something in the way of those convenient fictions we spoke of earlier, a single bold flight of invention,[1] which we may induce the community in general, and if possible the Rulers themselves, to accept?

What kind of fiction?

Nothing new; something like an Eastern tale of what, according to the poets, has happened before now in more than one part of the world. The poets have been believed; but the thing has not happened in our day, and it would be hard to persuade anyone that it could ever happen again.

You seem rather shy of telling this story of yours.

With good reason, as you will see when I have told it.

Out with it; don't be afraid.

Well, here it is; though I hardly know how to find the courage or the words to express it. I shall try to convince, first the Rulers and the soldiers,[2] and then the whole community, that all that nurture and education which we gave them was only something they seemed to experience as it were in a dream. In reality they were the whole time down inside the

---

[1] This phrase is commonly rendered by "noble lie," a self-contradictory expression no more applicable to Plato's harmless allegory than to a New Testament parable or the Pilgrim's Progress, and liable to suggest that he would countenance the lies, for the most part ignoble, now called propaganda.

[2] Note that the Guardians themselves are to accept this allegory, if possible. It is not "propaganda" foisted on the masses by the Rulers.

earth, being moulded and fostered while their arms and all their equipment were being fashioned also; and at last, when they were complete, the earth sent them up from her womb into the light of day. So now they must think of the land they dwell in as a mother and nurse, whom they must take thought for and defend against any attack, and of their fellow citizens as brothers born of the same soil.

You might well be bashful about coming out with your fiction.

No doubt; but still you must hear the rest of the story. It is true, we shall tell our people in this fable, that all of you in this land are brothers; but the god who fashioned you mixed gold in the composition of those among you who are fit to rule, so that they are of the most precious quality; and he put silver in the Auxiliaries, and iron and brass in the farmers and craftsmen. Now, since you are all of one stock, although your children will generally be like their parents, sometimes a golden parent may have a silver child or a silver parent a golden one, and so on with all the other combinations. So the first and chief injunction laid by heaven upon the Rulers is that, among all the things of which they must show themselves good guardians, there is none that needs to be so carefully watched as the mixture of metals in the souls of the children. If a child of their own is born with an alloy of iron or brass, they must, without the smallest pity, assign him the station proper to his nature and thrust him out among the craftsmen or the farmers. If, on the contrary, these classes produce a child with gold or silver in his composition, they will promote him, according to his value, to be a Guardian or an Auxiliary. They will appeal to a prophecy that ruin will come upon the state when it passes into the keeping of a man of iron or brass. Such is the story; can you think of any device to make them believe it?

Not in the first generation; but their sons and descendants might believe it, and finally the rest of mankind.

Well, said I, even so it might have a good effect in making them care more for the commonwealth and for one another; for I think I see what you mean.

So, I continued, we will leave the success of our story to the care of popular tradition; and now let us arm these sons of Earth and lead them, under the command of their Rulers, to the site of our city. There let them look round for the best place to fix their camp, from which they will be able to control any rebellion against the laws from within and to beat off enemies who may come from without like wolves to attack the fold. When they have pitched their camp and offered sacrifice to the proper divinities, they must arrange their sleeping quarters; and these must be sufficient to shelter them from winter cold and summer heat.

Naturally. You mean they are going to live there?

Yes, said I; but live like soldiers, not like men of business.

What is the difference?

I will try to explain. It would be very strange if a shepherd were to disgrace himself by keeping, for the protection of his flock, dogs who were so ill-bred and badly trained that hunger or unruliness or some bad habit or other would set them worrying the sheep and behaving no better than wolves. We must take every precaution against our Auxiliaries treating the citizens in any such way and, because they are stronger, turning into savage tyrants instead of friendly allies; and they will have been furnished with the best of safeguards, if they have really been educated in the right way.

But surely there is nothing wrong with their education.

We must not be too positive about that, my dear Glaucon; but we can be sure of what we said not long ago, that if they are to have the best chance of being gentle and humane to one another and to their charges, they must have the right education, whatever that may be.

We were certainly right there.

Then besides that education, it is only common sense to say that the dwellings and other belongings provided for them must be such as will neither make them less perfect Guardians nor encourage them to maltreat their fellow citizens.

True.

With that end in view, let us consider how they should live and be housed. First, none of them must possess any private property beyond the barest necessaries. Next, no one is to have any dwelling or store-house that is not open for all to enter at will. Their food, in the quantities required by men of temperance and courage who are in training for war, they will receive from the other citizens as the wages of their guardianship, fixed so that there shall be just enough for the year with nothing over; and they will have meals in common and all live together like soldiers in a camp. Gold and silver, we shall tell them, they will not need, having the divine counterparts of those metals always in their souls as a god-given possession, whose purity it is not lawful to sully by the acquisition of that mortal dross, current among mankind, which has been the occasion of so many unholy deeds. They alone of all the citizens are forbidden to touch and handle silver or gold, or to come under the same roof with them, or wear them as ornaments, or drink from vessels made of them. This manner of life will be their salvation and make them the saviours of the commonwealth. If ever they should come to possess land of their own and houses and money, they will give up their guardianship for the management of their farms and households and become tyrants at enmity with their fellow citizens instead of allies. And so they will pass all their lives in hating and being hated, plotting and being plotted against, in much greater fear of their enemies at home than of any foreign foe, and fast heading for the destruction that will soon overwhelm their country with themselves. For all these reasons let us say that this is how our Guardians are to be housed and otherwise provided for, and let us make laws accordingly.

By all means, said Glaucon.

Here Adeimantus interposed. Socrates, he said, how would you meet the objection that you are not making these people particularly happy? It is their own fault too, if they are not; for they are really masters of the state, and yet they get no good out of it as other rulers do, who own lands, build themselves fine houses with handsome furniture, offer private sacrifices to the gods, and entertain visitors from abroad; who possess, in fact, that gold and silver you spoke of, with everything else that is usually thought necessary for happiness. These people seem like nothing so much as a garrison of mercenaries posted in the city and perpetually mounting guard.

Yes, I said, and what is more they will serve for their food only without getting a mercenary's pay, so that they will not be able to travel on their own account or to make presents to a mistress or to spend as they please in other ways, like the people who are commonly thought happy. You have forgotten to include these counts in your indictment, and many more to the same effect.

Well, take them as included now.

And you want to hear the answer?

Yes.

We shall find one, I think, by keeping to the line we have followed so far. We shall say that, though it would not be surprising if even these people were perfectly happy under such conditions, our aim in founding the commonwealth was not to make any one class specially happy, but to secure the greatest possible happiness for the community as a whole. We thought we should have the best chance of finding justice in a state so constituted, just as we should find injustice where the constitution was of the worst possible type; we could then decide the question which has been before us all this time. For the moment, we are constructing, as we believe, the state which will be happy as a whole, not trying to secure the well-being of a select few; we shall study a state of the opposite kind presently. It is as if we were colouring a statue[3] and someone came up and blamed us for not putting the most beautiful colours on the noblest parts of the figure; the eyes, for instance, should be painted crimson, but we had made them black. We should think it a fair answer to say: Really, you must not expect us to paint eyes so handsome as not to look like eyes at all. This applies to all the parts: the question is whether, by giving each its proper colour, we make the whole beautiful. So too, in the present case, you must not press us to endow our Guardians with a happiness that will

---

[3]Greek statues were commonly tinted, wholly or in part.

make them anything rather than guardians. We could quite easily clothe our farmers in gorgeous robes, crown them with gold, and invite them to till the soil at their pleasure; or we might set our potters to lie on couches by their fire, passing round the wine and making merry, with their wheel at hand to work at whenever they felt so inclined. We could make all the rest happy in the same sort of way, and so spread this well-being through the whole community. But you must not put that idea into our heads; if we take your advice, the farmer will be no farmer, the potter no longer a potter; none of the elements that make up the community will keep its character. In many cases this does not matter so much: if a cobbler goes to the bad and pretends to be what he is not, he is not a danger to the state; but, as you must surely see, men who make only a vain show of being guardians of the laws and of the commonwealth bring the whole state to utter ruin, just as, on the other hand, its good government and well-being depend entirely on them. We, in fact, are making genuine Guardians who will be the last to bring harm upon the commonwealth; if our critic aims rather at producing a happiness like that of a party of peasants feasting at a fair, what he has in mind is something other than a civic community. So we must consider whether our aim in establishing Guardians is to secure the greatest possible happiness for them, or happiness is something of which we should watch the development in the whole commonwealth. If so, we must compel these Guardians and Auxiliaries of ours to second our efforts; and they, and all the rest with them, must be induced to make themselves perfect masters each of his own craft. In that way, as the community grows into a well-ordered whole, the several classes may be allowed such measure of happiness as their nature will compass.

I think that is an admirable reply. . . .

. . . In my judgement, then, the question under what conditions people born and educated as we have described should possess wives and children, and how they should treat them, can be rightly settled only by keeping to the course on which we started them at the outset. We undertook to put these men in the position of watch-dogs guarding a flock. Suppose we follow up the analogy and imagine them bred and reared in the same sort of way. We can then see if that plan will suit our purpose.

How will that be?

In this way. Which do we think right for watch-dogs: should the females guard the flock and hunt with the males and take a share in all they do, or should they be kept within doors as fit for no more than bearing and feeding their puppies, while all the hard work of looking after the flock is left to the males?

They are expected to take their full share, except that we treat them as not quite so strong.

Can you employ any creature for the same work as another, if you do not give them both the same upbringing and education?

No.

Then, if we are to set women to the same tasks as men, we must teach them the same things. They must have the same two branches of training for mind and body and also be taught the art of war, and they must receive the same treatment.

That seems to follow.

Possibly, if these proposals were carried out, they might be ridiculed as involving a good many breaches of custom.

They might indeed.

The most ridiculous—don't you think?—being the notion of women exercising naked along with the men in the wrestling-schools; some of them elderly women too, like the old men who still have a passion for exercise when they are wrinkled and not very agreeable to look at.

Yes, that would be thought laughable, according to our present notions.

Now we have started on this subject, we must not be frightened of the many witticisms that might be aimed at such a revolution, not only in the matter of bodily exercise but in the training of women's minds, and not least when it comes to their bearing arms and riding on horseback. Having begun upon these rules, we must not draw back from the harsher provisions. The wits may be asked to stop being witty and try to be serious; and we may remind them that it is not so long since the Greeks, like most foreign nations of the present day, thought it ridiculous and shameful for men to be seen naked. When gymnastic exercises were first introduced in Crete and later at Sparta, the humorists had their chance to make fun of them; but when experience had shown that nakedness is better uncovered than muffled up, the laughter died down and a practice which the reason approved ceased to look ridiculous to the eye. This shows how idle it is to think anything ludicrous but what is base. One who tries to raise a laugh at any spectacle save that of baseness and folly will also, in his serious moments, set before himself some other standard than goodness of what deserves to be held in honour.

Most assuredly.

The first thing to be settled, then, is whether these proposals are feasible; and it must be open to anyone, whether a humorist or serious-minded, to raise the question whether, in the case of mankind, the feminine nature is capable of taking part with the other sex in all occupations, or in none at all, or in some only; and in particular under which of these heads this business of military service falls. Well begun is half done, and would not this be the best way to begin?

Yes.

Shall we take the other side in this debate and argue against ourselves? We do not want the adversary's position to be taken by storm
for lack of defenders.

I have no objection.

Let us state his case for him. 'Socrates and Glaucon,' he will say, 'there
is no need for others to dispute your position; you yourselves, at the very
outset of founding your commonwealth, agreed that everyone should do
the one work for which nature fits him.' Yes, of course; I suppose we did.
'And isn't there a very great difference in nature between man and
woman?' Yes, surely. 'Does not that natural difference imply a corresponding difference in the work to be given to each?' Yes. 'But if so,
surely you must be mistaken now and contradicting yourselves when you
say that men and women, having such widely divergent natures, should
do the same things?' What is your answer to that, my ingenious friend?

It is not easy to find one at the moment. I can only appeal to you to
state the case on our own side, whatever it may be.

This, Glaucon, is one of many alarming objections which I foresaw
some time ago. That is why I shrank from touching upon these laws
concerning the possession of wives and the rearing of children.

It looks like anything but an easy problem.

True, I said; but whether a man tumbles into a swimming-pool or into
mid-ocean, he has to swim all the same. So must we, and try if we can
reach the shore, hoping for some Arion's dolphin or other miraculous
deliverance to bring us safe to land.[4]

I suppose so.

Come then, let us see if we can find the way out. We did agree that
different natures should have different occupations, and that the natures
of man and woman are different; and yet we are now saying that these
different natures are to have the same occupations. Is that the charge
against us?

Exactly.

It is extraordinary, Glaucon, what an effect the practice of debating has
upon people.

Why do you say that?

Because they often seem to fall unconsciously into mere disputes which
they mistake for reasonable argument, through being unable to draw the
distinctions proper to their subject; and so, instead of a philosophical
exchange of ideas, they go off in chase of contradictions which are purely
verbal.

I know that happens to many people; but does it apply to us at this
moment?

Absolutely. At least I am afraid we are slipping unconsciously into a

[4]The musician Arion, to escape the treachery of Corinthian sailors, leapt into the sea and
was carried ashore at Taenarum by a dolphin, Herod.

dispute about words. We have been strenuously insisting on the letter of our principle that different natures should not have the same occupations, as if we were scoring a point in a debate; but we have altogether neglected to consider what sort of sameness or difference we meant and in what respect these natures and occupations were to be defined as different or the same. Consequently, we might very well be asking one another whether there is not an opposition in nature between bald and long-haired men, and, when that was admitted, forbid one set to be shoemakers, if the other were following that trade.

That would be absurd.

Yes, but only because we never meant any and every sort of sameness or difference in nature, but the sort that was relevant to the occupations in question. We meant, for instance, that a man and a woman have the same nature if both have a talent for medicine; whereas two men have different natures if one is a born physician, the other a born carpenter.

Yes, of course.

If, then, we find that either the male sex or the female is specially qualified for any particular form of occupation, then that occupation, we shall say, ought to be assigned to one sex or the other. But if the only difference appears to be that the male begets and the female brings forth, we shall conclude that no difference between man and woman has yet been produced that is relevant to our purpose. We shall continue to think it proper for our Guardians and their wives to share in the same pursuits.

And quite rightly.

The next thing will be to ask our opponent to name any profession or occupation in civic life for the purposes of which woman's nature is different from man's.

That is a fair question.

He might reply, as you did just now, that it is not easy to find a satisfactory answer on the spur of the moment, but that there would be no difficulty after a little reflection.

Perhaps.

Suppose, then, we invite him to follow us and see if we can convince him that there is no occupation concerned with the management of social affairs that is peculiar to women. We will confront him with a question: When you speak of a man having a natural talent for something, do you mean that he finds it easy to learn, and after a little instruction can find out much. more for himself; whereas a man who is not so gifted learns with difficulty and no amount of instruction and practice will make him even remember what he has been taught? Is the talented man one whose bodily powers are readily at the service of his mind, instead of being a hindrance? Are not these the marks by which you distinguish the presence of a natural gift for any pursuit?

Yes, precisely.

Now do you know of any human occupation in which the male sex is not superior to the female in all these respects? Need I waste time over exceptions like weaving and watching over saucepans and batches of cakes, though women are supposed to be good at such things and get laughed at when a man does them better?

It is true, he replied, in almost everything one sex is easily beaten by the other. No doubt many women are better at many things than many men; but taking the sexes as a whole, it is as you say.

To conclude, then, there is no occupation concerned with the management of social affairs which belongs either to woman or to man, as such. Natural gifts are to be found here and there in both creatures alike; and every occupation is open to both, so far as their natures are concerned, though woman is for all purposes the weaker.

Certainly.

Is that a reason for making over all occupations to men only?

Of course not.

No, because one woman may have a natural gift for medicine or for music, another may not.

Surely.

Is it not also true that a woman may, or may not, be warlike or athletic?

I think so.

And again, one may love knowledge, another hate it; one may be high-spirited, another spiritless?

True again.

It follows that one woman will be fitted by nature to be a Guardian, another will not; because these were the qualities for which we selected our men Guardians. So for the purpose of keeping watch over the commonwealth, woman has the same nature as man, save in so far as she is weaker.

So it appears.

It follows that women of this type must be selected to share the life and duties of Guardians with men of the same type, since they are competent and of a like nature, and the same natures must be allowed the same pursuits.

Yes.

We come round, then, to our former position, that there is nothing contrary to nature in giving our Guardians' wives the same training for mind and body. The practice we proposed to establish was not impossible or visionary, since it was in accordance with nature. Rather, the contrary practice which now prevails turns out to be unnatural.

So it appears.

Well, we set out to inquire whether the plan we proposed was feasible and also the best. That it is feasible is now agreed; we must next settle whether it is the best.

Obviously.

Now, for the purpose of producing a woman fit to be a Guardian, we shall not have one education for men and another for women, precisely because the nature to be taken in hand is the same.

True.

What is your opinion on the question of one man being better than another? Do you think there is no such difference?

Certainly I do not.

And in this commonwealth of ours which will prove the better men— the Guardians who have received the education we described, or the shoemakers who have been trained to make shoes?

It is absurd to ask such a question.

Very well. So these Guardians will be the best of all the citizens?

By far.

And these women the best of all the women?

Yes.

Can anything be better for a commonwealth than to produce in it men and women of the best possible type?

No.

And that result will be brought about by such a system of mental and bodily training as we have described?

Surely.

We may conclude that the institution we proposed was not only practicable, but also the best for the commonwealth.

Yes

The wives of our Guardians, then, must strip for exercise, since they will be clothed with virtue, and they must take their share in war and in the other social duties of guardianship. They are to have no other occupation; and in these duties the lighter part must fall to the women, because of the weakness of their sex. The man who laughs at naked women, exercising their bodies for the best of reasons, is like one that 'gathers fruit unripe,' for he does not know what it is that he is laughing at or what he is doing. There will never be a finer saying than the one which declares that whatever does good should be held in honour, and the only shame is in doing harm.

That is perfectly true. . . .

So far, then, in regulating the position of women, we may claim to have come safely through with one hazardous proposal, that male and female Guardians shall have all occupations in common. The consistency of the argument is an assurance that the plan is a good one and also feasible. We are like swimmers who have breasted the first wave without being swallowed up.

Not such a small wave either.

You will not call it large when you see the next.

Let me have a look at the next one, then.

Here it is: a law which follows from that principle and all that has gone before, namely that, of these Guardians, no one man and one woman are to set up house together privately: wives are to be held in common by all; so too are the children, and no parent is to know his own child, nor any child his parent.

It will be much harder to convince people that that is either a feasible plan or a good one.

As to its being a good plan, I imagine no one would deny the immense advantage of wives and children being held in common, provided it can be done. I should expect dispute to arise chiefly over the question whether it is possible.

There may well be a good deal of dispute over both points.

You mean, I must meet attacks on two fronts. I was hoping to escape one by running away: if you agreed it was a good plan, then I should only have had to inquire whether it was feasible.

No, we have seen through that manoeuvre. You will have to defend both positions.

Well, I must pay the penalty for my cowardice. But grant me one favour. Let me indulge my fancy, like one who entertains himself with idle day-dreams on a solitary walk. Before he has any notion how his desires can be realized, he will set aside that question, to save himself the trouble of reckoning what may or may not be possible. He will assume that his wish has come true, and amuse himself with settling all the details of what he means to do then. So a lazy mind encourages itself to be lazier than ever; and I am giving way to the same weakness myself. I want to put off till later that question, how the thing can be done. For the moment, with your leave, I shall assume it to be possible, and ask how the Rulers will work out the details in practice; and I shall argue that the plan, once carried into effect, would be the best thing in the world for our commonwealth and for its Guardians. That is what I shall now try to make out with your help, if you will allow me to postpone the other question.

Very good; I have no objection.

Well, if our Rulers are worthy of the name, and their Auxiliaries likewise, these latter will be ready to do what they are told, and the Rulers, in giving their commands, will themselves obey our laws and will be faithful to their spirit in any details we leave to their discretion.

No doubt.

It is for you, then, as their lawgiver, who have already selected the men, to select for association with them women who are so far as possible of the same natural capacity. Now since none of them will have any private home of his own, but they will share the same dwelling and eat at common tables, the two sexes will be together; and meeting without restriction for exercise and all through their upbringing, they will surely be drawn towards union with one another by a necessity of their nature—necessity is not too strong a word, I think?

Not too strong for the constraint of love, which for the mass of mankind is more persuasive and compelling than even the necessity of mathematical proof.

Exactly. But in the next place, Glaucon, anything like unregulated unions would be a profanation in a state whose citizens lead the good life. The Rulers will not allow such a thing.

No, it would not be right.

Clearly, then, we must have marriages, as sacred as we can make them; and this sanctity will attach to those which yield the best results.

Certainly.

How are we to get the best results? You must tell me, Glaucon, because I see you keep sporting dogs and a great many game birds at your house; and there is something about their mating and breeding that you must have noticed.

What is that?

In the first place, though they may all be of good stock, are there not some that turn out to be better than the rest?

There are.

And do you breed from all indiscriminately? Are you not careful to breed from the best so far as you can?

Yes.

And from those in their prime, rather than the very young or the very old?

Yes.

Otherwise, the stock of your birds or dogs would deteriorate very much, wouldn't it?

It would.

And the same is true of horses or of any animal?

It would be very strange if it were not.

Dear me, said I; we shall need consummate skill in our Rulers, if it is also true of the human race.

Well, it is true. But why must they be so skilful?

Because they will have to administer a large dose of that medicine we spoke of earlier.[5] An ordinary doctor is thought good enough for a patient who will submit to be dieted and can do without medicine; but he must be much more of a man if drugs are required.

True, but how does that apply?

It applies to our Rulers: it seems they will have to give their subjects a considerable dose of imposition and deception for their good. We said, if you remember, that such expedients would be useful as a sort of medicine.

[5]In the *Laws* "Plato's view of marriage is very far from being merely physical. It has its moral and even its religious side."

Yes, a very sound principle.

Well, it looks as if this sound principle will play no small part in this matter of marriage and child-bearing.

How so?

It follows from what we have just said that, if we are to keep our flock at the highest pitch of excellence, there should be as many unions of the best of both sexes, and as few of the inferior, as possible, and that only the offspring of the better unions should be kept.[6] And again, no one but the Rulers must know how all this is being effected; otherwise our herd of Guardians may become rebellious.

Quite true.

We must, then, institute certain festivals at which we shall bring together the brides and the bridegrooms. There will be sacrifices, and our poets will write songs befitting the occasion. The number of marriages we shall leave to the Rulers' discretion. They will aim at keeping the number of the citizens as constant as possible, having regard to losses caused by war, epidemics, and so on; and they must do their best to see that our state does not become either great or small.[7]

Very good.

I think they will have to invent some ingenious system of drawing lots, so that, at each pairing off, the inferior candidate may blame his luck rather than the Rulers.

Yes, certainly.

Moreover, young men who acquit themselves well in war and other duties, should be given, among other rewards and privileges, more liberal opportunities to sleep with a wife,[8] for the further purpose that, with good excuse, as many as possible of the children may be begotten of such fathers.

Yes.

As soon as children are born, they will be taken in charge by officers

---

[6]That is, "kept *as Guardians.*" The inferior children of Guardians were to be "thrust out among the craftsmen and farmers."

[7]Plato seems to forget that these rules apply only to Guardians. If the much larger third class is to breed without restriction, a substantial rise in their numbers might entail suspension of all childbirth among Guardians, with a dysgenic effect. Plato, however, feared a decline, rather than a rise, in the birth rate. (The state described in the *Laws* is always to have 5,040 citizens, each holding one inalienable lot of land.)

The "number of marriages" may include both the number of candidates admitted at each festival and the frequency of the festival. But it is perhaps likely that the festivals are to be annual, so that women who had borne children since the last festival would be re-marriageable. If so, at each festival a fresh group will be called up, consisting of all who have reached the age of 25 for men or 20 for women since the previous festival. Some or all of these will be paired with one another or with members of older groups. The couples will cohabit during the festival, which might last (say) for a month. The marriages will then be dissolved and the partners remain celibate until the next festival at earliest.

[8]Not to have several wives at once, but to be admitted at more frequent intervals to the periodic marriage festivals, not necessarily with a different wife each time.

appointed for the purpose, who may be men or women or both, since offices are to be shared by both sexes. The children of the better parents they will carry to the crèche to be reared in the care of nurses living apart in a certain quarter of the city. Those of the inferior parents and any children of the rest that are born defective will be hidden away, in some appropriate manner that must be kept secret.[9]

They must be, if the breed of our Guardians is to be kept pure.

These officers will also superintend the nursing of the children. They will bring the mothers to the crèche when their breasts are full, while taking every precaution that no mother shall know her own child; and if the mothers have not enough milk, they will provide wet-nurses. They will limit the time during which the mothers will suckle their children, and hand over all the hard work and sitting up at night to nurses and attendants.

That will make child-bearing an easy business for the Guardians' wives.

So it should be. To go on with our scheme: we said that children should be born from parents in the prime of life. Do you agree that this lasts about twenty years for a woman, and thirty for a man? A woman should bear children for the commonwealth from her twentieth to her fortieth year; a man should begin to beget them when he has passed "the racer's prime in swiftness,"[10] and continue till he is fifty-five.

Those are certainly the years in which both the bodily and the mental powers of man and woman are at their best.

If a man either above or below this age meddles with the begetting of children for the commonwealth, we shall hold it an offence against divine and human law. He will be begetting for his country a child conceived in darkness and dire incontinence, whose birth, if it escape detection, will not have been sanctioned by the sacrifices and prayers offered at each marriage festival, when priests and priestesses join with the whole community in praying that the children to be born may be even better and more useful citizens than their parents.

You are right.

The same law will apply to any man within the prescribed limits who touches a woman also of marriageable age when the Ruler has not paired them. We shall say that he is foisting on the commonwealth a bastard, unsanctioned by law or by religion.

Perfectly right.

As soon, however, as the men and the women have passed the age prescribed for producing children, we shall leave them free to form a

---

[9]Infanticide of defective children was practised at Sparta; but the vague expression used does not imply that all children of inferior Guardians are to be destroyed. Those not defective would be relegated to the third class.

[10]A poetical quotation, which may, in its original context, have referred to a racehorse, brought to the stud when he had ceased to run.

connexion with whom they will, except that a man shall not take his daughter or daughter's daughter or mother or mother's mother, nor a woman her son or father or her son's son or father's father; and all this only after we have exhorted them to see that no child, if any be conceived, shall be brought to light, or, if they cannot prevent its birth, to dispose of it on the understanding that no such child can be reared.[11]

That too is reasonable. But how are they to distinguish fathers and daughters and those other relations you mentioned?

They will not, said I. But, reckoning from the day when he becomes a bridegroom, a man will call all children born in the tenth or the seventh month sons and daughters, and they will call him father. Their children again he will call grandchildren, and they will call his group grandfathers and grandmothers; and all who are born within the period during which their mothers and fathers were having children will be called brothers and sisters. This will provide for those restrictions on unions that we mentioned; but the law will allow brothers and sisters to live together, if the lot so falls out and the Delphic oracle also approves.[12]

---

[11]The unofficial unions might be permanent. The only unions barred as incestuous are between parents and children, or grandparents and grandchildren (all such are included, since, if a woman cannot marry her father's father, a man cannot marry his son's daughter). It seems to follow that Plato did not regard the much more probable connexions of brothers and sisters as incestuous; and if so, he would see no reason against legal marriage of real brothers and sisters, who would not know they were so related. Such unions were regular in Egypt; and some modern authorities deny that they are dysgenic. Greek law allowed marriage between brother and half-sister by a different mother.

[12]This last speech deals with two distinct questions: (1) avoidance of incestuous unions as above defined; (2) legal marriage of brothers and sisters.

(1) Since the elderly people forming unofficial unions are not to know who are their parents or children, they must avoid all persons who could possibly be so related to them. This is easy, if cohabitation in legal marriage is confined to the duration of a marriage festival and the children of any parent must therefore belong to a batch born in the seventh or tenth month after any festival at which that parent has been married. (Most ancient authorities denied that a child could be born in the eighth month.) If a register was kept, a man could be told all the dates in question without being told who were his real children.

(2) After explaining how incestuous unions can be avoided by a man treating certain whole groups as his parents or children or grandparents or grandchildren, Plato adds that all persons "born within the period during which their mothers and fathers (not *his* father and mother) were having children" will be called "brothers" and "sisters." If unions of real brothers and sisters are not incestuous, this clause has nothing to do with avoidance of incest. It only adds to the definition of nominal parents and children and grandparents and grandchildren, a definition of those who will call one another "brothers" and "sisters," whether they are really so related or not. Probably, it is meant that these will be all the Guardians born in the same generation (in a vague sense). Since there is no question of incest, these persons will never need to inquire about dates of marriage and birth, if they wish to form a union.

The last sentence refers to both topics of the previous one: (1) avoidance of incestuous unions, (2) legal marriage of real brothers and sisters. It has been held that Plato regarded such marriages as incestuous and that the Oracle was to guard against them. But either the Rulers knew how all Guardians were related or they did not. If (as seems likely) they did know, they could avoid arranging such marriages without invoking an oracle to negative their own proposals. If they did not (though it would be folly to keep no registers if *any* incest was to be avoided), then how could the Oracle know? Granted that Plato did not hold

Very good.

This, then, Glaucon, is the manner in which the Guardians of your commonwealth are to hold their wives and children in common. Must we not next find arguments to establish that it is consistent with our other institutions and also by far the best plan?

Yes, surely.

We had better begin by asking what is the greatest good at which the lawgiver should aim in laying down the constitution of a state, and what is the worst evil. We can then consider whether our proposals are in keeping with that good and irreconcilable with the evil.

By all means.

Does not the worst evil for a state arise from anything that tends to rend it asunder and destroy its unity, while nothing does it more good than whatever tends to bind it together and make it one?

That is true.

And are not citizens bound together by sharing in the same pleasures and pains, all feeling glad or grieved on the same occasions of gain or loss; whereas the bond is broken when such feelings are no longer universal, but any event of public or personal concern fills some with joy and others with distress?

Certainly.

And this disunion comes about when the words "mine" and "not mine," "another's" and "not another's" are not applied to the same things throughout the community. The best ordered state will be the one in which the largest number of persons use these terms in the same sense, and which accordingly most nearly resembles a single person. When one of us hurts his finger, the whole extent of those bodily connexions which are gathered up in the soul and unified by its ruling element is made aware and it all shares as a whole in the pain of the suffering part; hence we say that the man has a pain in his finger. The same thing is true of the pain or pleasure felt when any other part of the person suffers or is relieved.

Yes; I agree that the best organized community comes nearest to that condition.

And so it will recognize as a part of itself the individual citizen to whom good or evil happens, and will share as a whole in his joy or sorrow.

It must, if the constitution is sound.

It is time now to go back to our own commonwealth and see whether these conclusions apply to it more than to any other type of state. In all alike there are rulers and common people, all of whom will call one another fellow citizens.

---

marriage of brothers and sisters to be incestuous, the Rulers could sometimes knowingly arrange such marriages. The Oracle might be asked once for all to approve the whole scheme of marriage laws, or it might be formally invoked at each festival. If it raised no objection, the Rulers would be protected from any charge of violating religious law.

Yes.

But in other states the people have another name as well for their rulers, haven't they?

Yes; in most they call them masters; in democracies, simply the government.

And in ours?

The people will look upon their rulers as preservers and protectors.

And how will our rulers regard the people?

As those who maintain them and pay them wages.

And elsewhere?

As slaves.

And what do rulers elsewhere call one another?

Colleagues.

And ours?

Fellow Guardians.

And in other states may not a ruler regard one colleague as a friend in whom he has an interest, and another as a stranger with whom he has nothing in common?

Yes, that often happens.

But that could not be so with your Guardians? None of them could ever treat a fellow Guardian as a stranger.

Certainly not. He must regard everyone whom he meets as brother or sister, father or mother, son or daughter, grandchild or grandparent.

Very good; but here is a further point. Will you not require them, not merely to use these family terms, but to behave as a real family? Must they not show towards all whom they call "father" the customary reverence, care, and obedience due to a parent, if they look for any favour from gods or men, since to act otherwise is contrary to divine and human law? Should not all the citizens constantly reiterate in the hearing of the children from their earliest years such traditional maxims of conduct towards those whom they are taught to call father and their other kindred?

They should. It would be absurd that terms of kinship should be on their lips without any action to correspond.

In our community, then, above all others, when things go well or ill with any individual everyone will use that word "mine" in the same sense and say that all is going well or ill with him and his.

Quite true.

And, as we said, this way of speaking and thinking goes with fellow-feeling; so that our citizens, sharing as they do in a common interest which each will call his own, will have all their feelings of pleasure or pain in common.

Assuredly.

A result that will be due to our institutions, and in particular to our Guardians' holding their wives and children in common.

Very much so.

But you will remember how, when we compared a well-ordered community to the body which shares in the pleasures and pains of any member, we saw in this unity the greatest good that a state can enjoy. So the conclusion is that our commonwealth owes to this sharing of wives and children by its protectors its enjoyment of the greatest of all goods.

Yes, that follows.

Moreover, this agrees with our principle that they were not to have houses or lands or any property of their own, but receive sustenance from the other citizens, as wages for their guardianship, and to consume it in common. Only so will they keep to their true character; and our present proposals will do still more to make them genuine Guardians. They will not rend the community asunder by each applying that word "mine" to different things and dragging off whatever he can get for himself into a private home, where he will have his separate family, forming a centre of exclusive joys and sorrows. Rather they will all, so far as may be, feel together and aim at the same ends, because they are convinced that all their interests are identical.

Quite so.

Again, if a man's person is his only private possession, lawsuits and prosecutions will all but vanish, and they will be free of those quarrels that arise from ownership of property and from having family ties. Nor would they be justified even in bringing actions for assault and outrage; for we shall pronounce it right and honourable for a man to defend himself against an assailant of his own age, and in that way they will be compelled to keep themselves fit.

That would be a sound law.

And it would also have the advantage that, if a man's anger can be satisfied in this way, a fit of passion is less likely to grow into a serious quarrel.

True.

But an older man will be given authority over all younger persons and power to correct them; whereas the younger will, naturally, not dare to strike the elder or do him any violence, except by command of a Ruler. He will not show him any sort of disrespect. Two guardian spirits, fear and reverence, will be enough to restrain him—reverence forbidding him to lay hands on a parent, and fear of all those others who as sons or brothers or fathers would come to the rescue.

Yes, that will be the result.

So our laws will secure that these men will live in complete peace with one another; and if they never quarrel among themselves, there is no fear of the rest of the community being divided either against them or against itself.[13]

No.

There are other evils they will escape, so mean and petty that I hardly like

---

[13]"Revolution always starts from the outbreak of internal dissension in the ruling class."

to mention them: the poor man's flattery of the rich, and all the embarrass-
ments and vexations of rearing a family and earning just enough to maintain
a household; now borrowing and now refusing to repay, and by any and
every means scraping together money to be handed over to wife and servants to spend. These sordid troubles are familiar and not worth describing.

Only too familiar.

Rid of all these cares, they will live a more enviable life than the
Olympic victor, who is counted happy on the strength of far fewer bless-
ings than our Guardians will enjoy. Their victory is the nobler, since by
their success the whole commonwealth is preserved; and their reward of
maintenance at the public cost is more complete, since their prize is to
have every need of life supplied for themselves and for their children;
their country honours them while they live, and when they die they
receive a worthy burial.

Yes, they will be nobly rewarded.

Do you remember, then, how someone who shall be nameless re-
proached us for not making our Guardians happy: they were to possess
nothing, though all the wealth of their fellow citizens was within their
grasp? We replied, I believe, that we would consider that objection later,
if it came in our way: for the moment we were bent on making our
Guardians real guardians, and moulding our commonwealth with a view
to the greatest happiness, not of one section of it, but of the whole.

Yes, I remember.

Well, it appears now that these protectors of our state will have a life
better and more honourable than that of any Olympic victor; and we can
hardly rank it on a level with the life of a shoemaker or other artisan or
of a farmer.

I should think not.

However, it is right to repeat what I said at the time: if ever a Guardian
tries to make himself happy in such a way that he will be a guardian no
longer; if, not content with the moderation and security of this way of
living which we think the best, he becomes possessed with some silly and
childish notion of happiness, impelling him to make his power a means to
appropriate all the citizens' wealth, then he will learn the wisdom of
Hesiod's saying that the half is more than the whole.

My advice would certainly be that he should keep to his own way of
living.

You do agree, then, that women are to take their full share with men
in education, in the care of children, and in the guardianship of the other
citizens; whether they stay at home or go out to war, they will be like
watch-dogs which take their part either in guarding the fold or in hunting
and share in every task so far as their strength allows. Such conduct will
not be unwomanly, but all for the best and in accordance with the natural
partnership of the sexes.

Yes, I agree. . . .

Here, then, are some more evils which must not elude the vigilance of our Guardians and find their way into the commonwealth: riches and poverty. The one produces luxury and idleness, the other low standards of conduct and workmanship; and both have a subversive tendency.

True enough. But I should like to know, Socrates, how our state will be able to go to war, if it has no money, especially if it is forced to fight a rich and powerful enemy.

Obviously it would be hard to fight one such enemy, but easier to deal with two.

What do you mean by that?

In the first place, if they have to fight, they will be highly trained soldiers matched against rich men.

True, so far as that goes.

Well then, Adeimantus, would not a single boxer in perfect training easily be a match for two wealthy and corpulent antagonists who could not box?

Not for both at once perhaps.

Not even if he could give ground and then turn and plant a blow on whichever came up first? Suppose he kept on doing that under a burning sun, would he not get the better of even more than two?

It would certainly not be surprising.

Well, don't you think that rich people know more of the theory and practice of boxing than of the art of war?

I am sure they do.

In that case it will probably be an easy matter for our trained warriors to fight twice or three times their number.

I will grant you that; I believe you are right.

And now suppose they sent envoys to one of the two enemy countries to tell them what is in fact the truth: "We have no use for gold and silver; we are not allowed to possess them. But you are allowed; so join forces with us, and you may have the spoils of the other country."[14] After such an offer would anyone choose to fight against tough, wiry dogs sooner than join the dogs in attacking the fat and tender sheep?

I should say not. But if a single state amasses the wealth of all the others, will not that be a danger to a state that has none?

I congratulate you on your idea that any state other than the one we are constructing deserves the name.

Why, what should the others be called?

By some grander name, for each of them is not one state, but many: two at least, which are at war with one another, one of the rich, the other of the poor, and each of these is divided into many more. To treat them all as a single state is a complete mistake. If you treat them as many and offer

---

[14]This message is in the "laconic" style of Spartan diplomacy.

to make over to one class the wealth and power and even the persons of the others, you will always find that your allies outnumber your enemies. Consequently, so long as your commonwealth is ordered wisely on the lines we have laid down, it will be the greatest of all; I do not mean the most famous, but greatest in the literal sense, even though it have no more than a thousand men to fight in its defence. You will not easily find in Hellas or elsewhere a state of that size which is really one, though there are plenty which look like single states and are many times as large. Don't you agree?

I do indeed.

Here, then, our Rulers will find the best principle for determining the size of the state and the proportionate amount of territory, beyond which they will not go: the state should be allowed to grow only so far as it can increase in size without loss of unity.

An excellent rule.

So we must lay yet another command on our Guardians: they are to take all possible care that the state shall neither be too small nor yet one that seems great but has no unity.

You think that will be easy!

Not so hard as the duty we mentioned earlier, of moving down any inferior child born to the Guardians into the other classes and promoting from those classes any child who is good enough to be a Guardian. Our intention there was to set the other citizens to work, one man at one task for which his nature fitted him, so that by keeping to that one business he might come to be a single man and not many. In that way the state as a whole would grow to be a single community, and not many.

You may well call that not so easy!

No, but really, my good Adeimantus, we are not laying upon the Guardians a whole number of burdensome duties, as you might suppose. It will all be easy enough, if only they will see to 'the one great thing,' as the saying goes, though I would rather call it the one thing that is sufficient: education and nurture. If a sound education has made them reasonable men, they will easily see their way through all these matters as well as others which we will pass over for the moment, such as the possession of wives, marriage, and child-bearing, and the principle that here we should follow, as far as possible, the proverb which says that friends have all things in common.

Yes, all should go well then.

Moreover, when a community has once made a good start, its growth proceeds in a sort of cycle. If a sound system of nurture and education is maintained, it produces men of a good disposition; and these in their turn, taking advantage of such education, develop into better men than their forebears, and their breeding qualities improve among the rest, as may be seen in animals.

That is likely enough.

In short, then, those who keep watch over our commonwealth must take the greatest care not to overlook the least infraction of the rule against any innovation upon the established system of education either of the body or of the mind. When the poet says that men care most for "the newest air that hovers on the singer's lips," they will be afraid lest he be taken not merely to mean new songs, but to be commending a new style of music. Such innovation is not to be commended, nor should the poet be so understood. The introduction of novel fashions in music is a thing to beware of as endangering the whole fabric of society, whose most important conventions are unsettled by any revolution in that quarter. So Damon declares, and I believe him.

You may count me too among his supporters, said Adeimantus.

It seems, then, said I, that it is here, in the field of music and poetry, that our Guardians must build their watch-tower.

It is certainly there that lawlessness easily creeps in unobserved.

Yes, I said, in the guise of a pastime, which seems so harmless.

It would be harmless, he replied, were it not that, little by little, this lawless spirit gains a lodgement and spreads imperceptibly to manners and pursuits; and from thence with gathering force invades men's dealings with one another, and next goes on to attack the laws and the constitution with wanton recklessness, until it ends by overthrowing the whole structure of public and private life.

Really? said I. Is all that true?

So I believe, he replied.

Our children's pastimes, then, as I began by saying, must be kept from the first within stricter bounds; if any licence be admitted, they will catch the spirit and will never grow into law-abiding and well-conducted men. And so, when children have made a good beginning in their play and musical education has instilled a spirit of order, this reverence for law, in complete contrast to the licence you were describing just now, will attend them in all their doings and foster their growth, restoring any institutions that may earlier have fallen into decay.[15]

That is true.

As a consequence, they will rediscover rules of behaviour which their predecessors have let fall into disuse, including matters supposed to be of little importance: how the young should be silent in the presence of their elders, give up their seats to them, and take dutiful care of their parents; not to mention details of personal appearance, such as the way their hair is cut and the clothes and shoes they wear. It would be silly, I think, to make laws on these matters; such habits cannot be established or kept up by written legislation. It is probable, at any rate, that the bent given by education will determine the quality of later life, by that sort of attraction

---

[15]Plato is here thinking of a reformed Athens, rather than of the ideal state.

which like things always have for one another, till they finally mount up to one imposing result, whether for good or ill. For that reason I should not myself be inclined to push legislation to that length.

With good reason.

But now look here, what are we to do about business transactions, dealings between buyers and sellers, contracts with tradesmen, actions for foul language and assault, legal proceedings and the impanelling of juries, collection and payment of any market or harbour dues that may be needed, and generally regulations for markets, police, custom houses, and all that sort of thing? Can we go so far as to legislate on any of these matters?

No; there will be no need to dictate to men of good breeding. They will soon find out for themselves what regulations are needed.

Yes, my friend, I replied, provided that, by the grace of heaven, they preserve the institutions we have already described.

Quite so, he agreed. Otherwise they will spend their lives making a host of petty regulations and amending them in the hope of reaching perfection.

Living, in fact, like those invalids who are too self-indulgent to give up their unwholesome habits.

Exactly.

And a pretty sort of life they have of it. All they gain from being doctored is that their ailments grow more severe and complicated, though they are always expecting to be cured by every fresh remedy that someone recommends.

Yes, that is a good description of a certain type of invalid.

And another amusing thing about them is that they take for their worst enemy anyone who tells them frankly that until they give up eating and drinking too much and idleness and debauchery, no medicine or surgery and no charms or amulets will do them any good.

I see nothing very amusing in being in a rage with good advice.

You don't seem to be an admirer of people like that.

I certainly am not.

Then neither will you admire the same sort of behaviour in a whole society. You will find something very like those invalids in some states with a bad form of government, which forbid their citizens, under pain of death, to make any radical change in the constitution, and at the same time honour as a good and profoundly wise person any obsequious flatterer who, without attempting such drastic treatment, can minister agreeably to their humours, which he is clever enough to anticipate.

The resemblance is very close, and I have nothing to say for them.

And what of the men who are willing and eager to minister to these invalid states? Have you no admiration for such cool temerity?

Yes, except when they are deluded by popular applause into fancying themselves to be real statesmen.

Why, said I, can't you make some allowances for them? When a man who cannot measure is told by a lot of equally ignorant people that he is six feet high, you cannot expect him not to believe them.

No, not in that instance.

Don't be so hard upon them, then. Surely there is something very amusing in the way they go on enacting their petty laws and amending them, always imagining they will find some way to put an end to fraud in business and in all those other transactions I was speaking of. They have no idea that really they are cutting off the heads of a hydra.

It is true; that is all they are doing.

I should have thought that laws and institutions of that order do not deserve the attention of a law-giver worthy of the name, no matter whether the constitution be good or bad. If it is bad, they are useless and effect nothing; if good, some are such as anyone could devise, and the rest will follow of themselves from the practices we have already instituted.

Then, what is there left for us to do in the way of legislation?

For us, nothing; but there are institutions of the highest worth and importance that must be left to the Delphian Apollo.

What are they?

The founding of temples, sacrifices, and the cults of gods, demigods, and heroes; the burial of the dead, and services to propitiate the powers of the other world. These are matters we do not understand ourselves, and in founding our commonwealth we shall be wise to consult no other religious authority than our national divinity. Indeed in religious matters, the authority of this god, from his seat at the very navel of the earth, may be said to extend to all mankind.[16]

Good. Let us do so.

[16]Excavation at Delphi has brought to light in the temple of Apollo the *omphalos* *("navel"), a conical stone which had been supposed to mark the centre of the earth when the earth was imagined to be a circular disk surrounded by the stream of Ocean. The oracle was in fact sometimes consulted by non-Greek states.*

— 18 —

a utopian vision before the industrial revolution

Sir Thomas More's *Utopia,* written early in the sixteenth century, described the social and political conditions of a society that existed on an island named Utopia. The social organization of the society that More created for the island was intended to exemplify an ideal set of social arrangements.

Precisely what constitutes an ideal social organization is, however, a relative matter. Social arrangements that are ideal or even workable for a society operating at a particular level of technological development, and with certain values that define an individual's rights, are likely to be inappropriate for a society operating at a drastically different technological level and with different values concerning individual freedom. Social problems that are considered major in one society may not even exist in another. In a society in which a man must work 14 hours a day in order to produce enough food for his family, the problem of using leisure time is less likely to be pressing than it is in a cybernated society in which available employment keeps people busy only five hours a week.

More's Utopia was designed to improve on the society he understood best— his own—just as Socrates' Republic is a variation on the social organization of his society, and Bellamy's system (Chapter 19) is a variation on the social organization of an industrial society. More's social system seems to have been designed on a minimax principle—that is, a strategy (in this case, a plan for a social system) designed to guarantee a certain minimally satisfactory outcome against even the most adverse conditions. A military strategist who employs a minimax principle in planning a campaign or defense assumes that his enemy will behave in the most intelligent possible manner, will try to inflict any damage necessary to win, and will make no strategic errors. The strategist therefore designs a defense against the most potentially damaging offense, even if it is unlikely to occur.

More's utopia appears to have been created on a minimax principle in that the societal design can be understood as a possible solution to a *game against nature* in which the human contestants have at their disposal only certain weapons—their technology. "Game against nature" is a phrase that strategists use to describe a contest in which an individual or a group seeks a method to accomplish some end despite the actions of an idealized opponent: nature. The characteristics of the physical environment, particularly those that are variable—average yearly rainfall, temperature fluctuation, weather—are the weapons that nature can use to prevent its human opponent from succeeding.

Consider the following problem. A group of people lives in a small agricultural community. The community has no motorized farm equipment, no modern insecticides, and no source of food outside its own production. To ensure having enough food to guard against the effects of drought, the members of the community must grow enough food to carry them through the next two growing seasons. Given this large a food reserve, they can survive one season of drought and still have enough food to sustain themselves until the next season's crop is harvested. Two consecutive dry seasons will destroy them. Food cannot be stored for more than two seasons ahead, for their methods of food preservation are primitive and supplies spoil after this length of time.

The community can make itself more secure by building a dam and an irrigation system so that water can be stored and used in a dry season. The problem is that the members of the community must use all their energies to grow enough food to build up adequate supplies; if they divert effort to the construction of the irrigation system, they will not be able to produce enough food to protect themselves against a dry season. Even with all of the community's available labor force working on the irrigation project, it would take two growing seasons to complete the task.

The community is engaged in a game against nature. If its members gamble that the next two growing seasons will be rainy, they can afford to devote to construction the time usually allocated to farming for one season and then build up their food supplies during the following season. If they are able to repeat this process twice they will have completed the irrigation system and be less dependent on the vagaries of the weather. If, however, they gamble and find that the second growing season is dry, they will be unable to bring in a crop, will have exhausted their food supplies, and will starve. The problem for the community is to devise a strategy by which they can construct the irrigation system and not have to gamble on being destroyed or, at least, to find a strategy that reduces the likelihood of being destroyed.

The game for which More sought a solution was one in which the goal was to make a hostile physical environment (one with relatively poor soil and climate for agriculture) provide enough food for a population that operated at a low level of agricultural technology. More's problem was to devise a social system in which men who functioned at a certain level of agricultural technology could be virtually ensured of having the minimal commodities necessary to subsist and of never starving to death. The emphasis on the guarantee of a minimal outcome, prevention of starvation, distinguishes More's society. Given a society in which agriculture is conducted on a relatively primitive level (and in which, compared to modern standards, yield per acre and yield per man hour of labor are exceedingly low), how much of the energies of the work force must be devoted to agriculture, and in what manner should the society be organized to ensure survival for its members?

utopia

by Sir Thomas More

. . . There be in the island fifty-four large and fair cities, or shire towns, agreeing all together in one tongue, in like manners, institutions and laws. They be all set and situate alike, and in all points fashioned alike, as far forth as the place or plot suffereth.

Of these cities they that be nighest together be twenty-four miles asunder. Again there is none of them distant from the next above one day's journey afoot. There come yearly to Amaurote out of every city three old men wise and well experienced, there to entreat and debate, of the common matters of the land. For this city (because it standeth just in the midst of the island, and is therefore most meet for the ambassadors of all parts of the realm) is taken for the chief and head city. The precincts and bounds of the shires be so commodiously appointed out, and set forth for the cities, that never a one of them all hath of any side less than twenty miles of ground, and of some side also much more, as of that part where the cities be of farther distance asunder. None of the cities desire to enlarge the bounds and limits of their shires. For they count themselves rather the good husbands than the owners of their lands. They have in the country in all parts of the shire houses or farms builded, well appointed and furnished with all sorts of instruments and tools belonging to husbandry. These houses be inhabited of the citizens, which come thither to dwell by course. No household or farm in the country hath fewer than forty persons, men and women, besides two bondmen, which be all under the rule and order of the good man, and the good wife of the house, being both very sage and discreet persons. And every thirty farms or families have one head ruler, which is called a philarch, being as it were a head bailiff. Out of every one of these families or farms cometh every year into the city twenty persons which have continued two years before in the country. In their place so many fresh be sent thither out of the city, which of them that have been there a year already, and be therefore expert and cunning in husbandry, shall be instructed and taught. And they the next year shall teach other. This order is used for fear that either scarceness of victuals, or some other like incommodity should chance, through lack of knowledge, if they should be altogether new, and fresh, and unexpert in husbandry. This manner and fashion of yearly changing and renewing the occupiers of husbandry, though it be solemn and customably used, to the intent that no man shall be constrained against his will to continue long in that hard and sharp kind of life, yet many of them have such a pleasure and delight in husbandry, that they obtain a longer space of years. These husbandmen plough and till the ground, and breed up cattle, and make ready wood, which they carry to the city either by land, or water, as they may most conveniently. They bring up a great multitude of poultry, and that by a marvellous policy. For the hens do not sit upon the eggs: but by keeping them in a certain equal heat they bring life into them, and hatch them. The chickens, as soon as they be come out of the shell, follow men and women instead of the hens. They bring up very few horses: nor none, but very fierce ones: and for none other use or purpose, but only to excercise their youth in riding and feats of arms. For oxen be put to all the labour of ploughing and drawing. Which they grant to be not so good as horses at a sudden brunt, and (as we say) at a dead lift, but yet they hold opinion that they will abide and suffer much more labour and pain than horses will. And they think that they be not in danger and subject unto so many diseases, and that they be kept and maintained with much less cost and charge: and finally that they be good for meat, when they be past labour. They sow corn only for bread. For their drink is either wine made of grapes, or else of apples, or pears, or else it is clean water. And many times mead made of honey or liquorice sodden in water, for thereof they have great store. And though they know certainly (for they know it perfectly indeed) how much victuals the city with the whole country or shire round above it doth spend: yet they sow much more corn, and breed up much more cattle, than serveth for their own use, and the overplus they part among their borderers. Whatsoever necessary things be lacking in the country, all such stuff they fetch out of the city: where without any exchange they easily obtain it of the magistrates of the city. For every month many of them go into the city on the holy day. When their harvest day draweth near and is at hand, then the philarchs, which be the head officers and bailiffs of husbandry, send word to the magistrates of the city what number of harvest men is needful to be sent to them out of the city. The which company of harvest men being there ready at the day appointed, almost in one fair day despatcheth all the harvest work. . . .

Every thirty families or farms, choose them yearly an officer, which in their old language is called the syphogrant, and by a newer name, the philarch. Every ten syphogrants, with all their 300 families be under an officer which was once called the tranibore, now the chief philarch. Moreover as concerning the election of the prince, all the syphogrants, which be in number 200, first be sworn to choose him whom they think most meet and expedient. Then by a secret election, they name prince, one of those four whom the people before named unto them. For out of the four quarters of the city there be four chosen, out of every quarter one, to stand for the election: which be put up to the council. The prince's office continueth all his lifetime, unless he be deposed or put down for suspicion of tyranny. They choose the tranibores yearly, but lightly they change them not. All the other offices be but for one year. The tranibores every third day, and sometimes, if need be, oftener come into the council house with the prince. Their council is concerning the commonwealth. If there be any controversies among the commoners, which be very few, they despatch and end them by-and-by. They take ever two syphogrants to them in counsel, and every day a new couple. And it is provided that nothing touching the commonwealth shall be confirmed and ratified unless it have been reasoned of and debated three days in the council, before it be decreed. It is death to have any consultation for the commonwealth out of the council, or the place of the common election. This statute, they say, was made to the intent that the prince and tranibores might not easily conspire together to oppress the people by tyranny, and to change the state of the weal public. Therefore matters of great weight and importance be brought to the election house of the syphogrants, which open the matter to their families. And afterward, when they have consulted among themselves, they show their device to the council. Sometimes the matter is brought before the council of the whole island. Furthermore this custom also the council useth, to dispute or reason of no matter the same day that it is first proposed or put forth, but to defer it to the next sitting of the council. Because that no man when he hath rashly there spoken that cometh first to his tongue's end, shall then afterward rather study for reasons wherewith to defend and confirm his first foolish sentence, than for the commodity of the commonwealth: as one rather willing the harm or hindrance of the weal public than any loss or diminution of his own existimation. And as one that would not for shame (which is a very foolish shame) be counted anything overseen in the matter at the first. Who at the first ought to have spoken rather wisely, than hastily, or rashly. . . .

Husbandry is a science common to them all in general, both men and women, wherein they be all expert and cunning. In this they be all instruct even from their youth: partly in schools with traditions and precepts, and partly in the country nigh the city, brought up as it were in playing not only beholding the use of it, but by occasion of exercising their bodies practising it also. Besides husbandry, which (as I said) is common to them all, every one of them learneth one or other several and particular science, as his own proper craft. That is most commonly either clothworking in wool or flax, or masonry, or the smith's craft, or the carpenter's science. For there is none other occupation that any number to speak of doth use there. For their garments, which throughout all the island be of one fashion (saving that there is a difference between the man's garment and the woman's, between the married and the unmarried) and this one continueth for evermore unchanged, seemly and comely to the eye, no let to the moving and wielding of the body, also fit both for winter and summer: as for these garments (I say) every family maketh their own. But of the other foresaid crafts every man learneth one. And not only the men, but also the women. But the women, as the weaker sort, be put to the easier crafts: they work wool and flax. The other more laboursome sciences be committed to the men. For the most part every man is brought up in his father's craft. For most commonly they be naturally thereto bent and inclined. But if a man's mind stand to any other, he is by adoption put into a family of that occupation, which he doth most fantasy. Whom not only his father, but also the magistrates do diligently look to, that he be put to a discreet and an honest householder. Yea, and if any person, when he hath learned one craft, be desirous to learn also another, he is likewise suffered and permitted.

When he hath learned both, he occupieth whether he will: unless the city have more need of the one, than of the other. The chief and almost the only office of the syphogrants is, to see and take heed that no man sit idle: but that every one apply his own craft with earnest diligence. And yet for all that, not to be wearied from early in the morning, to late in the evening, with continual work, like labouring and toiling beasts.

For this is worse than the miserable and wretched condition of bondmen. Which nevertheless is almost everywhere the life of workmen and artificers, saving in Utopia. For they dividing the day and the night into twenty-four just hours, appoint and assign only six of those hours to work; three before noon, upon the which they go straight to dinner: and after dinner, when they have rested two hours, then they work three and upon that they go to supper. About eight of the clock in the evening (counting one of the clock at the first hour after noon) they go to bed: eight hours they give to sleep. All the void time, that is between the hours of work, sleep, and meat, that they be suffered to bestow, every man as he liketh best himself. Not to the intent that they should misspend this time in riot or slothfulness: but being then licensed from the labour of their own occupations, to bestow the time well and thriftly upon some other good science, as shall please them. For it is a solemn custom there, to have lectures daily early in the morning, where to be present they only be constrained that be namely chosen and appointed to learning. Howbeit a great multitude of every sort of people, both men and women, go to hear lectures, some one and some another, as every man's nature is inclined.

Yet, this notwithstanding, if any man had rather bestow this time upon his own occupation (as it chanceth in many, whose minds rise not in the contemplation of any science liberal) he is not letted, nor prohibited, but is also praised and commended, as profitable to the commonwealth. After supper they bestow one hour in play: in summer in their gardens: in winter in their common halls: where they dine and sup. There they exercise themselves in music, or else in honest and wholesome communication. Diceplay, and such other foolish and pernicious games they know not. But they use two games not much unlike the chess. The one is the battle of numbers, wherein one number stealeth away another. The other is wherein vices fight with virtues, as it were in battle array, or a set field. In the which game is very properly showed, both the strife and discord that vices have among themselves, and again their unity and concord against virtues. And also what vices be repugnant to what virtues: with what power and strength they assail them openly: by what wiles and subtlety they assault them secretly: with what help and aid the virtues resist and overcome the puissance of the vices: by what craft they frustrate their purposes: and finally by what sleight or means the one getteth the victory. But here lest you be deceived, one thing you must look more narrowly upon. For seeing they bestow but six hours in work, perchance you may think that the lack of some necessary things hereof may ensue. But this is nothing so. For that small time is not only enough but also too much for the store and abundance of all things that be requisite, either for the necessity, or commodity of life. The which thing you also shall perceive, if you weigh and consider with yourselves how great a part of the people in other countries liveth idle. First almost all women, which be the half of the whole number: or else if the women be anywhere occupied, there most commonly in their stead the men be idle. Besides this how great, and how idle a company is there of priests, and religious men, as they call them? put thereto all rich men, especially all landed men, which commonly be called gentlemen, and noblemen. Take into this number also their servants: I mean all that flock of stout bragging rush bucklers. Join to them also sturdy and valiant beggars, cloaking their idle life under the colour of some disease or sickness. And truly you shall find them much fewer than you thought, by whose labour all these things be gotten that men use and live by. Now consider with yourself, of these few that do work, how few be occupied, in necessary works. For where money beareth all the swing, there many vain and superfluous occupations must needs be used, to serve only for riotous superfluity and unhonest pleasure. For the same multitude that now is occupied in work, if they were divided into so few occupations as the necessary use of nature requireth; in so great plenty of things as then of necessity would ensue, doubtless the prices would be too little for the artificers to maintain their livings. But if all these, that be now busied about unprofitable occupations, with all the whole flock of them that live idly and slothfully, which consume and waste every one of them more of these things that come by other men's labour, than two of the workmen themselves do: if all these (I say) were set to profitable occupations, you easily perceive how little time would be enough, yea and too much to store us with all things that may be requisite either for necessity, or for commodity, yea or for pleasure, so that the same pleasure be true and natural. And this in Utopia the thing itself maketh manifest and plain. For there in all the city, with the whole country, or shire adjoining to it scarcely 500 persons of all the whole number of men and women, that be neither too old, nor too weak to work, be licensed from labour. Among them be the syphogrants which (though they be by the laws exempt and privileged from labour) yet they exempt not themselves: to the intent they may the rather by their example provoke other to work. The same vacation from labour do they also enjoy, to whom the people persuaded by the commendation of the priests, and secret election of the syphogrants, have given a perpetual license from labour to learning. But if any one of them prove not according to the expectation and hope of him conceived, he is forthwith plucked back to the company of artificers. And contrariwise, often it chanceth that a handicraftsman doth so earnestly bestow his vacant and spare hours in learning, and through diligence so profit therein, that he is taken from his handy occupation, and promoted to the company of the learned. Out of this order of the learned be chosen ambassadors, priests, tranibores, and finally the prince himself. Whom they in their old tongue call Barzanes, and by a newer name, Adamus. The residue of the people being neither idle nor occupied about unprofitable exercises, it may be easily judged in how few hours how much good work by them may be done towards those things that I have spoken of. This commodity they have also above other, that in the most part of necessary occupations they need not so much work, as other nations do. For first of all the building or repairing of houses asketh everywhere so many men's continual labour, because that the unth[r]ifty heir suffereth the houses that his father builded in continuance of time to fall in decay. So that which he might have upholden with little cost, his successor is constrained to build it again anew, to his great charge. Yea many times also the house that stood one man in much money, another is of so nice and so delicate a mind, that he setteth nothing by it. And it being neglected, and therefore shortly falling into ruin, he buildeth up another is another place with no less cost and charge. But among the Utopians, where all things be set in a good order, and the commonwealth in a good stay, it very seldom chanceth, that they choose a new plot to build an house upon. And they do not only find speedy and quick remedies for present faults: but also prevent them that be like to fall. And by this means their houses continue and last very long with little labour and small reparations: insomuch that this kind of workmen sometimes have almost nothing to do. But that they be commanded to hew timber at home, and to square and trim up stones, to the intent that if any work chance, it may the speedier rise. Now, sir, in their apparel, mark (I pray you) how few workmen they need. First of all, whilst they be at work, they be covered homely with leather or skins, that will last seven years. When they go forth abroad they cast upon them a cloak, which hideth the other homely apparel. These cloaks throughout the whole island be all of one colour, and that is the natural colour of the wool. They therefore do not only spend much less woollen cloth than is spent in other countries, but also the same standeth them in much less cost. But linen cloth is made with less labour, and is therefore had more in use. But in linen cloth only whiteness, in woollen only cleanliness is regarded. As for the smallness or fineness of the thread, that is nothing passed for. And this is the cause wherefore in other places four or five cloth gowns of divers colours, and as many silk coats be not enough for one man. Yea and if he be of the delicate and nice sort ten be too few: whereas there one garment will serve a man most commonly two years. For why should he desire more? Seeing if he had them, he should not be the better wrapped or covered from cold, neither in his apparel any whit the comelier. Wherefore, seeing they be all exercised in profitable occupations, and that few artificers in the same crafts be sufficient, this is the cause that plenty of all things being among them, they do sometimes bring forth an innumerable company of people to amend the highways, if any be broken. Many times also, when they have no such work to be occupied about, an open proclamation is made, that they shall bestow fewer hours in work. For the magistrates do not exercise their citizens against their wills in unneedful labours. For why? in the institution of that weal public, this end is only and chiefly pretended and minded, that what time may possibly be spared from the necessary occupations and affairs of the commonwealth, all that the citizens should withdraw from the bodily service to the free liberty of the mind, and garnishing of the same. For herein they suppose the felicity of this life to consist. . . .

But now will I declare how the citizens use themselves one towards another: what familiar occupying and entertainment there is among the people, and what fashion they use in distributing every thing. First the city consisteth of families most commonly be made of kindreds. For the women, when they be married at a lawful age, they go into their husbands' houses. But the male children with all the whole male offspring continue still in their own family and be governed of the eldest and ancientest father, unless he dote for age: for then the next to him in age is put in his room. But to the intent the prescript number of the citizens should neither decrease, nor above measure increase, it is ordained that no family which in every city be six thousand in the whole, besides them of the country, shall at once have fewer children of the age of fourteen years of thereabout than ten or more than sixteen, for of children under this age no number can be appointed. This measure or number is easily observed and kept, by putting them that in fuller families be above the number into families of smaller increase. But if chance be that in the whole city the store increase above the just number, therewith they fill up the lack of other cities. But if so be that the multitude throughout the whole island pass and exceed the due number, then they choose out of every city certain citizens, and build up a town under their own laws in the next land where the inhabitants have much waste and unocccupied ground, receiving also of the inhabitants to them, if they will join and dwell with them. They thus joining and dwelling together do easily agree in one fashion of living, and that to the great wealth of both the peoples. For they so bring the matter about by their laws, that the ground which before was neither good nor profitable for the one nor for the other, is now sufficient and fruitful enough for them both. But if the inhabitants of that land will not dwell with them to be ordered by their laws, then they drive them out of those bounds which they have limited, and appointed out for themselves. And if they resist and rebel, then they make war against them. For they count this the most just cause of war, when any people holdeth a piece of ground void and vacant, to no good nor profitable use, keeping other from the use and possession of it, which notwithstanding by the law of nature ought thereof to be nourished and relieved. If any chance do so much diminish the number of any of their cities, that it cannot be filled up again, without the diminishing of the just number of the other cities (which they say chanced but twice since the beginning of the land through a great pestilent plague) then they make up the number with citizens fetched out of their own foreign towns, for they had rather suffer their foreign towns to decay and perish, than any city of their own island to be diminished. But now again to the conversation of the citizens among themselves. The eldest (as I said) ruleth the family. The wives be ministers to their husbands, the children to their parents, and to be short the younger to their elders. Every city is divided into four equal parts. In the midst of every quarter there is a market place of all manner of things. Thither the works of every family be brought into certain houses. And every kind of thing is laid up in several barns or storehouses. From hence the father of every family, or every householder fetcheth whatsoever he and his have need of, and carrieth it away with him without money, without exchange, without any gage, or pledge. For why should any thing be denied unto him? Seeing there is abundance of all things, and that it is not to be feared, lest any man will ask more than he needeth. For why should it be thought that that man would ask more than enough which is sure never to lack? Certainly in all kinds of living creatures either fear of lack doth cause covetousness and ravin, or in man only pride, which counteth it a glorious thing to pass and excel other in the superfluous and vain ostentation of things. The which kind of vice among the Utopians can have no place. Next to the market places that I spake of, stand meat markets: whither be brought not only all sorts of herbs, and the fruits of trees, with bread, but also fish, and all manner of four-footed beasts, and wild fowl that be man's meat. But first the filthiness and ordure thereof is clean washed away in the running river without the city in places appointed meet for the same purpose. From thence the beasts [be] brought in killed, and clean washed by the hands of their bondmen. For they permit not their free citizens to accustom themselves to the killing of beasts, through the use whereof they think that clemency, the gentlest affection of our nature, doth by little and little decay and perish. Neither they suffer any thing that is filthy, loathsome, or uncleanly, to be brought into the city, lest the air by the stench thereof infected and corrupt, should cause pestilent diseases. Moreover every street hath certain great large halls set in equal distance one from another, every one known by a several name. In these halls dwell the syphogrants. And to every one of the same halls be appointed thirty families, on either side fifteen. The stewards of every hall at a certain hour come into the meat markets, where they receive meat according to the number of their halls. But first and chiefly of all, respect is had to the sick, that be cured in the hospitals. For in the circuit of the city, a little without the walls, they have four hospitals, so big, so wide, so ample, and so large, that they may seem four little towns, which were devised of that bigness partly to the intent the sick, be they never so many in number, should not lie too throng or strait, and therefore uneasily and incommodiously: and partly that they which were taken and holden with contagious diseases, such as be wont by infection to creep from one to another, might be laid apart far from the company of the residue. These hospitals be so well appointed, and with all things necessary to health so furnished, and moreover so diligent attendance through the continual presence of cunning physicians is given, that though no man be sent thither against his will, yet notwithstanding there is no sick person in all the city, that had not rather lie there than at home in his own house. When the steward of the sick hath received such meats as the physicians have prescribed, then the best is equally divided among the halls, according to the company of every one, saving that there is had a respect to the prince, the bishop, the tranibores, and to ambassadors and all strangers, if there be any, which be very few and seldom. But they also when they be there, have certain houses appointed and prepared for them. To these halls at the set hours of dinner and supper cometh all the whole syphogranty or ward, warned by the noise of a brazen trumpet: except such as be sick in the hospitals, or else in their own houses. Howbeit no man is prohibited or forbid, after the halls be served, to fetch home meat out of the market to his own house, for they know that no man will do it without a cause reasonable. For though no man be prohibited to dine at home, yet no man doth it willingly: because it is counted a point of small honesty. And also it were a folly to take the pain to dress a bad dinner at home, when they may be welcome to good and fine fare so nigh hand at the hall.

. . . Howbeit, a wise and indifferent esteemer of things will not greatly marvel perchance, seeing all their other laws and customs do so much differ from ours, if the use also of gold and silver among them be applied, rather to their own fashions than to ours. I mean in that they occupy not money themselves, but keep it for that chance, which as it may happen, so it may be that it shall never come to pass. In the meantime gold and silver, whereof money is made, they do so use, as none of them doth more esteem it, than the very nature of the thing deserveth. And then who doth not plainly see how far it is under iron: as without the which men can no better live than without fire and water. Whereas to gold and silver nature hath given no use, that we may not well lack: if that the folly of men had not set it in higher estimation for the rareness sake. But of the contrary part, nature as a most tender and loving mother, hath placed the best and most necessary things open abroad: as the air, the water and the earth itself. And hath removed and hid farthest from us vain and unprofitable things. Therefore if these metals among them should be fast locked up in some tower, it might be suspected, that the prince and the council (as the people is ever foolishly imagining) intended by some subtilty to deceive the commons, and to take same profit of it to themselves. Furthermore if they should make thereof plate and such other finely and cunningly wrought stuff: if at any time they should have occasion to break it, and melt it again, and therewith to pay their soldiers' wages, they see and perceive very well, that men would be loath to part from those things, that they once began to have pleasure and delight in. To remedy all this they have found out a means, which, as it is agreeable to all their other laws and customs, so it is from ours, where gold is so much set by and so diligently kept, very far discrepant and repugnant: and therefore incredible, but only to them that be wise. For whereas they eat and drink in earthen and glass vessels, which indeed be curiously and properly made, and yet be of very small value: of gold and silver they make commonly chamber pots, and other like vessels, that serve for most vile uses, not only in their common halls, but in every man's private house. Furthermore of the same metals they make great chains, with fetters, and gyves wherein they tie their bondmen. Finally whosoever for any offence be infamed, by their ears hang rings of gold, upon their fingers they wear rings of gold, and about their necks chains of gold, and in conclusion their heads be tied about with gold. Thus by all means that may be they procure to have gold and silver among them in reproach and infamy. And therefore these metals, which other nations do as grievously and sorrowfully forgo, as in a manner from their own lives: if they should altogether at once be taken from the Utopians, no man there would think that he had lost the worth of one farthing. They gather also pearls by the sea-side, and diamonds and carbuncles upon certain rocks, and yet they seek not for them: but by chance finding them they cut and polish them. And therewith they deck their young infants. Which like as in the first years of their childhood, they make much and be fond and proud of such ornaments, so when they be a little more grown in years and discretion, perceiving that none but children do wear such toys and trifles: they lay them away even of their own shamefacedness, without any bidding of their parents: even as our children, when they wax big, do cast away nuts, brooches, and puppets. Therefore these laws and customs, which be so far different from all other nations, how divers fantasies also and minds they do cause, did I never so plainly perceive, as in the ambassadors of the Anemolians.

These ambassadors came to Amaurote whilest I was there. And because they came to entreat of great and weighty matters, those three citizens apiece out of every city were come thither before them. But all the ambassadors of the next countries, which had been there before, and knew the fashions and manners of the Utopians, among whom they perceived no honour given to sumptuous and costly apparel, silks to be contemned, gold also to be infamed and reproachful, were wont to come thither in very homely and simple apparel. But the Anemolians, because they dwell far thence and had very little acquaintance with them, hearing that they were all apparelled alike, and that very rudely and homely: thinking them not to have the things which they did not wear: being therefore more proud, than wise: determined in the gorgeousness of their apparel to represent very gods, and with the bright shining and glistering of their gay clothing to dazzle the eyes of the silly poor Utopians. So there came in three ambassadors with one hundred servants all apparelled in changeable colours: the most of them in silks: the ambassadors themselves (for at home in their own country they were noblemen) in cloth of gold, with great chains of gold, with gold hanging at their ears, with gold rings upon their fingers, with brooches and aglets of gold upon their caps, which glistered full of pearls and precious stones: to be short, trimmed and adorned with all those things, which among the Utopians were either the punishment of bondmen, or the reproach of infamed persons, or else trifles for young children to play withal. Therefore it would have done a man good at his heart to have seen how proudly they displayed their peacock's feathers, how much they made of their painted sheaths, and how loftily they set forth and advanced themselves, when they compared their gallant apparel with the poor raiment of the Utopians. For all the people were swarmed forth into the streets. And on the other side it was no less pleasure to consider how much they were deceived, and how far they missed of their purpose, being contrariwise taken, than they thought they should have been. For to the eyes of all the Utopians, except very few, which had been in other countries for some reasonable cause, all that gorgeousness of apparel seemed shameful and reproachful. Insomuch that they most reverently saluted the vilest and most abject of them for lords: passing over the ambassadors themselves without any honour: judging them by their wearing of golden chains to be bondmen. Yea you should have seen children also, that had cast away their pearls and precious stones, when they saw the like sticking upon the ambassador's caps, dig and push their mothers under the sides, saying thus to them. Look, mother, how great a lubber doth yet wear pearls and precious stones, as though he were a little child still. But the mother, yea, and that also in good earnest: peace, son, saith she: I think he be some of the ambassador's fools. Some found fault at their golden chains, as to no use nor purpose, being so small and weak, that a bondman might easily break them, and again so wide and large, that when it pleased him, he might cast them off, and run away at liberty whither he would. But when the ambassadors had been there a day or two and saw so great abundance of gold so lightly esteemed, yea in no less reproach, than it was with them in honour: and besides that more gold in the chains and gyves of one fugitive bondman, than all the costly ornaments of them three was worth: they began to abate their courage, and for very shame laid away all that gorgeous array, whereof they were so proud. And specially when they had talked familiarly with the Utopians, and had learned all their fashions and opinions.

For they marvel that any men be so foolish, as to have delight and pleasure in the glistering of a little trifling stone, which may behold any of the stars, or else the sun itself. Or that any man is so mad, as to count himself the nobler for the smaller or finer thread of wool, which selfsame wool (be it now in never so fine a spun thread) did once a sheep wear: and yet was she all that time no other thing than a sheep. They marvel also that gold, which of the own nature is a thing so unprofitable, is now among all people in so high estimation, that man himself, by whom, yea and for the use of whom it is so much set by, is in much less estimation than the gold itself. Insomuch that a lumpish blockheaded churl, and which hath no more wit than an ass, yea and as full of worthlessness and foolishness, shall have nevertheless many wise and good men in subjection and bondage, only for this, because he hath a great heap of gold. Which if it should be taken from him by any fortune, or by some subtle wile of the law (which no less than fortune doth raise up the low and pluck down the high), and be given to the most vile slave and abject drudge of all his household, then shortly after he shall go into the service of his servant, as an augmentation or an overplus beside his money. But they much more marvel at and detest the madness of them which to those rich men, in whose debt and danger they be not, do give almost divine honours, for none other consideration, but because they be rich: and yet knowing them to be such niggardly penny-fathers, that they be sure as long as they live, not the worth of one farthing of that heap of gold shall come to them.

Now I have declared and described unto you, as truly as I could the form and order of that commonwealth, which verily in my judgment is not only the best, but also that which alone of good right may claim and take upon it the name of a commonwealth or public weal. For in other places they speak still of the commonwealth, but every man procureth his own private wealth. Here where nothing is private, the common affairs be earnestly looked upon. And truly on both parts they have good cause so to do as they do. For in other countries who knoweth not that he shall starve for hunger, unless he make some several provision for himself, though the commonwealth flourish never so much in riches? And therefore he is compelled even of very necessity to have regard to himself, rather than to the people, that is to say, to other. Contrariwise, there where all things be common to every man, it is not to be doubted that any man shall lack anything necessary for his private uses, so that the common storehouses and barns be sufficiently stored. For there nothing is distributed after a niggish sort, neither there is any poor man or beggar. And though no man have anything, yet every man is rich. For what can be more rich, than to live joyfully and merrily, without all grief and pensiveness; not caring for his own living, nor vexed or troubled with his wife's importunate complaints, not dreading poverty to his son, nor sorrowing for his daughter's dowry? Yea they take no care at all for the living and wealth of themselves and all theirs, of their wives, their children, their nephews, their children's children, and all the succession that ever shall follow in their posterity. And yet besides this there is no less provision for them that were once labourers and be now weak and impotent, than for them that do now labour and take pain. Here now would I see, if any man dare be so bold as to compare with this equity, the justice of other nations; among whom, I forsake God, if I can find any sign or token of equity and justice. For what justice is this, that a rich goldsmith, or an usurer, or to be short, any of them which either do nothing at all, or else that which they do is such that it is not very necessary to the commonwealth, should have a pleasant and a wealthy living, either by idleness, or by unnecessary business; when in the meantime poor labourers, carters, ironsmiths, carpenters and ploughmen, by so great and continual toil, as drawing and bearing beasts be scant able to sustain, and again so necessary toil, that without it no commonwealth were able to continue and endure one year, do yet get so hard and poor a living, and live so wretched and miserable a life, that the state and condition of the labouring beasts may seem much better and wealthier? For they be not put to so continual labour, nor their living is not much worse, yea to them much pleasanter, taking no thought in the mean season for the time to come. But these silly poor wretches be presently tormented with barren and unfruitful labour. And the remembrance of their poor indigent and beggarly old age killeth them up. For their daily wages is so little, that it will not suffice for the same day, much less it yieldeth any overplus, that may daily be laid up for the relief of old age. Is not this an unjust and an unkind public weal, which giveth great fees and rewards to gentlemen, as they call them, and to goldsmiths, and to such other, which be either idle persons, or else only flatterers, and devisers of vain pleasures; and of the contrary part maketh no gentle provision for poor ploughmen, colliers, labourers, carters, ironsmiths, and carpenters: without whom no commonwealth can continue. But when it hath abused the labours of their lusty and flowering age, at the last when they be oppressed with old age and sickness, being needy, poor, and indigent of all things, then forgetting their so many painful watchings, not remembering their so many and so great benefits, recompenseth and ac-quitteth them most unkindly with miserable death. And yet besides this the rich men not only by private fraud, but also by common laws, do every day pluck and snatch away from the poor some part of their daily living. So whereas it seemed before unjust to recompense with unkindness their pains that have been beneficial to the public weal, now they have to this their wrong and unjust dealing (which is yet a much worse point) given the name of justice, yea and that by force of a law. Therefore when I consider and weigh in my mind all these commonwealths, which nowa-days anywhere do flourish, so God help me, I can perceive nothing but a certain conspiracy of rich men procuring their own commodities under the name and title of the commonwealth. They invent and devise all means and crafts, first how to keep safely, without fear of losing, that they have unjustly gathered together, and next how to hire and abuse the work and labour of the poor for as little money as may be. These devices, when the rich men have decreed to be kept and observed for the common-wealth's sake, that is to say for the wealth also of the poor people, then they be made laws. But these most wicked and vicious men, when they have by their insatiable covetousness divided among themselves all those things, which would have sufficed all men, yet how far be they from the wealth and felicity of the Utopian commonwealth? Out of the which, in that all the desire of money with the use thereof is utterly secluded and banished, how great a heap of cares is cut away! How great an occasion of wickedness and mischief is plucked up by the roots! For who knoweth not, that fraud, theft, ravine, brawling, quarreling, brabling, strife, chiding, contention, murder, treason, poisoning, which by daily punishments are rather revenged than refrained, do die when money dieth? And also that fear, grief, care, labours and watchings do perish even the very same moment that money perisheth? Yea poverty itself, which only seemed to lack money, if money were gone, it also would decrease and vanish away. And that you may perceive this more plainly, consider with yourselves some barren and unfruitful year, wherein many thousands of people have starved for hunger. I dare be bold to say, that in the end of that penury so much corn or grain might have been found in the rich men's barns, if they had been searched, as being divided among them whom famine and pestilence have killed, no man at all should have felt that plague and penury. So easily might men get their living, if that same worthy princess, lady money, did not alone stop up the way between us and our living, which a God's name was very excellently devised and invented, that by her the way thereto should be opened. I am sure the rich men perceive this, nor they be not ignorant how much better it were to lack no necessary thing, than to abound with overmuch superfluity; to be rid out of innumerable cares and troubles, than to be besieged with great riches. And I doubt not that either the respect of every man's private commodity, or else the authority of our saviour Christ (which for his great wisdom could not but know what were best, and for his inestimable goodness could not but counsel to that which he knew to be best) would have brought all the world long ago into the laws of this weal public, if it were not that one only beast, the princess and mother of all mischief, pride, doth withstand and let it. She measureth not wealth and prosperity by her own commodities, but by the miseries and incommodities of other: she would not by her good will be made a goddess, if there were no wretches left, whom she might be lady over to mock and scorn; over whose miseries her felicity might shine, whose poverty she might vex, torment and increase by gorgeously setting forth her riches. This hell-hound creepeth into men's hearts, and plucketh them back from entering the right path of life, and is so deeply rooted in men's breasts, that she cannot be plucked out. This form and fashion of a weal public, which I would gladly wish unto all nations, I am glad yet that it hath chanced to the Utopians, which have followed those institutions of life, whereby they have laid such foundations of their commonwealth, as shall continue and last not only wealthily, but also, as far as man's wit may judge and conjecture, shall endure for ever. For seeing the chief causes of ambition and sedition with other vices be plucked up by the roots and abandoned at home, there can be no jeopardy of domestical dissension, which alone hath cast under foot and brought to nought the well fortified and strongly-defenced wealth and riches of many cities. But forasmuch as perfect concord remaineth, and wholesome laws be executed at home the envy of all foreign princes be not able to shake or move the empire, though they have many times long ago gone about to do it, being evermore driven back.

a utopia
under conditions
of affluence

Edward Bellamy's *Looking Backward,* written in 1888, describes a post-Industrial-Revolution world system of the year 2000. Bellamy's society is based on forms of industrial, economic, and social organization that differ substantially from the structure of any real modern society. When coupled with the production power of an industrialized economy, Bellamy's radical form of social organization results in a society in which the population is truly affluent.

Although present-day American society is frequently called "affluent," it is the *average* level of wealth in the country that is being acknowledged. Variations in the life styles of members of the society are so great that to use the term "affluent society" in any but a statistical sense is absurd. For example, in 1965 the average size of a household in the United States was between three and four persons. If the part of the country's gross national product devoted to personal consumption had been divided equally among all households, the average buying power of each household would have been about $8,000.[1] This figure hardly describes the economic condition of the poor in American society. In 1969 President Nixon proposed a new welfare system for the United States. Under this system, a family of four would be guaranteed a minimum yearly income of $1,600. While it might be reasonable to assert that the United States as a society is affluent, it is certainly incorrect to assert that the population of the society is necessarily affluent.

Based on the present rate of population growth and a reasonable estimate of the United States' rate of economic development, the share for each household of the personal consumption portion of the gross national product will be approximately $28,000 (1965 dollars) in the year 2000, the year in which Bellamy's society is described.[2] What this means is that if in the year 2000 the part of the

[1]This calculation is based on figures reported in Herman Kahn and Anthony J. Wiener, *The Year 2000* (New York: The Macmillan Company, 1967), p. 168.

country's gross national product devoted to personal consumption were *divided equally* among all families in the society, each would have the buying power of a 1965 family with an income of $28,000. However, will an accurate description of the economic condition of large numbers of families in the country come from a statistic based on an equal division of the available gross national product? Given our present social arrangements, it will probably be no more appropriate to do this in the year 2000 than it is to do so today. Under the set of social arrangements outlined by Bellamy, this statistic would be appropriate.

The social system Bellamy creates incorporates the principles that an individual should not benefit from or be disadvantaged for his entire life by his ancestors, and that there should be equality in the contribution a man is expected to make to his society and equality in the share of its rewards that he receives. The first principle was intended to lead to rules that would eliminate the effects of two variables known to have pervasive influences on major aspects of an individual's life in all real societies: class origins and inherited abilities. Although much attention has recently focused on the effects of one's parents' socioeconomic status on a person's chances for success in American society, no serious question has ever been raised concerning the legitimacy of the social effects that follow from genetic factors. Certainly there is acceptance of the idea that a society has a responsibility to provide some minimum care for members who are born with severe disabilities and even some recognition that a man should not be discriminated against because of a physical deformity. Bellamy raises a question about the other end of the spectrum—that is, about the justification for the advantages that accrue to those whose unusual characteristics, genetically determined, are socially valuable. Is it any more reasonable to reward a man relatively well because he has the good fortune to have been born with high intelligence than it is to punish another who is born mentally deficient?

The second principle, equal contribution and equal return, focused attention on the relationship between an individual's abilities and his efforts, and was the basis for determining work load and payment. It is easy to understand why men who possess scarce and valuable abilities and are willing to use them have come to command greater shares of the products of their societies than those who possess less unusual and less valuable personal characteristics. If the norms of a society do not prevent a man from doing so, he will attempt to exchange his labor for the maximal return. If a job requires special abilities or skills that are rare in the population, the person who has these abilities or skills can refuse to accept a job unless he is paid more than he could get by filling another job that also requires special characteristics or a job that could be filled by most people. Bellamy attempts to design a society in which the norms do not permit this type of free labor-reward market. It is, of course, easy to design a society in which all individuals share equally in the goods and services that the society is able to provide. The difficult problem is to design one that does not appear certain to collapse.

---

[2]The projections of gross national product and population growth are from *ibid.*, p. 168.

Bellamy develops a conception of the relationship between ability and effort that is used to define "work." He then proceeds to elaborate the mechanisms whereby work loads can be equalized in the society. How is it possible to compare the work done by two men and devise a method of adjusting work load so that each will be satisfied to receive the same pay as the other, even though one is an administrator who sits at a desk for eight hours a day, makes decisions, and worries, and the other is a laborer who spends six hours a day digging ditches. This is one problem that Bellamy must solve if the society he creates is to have any chance of survival.

As a vehicle for presenting his ideas on social organization, Bellamy uses the device of moving an adult male from Boston in 1887 to the same city in 2000. Although the method Bellamy uses to accomplish movement is not as interesting as the methods used by writers of straight science fiction to accomplish the same end, it provides a satisfactory device for comparing Mr. West's 1887 American society to Dr. Leete's American Society of 2000.

The discussion of differences in social organization between the two societies begins with an account of the transformation of West's society into Leete's.

looking backward

by Edward Bellamy

"I am impatient to know by what contradiction of natural sequence the peace and prosperity which you now seem to enjoy could have been the outcome of an era like my own," [I said].

"Since you are in the humor to talk rather than to sleep" [replied my host], "as I certainly am, perhaps I cannot do better than to try to give you enough idea of our modern industrial system to dissipate at least the impression that there is any mystery about the process of its evolution. The Bostonians of your day had the reputation of being great askers of questions, and I am going to show my descent by asking you one to begin with. What should you name as the most prominent feature of the labor troubles of your day?"

"Why, the strikes, of course," I replied.

"Exactly. But what made the strikes so formidable?"

"The great labor organizations."

"And what was the motive of these great organizations?"

"The workmen claimed they had to organize to get their rights from the big corporations," I replied.

"That is just it," said Doctor Leete. "The organization of labor and the strikes were an effect, merely, of the concentration of capital in greater masses than had ever been known before. Before this concentration began, while as yet commerce and industry were conducted by innumerable petty concerns with small capital, instead of a small number of great concerns with vast capital, the individual workman was relatively important and independent in his relations to the employer. Moreover, when a little capital or a new idea was enough to start a man in business for himself, workingmen were constantly becoming employers and there was no hard and fast line between the two classes. Labor unions were needless then, and general strikes out of the question. But when the era of small concerns with small capital was succeeded by that of the great aggregations of capital, all this was changed. The individual laborer, who had been relatively important to the small employer, was reduced to insignificance and powerlessness over against the great corporatpon, while at the same time the way upward to the grade of employer was closed to him. Self-defense drove him to union with his fellows.

"The records of the period show that the outcry against the concentration of capital was furious. Men believed that it threatened society with a form of tyranny more abhorrent than it had ever endured. They believed that the great corporations were preparing for them the yoke of a baser servitude than had ever been imposed on the race, servitude not to men but to soulless machines incapable of any motive but insatiable greed. Looking back, we cannot wonder at their desperation, for certainly humanity was never confronted with a fate more sordid and hideous than would have been the era of corporate tyranny which they anticipated.

"Meanwhile, without being in the smallest degree checked by the clamor against it, the absorption of business by ever-larger monopolies continued. In the United States there was not, after the beginning of the last quarter of the century, any opportunity whatever for individual enterprise in any important field of industry, unless backed by a great capital. During the last decade of the century, such small businesses as still remained were fast-failing survivals of a past epoch, or mere parasites on the great corporations, or else existed in fields too small to attract the great capitalists. Small businesses, as far as they still remained, were reduced to the condition of rats and mice, living in holes and corners, and counting on evading notice for the enjoyment of existence. The railroads had gone on combining till a few great syndicates controlled every rail in the land. In manufactories, every important staple was controlled by a syndicate. These syndicates, pools, trusts, or whatever their name, fixed prices and crushed all competition except when combinations as vast as themselves arose. Then a struggle, resulting in a still greater consolidation, ensued. The great city bazaar crushed its country rivals with branch stores, and in the city itself absorbed its smaller rivals till the business of a whole quarter was concentrated under one roof, with a hundred former proprietors of shops serving as clerks. Having no business of his own to put his money in, the small capitalist, at the same time that he took service under the corporation, found no other investment for his money but its stocks and bonds, thus becoming doubly dependent upon it.

"The fact that the desperate popular opposition to the consolidation of business in a few powerful hands had no effect to check it proves that there must have been a strong economical reason for it. The small capitalists, with their innumerable petty concerns, had in fact yielded the field to the great aggregations of capital because they belonged to a day of small things and were totally incompetent to the demands of an age of steam and telegraphs and the gigantic scale of its enterprises. To restore the former order of things, even if possible, would have involved returning to the day of stagecoaches. Oppressive and intolerable as was the regime of the great consolidations of capital, even its victims, while they cursed it, were forced to admit the prodigious increase of efficiency which had been imparted to the national industries, the vast economies effected by concentration of management and unity of organization, and to confess that since the new system had taken the place of the old the wealth of the world had increased at a rate before undreamed of. To be sure this vast increase had gone chiefly to make the rich richer, increasing the gap between them and the poor; but the fact remained that, as a means merely of producing wealth, capital had been proved efficient in proportion to its consolidation. The restoration of the old system with the subdivision of capital, if it were possible, might indeed bring back a greater equality of conditons, with more individual dignity and freedom, but it would be at the price of general poverty and the arrest of material progress.

"Was there, then, no way of commanding the services of the mighty wealth-producing principle of consolidated capital without bowing down to a plutocracy like that of Carthage? As soon as men began to ask themselves these questions, they found the answer ready for them. The movement toward the conduct of business by larger and larger aggregations of capital, the tendency toward monopolies, which had been so desperately and vainly resisted, was recognized at last, in its true significance, as a process which only needed to complete its logical evolution to open a golden future to humanity.

"Early in the last century the evolution was completed by the final consolidation of the entire capital of the nation. The industry and commerce of the country, ceasing to be conducted by a set of irresponsible corporations and syndicates of private persons at their caprice and for their profit, were entrusted to a single syndicate representing the people, to be conducted in the common interest for the common profit. The nation, that is to say, organized as the one great business corporation in which all other corporations were absorbed; it became the one capitalist in place of all other capitalists, the sole employer, ·the final monopoly in which all previous and lesser monopolies were swallowed up, a monopoly in the profits and economies of which all citizens shared. The epoch of trusts had ended in The Great Trust. In a word, the people of the United States concluded to assume the conduct of their own business, just as one hundred-odd years before they had assumed the conduct of their own government, organizing now for industrial purposes on precisely the same grounds that they had then organized for political purposes. At last, strangely late in the world's history, the obvious fact was perceived that no business is so essentially the public business as the industry and commerce on which the people's livelihood depends, and that to entrust it to private persons to be managed for private profit is a folly similar in kind, though vastly greater in magnitude, to that of surrendering the functions of political government to kings and nobles to be conducted for their personal glorification."

"Such a stupendous change as you describe," said I, "did not, of course, take place without great bloodshed and terrible convulsions."

"On the contrary," replied Doctor Leete, "there was absolutely no violence. The change had been long foreseen. Public opinion had become fully ripe for it, and the whole mass of the people was behind it. There was no more possibility of opposing it by force than by argument. On the other hand the popular sentiment toward the great corporations and those identified with them had ceased to be one of bitterness, as they came to realize their necessity as a link, a transition phase, in the evolution of the true industrial system. The most violent foes of the great private monopolies were now forced to recognize how invaluable and indispensable had been their office in educating the people up to the point of assuming control of their own business. Fifty years before, the consolidation of the industries of the country under national control would have seemed a very daring experiment to the most sanguine. But by a series of object lessons, seen and studied by all men, the great corporations had taught the people an entirely new set of ideas on this subject. They had seen for many years syndicates handling revenues greater than those of states, and directing the labors of hundreds of thousands of men with an efficiency and economy unattainable in smaller operations. It had come to be recognized as an axiom that the larger the business the simpler the principles that can be applied to it; that, as the machine is truer than the hand, so the system, which in a great concern does the work of the master's eye in a small business, turns out more accurate results. Thus it came about that, thanks to the corporations themselves, when it was proposed that the nation should assume their functions, the suggestion implied nothing which seemed impracticable even to the timid. To be sure, it was a step beyond any yet taken, a broader generalization, but the very fact that the nation would be the sole corporation in the field would, it was seen, relieve the undertaking of many difficulties with which the partial monopolies had contended."

Doctor Leete ceased speaking, and I remained silent, endeavoring to form some general conception of the changes in the arrangements of society implied in the tremendous revolution which he had described.

Finally I said, "The idea of such an extension of the functions of government is, to say the least, rather overwhelming."

"Extension!" he repeated. "Where is the extension?"

"In my day," I replied, "it was considered that the proper functions of government, strictly speaking, were limited to keeping the peace and defending the people against the public enemy, that is, to the military and police powers."

"And, in heaven's name, who are the public enemies?" exclaimed Doctor Leete. "Are they France, England, Germany, or hunger, cold, and nakedness? In your day governments were accustomed, on the slightest international misunderstanding, to seize upon the bodies of citizens and deliver them over by hundreds of thousands to death and mutilation, wasting their treasures the while like water; and all this oftenenst for no imaginable profit to the victims. We have no wars now, and our governments no war powers, but in order to protect every citizen against hunger, cold, and nakedness, and provide for all his physical and mental needs, the function is assumed of directing his industry for a term of years. No, Mr. West, I am sure on reflection you will perceive that it was in your age, not in ours, that the extension of the functions of governments was extraordinary. Not even for the best ends would men now allow their governments such powers as were then used for the most maleficent."

"Leaving comparisons aside," I said, "the demagoguery and corruption of our public men would have been considered, in my day, insuperable objections to any assumption by government of the charge of the national industries. We should have thought that no arrangement could be worse than to entrust the politicians with control of the wealth-producing machinery of the country. Its material interests were quite too much the football of parties as it was."

"No doubt you were right," rejoined Doctor Leete, "but all that is changed now. We have no parties or politicians, and as for demagoguery and corruption, they are words having only an historical significance."

"Human nature itself must have changed very much," I said.

"Not at all," was Doctor Leete's reply, "but the conditions of human life have changed, and with them the motives of human action. The organization of society with you was such that officials were under a constant temptation to misuse their power for the private profit of themselves or others. Under such circumstances it seems almost strange that you dared entrust them with any of your affairs. Nowadays, on the contrary, society is so constituted that there is absolutely no way in which an official, however ill-disposed, could possibly make any profit for himself or any one else by a misuse of his power. Let him be as bad an official as you please, he cannot be a corrupt one. There is no motive to be. The social system no longer offers a premium on dishonesty. But these are matters which you can only understand as you come, with time, to know us better."

"But you have not yet told me how you have settled the labor problem. It is the problem of capital which we have been discussing," I said. "After the nation had assumed conduct of the mills, machinery, railroads, farms, mines, and capital in general of the country, the labor question still remained. In assuming the responsibilities of capital the nation had assumed the difficulties of the capitalist's position."

"The moment the nation assumed the responsibilities of capital those difficulties vanished," replied Doctor Leete. "The national organization of labor under one direction was the complete solution of what was, in your day and under your system, justly regarded as the insoluble labor problem. When the nation became the sole employer, all the citizens, by virtue of their citizenship, became employees, to be distributed according to the needs of industry."

"That is," I suggested, "you have simply applied the principle of universal military service, as it was understood in our day, to the labor question."

"Yes," said Doctor Leete, "that was something which followed as a matter of course as soon as the nation had become the sole capitalist. The people were already accustomed to the idea that the obligation of every citizen, not physically disabled, to contribute his military services to the defense of the nation was equal and absolute. That it was equally the duty of every citizen to contribute his quota of industrial or intellectual services to the maintenance of the nation was equally evident, though it was not until the nation became the employer of labor that citizens were able to render this sort of service with any pretense either of universality or equity. No organization of labor was possible when the employing power was divided among hundreds or thousands of individuals and corporations, between which concert of any kind was neither desired, nor indeed feasible. It constantly happened then that vast numbers who desired to labor could find no opportunity, and on the other hand, those who desired to evade a part or all of their debt could easily do so."

"Service, now, I suppose, is compulsory upon all," I suggested.

"It is rather a matter of course than of compulsion," replied Doctor Leete. "It is regarded as so absolutely natural and reasonable that the idea of its being compulsory has ceased to be thought of. He would be thought to be an incredibly contemptible person who should need compulsion in such a case. Nevertheless, to speak of service being compulsory would be a weak way to state its absolute inevitableness. Our entire social order is so wholly based upon and deduced from it that if it were conceivable that a man could escape it, he would be left with no possible way to provide for his existence. He would have excluded himself from the world, cut himself off from his kind, in a word, committed suicide."

"Is the term of service in this industrial army for life?"

"Oh, no; it both begins later and ends earlier than the average working period in your day. Your workshops were filled with children and old men, but we hold the period of youth sacred to education, and the period of maturity, when the physical forces begin to flag, equally sacred to ease and agreeable relaxation. The period of industrial service is twenty-four years, beginning at the close of the course of education at twenty-one and terminating at forty-five. After forty-five, while discharged from labor, the citizen still remains liable to special calls, in case of emergencies causing a sudden great increase in the demand for labor, till he reaches the age of fifty-five, but such calls are rarely, in fact almost never, made. The fifteenth day of October of every year is what we call Muster Day, because those who have reached the age of twenty-one are then mustered into the industrial service, and at the same time those who, after twenty-four years' service, have reached the age of forty-five are honorably mustered out. It is the great day of the year with us, whence we reckon all other events, our Olympiad, save that it is annual."

"It is after you have mustered your industrial army into service," I said, "that I should expect the difficulty to arise, for there its analogy with a military army must cease. Soldiers have all the same thing, and a very simple thing, to do, namely, to practice the manual of arms, to march and stand guard. But the industrial army must learn and follow two or three hundred diverse trades and avocations. What administrative talent can be equal to determine wisely what trade or business every individual in a great nation shall pursue?"

"The administration has nothing to do with determining that point."

"Who does determine it, then?" I asked.

"Every man for himself in accordance with his natural aptitude, the utmost pains being taken to enable him to find out what his natural aptitude really is. The principle on which our industrial army is organized is that a man's natural endowments, mental and physical, determine what he can work at most profitably to the nation and most satisfactorily to himself. While the obligation of service in some form is not to be evaded, voluntary election, subject only to necessary regulation, is depended on to determine the particular sort of service every man is to render. As an individual's satisfaction during his term of service depends on his having an occupation to his taste, parents and teachers watch from early years for indications of special aptitudes in children. A thorough study of the national industrial system, with the history and rudiments of all the great trades, is an essential part of our educational system. While manual training is not allowed to encroach on the general intellectual culture to which our schools are devoted, it is carried far enough to give our youth, in addition to their theoretical knowledge of the national industries, mechanical and agricultural, a certain familiarity with their tools and methods. Our schools are constantly visiting our workshops, and often are taken on long excursions to inspect particular industrial enterprises. In your day a man was not ashamed to be grossly ignorant of all trades except his own, but such ignorance would not be consistent with our idea of placing everyone in a position to select intelligently the occupation for which he has most taste. Usually long before he is mustered into service a young man has found out the pursuit he wants to follow, has acquired a great deal of knowledge about it, and is waiting impatiently the time when he can enlist in its ranks."

"Surely," I said, "it can hardly be that the number of volunteers for any trade is exactly the number needed in that trade. It must be generally either under or over the demand."

"The supply of volunteers is always expected to fully equal the demand," replied Doctor Leete. "It is the business of the administration to see that this is the case. The rate of volunteering for each trade is closely watched. If there be a noticeably greater excess of volunteers over men needed in any trade, it is inferred that the trade offers greater attractions than others. On the other hand, if the number of volunteers for a trade tends to drop below the demand, it is inferred that it is thought more arduous. It is the business of the administration to seek constantly to equalize the attractions of the trades, so far as the conditions of labor in them are concerned, so that all trades shall be equally attractive to persons having natural tastes for them. This is done by making the hours of labor in different trades to differ according to their arduousness. The lighter trades, prosecuted under the most agreeable circumstances, have in this way the longest hours, while an arduous trade, such as mining, has very short hours. There is no theory, no a priori rule, by which the respective attractiveness of industries is determined. The administration, in taking burdens off one class of workers and adding them to other classes, simply follows the fluctuations of opinion among the workers themselves as indicated by the rate of volunteering. The principle is that no man's work ought to be, on the whole, harder for him than any other man's for him, the workers themselves to be the judges. There are no limits to the application of this rule. If any particular occupation is in itself so arduous or so oppressing that, in order to induce volunteers, the day's work in it had to be reduced to ten minutes, it would be done. If, even then, no man was willing to do it, it would remain undone. But of course, in point of fact, a moderate reduction in the hours of labor or addition of other privileges suffices to secure all needed volunteers for any occupation necessary to men. If, indeed, the unavoidable difficulties and dangers of such a necessary pursuit were so great that no inducement of compensating advantages would overcome men's repugnance to it, the administration would only need to take it out of the common order of occupations by declaring it 'extra hazardous,' and those who pursued it especially worthy of the national gratitude, to be overrun with volunteers. Our young men are very greedy of honor, and do not let slip such opportunities. Of course you will see that dependence on the purely voluntary choice of avocations involves the abolition in all of anything like unhygienic conditions or special peril to life and limb. Health and safety are conditions common to all industries. The nation does not maim and slaughter its workmen by thousands, as did the private capitalists and corporations of your day."

"When there are more who want to enter a particular trade than there is room for, how do you decide between the applicants?" I inquired.

"Preference is given to those who have acquired the most knowledge of the trade they wish to follow. No man, however, who through successive years remains persistent in his desire to show what he can do at any particular trade, is in the end denied an opportunity. Meanwhile, if a man cannot at first win entrance into the business he prefers, he has usually one or more alternative preferences, pursuits for which he has some degree of aptitude, although not the highest. Everyone, indeed, is expected to study his aptitudes so as to have not only a first choice as to occupation, but a second or third, so that if, either at the outset of his career or subsequently, owing to the progress of invention or changes in demand, he is unable to follow his first vocation, he can still find reasonably congenial employment. This principle of secondary choices as to occupation is quite important in our system. I should add, in reference to the counter-possibility of some sudden failure of volunteers in a particular trade, or some sudden necessity of an increased force, that the administration, while depending on the voluntary system for filling up the trades as a rule, holds always in reserve the power to call for special volunteers, or draft any force needed from any quarter. Generally, however, all needs of this sort can be met by details from the class of unskilled or common laborers."

"How is this class of common laborers recruited?" I asked. "Surely nobody voluntarily enters that."

"It is the grade to which all new recruits belong for the first three years of their service. It is not till after this period, during which he is assignable to do any work at the discretion of his superiors, that the young man is allowed to elect a special avocation. These three years of stringent discipline none are exempt from, and very glad our young men are to pass from this severe school into the comparative liberty of the trades. If a man were so stupid as to have no choice as to occupation, he would simply remain a common laborer; but such cases, as you may suppose, are not common."

"Having once elected and entered on a trade or occupation," I remarked, "I suppose he has to stick to it the rest of his life."

"Not necessarily," replied Doctor Leete. "While frequent and merely capricious changes of occupation are not encouraged or even permitted, every worker is allowed, of course, under certain regulations and in accordance with the exigencies of the service, to volunteer for another industry which he thinks would suit him better than his first choice. In this case his application is received just as if he were volunteering for the first time, and on the same terms. Not only this, but a worker may likewise, under suitable regulations and not too frequently, obtain a transfer to an establishment of the same industry in another part of the country which for any reason he may prefer. Under your system a discontented man could indeed leave his work at will, but he left his means of support at the same time, and took his chances as to future livelihood. We find that the number of men who wish to abandon an accustomed occupation for a new one, and old friends and associations for strange ones, is small. It is only the poorer sort of workmen who desire to change even as frequently as our regulations permit. Of course transfers or discharges, when health demands them, are always given."

"As an industrial system, I should think this might be extremely efficient," I said, "but I don't see that it makes any provision for the professional classes, the men who serve the nation with brains instead of hands. Of course you can't get along without the brain workers. How, then, are they selected from those who are to serve as farmers and mechanics? That must require a very delicate sort of sifting process, I should say."

"So it does," replied Doctor Leete. "The most delicate possible test is needed here, and so we leave the question whether a man shall be a brain or hand worker entirely to him to settle. At the end of the term of three years as a common laborer, which every man must serve, it is for him to choose, in accordance to his natural tastes, whether he will fit himself for an art or profession, or be a farmer or mechanic. If he feels that he can do better work with his brains than his muscles, he finds every facility for testing the reality of his supposed bent, of cultivating it, and, if fit, of pursuing it as his avocation. The schools of technology, of medicine, of art, of music, of histrionics, and of higher liberal learning are always open to aspirants without condition."

"Are not the schools flooded with young men whose only motive is to avoid work?"

Doctor Leete smiled a little grimly.

"No one is at all likely to enter the professional schools for the purpose of avoiding work, I assure you," he said. "They are intended for those with special aptitude for the branches they teach, and anyone without it would find it easier to do double hours at his trade than try to keep up with the classes. Of course many honestly mistake their vocation, and, finding themselves unequal to the requirements of the schools, drop out and return to the industrial service; no discredit attaches to such persons, for the public policy is to encourage all to develop suspected talents which only actual tests can prove the reality of. The professional and scientific schools of your day depended on the patronage of their pupils for support, and the practice appears to have been common of giving diplomas to unfit persons, who afterward found their way into the professions. Our schools are national institutions, and to have passed their tests is a proof of special abilities not to be questioned.

"This opportunity for a professional training," the doctor continued, "remains open to every man till the age of thirty is reached, after which students are not received, as there would remain too brief a period before the age of discharge in which to serve the nation in their professions. In your day young men had to choose their professions very young, and therefore, in a large proportion of instances, wholly mistook their vocations. It is recognized nowadays that the natural aptitudes of some are later than those of others in developing, and therefore, while the choice of profession may be made as early as twenty-four, it remains open for six years longer."

A question which had a dozen times before been on my lips now found utterance, a question which touched upon what, in my time, had been regarded the most vital difficulty in the way of any final settlement of the industrial problem. "It's an extraordinary thing," I said, "that you should not yet have said a word about the method of adjusting the wages. Since the nation is the sole employer, the government must fix the rate of wages and determine just how much everybody shall earn, from the doctors to the diggers. All I can say is, that this plan would never have worked with us, and I don't see how it can now unless human nature has changed. In my day, nobody was satisfied with his wages or salary. Even if he felt he received enough, he was sure his neighbor had too much, which was as bad. If the universal discontent on this subject, instead of being dissipated in curses and strikes directed against innumerable employers, could have been concentrated upon one, and that the government, the strongest ever devised would not have seen two pay days."

Doctor Leete laughed heartily.

"Very true, very true," he said, "a general strike would most probably have followed the first pay day, and a strike directed against a government is a revolution. . . . "

"How . . . can you adjust satisfactorily the comparative wages or remuneration of the multitide of avocations, so unlike and so incommensurable, which are necessary for the service of society? In our day the market rate determined the price of labor of all sorts, as well as of goods. The employer paid as little as he could, and the worker got as much. It was not a pretty system ethically, I admit; but it did, at least, furnish us a rough-and-ready formula for settling a question which must be settled ten thousand times a day if the world was ever going to get forward. There seemed to us no other practicable way of doing it."

"Yes," replied Doctor Leete, "it was the only practicable way under a system which made the interests of every individual antagonistic to those of every other; but it would have been a pity if humanity could never have devised a better plan, for yours was simply the application to the mutual relations of men of the devil's maxim, 'Your necessity is my opportunity.' The reward of any service depended not upon its difficulty, danger, or hardship, for throughout the world it seems that the most perilous, severe, and repulsive labor was done by the worst-paid classes, but solely upon the straits of those who needed the service."

"All that is conceded," I said. "But, with all its defects, the plan of settling prices by the market rate was a practical plan; and I cannot conceive what satisfactory substitute you can have devised for it. The government being the only possible employer, there is of course no labor market or market rate. Wages of all sorts must be arbitrarily fixed by the government. I cannot imagine a more complex and delicate function than that must be, or one, however performed, more certain to breed universal dissatisfaction."

"I beg your pardon," replied Doctor Leete, "but I think you exaggerate the difficulty. Suppose a board of fairly sensible men were charged with settling the wages for all sorts of trades under a system which, like ours, guaranteed employment to all, while permitting the choice of avocations. Don't you see that, however unsatisfactory the first adjustment might be, the mistakes would soon correct themselves? The favored trades would have too many volunteers, and those discriminated against would lack them till the errors were set right. But this is aside from the purpose, for, though this plan would, I fancy, be practicable enough, it is no part of our system."

"How, then, do you regulate wages?" I once more asked.

Doctor Leete did not reply till after several moments of meditative silence. "I know, of course," he finally said, "enough of the old order of things to understand just what you mean by that question; and yet the present order is so utterly different at this point that I am a little at a loss how to answer you best. You ask me how we regulate wages; I can only reply that there is no idea in the modern social economy which at all corresponds with what was meant by wages in your day."

"I suppose you mean that you have no money to pay wages in," said I. "But the credit given the worker at the government storehouse answers to his wages with us. How is the amount of the credit given respectively to the workers in different lines determined? By what title does the individual claim his particular share? What is the basis of allotment?"

"His title," replied Doctor Leete, "is his humanity. The basis of his claim is the fact that he is a man."

"The fact that he is a man!" I repeated, incredulously. "Do you possibly mean that all have the same share?"

"Most assuredly."

"You see," he said, smiling, "that it is not merely that we have no money to pay wages in, but, as I said, we have nothing at all answering to your idea of wages."

By this time I had pulled myself together sufficiently to voice some of the criticisms which, man of the nineteenth century as I was, came upper most in my mind, upon this, to me, astounding arrangement. "Some men do twice the work of others!" I exclaimed. "Are the clever workmen content with a plan that ranks them with the indifferent?"

"We leave no possible ground for any complaint of injustice," replied Doctor Leete, "by requiring precisely the same measure of service from all."

"How can you do that, I should like to know, when no two men's powers are the same?"

"Nothing could be simpler," was Doctor Leete's reply. "We require of each that he shall make the same effort; that is, we demand of him the best service it is in his power to give."

"And supposing all do the best they can," I answered, "the amount of the produce resulting is twice greater from one man than from another."

"Very true," replied Doctor Leete, "but the amount of the resulting product has nothing whatever to do with the question, which is one of desert. Desert is a moral question, and the amount of the product a material quantity. It would be an extraordinary sort of logic which should try to determine a moral question by a material standard. The amount of the effort alone is pertinent to the question of desert. All men who do their best, do the same. A man's endowments, however godlike, merely fix the measure of his duty. The man of great endowments who does not do all he might, though he may do more than a man of small endowments who does his best, is deemed a less deserving worker than the latter, and dies a debtor to his fellows. The Creator sets men's tasks for them by the faculties he gives them; we simply exact their fulfillment."

"No doubt that is very fine philosophy," I said. "Nevertheless it seems hard that the man who produces twice as much as another, even if both do their best, should have only the same share."

"Does it, indeed, seem so to you?" responded Doctor Leete. "Now, do you know, that seems very curious to me? The way it strikes people nowadays is that a man who can produce twice as much as another with the same effort, instead of being rewarded for doing so, ought to be punished if he does not do so. In the nineteenth century, when a horse pulled a heavier load than a goat, I suppose you rewarded him. Now, we should have whipped him soundly if he had not, on the ground that, being much stronger, he ought to. It is singular how ethical standards change." The doctor said this with such a twinkle in his eye that I was obliged to laugh.

"I suppose," I said, "that the real reason that we rewarded men for their endowments, while we considered those of horses and goats merely as fixing the service to be severally required of them, was that the animals, not being reasoning beings, naturally did the best they could, whereas men could only be induced to do so by rewarding them according to the amount of their product. That brings me to ask why, unless human nature has mightily changed in a hundred years, you are not under the same necessity."

"We are," replied Doctor Leete. "I don't think there has been any change in human nature in that respect since your day. It is so constituted still that special incentives in the form of prizes, and advantages to be gained, are requisite to call out the best endeavors of the average man in any direction."

"But what inducement," I asked, "can a man have to put forth his best endeavors when, however much or little he accomplishes, his income remains the same? High characters may be moved by devotion to the common welfare under such a system, but does not the average man tend to rest back on his oar, reasoning that it is of no use to make a special effort, since the effort will not increase his income, nor its withholding diminish it?"

"Does it then really seem to you," answered my companion, "that human nature is insensible to any motives save fear of want and love of luxury, that you should expect security and equality of livelihood to leave them without possible incentives to effort? Your contemporaries did not really think so, though they might fancy they did. When it was a question of the grandest class of efforts, the most absolute self-devotion, they depended on quite other incentives. Not higher wages, but honor and the hope of men's gratitude, patriotism and the inspiration of duty, were the motives which they set before their soldiers when it was a question of dying for the nation, and never was there an age of the world when those motives did not call out what is best and noblest in men. And not only this, but when you come to analyze the love of money which was the general impulse to effort in your day, you find that the dread of want and desire of luxury was but one of several motives which the pursuit of money represented; the others, and with many the more influential, being desire of power, of social position, and reputation for ability and success. So you see that though we have abolished poverty and the fear of it, and inordinate luxury with the hope of it, we have not touched the greater part of the motives which underlay the love of money in former times, or any of those which prompted the supremer sorts of effort. The coarser motives, which no longer move us, have been replaced by higher motives wholly unknown to the mere wage earners of your age. Now that industry, of whatever sort, is no longer self-service, but service of the nation, patriotism, passion for humanity, impel the worker as in your day they did the soldier. The army of industry is an army, not alone by virtue of its perfect organization, but by reason also of the ardor of self-devotion which animates its members.

"But as you used to supplement the motives of patriotism with the love of glory, in order to stimulate the valor of your soldiers, so do we. Based as our industrial system is on the principle of requiring the same unit of effort from every man, that is, the best he can do, you will see that the means by which we spur the workers to do their best must be a very essential part of our scheme. With us, diligence in the national service is the sole and certain way to public repute, social distinction, and official power. The value of a man's services to society fixes his rank in it. Compared with the effort of our social arrangements in impelling men to be zealous in business, we deem the object lessons of biting poverty and wanton luxury on which you depended a device as weak and uncertain as it was barbaric. The lust of honor even in your sordid day notoriously impelled men to more desperate effort than the love of money could."

"I should be extremely interested," I said, "to learn something of what these social arrangements are. . . . "

"You must understand in the first place," replied the doctor, "that the supply of incentives to effort is but one of the objects sought in the organization we have adopted for the army. The other, and equally important, is to secure for the file leaders and captains of the force, and the great officers of the nation, men of proved abilities, who are pledged by their own careers to hold their followers up to their highest standard of performance and permit no lagging. With a view to these two ends the industrial army is organized. First comes the unclassified grade of common laborers, men of all work, to which all recruits during their first three years belong. This grade is a sort of school and a very strict one, in which the young men are taught habits of obedience, subordination, and devotion to duty. While the miscellaneous nature of the work done by this force prevents the systematic grading of the workers which is afterward possible, yet individual records are kept, and excellence receives distinction corresponding with the penalties that negligence incurs. It is not, however, policy with us to permit youthful recklessness or indiscretion, when not deeply culpable, to handicap the future careers of young men, and all who have passed through the unclassified grade without serious disgrace have an equal opportunity to choose the life employment they have most liking for. Having selected this, they enter upon it as apprentices. The length of the apprenticeship naturally differs in different occupations. At the end of it the apprentice becomes a full workman, and a member of his trade or guild. Now not only are the individual records of the apprentices for ability and industry strictly kept, and excellence distinguished by suitable distinctions, but upon the average of his record during apprenticeship the standing given the apprentice among the full workmen depends.

"While the internal organizations of different industries, mechanical and agricultural, differ according to their peculiar conditions, they agree in a general division of their workers into first, second, and third grades, according to ability, and these grades are in many cases subdivided into first and second classes. According to his standing as an apprentice, a young man is assigned his place as a first-, second-, or third-grade worker. Of course only young men of unusual ability pass directly from apprenticeship into the first grade of the workers. The most fall into the lower grades, working up as they grow more experienced, at the periodical regradings. These regradings take place in each industry at intervals corresponding with the length of the apprenticeship to that industry, so that merit never need wait long to rise, nor can any rest on past achievements unless they would drop into a lower rank. One of the notable advantages of a high grading is the privilege it gives the worker in electing which of the various branches or processes of his industry he will follow as his specialty. Of course it is not intended that any of these processes shall be disproportionately arduous, but there is often much difference between them, and the privilege of election is accordingly highly prized. So far as possible, indeed, the preferences even of the poorest workmen are considered in assigning them their line of work, because not only their happiness but their usefulness is thus enhanced. While, however, the wish of the lower-grade man is consulted so far as the exigencies of the service permit, he is considered only after the upper-grade men have been provided for, and often he has to put up with second or third choice, or even with an arbitrary assignment when help is needed. This privilege of election attends every regrading, and when a man loses a grade he also risks having to exchange the sort of work he likes for some other less to his taste. The results of each regrading, giving the standing of every man in his industry, are gazetted in the public prints, and those who have won promotion since the last regrading receive the nation's thanks and are publicly invested with the badge of their new rank."

"What may this badge be?" I asked.

"Every industry has its emblematic device," replied Doctor Leete, "and this, in the shape of a metallic badge so small that you might not see it unless you knew where to look, is all the insigns which the men of the army wear, except where public convenience demands a distinctive uniform. This badge is the same in form for all grades of industry, but while the badge of the third grade is iron, that of the second grade is silver, and that of the first is gilt.

"Apart from the grand incentive to endeavor afforded by the fact that the high places in the nation are open only to the highest-class men, and that rank in the army constitutes the only mode of social distinction for the vast majority who are not aspirants in art, literature, and the professions, various incitements of a minor, but perhaps equally effective, sort are provided in the form of special privileges and immunities in the way of discipline, which the superior-class men enjoy. These, while intended to be as little as possible invidious to the less successful, have the effect of keeping constantly before every man's mind the great desirability of attaining the grade next above his own.

"It is obviously important that not only the good but also the indifferent and poor workmen should be able to cherish the ambition of rising. Indeed, the number of the latter being so much greater, it is even more essential that the ranking system should not operate to discourage them than that it should stimulate the others. It is to this end that the grades are divided into classes. The grades as well as the classes being made numerically equal at each regrading, there is not at any time, counting out the officers and the unclassified and apprentice grades, over one-ninth of the industrial army in the lowest class, and most of this number are recent apprentices, all of whom expect to rise. Those who remain during the entire term of service in the lowest class are but a trifling fraction of the industrial army, and likely to be as deficient in sensibility to their position as in ability to better it.

"It is not even necessary that a worker should win promotion to a higher grade to have at least a taste of glory. While promotion requires a general excellence of record as a worker, honorable mention and various sorts of prizes are awarded for excellence less than sufficient for promotion, and also for special feats and single performances in the various industries. There are many minor distinctions of standing, not only within the grades but within the classes, each of which acts as a spur to the efforts of a group. It is intended that no form of merit shall wholly fail of recognition.

"As for actual neglect of work, positively bad work, or other overt remissness on the part of men incapable of generous motives, the discipline of the industrial army is far too strict to allow anything whatever of the sort. A man able to duty, and persistently refusing, is sentenced to solitary imprisonment on bread and water till he consents.

"The lowest grade of the officers of the industrial army, that of assistant foreman, or lieutenants, is appointed out of men who have held their place for two years in the first class of the first grade. Where this leaves too large a range of choice, only the first group of this class are eligible. No one thus comes to the point of commanding men until he is about thirty years old. After a man becomes an officer, his rating of course no longer depends on the efficiency of his own work, but on that of his men. The foremen are appointed from among the assistant foremen, by the same exercise of discretion limited to a small eligible class. In the appointments to the still higher grades another principle is introduced, which it would take too much time to explain now.

"Of course such a system of grading as I have described would have been impracticable applied to the small industrial concerns of your day, in some of which there were hardly enough employees to have left one apiece for the classes. You must remember that, under the national organization of labor, all industries are carried on by great bodies of men, many of your farms or shops being combined as one. It is also owing solely to the vast scale on which industry is organized, with coordinate establishments in every part of the country, that we are able by exchanges and transfers to fit every man so nearly with the sort of work he can do best.

"And now, Mr. West, I will leave it to you, on the bare outline of its features which I have given, if those who need special incentives to do their best are likely to lack them under our system. Does it not seem to you that men who found themselves obliged, whether they wished or not, to work, would under such a system be strongly impelled to do their best?"

I replied that it seemed to me the incentives offered were, if any objection were to be made, too strong; that the pace set for the young men was too hot; and such, indeed, I would add with deference, still remains my opinion, now that by longer residence among you I have become better acquainted with the whole subject.

Doctor Leete, however, desired me to reflect, and I am ready to say that it is perhaps a sufficient reply to my objection, that the worker's livelihood is in no way dependent on his ranking, and anxiety for that never embitters his disappointments; that the working hours are short, the vacations regular, and that all emulation ceases at forty-five, with the attainment of middle life.

"There are two or three other points I ought to refer to," he added, "to prevent your getting mistaken impressions. In the first place, you must understand that this system of preferment given the most efficient workers over the less so, in no way contravenes the fundamental idea of our social system, that all who do their best are equally deserving, whether the best be great or small. I have shown that the system is arranged to encourage the weaker as well as the stronger with the hope of rising, while the fact that the stronger are selected for the leaders is in no way a reflection upon the weaker, but in the interest of the common weal.

"Do not imagine, either, because emulation is given free play as an incentive under our system, that we deem it a motive likely to appeal to the nobler sort of men, or worthy of them. Such as these find their motives within, not without, and measure their duty by their own endowments, not by those of others. So long as their achievement is proportioned to their powers, they would consider it preposterous to expect praise or blame because it chanced to be great or small. To such natures emulation appears philosophically absurd, and despicable in a moral aspect by its substitution of envy for admiration, and exultation for regret, in one's attitude toward the successes and the failures of others.

"But all men, even in the last year of the twentieth century, are not of this high order, and the incentives to endeavor requisite for those who are not must be of a sort adapted to their inferior natures. For these, then, emulation of the keenest edge is provided as a constant spur. Those who need this motive will feel it. Those who are above its influence do not need it.

"I should not fail to mention," resumed the doctor, "that for those too deficient in mental or bodily strength to be fairly graded with the main body of workers, we have a separate grade, unconnected with the others — a sort of invalid corps, the members of which are provided with a light class of tasks fitted to their strength. All our sick in mind and body, all our deaf and dumb, and lame and blind and crippled, and even our insane, belong to this invalid corps, and bear its insigns. The strongest often do nearly a man's work, the feeblest, of course, nothing; but none who can do anything are willing quite to give up. In their lucid intervals, even our insane are eager to do what they can."

"That is a pretty idea of the invalid corps," I said. "Even a barbarian from the nineteenth century can appreciate that. It is a very graceful way of disguising charity, and must be grateful to the feelings of its recipients."

"Charity!" repeated Doctor Leete. "Did you suppose that we consider the incapable class we are talking of objects of charity?"

"Why, naturally," I said, "inasmuch as they are incapable of self-support."

But here the doctor took me up quickly.

"Who is capable of self-support?" he demand. "There is no such thing in a civilized society as self-support. In a state of society so barbarous as not even to know family cooperation, each individual may possibly support himself, though even then for a part of his life only; but from the moment that men begin to live together, and constitute even the rudest of society, self-support becomes impossible. As men grow more civilized, and the subdivision of occupations and services is carried out, a complex mutual dependence becomes the universal rule. Every man, however solitary may seem his occupation, is a member of a vast industrial partnership, as large as the nation, as large as humanity. The necessity of mutual dependence should imply the duty and guarantee of mutual support; and that it did not in your day constituted the essential cruelty and unreason for your system."

"That may all be so," I replied, "but it does not touch the case of those who are unable to contribute anything to the product of industry."

"Surely I told you [earlier, at] least I thought I did," replied Doctor

Leete, "that the right of a man to maintenance at the nation's table depends on the fact that he is a man, and not on the amount of health and strength he may have, so long as he does his best."

"You said so," I answered, "but I supposed the rule applied only to the workers of different ability. Does it also hold of those who can do nothing at all?"

"Are they not also men?"

"I am to understand, then, that the lame, the blind, the sick, and the impotent, are as well off as the most efficient, and have the same income?"

"Certainly," was the reply.

"The idea of charity on such a scale," I answered, "would have made our most enthusiastic philanthropists gasp."

"If you had a sick brother at home," replied Doctor Leete, "unable to work, would you feed him on less dainty food, and lodge and clothe him more poorly, than yourself? More likely far, you would give him the preference; nor would you think of calling it charity. Would not the word, in that connection, fill you with indignation?"

"Of course," I replied, "but the cases are not parallel. There is a sense, no doubt, in which all men are brothers; but this general sort of brotherhood is not to be compared, except for rhetorical purposes, to the brotherhood of blood, either as to its sentiment or its obligations."

"There speaks the nineteenth century!" exclaimed Doctor Leete. "Ah, Mr. West, there is no doubt as to the length of time that you slept. If I were to give you, in one sentence, a key to what may seem the mysteries of our civilization as compared with that of your age, I should say that it is the fact that the solidarity of the race and the brotherhood of man, which to you were but fine phrases, are, to our thinking and feeling, ties as real and as vital as physical fraternity.

"But even setting that consideration aside, I do not see why it so surprises you that those who cannot work are conceded the full right to live on the produce of those who can. Even in your day, the duty of military service for the protection of the nation, to which our industrial service corresponds, while obligatory on those able to discharge it, did not operate to deprive of the privileges of citizenship those who were unable. They stayed at home, and were protected by those who fought, and nobody questioned their right to be, or thought less of them. So, now, the requirement of industrial service from those able to render it does not operate to deprive of the privileges of citizenship, which now implies the citizen's maintenance, him who cannot work. The worker is not a citizen because he works, but works because he is a citizen. As you recognize the duty of the strong to fight for the weak, we, now that fighting is gone by, recognize his duty to work for him.

"A solution which leaves an unaccounted-for residuum is no solution at all; and our solution of the problem of human society would have been none at all had it left the lame, the sick, and the blind outside with the beasts, to fare as they might. Better far have left the strong and well unprovided for than these burdened ones, toward whom every heart must yearn, and for whom ease of mind and body should be provided, if for no others. Therefore it is, as I told you this morning, that the title of every man, woman, and child to the means of existence rests on no basis less plain, broad, and simple than the fact that they are fellows of one race — members of one human family. The only coin current is the image of God, and that is good for all we have.

"I think there is no feature of the civilization of your epoch so repugnant to modern ideas as the neglect with which you treated your dependent classes. Even if you had no pity, no feeling of brotherhood, how was it that you did not see that you were robbing the incapable class of their plain right in leaving them unprovided for?"

"I don't quite follow you there," I said. "I admit the claim of this class to our pity, but how could they who produced nothing claim a share of the product as a right?"

"How happened it," was Doctor Leete's reply, "that your workers were able to produce more than so many savages would have done? Was it not wholly on account of the heritage of the past knowledge and achievements of the race, the machinery of society, thousands of years in contriving, found by you ready-made to your hand? How did you come to be possessors of this knowledge and this machinery, which represent nine parts to one contributed by yourself in the value of your product? You inherited it, did you not? And were not these others, these unfortunate and crippled brothers whom you cast out, joint inheritors, coheirs with you? What did you do with their share? Did you not rob them when you put them off with crusts, who were entitled to sit with the heirs, and did you not add insult to robbery when you called the crusts charity?

"Ah, Mr. West," Doctor Leete continued, as I did not respond, "what I do not understand is, setting aside all considerations either of justice or brotherly feeling toward the crippled and defective, how the workers of your day could have had any heart for their work, knowing that their children, or grandchildren, if unfortunate, would be deprived of the comforts and even necessities of life. It is a mystery how men with children could favor a system under which they were rewarded beyond those less endowed with bodily strength or mental power. For, by the same discrimination by which the father profited, the son, for whom he would give his life, being perchance weaker than others, might be reduced to crusts and beggary. How men dared leave children behind them, I have never been able to understand."